Women of Good Taste

Beta Sigma Phi

EDITORIAL STAFF

Managing Editor	Mary Cummings
Executive Editor	Debbie Seigenthaler
Editorial Manager	Georgia Brazil
Project Manager	Anita McKay
Editor	Jan Keeling
Associate Editors	Linda Bennie, Ginger Ryan Joy Wilson
Typographers	Jessie Anglin, Sara Anglin
Award Selection Judges	Bill Ross, Debbie Seigenthaler Charlene Sproles
Art Director	Steve Newman
Illustrator	Barbara Ball
Test Kitchen	Charlene Sproles
Essayist	Dana Schafer

Cover photograph: Hazelnut Marketing Board

© Favorite Recipes® Press, A Division of Heritage House, Inc. 1998
  P.O. Box 305141, Nashville, Tennessee 37230

ISBN: 0-87197-468-1

Manufactured in the United States of America
First Printing 1998

Recipe for Cover photograph is on page 200.

Contents

Linda Rostenberg

Dear Beta Sigma Phi Sisters:

You know and I know that when it comes to food, Beta Sigma Phis rule! We've just got a knack for ferreting out the best recipe to wow the sisters at the next pot luck. Proof positive of that came to me the other day, when *Better Homes and Gardens* called, and asked to include recipes from our last Beta Sigma Phi cookbook in their newest cookbook publication—a compendium of the best recipes published in club cookbooks throughout the U.S.!

That made me start thinking about doing a best-of-the-best cookbook for us—but where would I begin? ALL our recipes are so good. We really do live up to the name of our newest collection, *Beta Sigma Phi Women of Good Taste*. We've concentrated our collection on great ideas that don't take long to create; and have included a special section of recipes submitted by Beta Sigma Phi husbands and men friends, too. As usual, these cookbooks are priced right, so you can stock up on Holiday or birthday presents for friends and families who, like us, love good food.

Of course, Beta Sigma Phi could never create these fabulous menus without your help. Time and again, people tell me how they have found the perfect recipes in one of our cookbooks. So next time you're wondering what to make, turn that worry over to your favorite *Women of Good Taste*. Your sisters can solve any culinary crisis—and you'll come out smelling like a (yellow) rose!

Yours in Beta Sigma Phi,

Linda Rosentenberg
Vice President, Communications
Beta Sigma Phi International

Notable Menus

Drift back in time to the
most memorable meal of
your lifetime. Chances are,
it didn't happen by accident!
Whether it as a festive holiday dinner,
an elegant luncheon, a lavish celebration,
or a casual family gathering, there was
someone who planned the entire meal—assembling
a menu that captured the spirit of the occasion.
In our Notable Menus section, we've saved you that step
by coordinating an array of themed menus to suit
a variety of occasions. You'll find foods that are
not only great to eat, but that
taste great together.
Add your own
creative touches—linens,
tableware, decorations—
and put on a party
they won't forget!

Holiday Brunch

Baked Ham with Apple Glaze
Egg Casserole
Baked Cheese Grits
Best Banana Bread
Baked Fruit Compote
Wonderful Wassail
Orange Juice — Champagne
See index for similar recipes.

The delightful smells these dishes contribute to a holiday meal may be even more wonderful than the food itself. The Wonderful Wassail is especially pleasing at Christmastime.

Peggy Ascherl
Preceptor Laureate Gamma Theta
Bellaire, Texas

BAKED HAM WITH APPLE GLAZE

1 (6- to 10-pound) fully cooked ham	**1 tablespoon lemon juice**
Whole cloves	**1/4 teaspoon ground cloves**
1 cup apple jelly	
1 tablespoon prepared mustard	

Preheat the oven to 325 degrees. Score the ham and stud with the whole cloves. Combine the apple jelly, mustard, lemon juice and ground cloves in a saucepan. Bring to a boil, then remove from heat. Brush glaze over ham. Bake glazed ham for 1 1/2 hours to 140 degrees on a meat thermometer. Use the remaining glaze as a sauce. Yield: 12 to 16 servings.

EGG CASSEROLE

2 cups seasoned croutons	**1/2 teaspoon salt**
1 1/2 cups shredded Cheddar cheese	**1/2 teaspoon dry mustard**
6 eggs, beaten	**1/8 teaspoon onion powder**
2 cups milk	**1/8 teaspoon white pepper**

Preheat the oven to 350 degrees. Place the croutons in a greased 6-by-10-inch baking dish and sprinkle the cheese over the croutons. Combine the eggs, milk, salt, mustard, onion powder and white pepper; mix well and pour over the cheese. Bake for 25 minutes or until puffed and golden. Yield: 10 servings.

BAKED CHEESE GRITS

6 cups water	**1/2 teaspoon garlic powder**
1 teaspoon salt	**2 tablespoons Worcestershire sauce**
1 1/2 cups regular grits	
1/2 cup butter or margarine	**1/2 teaspoon hot pepper sauce**
1 cup shredded Cheddar cheese	**3 eggs, beaten**
2 tablespoons sherry	

Preheat the oven to 350 degrees. Bring the water and salt to a boil in a saucepan; gradually add the grits, stirring constantly until thickened (read package directions). Add the butter, cheese, sherry, garlic powder, Worcestershire sauce, hot pepper sauce and eggs to grits. Pour the mixture into a greased 2 1/2-quart baking dish. Bake for 45 minutes.
Yield: 10 to 12 servings.

BEST BANANA BREAD

3/4 cup margarine	**3/4 teaspoon salt**
1 1/2 cups sugar	**1 teaspoon baking soda**
3 or 4 medium bananas	**3/4 cup chopped pecans or walnuts**
2 eggs, beaten	
1 teaspoon vanilla extract	**1/2 cup buttermilk or sour cream**
2 cups all-purpose flour	

Preheat the oven to 325 degrees. Cream the margarine and sugar until light and fluffy. Mash the bananas to make 1 1/2 cups. Blend the mashed bananas, eggs, vanilla and buttermilk into the margarine and sugar. Mix the flour, salt and soda and add to banana mixture. Fold in the nuts. Pour the batter into a greased and floured bundt pan or a 5-by-9-inch loaf pan. Bake for 1 1/4 hours. Cool for 10 minutes. Remove from pan. Yield: 10 to 12 servings.

BAKED FRUIT COMPOTE

8 soft macaroons, crumbled	**1 (17-ounce) can apricot halves, drained**
1 (16-ounce) can pitted dark sweet cherries, drained	**1 (16-ounce) can pear halves, drained**
1 (16-ounce) can sliced peaches, drained	**1 (21-ounce) can cherry pie filling**
1 (15-ounce) can pineapple chunks, drained	**1/2 cup brandy or apple juice**
	1 tablespoon butter or margarine

Preheat the oven to 400 degrees. Toast the crumbled macaroons in the oven for 3 to 4 minutes. Turn the oven down to 350 degrees. Sprinkle half the macaroon crumbs on the bottom of a 9-by-12-inch baking dish. Layer the cherries, peaches, pineapple, apricots, pears and cherry pie filling over the macaroon crumb layer; sprinkle the remaining macaroon crumbs over the top. Pour the brandy over the fruit and dot with butter. Bake for 40 minutes. Yield: 12 servings.

WONDERFUL WASSAIL

2 quarts apple juice
2¼ cups pineapple juice
1 cup lemon juice
2 cups orange juice
½ cup sugar
3 sticks cinnamon
1 teaspoon whole cloves

Combine all the ingredients in a large kettle. Simmer, covered, for 30 minutes. Uncover the kettle and simmer for 30 minutes longer. Strain out the spices. Serve hot. Reheat as needed. Yield: 24 servings.

Dorothy Woodburn, Preceptor Psi, Vancouver, Washington, entertains with a Never-Fail Dinner of tossed summer salad, baked chicken breasts in orange sauce, spinach madeleine, baked rice pilaf, and cherry dessert squares. The menu may be prepared ahead and served with rolls and drinks.

Corny Chicken Supper

Your Favorite Salad — Corny Chicken
Toasted French Bread
Fruit Cobbler for a Busy Day with
Vanilla Ice Cream
See index for similar recipes.

The Corny Chicken recipe was given to me by my mother-in-law. All the men in my family love it. You can save time on the day you serve this meal by planning ahead. Add salad, bread, and dessert, and it becomes a meal that everybody loves.

Dorothy L. Fiske, Eta
Winnemucca, Nevada

CORNY CHICKEN

I cook the chicken a day ahead, remove the meat from the bones, and let the meat and broth chill separately in the refrigerator. The next day I skim the fat from the broth and use a cup of the broth in the recipe. If there is any leftover broth, I freeze it for use in another recipe. You may substitute 8 ounces of shredded Monterey Jack cheese for the 8 ounces shredded Cheddar cheese.

1 (3- to 4-pound)
*   chicken, stewed*
1 (12-count) package
*   corn tortillas*
1 (15-ounce) can chili
*   con carne without*
*   beans*
1 (10-ounce) can cream
*   of chicken soup*
1 (10-ounce) can cream
*   of mushroom soup*
1 (8-ounce) can tomato
*   sauce or hot*
*   enchilada sauce*
4 cups shredded Cheddar
*   cheese*
1 cup chicken broth

Preheat the oven to 350 degrees. Remove the chicken meat from the bones. Butter a 9-by-13-inch baking dish and line it with the corn tortillas. Layer half the chicken over the tortillas. Combine the chili con carne, chicken soup, mushroom soup and tomato sauce; pour half the mixture over the chicken. Sprinkle half the cheese over the top. Repeat the chicken, soup and cheese layers. Pour the chicken broth over all. Bake uncovered for about 30 minutes or until bubbly. Yield: 12 servings.

FRUIT COBBLER FOR A BUSY DAY

I use fresh fruit or berries in season, blackberries whenever I can. If there is an abundance of fruit, I freeze some of it for later use. The cobbler made with frozen berries gives a refreshing taste of summer on a cold winter's day. All six of my children loved it, especially when served with ice cream. When I served the cobbler for dessert, it was always gone by bedtime. Use a 9-by-13-inch pan if you double the recipe.

½ cup all-purpose flour
½ cup milk
1 teaspoon baking
*   powder*
1 cup sugar
2 to 3 cups fruit of
*   choice, fresh or*
*   canned*

Preheat the oven to 350 degrees. Mix together the flour, milk, baking powder and ½ cup of the sugar. Pour the batter into a well-greased 9-by-9-inch baking pan and place the fruit over the batter. Sprinkle the remaining sugar over the fruit. Bake for about 30 minutes or until the crust rises to the top and browns. Yield: 9 to 12 servings.

✤ Memories of Home

Dad's Red Onion Strawberry Salad
Mom's Chicken Casserole
Everybody's Favorite Broccoli Casserole
Claire's Fluffy Rolls
Uncle Bob's Best Chocolate Cake

See index for similar recipes.

This is the menu I serve when I invite my family over for a special dinner. I prepare a favorite dish for each family member so that everyone feels extra-special. The chicken, broccoli, and cake can be prepared the night before, and the roll mixture can be set out the night before as well.

Jo Prusha
Omaha, Nebraska

DAD'S RED ONION STRAWBERRY SALAD

The dressing and strawberries add a delightful taste to this salad. Raspberries can be substituted for the strawberries. This is a refreshing salad in summer, but it can also add a sunny touch to a cold winter day.

3/4 cup mayonnaise-type salad dressing	1 tablespoon milk
2 teaspoons poppy seeds	1/2 cup sugar
2 teaspoons raspberry vinegar	1 head romaine lettuce
	1 pint fresh strawberries
	1 medium red onion

Combine the salad dressing, poppy seeds, vinegar, milk and sugar. Chill for 3 hours. Clean and slice the lettuce and strawberries. Slice the onion in 1/2-inch rings. Toss together the lettuce, strawberries and onion rings. Top with the dressing. Yield: 12 servings.

MOM'S CHICKEN CASSEROLE

3 to 4 whole chicken breasts, split	16 ounces sour cream
3 packages butter crackers, crushed	2 tablespoons poppy seeds
2 cups melted butter or margarine	1 tablespoon bottled minced garlic
2 (10-ounce) cans cream of chicken soup	2 tablespoons bottled minced onion

Boil the chicken breasts until cooked through, then allow them to cool. Preheat the oven to 350 degrees. Combine the crushed butter crackers and melted butter. Press 2/3 of the cracker mixture into a 9-by-13-inch baking dish. Set aside. Chop the cooked chicken breasts in small pieces. Mix the chicken with the cream of chicken soup, sour cream, poppy seeds, minced garlic and minced onion. Place the chicken mixture in the cracker crust in the dish. Sprinkle the remaining cracker mixture over the top. Bake uncovered for 1 hour. Yield: 12 servings.

BROCCOLI CASSEROLE

If you want to make this casserole into a one-dish meal, add 2 cups of chopped cooked ham or chicken.

1 (10-ounce) package frozen chopped broccoli	1 (10-ounce) can cream of chicken soup
1 1/2 cups quick-cooking rice	1 soup can of milk
1 (10-ounce) can cream of mushroom soup	2 cups shredded mild Cheddar cheese

Preheat the oven to 325 degrees. Cook the frozen broccoli using package directions and drain. Stir together the rice, soups, milk, broccoli and 1 cup of the shredded cheese. Pour the mixture into a 1 1/2-quart baking dish and sprinkle with the remaining cheese. Bake for 30 minutes or until the cheese starts to brown. Yield: 6 to 8 servings.

CLAIRE'S FLUFFY ROLLS

1 package dry yeast	1/2 cup vegetable oil
1/4 cup warm water	1/2 teaspoon baking soda
1 cup milk, scalded and cooled	1 teaspoon salt
1/2 cup sugar	2 eggs, beaten
	4 cups all-purpose flour

Dissolve the yeast in the warm water in a large bowl. Add the milk, sugar, oil, baking soda, salt and eggs. Beat well. Add the flour and beat again. Cover the bowl and allow to rest on a counter or in a cupboard overnight. Next morning, turn out the dough onto a lightly floured board. Divide the dough into 3 balls; roll 1 of the balls to the size and shape of a pie crust about 1/2 inch thick. (Remainder of the dough may be kept in the refrigerator for use 1 or 2 days later.) Cut the circle into 12 wedges. Roll each wedge into a crescent shape, ending with the point on the outside of the roll. Place crescents 1 inch apart on greased cookie sheet. Let rise for at least 2 hours. Preheat the oven to 350 degrees. Bake rolls for 15 minutes or until lightly browned. Yield: 12 servings.

UNCLE BOB'S BEST CHOCOLATE CAKE

This is a moist, brownielike cake. Kids love it—especially served with peppermint ice cream!

2 cups sugar	*1 teaspoon vanilla*
2 cups all-purpose flour	* extract*
1/2 teaspoon salt	*1/2 teaspoon cinnamon*
2 sticks margarine	*1/2 cup buttermilk*
1 cup water	*Cocoa Frosting*
3 tablespoons cocoa	*1/2 cup chopped pecans*
2 eggs	* or walnuts (optional)*
1 teaspoon baking soda	

Preheat the oven to 350 degrees. Mix together the sugar, flour and salt in a medium bowl. Put the margarine, water and cocoa in a saucepan; bring just to a boil. Pour over the flour mixture and blend well. Add the eggs, baking soda, vanilla, cinnamon and buttermilk; mix well. Pour the batter into an ungreased jelly roll pan. Bake for 20 minutes. After it cools, spread with Cocoa Frosting; sprinkle with pecans. Yield: 8 to 12 servings.

COCOA FROSTING

1 stick butter or	*1 teaspoon vanilla*
* margarine*	* extract*
6 tablespoons milk	*Powdered sugar*
3 tablespoons cocoa	

Melt butter in a saucepan on low heat; stir in milk and cocoa. Remove from heat. Add vanilla and enough powdered sugar to make the desired consistency. Yield: 8 to 12 servings.

Monte's Favorite Salmon Supper

Salmon Cakes
Fried Potatoes and Spinach
Corn on the Cob
Chocolate Cake with Applesauce
See index for similar recipes.

The unusual combinations of ingredients make a memorable meal. It is simple, nourishing, and delicious—likely to become somebody's favorite!

Pam Moon
Sedalia, Missouri

SALMON CAKES

1 (15-ounce) can salmon	*4 to 6 saltine crackers*
1 egg	*Vegetable oil*

Drain the salmon, reserving the juice, and remove the bones. Place the salmon in a medium bowl. Add the egg. Crumble the saltines into the salmon mixture and stir together. Add some of the juice if the mixture is too dry to form patties. Form 4 to 6 patties and panfry to a golden brown in a small amount of vegetable oil. Yield: 4 to 6 servings.

FRIED POTATOES AND SPINACH

4 to 6 large potatoes	*1 medium onion,*
Vegetable oil	* chopped*
1 (14-ounce) can	*1 teaspoon vinegar*
* chopped spinach*	*Salt and pepper*

Peel the potatoes and cut them into thin slices. Panfry the potato slices in a small amount of vegetable oil in a skillet over medium heat. Fry until golden brown, turning when necessary to prevent burning. Warm the spinach and place 1/4 of the spinach over each serving of potatoes. Top with the desired amount of chopped onion and pour 1/4 teaspoon vinegar over onion for each serving. Salt and pepper to taste. Yield: 4 servings.

CHOCOLATE CAKE WITH APPLESAUCE

1 (2-layer) chocolate	*1 (25-ounce) jar*
* cake mix*	* applesauce*
Packaged chocolate	*1/4 cup sugar*
* frosting*	*1 teaspoon cinnamon*

Bake the chocolate cake according to package directions. Cool the cake, then spread with the frosting. Pour the applesauce into a medium bowl. Add sugar and cinnamon and stir until blended. To serve, spoon some of the applesauce mixture over each slice of cake. Yield: 12 to 16 servings.

Linda Werkheiser, Xi Nu Alpha, Lena, Illinois, does a rather deceptive Dinner-on-the-Double by preparing a slow-cooker chicken stew in the morning and mixing up some quick corn muffins and a chocolate pudding cake when she gets home. She says she has dinner on the table just 20 minutes after she gets home and it looks as if she has cooked all day.

Tara Smith, Alpha Rho Theta, Friendswood, Texas, tells of a chapter Hollywood Party with a menu of Lana Turnovers, Imogene Coconut Salad, Bogie Hoagies, Apple Betty Davis, Vivian Leigh Tea, and Deanna Durbin Bourbon. Make up your own menu to include your favorite stars.

Night in Chinatown

Green Tea — Braised Honeyed Chicken
Chicken Corn Soup — Chinese Stir-Fry
Fried Rice — Filled Chocolate Meringues
See index for similar recipes.

A special Chinese night makes a wonderful chapter meeting. When I served this meal, some of us dressed for the occasion and all of us sat on the floor on pillows. The food can be prepared days ahead and reheated just before guests arrive. You can usually find green tea at the grocery store.

Donna S. Russell
Alvin, Texas

BRAISED HONEYED CHICKEN

2 pounds chicken wings (12 wings)
2 tablespoons oil, peanut if possible
2 green onions, cut into 1½-inch pieces
1 tablespoon thin strips of gingerroot
⅓ cup sherry
2 tablespoons honey
2 tablespoons low-sodium soy sauce

Cut each wing at the joints into 3 sections (or use pre-cut wings). Heat the oil in a heavy skillet. Stir-fry the onions and gingerroot for 3 minutes to flavor the oil. Remove the onions and gingerroot with a slotted spoon and discard. Brown the chicken pieces quickly in the flavored oil; remove chicken and set aside. Drain the skillet. Add the sherry, honey and soy sauce to the skillet; bring to a boil. Stir in the chicken. Reduce the heat, cover and simmer for 15 minutes, turning the chicken every 5 minutes as the sauce thickens. Serve immediately; or arrange on a platter, cover, chill in the refrigerator and serve cold.
Yield: 6 servings.

CHICKEN CORN SOUP

Ground beef or pork can be substituted for the chicken in this recipe. Increase the cooking time to 20 minutes and skim off the fat. If you are preparing a pork roast for use in a pork stir-fry, you can use part of the roast in this soup.

4 cups chicken broth
1 chicken breast, skinned, boned, minced
1 (17-ounce) can cream-style corn
½ cup minced water chestnuts
2 tablespoons dry sherry
1 tablespoon soy sauce
2 tablespoons cornstarch
¼ cup water
¼ cup chopped green onion

Put the broth, chicken, corn, water chestnuts, sherry and soy sauce in a saucepan; bring to a boil, stirring to break up the chicken. Reduce the heat and simmer for about 2 minutes. Blend together the cornstarch and water. Stir the cornstarch mixture into the soup, stirring until the soup thickens (about 2 minutes). Sprinkle with green onion. Serve hot.
Yield: 6 servings.

CHINESE STIR-FRY

Be sure that the pork is cooked all the way through. You can use either plain or Chinese cabbage. Dark sesame oil and rice vinegar can be found in the Chinese food section at the grocery store.

2 to 3 cups cubed pork roast
Sesame oil, dark
1 medium onion, coarsely chopped
3 or 4 ribs celery, diagonally sliced
1½ to 2 cups shredded cabbage
1½ to 2 cups shredded carrots
1 (4-ounce) can sliced mushrooms
1 tablespoon cornstarch
1 cup cold chicken broth or roast drippings
Soy sauce to taste
Rice vinegar to taste
Chopped peanuts (optional)
Chow mein noodles or rice

Prepare all ingredients before stir-frying. Stir-fry the cubed pork in a small amount of sesame oil until lightly browned; remove the pork to a separate bowl. Stir-fry the onion, celery, cabbage and carrots in a small amount of sesame oil until the vegetables are slightly tender. Stir in the pork and mushrooms and bring to a simmer. Blend together the cornstarch and cold broth, then add to the pork and vegetables. Add the soy sauce and rice vinegar. Cook, stirring, until all ingredients are tender and sauce is thickened. Sprinkle with peanuts if desired. Serve over chow mein noodles or rice. Yield: 4 to 6 servings.

FRIED RICE

Cooked shrimp or any cooked meat may be substituted for the ham.

3 tablespoons vegetable oil, peanut if possible	**1/2 cup chopped onions**
4 eggs, beaten	**4 cups cooked white rice**
3/4 cup frozen peas, thawed	**1/2 teaspoon salt**
1 cup chopped cooked ham	**1/4 teaspoon garlic powder**
	Dash of pepper
	2 tablespoons soy sauce

Heat 2 tablespoons of the oil in a large skillet. Add the eggs, cooking and stirring until softly set. Remove the eggs from the skillet and set aside. Add the remaining tablespoon of oil to the skillet and add the peas, ham and onions. Stir-fry for 2 minutes. Stir in the eggs, cooked rice, salt, garlic powder, pepper and soy sauce. Be sure the mixture is thoroughly blended. Yield: 6 to 8 servings.

FILLED CHOCOLATE MERINGUES

2 egg whites, room temperature	**1/2 teaspoon vanilla extract**
1/4 teaspoon cream of tartar	**2 teaspoons cocoa**
Dash of salt	**Chocolate Cheese Filling**
1/2 cup sugar	**24 raspberries**
	24 mint leaves

Preheat the oven to 275 degrees. Line cookie sheets with parchment paper. Beat the egg whites with the cream of tartar and salt in a small mixing bowl until soft peaks form. Beat in the sugar, 1 tablespoon at a time, until stiff, glossy peaks form. Fold in the vanilla. Sift the cocoa over the top of the egg white mixture; gently fold in the cocoa until combined with egg whites. Drop by tablespoons onto the parchment paper. Make indentations in the center of each mound with the back of a small spoon. Bake for 45 minutes or until the meringue turns a light cream color and feels dry to the touch. Carefully peel the meringues off the parchment paper. Cool them completely on wire racks. To serve, spoon or pipe about 2 tablespoons of Chocolate Cheese Filling into the center of each meringue. Garnish each with a raspberry and a mint leaf. Yield: 24 meringues.

CHOCOLATE CHEESE FILLING

1 cup part-skim ricotta cheese	**1 tablespoon sugar**
2 tablespoons cocoa	**1/2 teaspoon vanilla extract**

Combine the ricotta cheese, cocoa, sugar and vanilla in a blender or food processor container; process until smooth. Refrigerate, covered, until serving time. Yield: 1 1/4 cups.

Christmas Brunch

Assorted Fruits and Juices
Assorted Breads and Muffins
Baked Eggs — Coffee
See index for similar recipes.

Christmas Brunch leftovers reheat beautifully in a microwave oven. My sister (also a Beta Sigma Phi) gave me this recipe many years ago. Because it is so quick and easy to prepare, it has become a Christmas tradition. It can be adapted easily for dieters by using an egg substitute, fat-free cottage cheese, and low-fat cheese.

Lucille Jenks, Laureate Omicron
Pahrump, Nevada

BAKED EGGS

10 eggs	**1/2 (4-ounce) can mild chopped chiles**
1/2 cup all-purpose flour	
1 teaspoon baking powder	**1/2 (2-ounce) jar pimientos (optional)**
1/2 teaspoon salt	**1/2 cup melted butter or margarine**
1 pint cottage cheese	
4 cups shredded Monterey Jack cheese	

Preheat the oven to 350 degrees. Beat the eggs in a large mixing bowl. Combine the flour, baking powder and salt; add to the eggs and beat together well. Add the cottage cheese, Monterey Jack cheese, chiles, pimientos and melted butter; beat well. Pour into a 9-by-11-inch baking dish. Bake for 35 minutes. Remove from the oven and let set for 5 minutes. Cut into squares and serve. Yield: 8 to 10 servings.

Rhonda Jo Kimble, Alpha Phi, Watertown, South Dakota, says it is healthier and cheaper to use a mixture of 1/4 cup vegetable oil and 1 tablespoon liquid lecithin from the health food store for greasing pans.

Swiss Fondue Evening

Paté and Crackers
Swiss Fondue
Fruit Salad
Phyllo Cups with
Ice Cream and Rhubarb Sauce
Dry White Wine or Vin Rosé
Hot Tea
See index for similar recipes.

We were introduced to Swiss Fondue by a European couple who had emigrated to Canada. They showed us how to dip a bread piece in the kirsch, then in the fondue, and finally in ground black pepper. Serve the fondue with extra kirsch for dipping. There's something about fondue that makes any evening a special occasion. Gathering around a single pot to share food is guaranteed to break the ice.

Delma J. Waller, Preceptor Alpha Sigma
Waterloo, Ontario, Canada

SWISS FONDUE

1 clove of garlic	*1 ounce kirsch*
2 cups dry white wine	*⅛ teaspoon white*
12 ounces finely	*pepper*
shredded Gruyère or	*⅛ teaspoon nutmeg*
Swiss cheese	*Dash of paprika*
8 ounces finely shredded	*(optional)*
Emmentaler cheese	*French bread cut into*
1 teaspoon cornstarch	*small cubes*

Rub a large saucepan with the clove of garlic. Heat the white wine in the saucepan over medium heat. Combine the Gruyère and the Emmentaler cheeses. Add ⅓ of the cheese mixture to the wine; bring slowly to a boil, stirring constantly. Add the remaining cheese slowly, stirring until all the cheese is melted. Stir the cornstarch into the kirsch, then stir the kirsch mixture into the fondue. Stir in the white pepper, nutmeg and paprika. Pour the mixture into a fondue pot. Keep the mixture bubbling gently over the fondue burner. Serve with the French bread pieces. Yield: 4 servings.

FRUIT SALAD

Serve the fruit salad after the fondue.

1 medium grapefruit,	*1 (16-ounce) can lychees,*
pared and sectioned	*drained and halved*
1 medium orange, pared	*1 teaspoon lemon juice*
and sectioned	
1 (16-ounce) can	
pineapple cubes,	
drained	

Cut the grapefruit and orange sections into quarters. Combine the orange and grapefruit sections with the pineapple and lychees in a glass bowl. Sprinkle the lemon juice over the fruit and mix lightly. Chill until serving time. Yield: 4 to 8 servings.

PHYLLO CUPS WITH RHUBARB SAUCE

This pastry is fragile. The custard cups must be buttered well in order to remove the phyllo without breaking.

4 sheets frozen phyllo	*Vanilla ice cream*
dough, thawed	*Rhubarb Sauce*
3 tablespoons melted	
butter or margarine	

Stack the sheets of phyllo, one on top of the other, on the work surface. Using a sharp knife, cut the stack lengthwise, then crosswise into quarters. Grease 4 custard cups with butter. Place 1 quarter-sheet of phyllo on top of another. Brush the top sheet with melted butter. Arrange the 2 quarter-sheets of phyllo in a custard cup. Stack another 2 quarter-sheets of phyllo and brush the top one with melted butter. Place these crosswise over the phyllo in the custard cup, and arrange to form a cup. Repeat the process with 3 more custard cups, making 4 cups of phyllo. Place the custard cups on a baking sheet. Bake for 10 to 12 minutes or until the phyllo is crisp and golden. Cool in the cups. Make the Rhubarb Sauce. Remove the cooled phyllo from the custard cups and place on dessert plates. Spoon the ice cream into the phyllo cups and top with Rhubarb Sauce. Yield: 4 servings.

RHUBARB SAUCE

2 teaspoons	*½ pound fresh or frozen*
cornstarch	*rhubarb, chopped*
2 tablespoons water	*½ cup sugar*

Stir the cornstarch and the water together in a saucepan. Add the rhubarb. Cook over medium heat, stirring, until the mixture thickens. Stir in the sugar. Let cool.

Doreen C. Saunders, Laureate Alpha Alpha, Kingston, Ontario, Canada, likes the idea of a Late Summer Luncheon that makes the summer bounty-at-its-best shine. With a simple entrée of chicken breasts, she presents sliced marinated tomatoes, a salad of crisp young spinach leaves, and a dessert accompanied by fresh strawberries, grapes, pineapple, raspberries, blueberries, and bananas.

Casserole Brunch

Spicy Egg Casserole
Crunchy Sausage Casserole
Amaretto Hot Fruit Compote
See index for similar recipes.

Every December our chapter gathers together to eat brunch, to exchange ornaments and secret sister gifts, and to share our hopes for Christmas.

Anne Rottmann, Xi Zeta Phi
Jefferson City, Missouri

SPICY EGG CASSEROLE

The bread crusts may be removed, but it is easier to prepare the bread if the crusts are left on.

3 cups shredded Cheddar cheese	1½ teaspoons salt
3 cups shredded Monterey Jack cheese	½ teaspoon onion powder
10 slices white bread, buttered and cubed	¼ teaspoon black pepper
8 eggs, slightly beaten	⅛ teaspoon cayenne pepper
3½ cups milk	1 teaspoon Worcestershire sauce
1 teaspoon light brown sugar	1 teaspoon dry mustard
¼ teaspoon paprika	

Grease an 11-by-13-inch baking pan. Combine the shredded cheeses. Line the pan with half the bread cubes, then sprinkle half the cheese mixture over the bread. Repeat bread and cheese layers. Combine the eggs, milk, brown sugar, paprika, salt, onion powder, pepper, cayenne pepper, Worcestershire sauce and mustard; pour over bread and cheese layers.

Refrigerate, covered, for 8 to 48 hours. Preheat the oven to 325 degrees. Bake for 1 hour or until set. Yield: 12 servings.

CRUNCHY SAUSAGE CASSEROLE

1 (6-ounce) package long grain and wild rice mix	1 (8-ounce) can sliced water chestnuts, drained
1 pound bulk pork sausage	3 tablespoons soy sauce
1 pound ground beef	1 (2-ounce) package sliced almonds
1 large onion, chopped	Lemon slices (optional)
1 (8-ounce) can sliced mushrooms, drained	Parsley sprigs (optional)

Prepare the rice mix using package directions and set aside. Brown the meat well; drain. Add the rice, onion, mushrooms, water chestnuts and soy sauce to the browned meat. Stir well and spoon into an ungreased 2-quart baking dish. Chill, covered, in the refrigerator for 8 to 10 hours. Preheat the oven to 325 degrees. Remove the baking dish from the refrigerator and allow it to rest at room temperature for 30 minutes. Sprinkle the almonds on top. Bake uncovered for 50 minutes. Garnish with lemon slices and parsley if desired. Yield: 10 servings.

AMARETTO HOT FRUIT COMPOTE

1 (16-ounce) can peach halves, drained	2 bananas, sliced
1 (16-ounce) can pear halves, drained	1 teaspoon lemon juice
1 (15-ounce) can pineapple chunks, drained	12 soft coconut macaroons, crumbled
1 (17-ounce) can apricot halves, drained	1 (2-ounce) package sliced almonds, toasted
1 (16-ounce) can pitted dark sweet cherries, drained	¼ cup butter or margarine
	⅓ cup amaretto

Preheat the oven to 350 degrees. Combine the canned peaches, pears, pineapple, apricots and cherries in a large bowl. Combine the bananas and lemon juice and add to the fruit mixture. Layer half the fruit mixture and half the macaroon crumbs in a 2½-quart baking dish. Sprinkle with 3 tablespoons of the toasted almonds and dot with 2 tablespoons butter. Repeat the fruit and macaroon layers. Sprinkle with another 3 tablespoons of almonds and dot with the remaining butter. Pour the amaretto evenly over mixture. Bake for 30 minutes. Sprinkle with the remaining almonds. Stir before serving. Yield: 10 servings.

❖ Luncheon with the Ladies

Iced Tea with Mint
Mushroom Spinach Salad
Hot Chicken Salad — Krispy Rolls
Brownie Sundae — Coffee
See index for similar recipes.

This is a delightful luncheon to serve when getting together with old high school chums. Everything except the rolls can be prepared the day before.

Susan R. Raber
Ballwin, Missouri

MUSHROOM SPINACH SALAD

Even though the salad can be prepared a day ahead of time, I prefer to prepare the mushrooms on the day of the luncheon. Be sure to add the dressing to the salad just before serving.

6 to 8 ounces fresh
  mushrooms
1/2 pound fresh spinach
1/2 cup radishes
4 tablespoons olive oil
2 tablespoons wine
  vinegar
1 clove of garlic, finely
  minced
1/2 teaspoon salt
Freshly ground black
  pepper to taste

Rinse the mushrooms, spinach and radishes; pat dry. Slice the mushrooms, tear the spinach and slice the radishes. Put all in a salad bowl. Combine the oil, vinegar, garlic, salt and pepper; mix well. Pour over the vegetables and toss. Yield: 6 servings.

HOT CHICKEN SALAD

4 cups chopped cooked
  chicken
3/4 cup mayonnaise
1 (10-ounce) can cream
  of chicken soup
2 cups chopped celery
4 hard-cooked eggs
1 teaspoon salt
1 tablespoon chopped
  onion
2 tablespoons lemon
  juice
1 (2-ounce) jar chopped
  pimientos
1 can slivered almonds
1/2 (8-ounce) bag frozen
  peas (optional)
2 to 3 ounces shredded
  Cheddar cheese
Potato chips, crushed

Preheat the oven to 375 degrees. Combine the chicken, mayonnaise, cream of chicken soup, celery, hard-cooked eggs, salt, onion, lemon juice, pimientos, almonds and frozen peas in a 9-by-12-inch baking dish. Top with the shredded cheese and enough crushed potato chips to cover. Bake for 25 minutes. Yield: 10 servings.

KRISPY ROLLS

1 (12-ounce) can
  refrigerated
  biscuits
2 cups crisp rice cereal,
  crushed
1 to 2 tablespoons
  poppy seeds
1 cup grated Parmesan
  cheese
1/2 cup milk

Preheat the oven to the temperature specified on the biscuit package directions. Combine the crushed cereal, poppy seeds and Parmesan cheese in a shallow bowl. Dip each biscuit in milk and roll in the cereal mixture. Place on a baking sheet and bake according to package directions. Yield: 10 rolls.

BROWNIE SUNDAE

2 sticks butter or
  margarine
2 cups sugar
4 eggs
1 1/2 cups all-purpose
  flour
4 tablespoons cocoa
1 teaspoon vanilla
  extract
1/2 cup chopped pecans
Vanilla ice cream
1 (8- to 12-ounce) jar
  fudge topping

Preheat the oven to 350 degrees. Grease an 8-by-8-inch baking pan. Cream the butter and sugar together in a medium bowl, then beat the eggs into the butter and sugar. Add the flour, cocoa, vanilla and pecans to the egg mixture and mix thoroughly. Spread the cocoa mixture in a greased pan and bake for 30 minutes. After cooling, cut into 2-by-2-inch squares. Serve each brownie topped with a medium-size scoop of ice cream and a tablespoon of hot fudge. Yield: 16 brownies.

Sandra Kourik, Xi Alpha Delta, Henderson, Nevada, likes parties with a foreign flair. She suggests a Hawaiian Party with leis for the guests and a menu that includes rumaki, baked bananas, oriental-flavored kabobs, lumpia, fish baked in a macadamia coating, and other tropical-style dishes such as a coconut dessert. Other theme menus might be a German Dinner focusing on sauerbraten with red cabbage and potato pancakes, or a Spanish Dinner featuring arroz con pollo and flan.

Working Woman's Prime Rib Dinner

Caesar Salad with Cleopatra Dressing
Prime Rib of Beef
Baked Potatoes
Steamed Broccoli Florets
See index for similar recipes.

Select a choice cut of prime rib for this delicious meal. Put the beef in the oven before leaving for work and it will be ready when you return home.

Marie Rita Schmidt
Lakeland, Florida

CAESAR SALAD

Romaine lettuce,
   chopped or whole
Iceberg lettuce, chopped

Croutons
Parmesan cheese

Toss together the romaine lettuce, iceberg lettuce, croutons and Parmesan cheese. Serve with Cleopatra Dressing. Yield: variable.

CLEOPATRA DRESSING

3 or 4 eggs
4 or 5 anchovies
1 or 2 cloves of garlic

1 cup light vegetable oil
1 tablespoon fresh or
   bottled lemon juice

Place the eggs, anchovies and garlic in a blender and blend until smooth. With the blender running, slowly pour in the oil. The dressing will thicken as you pour. Add the lemon juice, stirring with a spoon. Pour desired amount of dressing over the salad greens. Yield: 2 cups.

PRIME RIB OF BEEF

5 pounds (or more)
   prime rib

Preheat the oven to 500 degrees. Place the beef in a roasting pan in the oven; bake for 5 to 7 minutes (5 minutes for Rare, 7 for Medium Rare). Reduce heat to the lowest setting and continue to cook for 8 to 10 hours. Yield: 10 to 12 servings.

Mary Beth's Unusual Birthday Surprise

Salad
Grilled Pork Chops
Pineapple Bake
Sautéed Brussels Sprouts
Rolls
See index for similar recipes.

A friend prepared this unusual dinner for me on my birthday because I love brussels sprouts! The salad and rolls are optional.

Mary Beth Lemons, Preceptor Alpha Kappa
Phoenix, Arizona

PINEAPPLE BAKE

When it comes to side dishes for pork, I like alternatives to the old standbys like applesauce and cranberry sauce. Pineapple Bake makes a good side dish for pork, chicken, or turkey.

4 slices white bread
½ cup butter or
   margarine, softened
¾ cup sugar

4 eggs
1 (16-ounce) can crushed
   pineapple

Preheat the oven to 350 degrees. Remove the bread crusts and cut the bread into cubes. Cream the butter and sugar in a large bowl until light and fluffy. Add eggs one at a time, beating them into the butter mixture. Stir in the pineapple and bread cubes. Pour into a greased 9-inch baking dish and bake for about an hour or until lightly browned. Yield: 4 to 6 servings.

SAUTEED BRUSSELS SPROUTS

1½ cups brussels
   sprouts
2 teaspoons butter or
   margarine
Salt and pepper

Pinch of nutmeg
2 teaspoons lemon juice
1 tablespoon chopped
   parsley

Boil the brussels sprouts for 20 minutes or until tender. For best flavor, cut the cooked sprouts in half. Sauté the sprouts in butter with the salt, pepper and nutmeg. When the butter begins to brown, add the lemon juice and parsley. Yield: 4 servings.

Winter Warmup

Zesty Onion Meat Loaf
Frozen Vegetable Medley
Hearty Wheat Bread
Peach Bread Pudding
See index for similar recipes.

This meal is delicious any time of the year, but it is especially satisfying on a cold, dark winter evening. You may substitute canned or frozen peaches for ripe peaches.

Mary Agler, Delta Gamma
Alliance, Nebraska

ZESTY ONION MEAT LOAF

If you would rather not shape a free-standing meat loaf, use a loaf pan for baking. Using a loaf pan may mean an extra 10 minutes baking time.

1½ pounds ground beef	**1 egg**
1 (10-ounce) can Italian	**2 tablespoons**
tomato soup	**Worcestershire sauce**
1 (3-ounce) can French-	**¾ teaspoon salt**
fried onion rings	**¼ teaspoon pepper**

Preheat the oven to 350 degrees. Mix together the beef, ⅓ cup of the tomato soup, half the French-fried onion rings, egg, Worcestershire sauce, salt and pepper. Shape into a 4-by-8-inch loaf on a shallow baking dish. Bake for 1 hour or until completely cooked. Pour off the fat. Spoon the remaining tomato soup over the meat loaf and top with the remaining French-fried onions. Bake for another 5 minutes or until onions are golden. Yield: 6 servings.

PEACH BREAD PUDDING

3 eggs	**2 tablespoons butter or**
¾ cup sugar	**margarine**
1½ cups milk	**3 or 4 ripe peaches**
2 teaspoons vanilla	**2 tablespoons lemon**
extract	**juice**
6 thick slices white	
bread	

Preheat the oven to 350 degrees. Beat together the eggs and ½ cup of the sugar in a medium bowl. Gradually add the milk, continuing to beat well. Add the vanilla. Tear the bread into large pieces. Melt the butter in a skillet over medium heat, and brown the bread in the butter until golden. Remove the pan from the heat and cool. Peel, pit and slice the peaches. Toss the peach slices with the remaining ¼ cup of sugar and the lemon juice. Add the peaches to the bread and gently toss together. Pour the peaches and bread into a glass 8-by-8-inch baking pan and pour the egg mixture over all. Bake for 45 minutes or until lightly browned. Yield: 10 to 16 servings.

Birthday Celebration

Tossed Salad — Chicken Curry
Rice Pilaf — Sugar Snap Peas
Angel Food Cake with Rainbow Sherbet
See index for similar recipes.

I created this dinner to celebrate my husband's forty-first birthday. He loved it!

Cathy Beaver, Preceptor Gamma Eta
Tulsa, Oklahoma

CHICKEN CURRY

An easy way to prepare the chicken is to broil skinless, boneless chicken breasts, refrigerate until firm, then dice the cooled chicken. For an extra-special curry, top with raisins, chopped almonds, and shredded fresh coconut. Serve hot over rice pilaf made from a mix.

1 tablespoon margarine	**2½ teaspoons curry**
1 cup chopped apple	**powder**
1 cup chopped celery	**¾ cup chicken broth**
½ cup chopped sweet	**2 cups milk**
onion	**2 cups diced cooked**
1 clove of garlic, minced	**chicken**
2 tablespoons	**1 (3-ounce) can**
cornstarch	**mushrooms**

Melt the margarine in a saucepan. Add the apple, celery, onion and garlic to the pan; sauté in the margarine until tender. Combine the cornstarch, curry powder and chicken broth; stir into the apple mixture. Add the milk slowly, cooking and stirring until thick and bubbly. Stir in the chicken and mushrooms and heat all the way through.
Yield: 6 servings.

Victorian Ladies' Luncheon

Fresh Fruit Salad with
Poppy Seed Dressing
Shrimp Bisque
Cranberry Chicken Salad
Parmesan Breadsticks
Frozen Daiquiri Dessert
See index for similar recipes.

My chapter served this luncheon when we enter-
tained another chapter. We had parlor games
after lunch. The Shrimp Bisque makes 4 large
servings; to serve a crowd, serve the bisque in
small cups.

Julie Parnell, Preceptor Xi Pi
Houston, Texas

SHRIMP BISQUE

Be sure to let the cooked vegetables cool before purée-
ing them in the blender. If you think they are still too
hot and may cause a blender "explosion," try remov-
ing the center of the lid and covering it with a towel
before turning on the blender. The towel will allow
any hot burst of steam to escape but will catch any
food that flies up while being blended.

1 cup chicken broth	1/2 bay leaf, crumbled
1 (19-ounce) can tomatoes	1 teaspoon salt
1/2 cup chopped onions	2 tablespoons long grain rice
1/2 cup chopped celery	1/4 cup sherry
1 cup sliced carrots	1 cup half-and-half
Dash of ground cloves	1/2 pound shrimp, cooked, shelled, deveined
1/8 teaspoon black pepper	

Place the chicken broth, tomatoes, onions, celery, carrots, cloves, pepper, bay leaf, salt and rice in a 2-quart
saucepan. Bring to a boil. Simmer, covered, very
slowly for about 35 minutes or until vegetables are
tender. Purée the cooked vegetable mixture in a
blender until it is very smooth. Pour the blended
mixture into the top of a double boiler. Heat over
boiling water. Just before serving, add the sherry,
half-and-half and shrimp. Yield: 4 servings.

CRANBERRY CHICKEN SALAD

1 (2- to 3-pound) chicken	1/2 cup water
1 cup mayonnaise	1/4 cup boiling water
1 cup finely chopped celery	1 (3-ounce) box lemon gelatin
1 onion, finely chopped	3/4 cup boiling water
1/2 teaspoon salt	1 cup whole cranberry sauce
1/4 teaspoon pepper	1/4 cup orange juice
1/2 teaspoon basil	
1 envelope unflavored gelatin	

Cook the chicken. Remove the meat from the bones
and chop it into small pieces. Combine the chopped
chicken with the mayonnaise, celery, onion, salt, pepper and basil. Soften the gelatin in 1/2 cup water, then
add 1/4 cup boiling water to dissolve it. Stir the
gelatin into the chicken mixture. Spoon into an 8-by-
8-inch pan. Chill, covered, in the refrigerator for at
least several hours or until firm. Dissolve the lemon
gelatin in 3/4 cup boiling water; add the cranberry
sauce and orange juice. Spoon the cranberry mixture
over the chilled chicken salad. Yield: 12 to 16 servings.

PARMESAN BREADSTICKS

1 (10-count) package hot dog buns	Parmesan cheese
2 sticks butter or margarine, melted	

Preheat the oven to 250 degrees. Cut the buns lengthwise into thirds, then cut each long "breadstick" in
half. Line a baking sheet with foil. Lay the breadsticks on the foil. Using a pastry brush, liberally
spread the butter on all the breadsticks. Sprinkle with
Parmesan cheese. Bake for 30 to 60 minutes or until
the breadsticks are brown and crunchy.
Yield: Each bun makes 12 breadsticks.

FROZEN DAIQUIRI DESSERT

1 (8-ounce) package cream cheese, softened	1 1/2 jiggers rum
1 (6-ounce) can frozen limeade	1 (20-ounce) can crushed pineapple, drained
1 (3-ounce) package custard mix	1 (8-ounce) jar maraschino cherries, drained and chopped
	1/2 cup chopped pecans

Blend the cream cheese, limeade, custard mix and
rum in a blender. Mix together the crushed pineapple, cherries and pecans in a large bowl. Add the
blender mixture and mix well. Spread in a 9-by-13-
inch pan and freeze. Yield: 12 to 16 servings.

Old-Fashioned Easter Dinner

Orange Pearl Delight Salad
Baked Ham
Tossed Vegetable Medley
Scalloped Potatoes
Freshly Cooked Applesauce
Icebox Dinner Rolls
Strawberry Wonder Cake
Iced Tea with Fresh Lemon
Coffee
See index for similar recipes.

This is the traditional dinner that my family always requests for Easter. I prefer to use a bone-in shank or butt ham, and I use an oven bag for cooking. A ham cooks more quickly in an oven bag and is more tender and moist—and a cinch to clean up!

Darice Hostetler
Burlington, Colorado

ORANGE PEARL DELIGHT SALAD

1 (11-ounce) can
 mandarin oranges
1 (3-ounce) package
 orange gelatin
2 (3-ounce) packages
 tapioca pudding mix

1 (8-ounce) package
 whipped topping
1/2 cup chopped pecans
 or walnuts

Drain the mandarin oranges and reserve the liquid. Place the orange segments in a covered container in the refrigerator. Mix together the reserved mandarin orange liquid and enough water to make 3 1/2 cups liquid. Place the liquid in a saucepan with the gelatin and pudding mix and mix well. Cook over medium heat until the mixture comes to a full boil, stirring constantly. Pour into a large serving bowl and chill, covered, in the refrigerator for several hours or until firm. When ready to serve, fold the whipped topping, mandarin oranges and nuts into the chilled gelatin mixture. Yield: 8 servings.

TOSSED VEGETABLE MEDLEY

1 head cauliflower,
 broken into florets
1 bunch broccoli, broken
 into florets
1 pint cherry tomatoes,
 halved

Ranch dressing to taste
Freshly grated
 Parmesan cheese

Place the cauliflower, broccoli, tomatoes and ranch dressing in a large serving bowl. Toss with the Parmesan cheese.

SCALLOPED POTATOES

6 to 8 (depending on
 size) russet or Idaho
 potatoes, peeled
1 1/2 cups milk, scalded
1/2 cup margarine

1 tablespoon instant
 onion
Salt and pepper to taste
1 cup shredded sharp
 Cheddar cheese

Preheat the oven to 350 degrees. Slice the potatoes into thin slices. Layer them with the milk, margarine and onion in a greased 9-by-13-inch baking pan, adding salt and pepper to each layer to taste. Dot with margarine and top with the cheese. Bake for 1 1/2 hours or until golden brown. Yield: 8 servings.

FRESHLY COOKED APPLESAUCE

10 cooking apples,
 peeled and cored
1/4 cup sugar

1 teaspoon cinnamon
1/4 cup water

Cut the apples into quarters and place in a heavy saucepan. Add the sugar, cinnamon and water. Simmer until all the ingredients are steaming hot. Remove the pan from the heat and cover. The apples will finish cooking in the covered pan as they rest about 15 minutes. Yield: 8 servings.

ICEBOX DINNER ROLLS

This dough can be kept in the refrigerator for up to 10 days.

1 envelope dry yeast
1/2 cup warm water
1 quart milk, scalded
 and cooled
1 cup mashed potatoes
1 cup sugar
1 cup melted or liquid
 shortening

2 cups all-purpose flour,
 sifted
1 teaspoon baking
 powder
1 teaspoon baking soda
1 teaspoon salt

Soften the yeast in the warm water. Combine the cooled milk, potatoes, sugar and shortening in a large bowl; mix thoroughly. Add the yeast mixture.

Stir in the flour, baking powder, baking soda and salt. Let the dough rise in a warm place until it appears full of gas bubbles. Stir in more flour, enough to make a stiff dough. Knead the dough until smooth and elastic and place in a greased bowl; cover and place in refrigerator. When ready to bake rolls, cut or pinch off the desired amount of dough. Let the dough rise for 1 hour at room temperature. Shape into rolls. Preheat the oven to 425 degrees. Let the shaped rolls rise for 1 hour. Finally, bake for 12 to 15 minutes or until lightly browned. Yield: 1 dozen rolls.

STRAWBERRY WONDER CAKE

1 (6-ounce) package
    strawberry gelatin
2 cups boiling water
2 (16-ounce) packages
    frozen strawberries,
    thawed and drained
2 (4-ounce) packages
    vanilla instant
    pudding mix

2 cups milk
1 pint vanilla ice cream,
    softened
1 prepared angel food
    cake, cut or torn into
    small pieces

Dissolve the gelatin in the boiling water in a bowl. Chill, covered, in the refrigerator until partially set. Fold the strawberries into the gelatin mixture. Combine the pudding mix and milk in a large bowl; blend well. Stir the ice cream into the pudding mixture. Layer the cake, pudding mixture and gelatin mixture in a serving dish. Chill well until serving time. Yield: 16 servings.

Summertime Delight

Caesar Salad
Heart-Healthy Vegetable Pizza
Grilled Salmon with Capers
Baked Potatoes
See index for similar recipes.

The pizza on this menu serves a small crowd. If you are indeed serving a small crowd, buy more salmon fillets and increase the other ingredient amounts in the salmon recipe.

Lois Franz, Preceptor Epsilon
Hayden Lake, Idaho

HEART-HEALTHY VEGETABLE PIZZA

1/2 package active dried
    yeast
3/4 cup warm water
2 tablespoons olive oil
1 teaspoon salt
1/2 teaspoon minced
    fresh parsley
2 to 2 1/2 cups all-purpose
    flour
2 tablespoons
    mayonnaise
1 package ranch
    dressing mix

1 (8-ounce) package
    cream cheese,
    softened
Small cucumber, cut
    into small pieces
1/4 to 1/2 cup coarsely
    chopped broccoli
1/4 to 1/2 cup coarsely
    chopped cauliflower
Green tomato, chopped
2 to 4 green onions,
    chopped

Preheat the oven to 425 degrees. Dissolve the yeast in the warm water in a large bowl and let stand for 5 to 10 minutes. Grease a pizza pan or a 9-by-13-inch baking pan. Stir the olive oil, salt and parsley into the yeast mixture. Slowly add flour until the dough is smooth and not too sticky. Knead the dough for a few minutes, adding flour as necessary to prevent sticking. Spread or roll out the dough to cover the entire greased pan. Bake for about 20 minutes or until just beginning to brown. Remove from the oven and allow to cool for 30 minutes. Mix together the mayonnaise, ranch dressing mix and cream cheese; spread over the cooled crust. Scatter the broccoli, cauliflower, tomato and green onion over the top. Yield: 12 to 15 servings.

GRILLED SALMON WITH CAPERS

3 salmon fillets
1/2 cup packaged pesto
    sauce mix
1/2 teaspoon vegetable
    oil
1/2 cup butter or
    margarine

1/2 cup white wine
2 tablespoons drained
    capers
Dash of salt and pepper
1 cup sour cream
1 teaspoon all-purpose
    flour

Preheat the grill. Wash the salmon fillets. Pour the pesto mix and the oil into a shallow baking dish. Add the salmon fillets, turning them over until they are covered with the mixture. Grill for 6 to 10 minutes, depending on the thickness of the fillets. To make the sauce, melt the butter in a small saucepan. Add the white wine, capers, salt and pepper. Stir together the sour cream and flour and add to the butter mixture. Pour over the grilled salmon. Yield: 3 servings.

✤ Holiday Chapter Meeting

Guacamole with Tortilla Chips
Pineapple Salad Mold
Deviled Ham Spread — Tuna Mold
Assorted Chips and Crackers
Festive Fruitcake
Floating Island Eggnog
English Wassail
See index for similar recipes.

This festive mixture of colors, textures, and aromas will give everyone the feeling of an old-time Christmas.

Mary D. Stockwell, Xi Lambda
Baton Rouge, Louisiana

GUACAMOLE

3 ripe avocados	Dash of hot pepper
1/8 teaspoon bottled	sauce
minced garlic	1/2 small onion, finely
1/8 teaspoon canned	chopped
chopped jalapeño	3 tablespoons sour
peppers	cream
1/4 teaspoon lemon juice	Tortilla chips

Mash the avocados in a medium bowl until the mixture has a coarse texture. Blend in the garlic, jalapeño peppers, lemon juice, hot pepper sauce and onion. Blend in the sour cream and chill until ready to serve. Serve with tortilla chips. Yield: 2 cups.

PINEAPPLE SALAD MOLD

1 envelope unflavored	Dash of salt
gelatin	1 cup shredded Cheddar
1/2 cup cold water	cheese
1 (9-ounce) can crushed	1/2 cup whipping cream,
pineapple	whipped
2 tablespoons lemon	Walnuts
juice	Maraschino cherries
1/4 cup sugar	Endive

Early in the day, sprinkle the gelatin on the cold water to soften. Heat the pineapple with the lemon juice, sugar and salt in a saucepan over medium heat. Add the gelatin mixture; stir until dissolved. Chill, covered, until partially thickened; fold in the cheese

and whipped cream. Turn into a 1-quart mold. Chill, covered, until firmly set. Unmold the salad onto a serving plate. Garnish with cherries and walnuts. Tuck endive around the bottom of the salad. Yield: 6 to 8 servings.

DEVILED HAM SPREAD

2 (2 1/2-ounce) cans	1 teaspoon lemon juice
deviled ham	1 teaspoon horseradish
2 (3-ounce) packages	Pretzels and corn chips
cream cheese, softened	

Combine the deviled ham, cream cheese, lemon juice and horseradish. Serve in a 2-cup quiche dish alongside pretzels and corn chips. Yield: 1 1/2 cups.

TUNA MOLD

2 envelopes unflavored	2 hard-cooked eggs,
gelatin	chopped
1/2 cup cold water	2 cups mayonnaise
2 (6-ounce) cans tuna,	Red pepper to taste
drained, flaked	Assorted crackers
5 green onions, chopped	

Stir the gelatin into the cold water to soften, then heat in a small saucepan, stirring to dissolve. Set aside to cool. Combine the tuna, onions, eggs, mayonnaise and red pepper; mix thoroughly. Stir in the cooled gelatin mixture. Spray a 2-quart mold with nonstick cooking spray and pour the tuna mixture into the mold. Chill, covered, in the refrigerator until set. Unmold on a serving tray and serve with assorted crackers. Yield: 20 servings.

FESTIVE FRUITCAKE

1 (loaf) cranberry quick	8 ounces candied
bread mix	pineapple chunks
1 (loaf) nut quick bread	4 ounces red candied
mix	cherries
2 eggs, beaten	4 ounces green candied
2 tablespoons vegetable	cherries
oil	2 cups chopped walnuts
2 cups water	
16 ounces mixed candied	
fruit, chopped	

Preheat the oven to 350 degrees. Pour both quick bread mixes into a large bowl. Add the eggs, oil and water; stir until the dry ingredients are moistened. Add the candied ingredients and walnuts, blending well. Pour the batter into a bundt cake pan that has been well greased and floured. Bake for 75 to 85 minutes or until an inserted toothpick comes out clean. Yield: 24 to 36 servings.

FLOATING ISLAND EGGNOG

4 eggs
4 tablespoons sugar
1 quart milk
1 tablespoon vanilla
extract

Dash of confectioners'
sugar
Dash of cinnamon
Dash of nutmeg

Separate the eggs. Beat the egg yolks with the sugar until very light. Bring the milk just to a boil in a 2-quart Dutch oven over high heat; stir the egg yolk mixture into the milk as it begins to boil. Reduce the heat to medium and let the mixture thicken as you stir for 1 minute. Remove from heat, add the vanilla and set aside to cool. Chill, covered, in the refrigerator for 2 or 3 hours or until very cold. Beat the egg whites to a stiff froth. Ladle the cold eggnog into a glass punch bowl. Heap the egg whites on top. Dust with remaining ingredients. Yield: 8 servings.

ENGLISH WASSAIL

1 (64-ounce) bottle apple
juice
1 (32-opunce) bottle
cranberry juice
2 cups orange juice
3/4 cup (about) sugar
(optional)

1 cup rum (optional)
2 cinnamon sticks
1 teaspoon whole
allspice
1 teaspoon whole cloves
1 lemon, thinly sliced
1 orange, thinly sliced

Pour the apple juice, cranberry juice and orange juice into a slow cooker. Stir in sugar and rum if desired. Break the cinnamon sticks in half and place in a large tea ball with the allspice and cloves. Float the tea ball, lemon slices and orange slices in the juices. Cook on High for 1 hour. Turn down to Low and cook for another 4 to 8 hours. Yield: 20 servings.

Slow-Cooker Ham Dinner

Triple-Orange Salad
Slow Cooker Foil-Baked Ham
Confetti Scalloped Potatoes
See index for similar recipes.

My family (especially the kids) adores this meal—and there aren't a lot of dishes to do when it's over!

Michelle A. Doyle, Xi Omega
Worland, Wyoming

TRIPLE-ORANGE SALAD

For other tasty varieties of this salad, try different flavors of gelatin, juice, and fruit.

1 (6-ounce) package
orange gelatin
2 cups boiling water
1 (6-ounce) can frozen
orange juice
concentrate

1 (20-ounce) can crushed
pineapple, undrained
1 (11-ounce) can
mandarin orange
sections, drained

Dissolve the gelatin in the boiling water. Stir in the orange juice concentrate until it is thawed, then stir in the pineapple and mandarin oranges. Chill until set. Yield: 12 servings.

SLOW-COOKER FOIL-BAKED HAM

I cube the leftover ham and place the cubes in freezer bags, 1 cup per bag, to store in the freezer for use in other recipes such as scalloped potatoes.

3- to 4-pound precooked
ham

1/2 cup water

Wrap ham in foil. Pour 1/2 cup water in a slow cooker. Place ham in the slow cooker. Cover and cook on High for 1 hour. Reduce heat to Low and cook for 6 to 7 hours longer. Yield: 6 to 8 servings.

CONFETTI SCALLOPED POTATOES

1/2 cup butter or
margarine
1/2 cup chopped onion
1 (16-ounce) package
frozen hash brown
potatoes
1 (10-ounce) can cream
of celery soup

1 soup can milk
1 cup shredded Cheddar
cheese
1 (11-ounce) can
Mexicorn, drained
1 cup cheese cracker
crumbs, divided

Preheat the oven to 375 degrees. Melt the butter in a large skillet over medium heat. Add the onion and sauté until tender. Stir in the hash browns, soup and milk. Add the cheese, Mexicorn and 1/2 cup of the cracker crumbs. Pour the mixture into a 9-by-13-inch baking dish and top with remaining crumbs. Bake for 35 to 40 minutes until browned. Yield: 6 to 8 servings.

Johnnie Stanford, Laureate Zeta Eta, Bryan, Texas, submits a Guest Day Tea menu which includes a crab meat appetizer, chicken salad sandwiches, cream cheese brownies, sugar cookies, apricot balls, and salted pecans to go with a choice of fruit punch or Earl Grey tea.

Bayou Banquet

"LSU" (Layered Salad Unlimited)
Creole Bread — Crawfish New Orleans
Louisiana Sunshine Dessert
Cajun Champagne
See index for similar recipes.

From salad to champagne, this menu is perfect for any exciting celebration . . . especially in Bayou country!

Cheryl Magee, Xi Eta
McComb, Mississippi

"LSU" (LAYERED SALAD UNLIMITED)

You may add boiled shrimp to this recipe if you like.

½ head lettuce	1 (8-ounce) can English
1 cup shredded or diced	peas, drained
carrots	2 cups mayonnaise
½ cup diced green bell	1 tablespoon sugar
pepper	2 cups shredded Cheddar
1 cup sliced cucumber	cheese
½ cup each diced celery,	Bacon bits
onion and radishes	Diced tomatoes

Wash the lettuce and tear into bite-size pieces; place in a bowl of water with 5 or 6 pieces of ice. Set aside. Wash and prepare the carrots, bell pepper, cucumber, celery, onion and radishes. Drain the lettuce and place it in a deep 11-by-14-inch baking dish. Layer the carrots, bell pepper, cucumber, celery, onion, radishes and peas over the lettuce. Mix together the mayonnaise and sugar and spread over the peas. Spread the cheese over the mayonnaise layer. Garnish with bacon bits and diced tomatoes. Chill, covered, in the refrigerator until ready to serve. Yield: 10 to12 servings.

CREOLE BREAD

1 large loaf French bread	2 cups shredded
½ cup melted butter or	mozzarella cheese
margarine	(optional)
1 tablespoon garlic	Paprika (optional)
powder	

Preheat the oven to 350 degrees. Slice the French bread in half lengthwise. Mix the garlic powder with the melted butter and spread over the cut sides of the bread. Sprinkle the cheese over the butter if desired. Place on a baking sheet. Bake for 15 to 20 minutes or until golden brown. Sprinkle paprika over the bread if you want more color. Yield: 10 servings.

CRAWFISH NEW ORLEANS

This dish may be prepared ahead of time and frozen without the process cheese and onion rings.

8 ounces cream cheese	2 cups cooked rice
½ cup plus 2	1 tablespoon garlic
tablespoons butter or	powder
margarine	Red and black pepper to
2 pounds crawfish tails	taste
1 large onion, diced	2 cups shredded process
1 large green pepper	cheese
8 ounces fresh or canned	1 (6-ounce) can French-
mushrooms	fried onion rings
1 (10-ounce) can	
mushroom soup	

Preheat the oven to 350 degrees. Melt the cream cheese and ½ cup of the butter together in the microwave. Sauté the crawfish tails, onion, bell pepper and mushrooms in the remaining 2 tablespoons butter until the crawfish turns bright red. Stir in the soup, rice, garlic powder and red and black pepper. Add the cream cheese mixture. Pour into a greased 11-by-14-inch baking dish and top with the process cheese. Bake for 20 minutes. Top with the onion rings and bake for 15 to 20 minutes. Yield: 12 servings.

LOUISIANA SUNSHINE DESSERT

Making the crust the night before will speed up the final preparation of this dessert.

1 cup all-purpose flour	1 (8-ounce) container
½ cup melted butter or	whipped topping
margarine	3 egg yolks
¼ cup sugar	1 (14-ounce) can
1 cup chopped pecans or	sweetened condensed
walnuts	milk
1 (8-ounce) package	Juice of 4 lemons
cream cheese,	1 (8-ounce) container
softened	whipped topping
2 cups powdered sugar	½ cup chopped pecans
2 teaspoons vanilla	or walnuts
extract	

Preheat the oven to 350 degrees. Combine the flour with the butter, sugar and nuts. Pat the mixture evenly into an 11-by-14-inch baking pan and bake for 15 to 20 minutes or until lightly browned. Let cool completely. To make the cream cheese filling, mix the cream cheese with the powdered sugar, vanilla and 1 container of the whipped topping. Pour the mixture into the crust. Combine the egg yolks with the condensed milk and lemon juice. Pour over the cream cheese filling. Spread remaining whipped topping over the lemon filling and sprinkle nuts over the top. Chill for 1 hour before serving. Yield: 16 servings.

CAJUN CHAMPAGNE

3 family-size tea bags
4 cups bottled water
1 cup sugar

Crushed ice
Lemon slices
1 liter club soda, chilled

Place the tea bags in the bottled water and bring to a rolling boil; remove the pan from the heat. Let the tea rest for 10 minutes. Put the sugar in a half-gallon pitcher. Pour the tea into the pitcher and stir. Fill glasses half-full of tea. Add ¼ cup crushed ice to each glass and garnish with a lemon slice. Fill the glasses with chilled club soda. Yield: 8 to 12 servings.

Bea Cummins of Jefferson City, Missouri, suggests a colorful Post-Holiday Luncheon as a good way to use leftovers. Serve chicken or turkey and stuffing casserole, cranberry gelatin salad, glazed carrots with broccoli, and fruitcake served with ice cream.

Complete Do-Ahead Holiday Party

Orange Endive Salad
Turkey Tetrazzini
Spiced Cranberry Chutney
Classic Tiramisu
See index for similar recipes.

I have many pleasant memories of holiday parties made easy with this menu. Turkey Tetrazzini is the perfect dish for making use of leftover Thanksgiving turkey, and it freezes beautifully for up to one month.

Lois Bolan, Eta Nu
Boyne City, Michigan

ORANGE ENDIVE SALAD

You can wash and dry the salad greens and place them in a plastic bag in the refrigerator the day before.

2 navel oranges, peeled
and sectioned
1 small red onion
12 cups endive and other
greens
2 cloves of garlic,
minced

12 tablespoons olive oil
4 tablespoons tarragon
vinegar
2 teaspoons sugar
2 teaspoons salt
2 teaspoons paprika

Cut the orange sections in thirds. Slice the onion into thin rings. Toss the salad greens, oranges and onion slices together in a large salad bowl. To make the dressing, put the garlic, olive oil, vinegar, sugar, salt and paprika in a glass jar with a tight lid. Shake well and pour over the salad when ready to serve. Yield: 12 servings.

TURKEY TETRAZZINI

½ cup butter or
margarine
½ cup diced onion
½ cup diced celery
½ cup diced green
pepper
1 clove of garlic, crushed
1 cup sliced mushrooms
½ cup all-purpose flour
3 cups canned chicken
broth, defatted
¾ cup half-and-half
¼ cup sherry
1 teaspoon tarragon

1½ teaspoons salt
½ teaspoon pepper
½ cup canned slivered
pimientos
1 (16-ounce) package dry
spaghetti
3 pounds cubed cooked
turkey
1 cup grated Parmesan
cheese
2 cups (½-inch) bread
cubes made from firm
white bread
Paprika

Preheat the oven to 350 degrees. Butter one 12-by-16-inch baking dish or two 7-by-11-inch baking dishes. Melt the butter in a skillet and sauté the onion, celery, green pepper and garlic for 5 minutes. Add the mushrooms and cook for 3 minutes longer. Add the flour; cook, stirring, over low heat for 2 minutes. Add the broth; increase the heat to Medium and stir well. Add the half-and-half, sherry, tarragon, salt, pepper and pimientos; cook, stirring, until smooth and thickened. Remove from heat. Cook the spaghetti according to package directions and drain. Place half the pasta in the baking dish, spread half the turkey over the pasta, pour half the cream sauce over the turkey and sprinkle with ⅓ of the Parmesan cheese. Repeat the layers, top with the bread cubes and sprinkle with the remaining Parmesan cheese. Sprinkle lightly with paprika. Bake for 30 to 40 minutes or until bubbly. Yield: 12 servings.

SPICED CRANBERRY CHUTNEY

Prepare this chutney for Thanksgiving dinner—you can freeze the leftovers and use them later for your holiday party.

2 cups cider vinegar
1 medium onion, chopped
1/2 cup water
1 teaspoon ground fresh ginger
2 teaspoons grated orange peel
1 1/2 teaspoons salt
1/2 teaspoon cinnamon
1 clove of garlic, minced
1/2 teaspoon dry mustard

1/4 teaspoon dried red pepper
3 cups firmly packed light brown sugar
2 pears, peeled, cored, diced
1 large Granny Smith apple, peeled, cored, diced
2 cups cranberries
1/2 cup raisins

Place vinegar, onion, water, ginger, orange peel, salt, cinnamon, garlic, mustard and red pepper in a medium saucepan; bring to a boil, stirring often. Cook for 15 minutes over medium heat. Add brown sugar, pears, apple, cranberries and raisins. Simmer, uncovered, for 1 hour or until the mixture thickens slightly. The mixture will thicken even more as it cools. The chutney can be kept in the refrigerator for 4 days, or it can be frozen. Yield: 6 cups (24 servings).

CLASSIC TIRAMISU

This dessert should be prepared the day before serving.

6 egg yolks
1 1/4 cups sugar
1 1/4 cups Cheese Mixture or mascarpone cheese
2 cups whipping cream
2 (3-ounce) packages ladyfingers, halved

1/3 cup coffee liqueur, or
1/2 cup hot water mixed with
2 teaspoons instant coffee granules
1/4 cup unsweetened cocoa powder
Chocolate curls

Combine the egg yolks and sugar and whip for about 1 minute or until thick and lemon-colored. Place in the top of a double boiler over boiling water and cook for 8 to 10 minutes, stirring constantly. Remove from the heat and add the Cheese Mixture, beating well. Whip 1 3/4 cups of the cream until stiff peaks form; fold into the yolk mixture and set aside. Line the bottom of a 3-quart dish with the ladyfinger halves. Brush the ladyfingers with half the coffee liqueur. Spoon half the yolk mixture over the ladyfingers. Repeat the layers. Sift the cocoa powder over all. Chill, covered, in the refrigerator for 8 to 10 hours. Garnish with additional whipped cream and chocolate curls if desired. Yield: 6 servings.

CHEESE MIXTURE

1 (8-ounce) package cream cheese, softened

1/4 cup sour cream
2 tablespoons whipping cream

Mix all ingredients in a bowl until fluffy.

Spring-Summer Party Buffet

Springtime Punch — Summer Salad
Orange Wedges — Pasta with Asparagus
Spaghettini with Garlic and Oil
Fresh Sliced Tomatoes
Cow Pies — Comeback Cake

See index for similar recipes.

This spaghettini recipe is perfect for a party buffet. It is delicious and simple—what some call a "throw-together" dish.

Joycee Davis, Preceptor Zeta
Lowell, Arizona

SPAGHETTINI WITH GARLIC AND OIL

Serve the pasta with fresh tomatoes drizzled with a balsamic vinaigrette.

12 ounces spaghettini
3 tablespoons olive oil
6 cloves of garlic, minced
1/2 cup reduced-sodium chicken broth, defatted
3 tablespoons fresh lemon juice
3 tablespoons chopped fresh parsley

3 tablespoons snipped fresh chives
1 teaspoon grated lemon zest
3/4 teaspoon salt
1/4 teaspoon freshly ground black pepper
2 tablespoons grated Parmesan cheese
1 tablespoon plain dried bread crumbs

Cook the spaghettini according to package directions just until tender; drain well. Heat the olive oil in a large skillet over low heat. Add the garlic and sauté for 5 minutes or until tender, stirring frequently. Stir in the next 7 ingredients. Cook for 1 minute or until the mixture is heated through. Remove the spaghettini to a large bowl; add the garlic sauce and toss to combine. Sprinkle with the Parmesan cheese and bread crumbs and toss again. Yield: 6 servings.

Appealing Appetizers and Beverages

"There's never a second chance to make a first impression,' and so it is with appetizers. Delectable appetizers set the stage for the dining experience, whetting the appetite and offering a foretaste of pleasures to come.
A mouth-watering platter of hors d'oeuvres satisfies the desire to munch while anticipating the appearance of the main meal. More substantial appetizers can serve as little meals in themselves.
As the prelude to any menu, invite your guests to sample the sumptuous selections offered here.
Whip up one of the many tasty beverages as an accompaniment—and let the party begin!

ARTICHOKE PARMESAN PUFFS

This recipe makes enough puffs for a large party.

1 cup water
2 tablespoons butter or
   margarine
1 cup all-purpose flour
1 teaspoon garlic salt
2 eggs
1 (14-ounce) can
   artichoke hearts,
   drained, finely
   chopped
1/4 cup grated Parmesan
   cheese

Preheat the oven to 375 degrees. Bring the water and butter to a boil in a large saucepan. Reduce heat to low. Add the flour and garlic salt all at once, stirring vigorously until the mixture forms a ball; remove from heat. Add the eggs; beat until well blended. Beat in the artichoke hearts and Parmesan cheese. Drop heaping teaspoons of the batter onto a baking sheet lined with parchment paper. Bake for 25 to 28 minutes or until lightly browned. Serve warm. Yield: 5 dozen.

Judith Murrill, Preceptor Sigma
Corvallis, Montana

ANTIPASTO

This recipe can be a lifesaver when you have unexpected company.

1 (4-ounce) jar
   pimientos, drained,
   chopped
3 green peppers, chopped
1/4 cup vegetable oil
1 (7-ounce) can tuna,
   drained
1/2 cup vinegar
1 (10-ounce) can sliced
   mushrooms, drained,
   chopped
1 cup sweet pickles,
   drained, chopped
12 to 20 green and black
   olives, sliced
1 cup catsup
1 cup bottled chili sauce
2 cloves of garlic,
   crushed
Pinch of cinnamon
1 bay leaf

Prepare canning jars as for preserving. Sauté the pimientos and green peppers in the oil over low heat for 10 minutes. Add the tuna, vinegar, mushrooms, pickles, olives, catsup, chili sauce, garlic, cinnamon and bay leaf; simmer for 10 minutes. Remove the bay leaf. Pour into the canning jars. Refrigerate. Yield: 5 pint jars.

Lorna Wright, Laureate Beta Gamma
Lively, Ontario, Canada

TACO CHICKEN WINGS

1 package taco
   seasoning mix
1/4 cup cornmeal
2 teaspoons parsley
   flakes
3/4 teaspoon salt
2 pounds chicken wings
   or legs
Bleu cheese dressing

Preheat the oven to 350 degrees. Combine the taco seasoning mix, cornmeal, parsley flakes and salt in a plastic bag. Add the chicken wings. Close the bag and shake well until wings are coated. Arrange the wings on a baking sheet. Bake for 25 minutes. If wings are not brown after 25 minutes, turn and bake for 10 minutes longer. Serve with bleu cheese dressing. Yield: 12 to 15 servings.

Margaret Belleau, Lambda Mu
Gravenhurst, Ontario, Canada

CRUNCHY BACON BITES

I always use aluminum foil on top of the cookie sheet—it makes for easy cleanup.

1 pound sliced turkey or
   pork bacon strips
2 (8-ounce) cans water
   chestnuts
Wooden toothpicks
1/3 cup packed light
   brown sugar
1/2 cup catsup

Preheat the oven to 250 degrees. Cut the bacon strips in half crosswise, and again lengthwise. Wrap each small bacon strip around a water chestnut; secure with a wooden toothpick. Arrange on a baking sheet. Bake for 1 hour. Mix the brown sugar and catsup in a small bowl. Dip the slightly cooled bacon bites into the mixture. Return them to the baking sheet and bake for 1 hour longer. Yield: 24 to 30 pieces.

Dee Lourenco, Rho Beta
Belleview, Florida

BACON ROLLUPS

We serve only appetizers for Christmas dinner—and these are great ones.

1/2 cup margarine
1 cup water
3 cups herb-seasoned
   stuffing mix
2 eggs, beaten
1/4 pound ground beef,
   browned, crumbled
1/4 pound sausage,
   browned, crumbled
1 pound sliced bacon

Preheat the oven to 375 degrees. Melt the margarine in the 1 cup water in a saucepan over medium heat. Remove from heat. Mix in the stuffing mix; blend well. Chill, covered, in the refrigerator for 1 to 2 hours. Add the eggs, ground beef and sausage; mix well. Roll into pecan-shaped balls. Cut the bacon slices into thirds; wrap each third around a stuffing roll and secure with a toothpick. Arrange the rollups on a baking sheet. Bake for 35 minutes or until bacon is crisp. Yield: 6 dozen.

Helen Sidebottom, Upsilon Nu
Versailles, Missouri

BROCCOLI CHEESE SQUARES

You may also use low-fat cheese, skim milk, no-salt butter, and egg substitute, and skip the seasoned salt altogether. It's delicious!

3 tablespoons butter or margarine	1 cup all-purpose flour
2 (10-ounce) packages frozen chopped broccoli	1 teaspoon salt
	4 cups mild or sharp shredded Cheddar cheese
3 eggs	2 tablespoons chopped onion
1 cup milk	
1 teaspoon baking powder	Seasoned salt to taste

Preheat the oven to 350 degrees. Melt the butter in a 9-by-13-inch baking dish. Prepare the broccoli according to package directions, but undercook it slightly. Cool and press dry. Beat the eggs with the milk until the mixture is frothy. Stir the baking powder, flour and salt into the egg mixture. Fold in the broccoli, cheese and onion. Spoon into the baking dish, spreading evenly. Sprinkle with seasoned salt. Bake for 35 minutes. Remove from the oven and let stand for 5 minutes. Cut into 1½-inch squares. Serve hot or cold. Yield: 4 dozen.

Anita Sue Maynard, Preceptor Theta
Williamson, West Virginia

CHEESE PUFFS

2 cups grated Cheddar cheese	½ teaspoon salt
½ cup margarine	1 teaspoon paprika
1 cup all-purpose flour	48 small stuffed green olives, drained

Preheat the oven to 400 degrees. Cream the Cheddar cheese and margarine in a large bowl until light and fluffy. Add the flour, salt and paprika; blend well. Form 1 teaspoon of the mixture into a ball and shape it around an olive. Continue until all the olives are covered with the cheese mixture; arrange them on a baking sheet. Bake for 15 minutes. Pierce with toothpicks and serve hot. Yield: 4 dozen.

Andrea Duckworth
Dexter, Missouri

CHEESY KRISPS

1 cup butter or margarine, softened	1 cup shredded sharp Cheddar cheese
1 cup shredded mild Cheddar cheese	2 cups all-purpose flour
	2 cups crisp rice cereal

Preheat the oven to 400 degrees. Cream the butter and mild and sharp Cheddar cheese in a large bowl until fluffy. Add the flour and rice cereal; combine to make a stiff dough. Roll the dough into walnut-size (or smaller) balls using your palms. Place the balls 2 inches apart on a greased baking sheet; flatten with a fork. Bake for 10 minutes or until edges are slightly brown. Yield: 5 dozen.

Bonnie Arie, Laureate Alpha Phi
Watseka, Illinois

POLYNESIAN CHICKEN WINGS

3 pounds chicken wings	¼ cup dry sherry
1 cup soy sauce	3 cloves of garlic, crushed
½ cup pineapple juice	
½ cup orange juice	1 tablespoon honey or light brown sugar
¼ cup lemon juice	

Cut off the tips of the wings and discard. Cut the wings at the joint. Mix the soy sauce, pineapple juice, orange juice, lemon juice, sherry, garlic and honey in a 9-by-13-inch baking dish. Add the wings; marinate, covered, in the refrigerator for several hours. Preheat the oven to 325 degrees. Pour off half the marinade, reserving it. Bake the wings, uncovered, for 1 hour. Broil for a few minutes, turning, until both sides are crispy. Add some of the reserved marinade if the wings seem too dry. Yield: 21 to 24 servings.

Lorraine Ondriezek
Deadwood, South Dakota

CHICKEN RANCH NACHOS

¼ cup butter or margarine	8 ounces shredded Monterey Jack or Cheddar cheese
Salt and pepper to taste	
½ pound boneless chicken strips, cubed	1 (6-ounce) can black olives, drained
1 (16-ounce) bag tortilla chips	½ cup diced tomatoes
	½ cup chopped chives
1 (16-ounce) package ranch dressing	Jalapeño peppers (optional)

Melt the butter in a medium skillet over high heat. Add salt and pepper to taste and the cubed raw chicken; sauté until the chicken is completely cooked. Layer the chips to cover a microwave-safe platter. Layer the cooked chicken over the chips; squeeze the dressing over the chicken. Sprinkle the cheese over the dressing, and layer ¾ of the black olives, the tomatoes and the chives over the cheese. Top with the remaining olives and the jalapeño peppers. Microwave on High for 3 to 5 minutes or until the cheese is melted. Yield: 12 to 15 servings.

Amber Lynn Stockstill
Porter, Texas

CHILE SQUARES

2 (5-ounce) cans
    chopped green chiles
8 ounces shredded sharp
    Cheddar cheese

8 ounces shredded
    mozzarella cheese
6 eggs

Preheat the oven to 350 degrees. Rinse the chiles well in cold water; drain and pat dry. Combine the shredded cheeses in a bowl. Grease an 8-by-8-inch baking pan. Spread ½ of the combined cheeses in the bottom of the pan. Layer the chiles over the cheese, then add the rest of the cheese. Beat the eggs for ½ minute; pour evenly over the cheese and chiles. Bake for 35 minutes or until lightly browned. Let stand for 30 minutes; cut into 1-inch squares. Yield: 20 servings.

Joan E. Petainen
Sault Ste. Marie, Ontario, Canada

MEXICAN FUDGE

3 eggs, beaten
½ cup green taco sauce
2 cups shredded
    Monterey Jack cheese

2 cups shredded Cheddar
    cheese

Preheat the oven to 350 degrees. Combine the eggs and taco sauce. Mix or shake the Jack cheese and Cheddar cheese together; a large sealable plastic bag works well for this. Place half the cheese mixture in the bottom of a quiche pan. Pour the egg mixture on top. Spread the rest of the cheese mixture over the egg mixture. Bake for 30 minutes. Let set before cutting with a pizza cutter. Serve with crackers. Yield: 20 to 30 servings.

Judie Fair, Xi Eta
Birmingham, Alabama

FRIED RAVIOLI APPETIZERS

1 egg
2 tablespoons water
½ cup fine dry bread
    crumbs
2 tablespoons Parmesan
    cheese
½ teaspoon oregano
    leaves

1 package frozen ravioli,
    thawed
Vegetable oil for frying
2 cups prepared
    spaghetti sauce

Beat the egg and water together in a small bowl with a fork or wire whisk; set aside. Stir together the bread crumbs, Parmesan cheese and oregano in another small bowl. Dip each thawed ravioli into the egg mixture, then coat with the crumb mixture. Heat ½ inch oil to 375 degrees in a 10-inch skillet. Fry the ravioli, a few at a time, for 1 minute on each side or until golden. Heat the spaghetti sauce in a 1-quart saucepan over medium heat. Drain the ravioli on paper towels; stir into the spaghetti sauce. Yield: 12 servings.

Michelle Slavens
Eldon, Missouri

FIESTA SHRIMP

If you don't want to skewer these appetizers, barbecue them in a wok-type basket made for the grill.

¼ cup tequila
1 tablespoon fresh
    cilantro
2 tablespoons fresh lime
    juice
Hot pepper sauce to
    taste

1 tablespoon honey
1 tablespoon orange or
    lemon peel
2 tablespoons olive oil
24 medium shrimp,
    shelled, deveined
2 limes, sliced

Mix the tequila, cilantro, lime juice, hot pepper sauce, honey, orange peel and olive oil in a large sealable plastic bag. Add the shrimp; marinate in the closed bag in the refrigerator for 1 to 3 hours. Preheat the grill. Alternate shrimp and lime slices on skewers. Grill for 2 to 3 minutes on each side, brushing with marinade. Yield: 12 servings.

Kate Tyner, Xi Pi
Kodiak, Alaska

ZUCCHINI APPETIZERS

4 small zucchini,
    unpared, thinly sliced
1 cup baking mix
¼ cup finely chopped
    onion
½ cup grated Parmesan
    cheese
½ teaspoon oregano

2 tablespoons snipped
    parsley
½ teaspoon salt
Dash of pepper
1 clove of garlic, finely
    chopped
½ cup vegetable oil
4 eggs, slightly beaten

Preheat the oven to 350 degrees. Combine the ingredients in a large bowl; mix well. Spread the mixture in a greased 9-by-13-inch baking dish. Bake for about 25 minutes or until golden. Cut into 2-inch squares. Yield: 24 servings.

Bettie Paoletta
San Antonio, Texas

Janice L. Jacobson, Iota Phi, Fayetteville, North Carolina, makes Cucumber Canapés by mixing 12 ounces cream cheese with an envelope of Italian salad dressing mix to chill overnight. After spreading slices of party rye bread with the mixture, top each with a thin slice of cucumber and a pinch of dillweed.

SPINACH BALLS

These are even better served cold.

2 (10-ounce) packages
  frozen chopped
  spinach, cooked,
  drained
1 (6-ounce) package
  stovetop stuffing mix
  (chicken or
  cornbread)
½ cup melted margarine

4 eggs, well beaten
1 onion, chopped
½ teaspoon garlic
  powder
¼ teaspoon thyme
½ cup grated Parmesan
  cheese
½ teaspoon pepper
Salt to taste

Mix the spinach, stuffing mix (uncooked), margarine, eggs, onion, garlic powder, thyme, Parmesan cheese, pepper and salt in a large bowl. Chill, covered, in the refrigerator for at least 1 hour; 8 to 10 hours is better. Preheat the oven to 350 degrees. Shape into balls by teaspoon. Place on a greased baking sheet. Bake for 20 minutes. Yield: 20 to 30 servings.

Mary Clark, Xi Xi Psi
Forth Worth, Texas

PARMESAN ARTICHOKE APPETIZERS

1 (14-ounce) can
  artichokes, drained,
  chopped
¾ cup grated Parmesan
  cheese
¾ cup grated
  mozzarella cheese

½ cup mayonnaise
2 (4-count) cans
  refrigerated crescent
  dinner rolls
½ red bell pepper, cut in
  strips

Preheat the oven to 375 degrees. Combine the artichokes, Parmesan cheese, mozzarella cheese and mayonnaise. Unroll the crescent roll dough into rectangles; press into the bottom of an ungreased 10-by-15-inch pan. Bake for 10 minutes. Spread the artichoke mixture over the crust; bake for 15 minutes longer. Cut into triangles and garnish with the pepper strips. Serve warm. Yield: 32 servings.

Frances Moore
Paris, Ontario, Canada

ARTICHOKE CROSTINI

For a quicker version, mix all the ingredients, bake at 350 degrees, and serve as a dip. It's great with pita chips, crackers, or bruschetta.

1 (14-ounce) can
  artichokes, chopped
2 cups shredded
  mozzarella cheese
1 cup grated Parmesan
  cheese

1 cup mayonnaise
½ teaspoon garlic salt
½ teaspoon onion salt
1 baguette

Preheat the broiler. Mix the artichokes with the next 5 ingredients. Slice the baguette and arrange on a baking sheet in a single layer. Drop a heaping tablespoon of the artichoke mixture on each slice. Broil for 10 minutes or until golden brown.
Yield: 15 to 20 servings.

Tamara Hinrichs, Xi Iota Kappa
St. Charles, Missouri

HOT CHEESE CRABBIES

1 (4-ounce) can crab,
  drained
1 (5-ounce) jar Old
  English cheese spread
½ cup margarine,
  softened
2 tablespoons
  mayonnaise

½ teaspoon garlic
  powder
1 tablespoon dehydrated
  minced onion
Salt and pepper to taste
1 (6-count) package
  sourdough English
  muffins, split

Mix the crab, cheese spread, margarine, mayonnaise, garlic powder, dehydrated onion, salt and pepper in a bowl. Spread over split English muffins. Flash-freeze, covered, for 30 minutes to set the mixture for easy cutting. Preheat the broiler. Cut each muffin half into 6 bite-size pieces. Broil until the mixture bubbles and is lightly browned. Yield: 8 dozen.

Lois Perovich, Xi Delta Xi
Long Beach, California

CRAB CANAPES

This recipe is fast if you use the melba toast, but to make an eye-catching appetizer for guests, use crinkle-cut cucumbers!

⅔ cup nonfat cream
  cheese, softened
2 teaspoons lemon juice
1 teaspoon hot pepper
  sauce
1 (8-ounce) package
  imitation crab or
  lobster meat, flaked
⅓ cup chopped red bell
  pepper

2 green onions with
  tops, sliced
  (about ¼ cup)
2½ medium cucumbers,
  cut into 64 (⅜-inch-
  thick) slices, or 64
  melba toast rounds
Parsley (optional)

Combine the cream cheese, lemon juice and hot pepper sauce in a medium bowl; mix well. Stir in the crab meat, bell pepper and green onions. Chill, covered, until ready to serve. When ready to serve, spoon 1½ teaspoons crab mixture on each cucumber slice. Arrange on a serving plate; garnish with parsley. Yield: 16 servings.

Terry Patlovany, Delta Sigma
Westminster, Colorado

CRAB CROSTINI

8 ounces lump crab meat
1/2 cup diced red or green bell pepper
2 tablespoons plus 2 teaspoons reduced-calorie mayonnaise
2 tablespoons chopped cilantro
1 tablespoon chopped chives
1 tablespoon fresh lime juice
1 tablespoon Dijon mustard
2 teaspoons grated Parmesan cheese
4 to 5 drops hot pepper sauce
4 ounces Italian bread, cut in 16 slices

Preheat the broiler. Line a broiler pan with foil. Pick over the crab meat to remove any cartilage. Combine the crab meat, bell pepper, mayonnaise, cilantro, chives, lime juice, Dijon mustard, Parmesan cheese and hot pepper sauce in a medium bowl; blend well. Spread 1 tablespoon of the crab mixture on each slice of bread. Arrange the slices on the broiler pan. Broil 4 inches from the heat for 5 to 6 minutes or until browned. Serve with fresh fruit. Yield: 16 servings.

Sandra Johnson
Stanberry, Missouri

ENGLISH MELTS

1 cup butter or margarine, softened
2 (5-ounce) jars Old English sharp cheese spread
4 tablespoons mayonnaise
1 pound crab meat
1 teaspoon seasoned salt
1 teaspoon garlic powder
1 (6-count) package English muffins
Paprika

Mix the butter, cheese spread, mayonnaise, crab meat, seasoned salt and garlic powder in a medium bowl. Slice the muffins in half. Spread the crab mixture on the muffin halves. Arrange on a baking sheet; sprinkle with paprika. Broil for 5 to 8 minutes or until brown. Remove from the baking sheet; cut each muffin in half again. Yield: 12 to 24 servings.

Linda Tiller, Laureate Sigma
Virginia Beach, Virginia

Bertha R. Hall, Alpha Master, Hanahan, South Carolina, makes Crab Meat Rollups with a mixture of 16 ounces cream cheese, 1/3 cup mayonnaise, 2 tablespoons chopped green onions, 1/4 cup chopped red bell pepper, 1 cup shredded Cheddar cheese, and a can of crab meat spread on large flour tortillas, rolled up, chilled, and cut into slices.

CRAB MELTAWAYS

1 (6-count) package English muffins
1/2 pound crab meat or 1 (7-ounce) can crab meat
1/2 cup butter or margarine
1 (7-ounce) jar Old English sharp cheddar cheese
2 tablespoons mayonnaise
1/2 teaspoon seasoned salt

Slice each muffin in half. Cut each half into quarters. Arrange on a baking sheet. Combine the crab meat, butter, cheese spread, mayonnaise and seasoned salt in a bowl; beat well with an electric mixer. Spread the mixture on the cut muffins. Freeze, covered, for at least 30 minutes or up to 3 weeks. Just before serving, broil until puffy and bubbly and slightly golden brown. Be sure not to overbrown. Yield: 24 servings.

Chris Pickett, Psi Zeta
Stewartsville, Missouri

VEGGIE PIZZA

2 (8-count) packages crescent rolls
2 (8-ounce) packages cream cheese
3/4 cup mayonnaise
1 envelope ranch salad dressing mix
1 bunch broccoli, cut into pieces
1 bunch carrots, sliced
1 head cauliflower, cut or broken
1 or 2 green peppers, sliced
1 (8-ounce) package shredded mozzarella or Cheddar cheese

Preheat the oven to 375 degrees. Open the crescent roll packages. Press the dough on a pizza pan and roll out to desired thickness. Bake as directed on the package; let cool. Mix the cream cheese, mayonnaise, and salad dressing mix in a bowl until well blended. Spread the mixture on top of the cooled crust. Spread the broccoli, carrots, cauliflower and green pepper over the cream cheese mixture. Cover with the shredded cheese. Return to the oven for 5 minutes. Cut into wedges. Yield: 8 to 24 servings.

Kim Hoendorf, Legacy Member
Gladstone, Missouri

COCKTAIL PIZZAS

2 tablespoons plus 2 teaspoons vegetable oil
1/2 small onion, chopped
3 tablespoons vinegar
1 (4-ounce) can diced green chiles
1 (4-ounce) can chopped black olives
16 ounces shredded sharp Cheddar cheese
1 or 2 loaves buffet-size or cocktail-size rye bread, sliced

Combine the vegetable oil, onion, vinegar, chiles, olives and cheese in a bowl; mix well. Spread on the bread slices, leaving a narrow empty border next to the crust to allow the mixture to melt and spread. (If making ahead of time, cover at this point and refrigerate until ready to serve.) Broil for about 5 minutes or until cheese melts. Yield: 2 dozen or more.

Donna Hughes
Bend, Oregon

MUSHROOM CROUSTADES

The croustades may be filled and frozen before baking if desired.

24 slices of white bread	1/2 teaspoon salt
4 tablespoons butter or margarine	1/8 teaspoon cayenne pepper
3 tablespoons finely chopped shallots	1 tablespoon finely chopped parsley
8 ounces finely chopped mushrooms	1 1/2 tablespoons finely chopped chives
2 tablespoons all-purpose flour	1/2 teaspoon lemon juice
1 cup heavy cream	1 tablespoon grated Parmesan cheese

Preheat the oven to 400 degrees. Cut a round from the center of each slice of bread with a 3-inch round cookie cutter or drinking glass. Grease 2 (12-muffin) tins that have 2-inch muffin cups. To form the croustades, push the bread rounds into the tins, molding them to form perfect cups. Bake for 10 minutes or until light brown. Let cool. Melt the butter in a heavy 10-inch skillet. Add the shallots, stirring constantly over moderate heat for about 4 minutes; do not brown. Stir in the mushrooms, coating them thoroughly with butter and allowing them to cook for a few minutes without stirring. Begin to stir them after they have given off a good deal of liquid; continue to cook, stirring occasionally, for 10 to 15 minutes or until all moisture has evaporated. Remove from heat and sprinkle the flour over the mixture; stir thoroughly. Return to heat and pour the cream over the mixture, stirring constantly. Bring to a boil; lower heat until mixture is barely simmering and cook for a minute or 2 longer to remove any taste of raw flour. Remove from heat and add the salt, cayenne pepper, parsley, chives and lemon juice. Remove to a bowl and chill, covered, in the refrigerator until ready to fill the croustades. Fill the croustades with the mushroom mixture and bake for about 10 minutes. Sprinkle Parmesan cheese over each.
Yield: 24 servings.

Jean Poynor, Epsilon Master
Eureka Springs, Arkansas

SAUSAGE SQUARES

1 cup baking mix	2 tablespoons mayonnaise
1 cup milk	
2 tablespoons mayonnaise	1 egg
1 pound sausage	2 cups shredded Cheddar cheese
3 tablespoons chopped onion	1 (4-ounce) can chopped green chiles

Preheat the oven to 375 degrees. Combine the baking mix, milk and 2 tablespoons mayonnaise; spread in a greased 9-by-13-inch pan. Sauté the sausage and onion until sausage is cooked completely through. Drain well and spread over the baking mix mixture. Mix 2 tablespoons mayonnaise, the egg, cheese and green chiles in a bowl; spread over the top of the sausage layer. Bake for 25 minutes. Yield: 8 dozen.

Dean Jones, Xi Beta Alpha
Bowling Green, Kentucky

TURKEY DIVINE TARTLETTES

1 (20-count) can refrigerated dinner rolls	1/4 cup chopped onion
	1/4 cup shredded Cheddar cheese
1 cup chopped cooked turkey	Salt and pepper to taste
1/4 cup chopped celery	1/4 to 1/2 cup mayonnaise-type salad dressing
1/4 cup green pepper	

Preheat the oven to 375 degrees. Open the package of dinner rolls; lightly roll the dough into a rectangle with a rolling pin. Cut to make 12 squares. Press the dough into bottoms and sides of the cups of a 12-cup muffin tin, forming 12 dough cups. Mix the turkey, celery, green pepper, onion, Cheddar cheese, salt and pepper in a bowl; add the salad dressing, stirring just until the other ingredients are moistened. Fill the lined muffin cups with the mixture. Bake for 10 to 15 minutes or until brown and bubbly.
Yield: 12 servings.

Cecilia Boyd-Bernier, Theta Iota
Chase, British Columbia, Canada

Nancy Auf Der Heide, Pi Iota, Shawnee, Kansas, makes Crispy Creamy Rollups by trimming crusts from white bread slices, rolling the slices thin, spreading with a can of any cream soup, and rolling up. Wrap a half slice of bacon around each and bake in a preheated 375-degree oven for 15 minutes or until light brown. Drain well and serve warm.

BOODEGGS

1½ pounds Muenster
  cheese, shredded
3 to 4 eggs, beaten

1 package phyllo dough
1 cup melted butter

Preheat the oven to 350 degrees. Combine the cheese and eggs in a bowl. Cut the phyllo dough in 3 sections, then cut each section stack in half. Keep the phyllo covered with a damp cloth to keep it from drying out. Brush 3 sheets of phyllo dough with melted butter, then place one on top of the other to make a stack of 3. Place 1 teaspoon of the cheese mixture in the center of the top sheet of phyllo, then fold up all 3 sheets at the same time, enclosing the ends so the cheese mixture is encased. Arrange the appetizers on buttered cookie sheets; bake for 20 minutes or until brown on top. Yield: 45 to 50 servings.

Edith Green
Portland, Indiana

TIROPITA (CHEESE PIE)

12 ounces feta cheese,
  crumbled
12 ounces low-fat or
  regular cottage cheese
1 egg, well beaten

Dash of pepper
1 package phyllo dough
1 to 1½ cups melted
  butter

Preheat the oven to 350 degrees. Mix the feta cheese, cottage cheese, egg and pepper in a medium bowl; set aside. Cut the phyllo sheets into 2-inch strips, using a cutting board and a ruler to make straight lines. Put a damp towel over the strips to keep them from drying out. Brush 2 strips with melted butter and place one on top of the other. Put 1 teaspoon of the cheese mixture in the corner of the double strip and fold several times until it becomes a triangle. Brush the triangle ends with butter to seal the fold. Arrange triangles on a baking sheet. Bake for 10 minutes or until golden brown. Yield: 45 to 50 servings.

Delores Miller, Laureate Nu
Cody, Wyoming

Lee Ann Stump, Epsilon Eta, Muncy, Pennsylvania, says that her sister's Sweet and Spicy Wings are outstanding. She bakes 2 pounds of salt-and-peppered wings in a preheated 350-degree oven for 45 minutes. Drain well and cover with a sauce of 8 ounces cream cheese, ½ cup each apple jelly and pineapple preserves, 1 teaspoon dry mustard, ½ teaspoon red pepper flakes, and 1 tablespoon horseradish. Bake, covered, for 20 minutes.

CHICKEN PUFFS

You may add onion flakes, pimientos, and chopped green pepper to the chicken mixture if you like.

2 cups chopped cooked
  chicken (white
  meat)
1 (8-ounce) package
  cream cheese

4 tablespoons butter or
  margarine, softened
2 (8-count) packages
  refrigerated crescent
  rolls

Preheat the oven to 350 degrees. Mix the chicken, cream cheese and butter in a bowl until blended. Separate the crescent roll dough where perforated. Place a heaping tablespoon of the chicken mixture on each piece. Fold over the dough, wrapping the filling into a triangular package; pinch closed. Bake on a baking sheet until nicely browned. Serve warm or cooled. Yield: 16 servings.

Patricia A. Siron
Mexico, Missouri

MEXICAN STUFFED PEPPERS

Make these early and bake just before serving.

1 tablespoon margarine
¼ cup chopped green
  onion
¾ pound ground turkey
¼ teaspoon salt
⅛ teaspoon pepper

2 tablespoons chopped
  fresh cilantro
1 cup shredded
  mozzarella cheese
4 fresh Anaheim peppers
1 teaspoon vegetable oil

Preheat the oven to 350 degrees. Spray a 2-quart baking dish with nonstick cooking spray. Melt the margarine in a medium skillet over medium-high heat. Stir in the green onion, ground turkey, salt, pepper and 1 tablespoon of the cilantro. Sauté for 3 to 5 minutes or until turkey is cooked through. Stir in half the cheese; mix well. Remove from heat. Cut each pepper lengthwise down 1 side to within ½ inch of the tip; remove the seeds. Spoon ¼ of the turkey mixture into each pepper; close the pepper to seal in the filling. Brush with oil. Turn into the baking dish and bake for 15 minutes. Sprinkle the remaining cilantro and remaining cheese over the peppers. Bake for 8 to 10 minutes or until the cheese melts. Yield: 4 servings.

Dorothy Thompson, Laureate Beta Sigma
St. Charles, Missouri

Carolyn Ellis, Xi Beta Iota, Mineral Wells, Texas, rinses, drains, and chops a jar of dried beef to mix with 16 ounces cream cheese, 1 cup salsa, a bunch of chopped green onions, and chili powder to taste to make Hocus Pecos Dip.

GOOBERS (PORK DUMPLINGS) WITH AUNT BELL'S MUSTARD

When my sister introduced me to Goobers, I discovered that my Great-Aunt Bell's mustard was the perfect accompaniment. To save time, ask your husband to help make the Goobers. Make it a social event with a glass or two of wine!

2 (12-ounce) packages won ton wrappers	1/4 cup finely chopped celery
2 pounds lean ground pork, cooked	1/4 teaspoon ground ginger
14 ounces shrimp, chopped	3 tablespoons soy sauce
1/2 cup finely chopped fresh mushrooms	2 tablespoons cornstarch
1/3 cup finely chopped green onion	Soy sauce for dipping
	Aunt Bell's Mustard

Cut the won ton wrappers into circles, using a small glass as a guide. Combine the ground pork, shrimp, mushrooms, green onion, celery and ginger in a large bowl. Combine the soy sauce and cornstarch in a small bowl; add to the pork mixture. Mix well with your hands. Spread about 1 teaspoon of the pork mixture in the center of each won ton circle; gently fold toward the center to form a "top hat" package. Arrange on cookie sheets. Freeze, covered, on a baking sheet for about 1 hour or until the Goobers are easy to handle. Place them in storage containers to be returned to the freezer until ready to cook. To cook, place the frozen Goobers in a vegetable steamer sprayed with nonstick cooking spray. Cover and steam on medium heat for about 20 minutes. Serve with soy sauce and Aunt Bell's Mustard for dipping. Yield: 8 dozen.

AUNT BELL'S MUSTARD

This mustard is also delicious with baked ham, beef or ham sandwiches, hot dogs, and hamburgers.

6 tablespoons all-purpose flour	1/2 teaspoon salt
6 tablespoons sugar	6 tablespoons white vinegar
3 tablespoons dry mustard	6 tablespoons evaporated milk

Combine the flour, sugar, dry mustard, salt, vinegar and evaporated milk; mix well. Chill before serving.

Lori Whitlock, Xi Beta Alpha
Port Coquitlam, British Columbia, Canada

CHINESE BARBECUED PORK

2 pounds whole pork tenderloin, 1- to 1 1/2-inch pieces	1/2 cup honey
1 teaspoon red food coloring	1/3 cup finely chopped preserved ginger
1 1/2 teaspoons seasoned salt	1/3 cup preserved ginger syrup
1/2 cup sherry	2 tablespoons cornstarch
1/4 cup soy sauce	Chinese hot mustard (optional)
1/2 cup pineapple juice or sherry	Sesame seeds

Preheat the oven to 325 degrees. Brush the pork tenderloin with the red food coloring (or put the tenderloin with the food coloring in a sealable plastic bag, working the bag to coat the tenderloin). Sprinkle the seasoned salt over the tenderloin. Remove from the bag. Place in a roasting pan and roast in the oven until cooked through. Combine the sherry, soy sauce, honey, ginger, ginger syrup and cornstarch in a saucepan. Cook over medium-low heat, stirring constantly until thick and clear. Brush the pork with a small amount of the sauce for the last 20 minutes of roasting time. Slice very thin. Serve hot or cold with the sauce or with Chinese hot mustard and sesame seeds. Yield: 10 servings.

Dorothy L. Lind, Laureate Beta Sigma
Puyallup, Washington

HEAVENLY SAUSAGE STARS

2 cups cooked, crumbled sausage	1 (3-ounce) can sliced black olives
1 1/2 cups (6 ounces) shredded sharp Cheddar cheese	1/2 cup chopped red pepper
1 1/2 cups (6 ounces) shredded Monterey Jack cheese	1 (12-ounce) package fresh or frozen won ton wrappers
1 cup prepared ranch salad dressing	Vegetable oil for brushing wrappers

Preheat the oven to 350 degrees. Blot the sausage dry with paper towels; combine with the Cheddar cheese, Monterey Jack cheese, salad dressing, olives and red pepper; mix well. Grease four 12-cup muffin tins and press 1 won ton wrapper in each cup. Brush with oil. Bake for 5 minutes or until golden. Remove the won ton wrappers from the cups and place on baking sheets. Fill with the sausage mixture. Bake for 5 minutes or until bubbly. Yield: 4 dozen.

Virginia Crowell
Newport, Oregon

TORTILLA BLOSSOMS

10 (8- or 10-inch) flour tortillas	1/2 cup chopped black olives
1 cup mayonnaise	1/4 cup chopped green onion
1 cup shredded sharp Cheddar cheese	Salsa for garnish
1 (5-ounce) can chopped green chiles	

Preheat the oven to 350 degrees. Cut the tortillas into quarters; heat to soften. Press each tortilla into a muffin cup to form a "blossom." Combine the next 5 ingredients in a bowl; mix well. Fill each prepared tortilla "blossom" with about 2 tablespoons of the filling. Bake for 20 minutes. Remove to a serving platter and top with salsa. Yield: 2 dozen.

Ginny Fletcher, Psi Psi
Milan, Missouri

SPINACH PUFFS

To save time, spread the crescent rolls with the spinach mixture, roll jelly roll style, and cut to make roll-type appetizers.

1 (10-ounce) package frozen chopped spinach, thawed, drained	1 (14-ounce) box vegetable soup mix
1 (8-ounce) can water chestnuts, drained, finely chopped	1¼ cups sour cream
	1 cup shredded Cheddar cheese
1 cup mayonnaise	2 (8-count) packages refrigerated crescent rolls

Preheat the oven to 375 degrees. Combine the first 6 ingredients in a large bowl; mix well. Press the seams of each package of dough to make a rectangle. Cut each rectangle into 24 pieces. Spray 4 mini-muffin pans with nonstick cooking spray. Roll each dough piece into a ball and place in the mini-muffin pans. Create tarts with a tart shaper. Spoon some of the spinach mixture into each tart. Bake for 12 to 15 minutes or until crust is golden. Yield: 4 dozen.

Tammy Kern, Lambda
Meridian, Idaho

Susan Laitner, Preceptor Epsilon Delta, Independence, Missouri, makes a Taco-Seasoned Cheese Ball by mixing 16 ounces of cream cheese with 2 cups shredded Cheddar cheese, 2 tablespoons Worcestershire sauce, a tablespoon of minced onion, and 1/2 cup chopped pecans. Shape into a ball and coat with taco seasoning mix.

PHYLLO VEGETABLE PURSES

2 teaspoons vegetable oil	1/2 cup chopped roasted red peppers
3/4 cup chopped leeks	1/4 cup sun-dried tomatoes, softened in warm water
1/2 cup finely chopped carrots	
2 teaspoons minced garlic	3 tablespoons grated Parmesan cheese
1/2 cup chopped mushrooms	4 sheets phyllo pastry dough
1/3 cup light cream cheese, softened	2 teaspoons melted butter or margarine
1/2 cup chopped fresh coriander	

Preheat the oven to 400 degrees. Heat the oil in a nonstick saucepan over medium-low heat. Add the leeks, carrots and garlic; sauté for 5 minutes. Stir in the mushrooms; sauté, stirring, for 3 minutes longer. Remove from heat. Stir in the cream cheese until it melts. Stir in the coriander, red peppers, sun-dried tomatoes and Parmesan cheese. Layer 2 sheets of phyllo on a work surface; brush with melted butter. Cut each sheet into 12 squares. Put about 2 teaspoons of the cream cheese filling in the center of each square; bring up the corners of the square and pinch the corners together in the center. Brush the tops of the "purses" with the remaining melted butter. Arrange on a well-greased cookie sheet. Bake for 8 to 10 minutes or until lightly browned. Yield: 2 dozen.

Carol Kay, Preceptor Lambda
Kitchener, Ontario, Canada

ASPARAGUS BUNDLES

1 loaf white bread, sliced, crusts removed	1 egg, beaten
1 (8-ounce) package plus 1 (3-ounce) package cream cheese, softened	1 tablespoon mayonnaise
	20 fresh asparagus spears or 2 (15-ounce) cans asparagus spears
3 ounces bleu cheese, crumbled	1/2 cup melted margarine

Preheat the oven to 350 degrees. Roll the bread slices with a rolling pin until flat. Mix the cream cheese, egg and mayonnaise until well blended. Spread the cheese mixture over the flattened bread slices. Place an asparagus spear along one side of each slice of bread and roll up like a jelly roll. Cut each roll into 3 pieces. Dip each bundle in melted margarine and arrange on baking sheets. Bake for 15 to 20 minutes. Yield: 5 dozen.

Sandy Stretcher, Xi Rho Psi
Port Neches, Texas

BLEU CHEESE ASPARAGUS SPEARS

Use fresh asparagus whenever possible.

**20 slices thin white
bread, crusts removed
3 ounces bleu cheese
1 (8-ounce) package
cream cheese,
softened
1 egg, slightly beaten**

**20 fresh asparagus
spears or
2 (15-ounce) cans
asparagus spears
Melted butter or
margarine for dipping**

Roll the bread slices with a rolling pin until flat. Combine the bleu cheese, cream cheese and egg; mix well. Spread the bleu cheese mixture over the flattened bread slices. Place an asparagus spear along one side of each slice of bread and roll up like a jelly roll. Cut each roll into 3 pieces. Dip in melted butter and freeze, covered, on baking sheets. Bake when ready to serve, for 15 to 20 minutes in a 400-degree oven. Yield: 5 dozen.

*Beth Buske, Eta Omicron
Ruston, Louisiana*

GRATED CARROT SANDWICHES

Brown bread is very tasty for this recipe.

**1 (8-ounce) package
cream cheese,
softened
2 small carrots, finely
grated
1 tablespoon onion juice**

**Salt and pepper to taste
Mayonnaise
1/4 cup chopped toasted
pecans
Loaf of bread, sliced,
crusts removed**

Mix the cream cheese and carrots in a bowl; add the onion juice, salt, pepper and enough mayonnaise to moisten. Stir in the pecans. Spread each bread slice with cream cheese filling, roll like a jelly roll, chill for at least 1 hour and slice; or cut the bread slices into shapes and spread with the cream cheese filling. Yield: 4 to 5 dozen.

*Carolyn H. Waters, Xi Psi
Crestview, Florida*

CHICKEN PINWHEELS

**1 teaspoon dried
basil
1/2 teaspoon salt
1/4 teaspoon pepper
1/2 teaspoon garlic
powder**

**4 boneless, skinless
chicken breast halves
4 very thin slices ham
2 tablespoons lemon
juice
Paprika**

Preheat the oven to 350 degrees. Combine the basil, salt, pepper and garlic powder in a small bowl; set aside. Pound the chicken breasts between 2 sheets of plastic wrap to about 1/4 inch thick. Sprinkle the garlic mixture over the chicken breasts and place a slice of ham over each. Roll up tightly and secure with toothpicks. Place seam side down in a baking dish; drizzle with the lemon juice and sprinkle with paprika. Bake for 20 to 25 minutes. Let cool. Slice into rounds. Yield: 4 dozen.

*Anita Foley, Xi Alpha Psi
Loudon, Tennessee*

DOUG'S DELICIOUS SMOKED SALMON AND SHRIMP SPIRALS

This recipe serves a large crowd; halve it if necessary.

**2 cups spreadable cream
cheese
2 cups sour cream
1 1/2 cups barbecue-
smoked salmon
1/2 pound fresh shrimp,
cooked, chopped**

**5 green onions, chopped
Lemon pepper to taste
10 (10-inch) flour
tortillas**

Combine the cream cheese, sour cream, salmon, shrimp, onions and lemon pepper in a bowl. Spread the mixture thinly over each tortilla and roll tightly. Chill for 1 hour. Cut into 1-inch slices; allow each slice to relax into a spiral. Serve cold. Yield: 5 dozen.

*Linda L. Smith
Campbell River, British Columbia, Canada*

FIESTA APPETIZERS

**2 (3-ounce) packages
cream cheese,
softened
1 envelope ranch salad
dressing mix
1 (5-ounce) can chopped
green chiles**

**2 green onions
1/2 cup sliced black
olives
1 (2-ounce) jar
pimientos
1 (10-count) package
large flour tortillas**

Mix the cream cheese and salad dressing mix. Stir in the chiles, green onions, black olives and pimientos; mix well. Spread the mixture over the tortillas, roll tightly and slice into 1-inch slices. Yield: 5 dozen.

*Sheila H. Kilbourne
Staunton, Virginia*

Jean M. Nodland, Zeta Master, Colorado Springs, Colorado, makes a Hot Artichoke Chile Dip to serve with crackers and rye bread. She chops a 15-ounce can of drained artichoke hearts to mix with 1 cup mayonnaise, 1 cup grated Parmesan cheese, and a 4-ounce can of chopped green chiles. Bake in a pre-heated 350-degree oven for 30 minutes.

MEXICAN ROLLUPS

Slicing is a breeze when you use an electric knife.

1 (8-ounce) package
  cream cheese,
  softened
1 (8-ounce) container
  sour cream
1/2 cup finely chopped
  green onion
1/2 teaspoon black
  pepper
1/2 teaspoon garlic
  powder
1/2 teaspoon seasoned
  salt
1 (4-ounce) can chopped
  black olives
1 (4-ounce) can chopped
  green chiles
8 ounces shredded
  Cheddar cheese
Hot pepper sauce to
  taste (optional)
1 (10-count) package
  large flour tortillas
Salsa

Combine the cream cheese, sour cream, green onion, pepper, garlic powder and seasoned salt in a bowl; blend well. Add the olives and chiles to the cream cheese mixture; blend well. Fold in the Cheddar cheese and hot pepper sauce. Spread the mixture thinly over each tortilla; roll up tightly. Place each roll seam side down on a baking sheet. Cover with plastic wrap and chill for 1 to 2 hours. Slice to desired thickness and arrange on a serving tray. Serve with salsa. Yield: 4 to 5 dozen.

Gloria Hinrichs
Orleans, Nebraska

PAULINE'S TAQUITAS

I usually freeze these appetizers and bake them straight from the freezer until crisp. Serve with salsa. These are great appetizers during football Sunday. It's very easy to double the recipe.

2 pounds lean ground
  beef
2 pounds lean ground
  pork
1 envelope chili
  seasoning
1 pound process cheese,
  cubed
40 to 48 corn tortillas
Hot vegetable oil
Salsa

Preheat the oven to 400 degrees. Brown the beef and pork in a saucepan until cooked through. Drain well. Add the chili seasoning; stir well. Add the cheese and heat, stirring, until melted. Let cool. Dip the tortillas into hot oil to soften; drain on paper towels. Place 1 tablespoon meat mixture on each tortilla. Roll tightly and fasten with toothpicks. Arrange on a baking sheet and bake for 20 minutes. Serve with salsa for dipping. Yield: 3 to 4 dozen.

Julie Collins, Eta Delta
Ponca City, Oklahoma

TACO ROLLUPS

Serve with picante sauce for dipping.

2 (8-ounce) packages
  cream cheese,
  softened
1 (8-ounce) carton sour
  cream
1/2 envelope dry onion
  soup mix
2 tablespoons dry taco
  seasoning mix
1/4 to 1/2 cup picante
  sauce
1 (4-ounce) can chopped
  black olives
1 (10-count) package
  large flour tortillas
8 ounces shredded
  Cheddar cheese

Combine the cream cheese, sour cream, onion soup mix, taco seasoning mix, picante sauce and olives; mix well. Spread on the tortillas; roll up tightly. Chill, covered, for at least 1 hour. Slice to desired thickness and serve. Yield: 4 to 5 dozen.

Pat Lollar, Psi Zeta
Stewartsville, Missouri

TORTILLA PINWHEELS

2 (8-ounce) packages
  cream cheese,
  softened
3 to 4 small green
  onions, chopped
3 to 4 tablespoons sour
  cream
1 (4-ounce) can chopped
  green chile peppers,
  drained
1 teaspoon lemon juice
3 tablespoons mild or
  medium picante
  sauce
1/4 teaspoon garlic
  powder
1/2 teaspoon
  Worcestershire sauce
1/2 cup chopped pecans
1 dozen large flour
  tortillas

Combine the cream cheese, green onions, sour cream, chile peppers, lemon juice, picante sauce, garlic powder, Worcestershire sauce and pecans; mix well. Chill, covered, for several hours or overnight. Spread the mixture very thickly on the tortillas; roll up tightly and secure with a toothpick. Cover with plastic wrap and chill for 8 to 10 hours. Slice 1/2 inch thick to serve. Yield: 6 dozen or more.

Charlotte Wilson
Santa Fe, New Mexico

Lisa Dorschner, Theta, Pierre, South Dakota, suggests making your own delicious Homemade Tortilla Chips from the array of flavored tortillas available. Spray a baking stone or baking sheet with cooking spray. Cut the tortillas into strips or wedges, and arrange in a single layer to bake in a preheated 400-degree oven for 6 to 8 minutes or until light brown and crisp.

SPINACH ROLLUPS

2 (10-ounce) boxes
  frozen chopped
  spinach, drained
1 cup sour cream
1 cup mayonnaise
1 (8-ounce) can water
  chestnuts, chopped
1 (4-ounce) can chopped
  black olives

1 bunch green onions,
  chopped
1 (2-ounce) jar real
  bacon bits
1 envelope ranch salad
  dressing mix
1 (10-count) package
  large flour tortillas

Mix the spinach, sour cream, mayonnaise, water chestnuts, olives, green onions, bacon bits and salad dressing mix in a bowl; blend well. Chill, covered, for 2 to 3 hours. Spread the mixture thinly on the tortillas; roll up like jelly rolls. Slice into 1/2-inch pieces and serve. Yield: 15 to 20 servings.

Kimberly Crain
Antioch, Tennessee

CRISPIX PARTY MIX

1/2 cup margarine
1 cup packed light
  brown sugar
1/4 cup light corn syrup
1 teaspoon vanilla
  extract
1 teaspoon baking soda
1 (12-ounce) box Crispix

2 cups unsalted dry
  roasted peanuts
8 ounces fat-free
  pretzels
1 (16-ounce) bag
  "M & M's" Peanut
  Chocolate Candies

Melt the margarine in a medium bowl in the microwave. Add the brown sugar, corn syrup and vanilla. Microwave on High, uncovered, for 2 minutes. Add the baking soda; blend well. Pour the Crispix into a small to medium-size brown paper bag. Add the sugar mixture; holding the bag closed, shake the bag well. Microwave the bag for 1 1/2 minutes; shake again. Microwave for 1 1/2 minutes longer. Pour into a large bowl. Stir in the peanuts and pretzels. Cool for 2 hours. Stir in the chocolate candies. Store in an airtight container. Yield: 8 cups.

Karen Vander Laan, Omicron Chi
Spirit Lake, Iowa

Pat Novak, Beta Delta, Waukon, Iowa, makes Festive Ham Appetizers by mixing 1/2 cup brown sugar, 1 tablespoon cornstarch, 1/4 teaspoon cloves, a dash of ginger, and 1/2 cup lemon juice in a saucepan and cooking until thickened, stirring constantly. Stir in 3 cups cubed ham, 2 large apples, cubed, and a cup of small cooked mushrooms. Serve with toothpicks from a fondue pot or chafing dish.

HAWAIIAN COCONUT CRUNCH

I add chocolate chips to this recipe!

3 cups honey graham
  cereal
1 cup salted peanuts
1 cup raisins
1 cup dried banana chips
2 tablespoons honey

2 tablespoons butter or
  margarine
1/2 teaspoon cinnamon
1/4 teaspoon salt
4 cups popped popcorn
1 cup flaked coconut

Preheat the oven to 300 degrees. Mix the first 4 ingredients in a jelly roll pan. Heat the honey and butter in a saucepan over low heat; stir in the cinnamon and salt. Pour the butter mixture over the cereal mixture; toss until evenly coated. Bake for 10 minutes, stirring once after 5 minutes. Remove from the oven. Stir in the popcorn and coconut. Store in an airtight container. Yield: 10 to 12 cups.

Susan Cromer
Pittsburgh, Pennsylvania

TOASTED SNACK MIX

3 cups Malt-o-Meal
  Toasty O's cereal
2 cups miniature
  shredded wheat
  pieces, cut in half
1/2 cup pretzel sticks,
  broken
1/2 cup walnuts, pecans,
  or peanuts

1 tablespoon
  Worcestershire sauce
1/2 teaspoon garlic
  powder
1/2 teaspoon onion salt
6 tablespoons melted
  butter or margarine

Preheat the oven to 250 degrees. Combine the Toasty O's, shredded wheat, pretzel sticks and nuts in a large bowl. Combine the remaining ingredients in a small bowl. Pour the butter mixture over the cereal mixture, tossing to coat evenly. Spoon into a 10-by-15-inch jelly roll pan. Bake, stirring occasionally, for 45 minutes or until lightly toasted. Let it cool completely. Yield: 6 cups.

Deborah McNett, Zeta Iota
Silver City, New Mexico

Edy Mohler, Laureate Alpha Upsilon, Oro Valley, Arizona, makes the easiest appetizer, Cream Cheese Sesame Block, by placing an 8-ounce block of cream cheese on a plate and making wavy lines over the surface with a a fork. She then pats toasted sesame seeds over the surface and pours a generous amount of soy sauce over the top. Refrigerate for several hours, turning occasionally and basting with the soy sauce. Serve with crackers.

PRALINE PECANS

These pecans can be stored up to 2 weeks in an air-tight container.

1 egg white	1 teaspoon cinnamon
1 teaspoon water	1 teaspoon salt
2 pounds pecan halves	1/2 teaspoon cocoa
1 cup sugar	

Preheat the oven to 325 degrees. Beat the egg white and water in a large bowl. Add the pecan halves; toss quickly to coat. Mix the sugar, cinnamon, salt and cocoa; pour over the pecans and toss quickly. Pour the mixture onto a greased 11-by-17-inch baking sheet. Bake for 45 minutes, stirring every 10 minutes. Loosen the pecans from the baking sheet with spatula as soon as you remove from the oven. Let cool. Yield: 6 cups.

Janice Waryk, Preceptor Zeta Zeta
Strongsville, Ohio

❖ MUSHROOM STRUDEL

3 tablespoons butter	1/2 cup sour cream
1 pound fresh mushrooms, sliced	3 tablespoons chopped water chestnuts
1/4 cup chopped onion	2 large cloves of garlic, minced
1 tablespoon dry sherry	
1 teaspoon salt	2 teaspoons fresh lemon juice
1 (8-ounce) package cream cheese, cut in small pieces	1/2 teaspoon ground black pepper
1 cup fine bread crumbs	20 phyllo pastry sheets
1/2 cup plain yogurt	1/2 cup melted butter

Preheat the oven to 375 degrees. Melt the 3 tablespoons butter in a large skillet over medium-high heat. Add the mushrooms and onion. Sauté, stirring frequently, until the vegetables are golden and the juices have evaporated. Stir in the sherry and salt; cook until the sherry is absorbed. Remove from heat and drain well. Return the mixture to the skillet. Add the cream cheese and stir until melted. Blend in the bread crumbs, yogurt, sour cream, water chestnuts, garlic, lemon juice and pepper. Grease a large rimmed baking sheet or jelly roll pan. Place one phyllo sheet on your work surface. Brush with melted butter. Top with a second phyllo sheet; brush it with melted butter. Repeat to form a stack of 10 buttered sheets. Spoon half the mushroom mixture in a strip along 1 long edge of the phyllo, leaving a 3-inch margin at each end. Roll up the phyllo to enclose the filling, tucking in the ends. Place seam side down on the prepared baking sheet. Brush with melted butter. Form a second roll with the remaining phyllo and mushroom mixture. Bake 25 minutes or until crisp and browned. Let cool for 5 minutes; slice. Serve immediately. Yield: 15 to 18 servings.

Judy Livingston, Xi Epsilon Alpha
Paonia, Colorado

SWEET AND SOUR MUSHROOMS

The leftover dressing can be used on vegetable salads.

3/4 cup sugar	2 (4-ounce) jars whole mushrooms, drained, liquid reserved
1/4 cup vinegar	
3/4 cup vegetable oil	
1/3 cup catsup	1 medium onion, sliced, separated into rings
2 tablespoons Worcestershire sauce	

Combine the sugar and vinegar in a medium saucepan; cook over medium heat until the sugar dissolves. Remove from heat. Add the oil, catsup, Worcestershire sauce and 1/4 cup of the reserved mushroom liquid. Shake well in the pan, covered, or blend at medium speed in a blender until smooth. Stir in the mushrooms and onion rings. Chill, covered, in the refrigerator for 6 hours or overnight. Before serving, drain off the dressing, reserving it. Serve the mushrooms with toothpicks and with the reserved dressing for dipping. Yield: 4 dozen.

Veronica Filipek
Minot, North Dakota

MUSHROOM TARTS

2 loaves sliced white bread	1 tablespoon cornstarch
Butter or margarine	1 cup cream
3/4 cup chopped onion	1 tablespoon lemon juice
2 tablespoons margarine	1/2 teaspoon pepper
1 pound mushrooms, chopped	6 ounces shredded mozzarella cheese

Preheat the oven to 350 degrees. Butter both sides of each slice of bread. Cut the slices into circles and place each circle in one of the cups of a muffin tin. Bake for 10 minutes or until lightly browned. Sauté the onion, margarine and mushrooms in a skillet for 3 or 4 minutes. Drain a small amount of the liquid into a medium saucepan. Combine the cornstarch with the mushroom liquid and heat over medium heat until slightly thickened. Add the cream and the mushroom mixture to the cornstarch mixture; bring to a boil. Remove from heat. Stir in the lemon juice and pepper. Pour into the bread cups and sprinkle with the cheese. Yield: 36 servings.

Sandra Simpson, Preceptor Gamma Beta
Port Alberni, British Columbia, Canada

CHINESE STUFFED MUSHROOMS

100 fresh mushrooms	1 teaspoon ginger
2 packages Farmer John sausage	2 tablespoons soy sauce
4 or 5 green onions, sliced small	1 egg
1 (8-ounce) can water chestnuts, minced	5 or 6 saltine crackers, crushed
	Parmesan cheese

Preheat the oven to 350 degrees. Clean the mushrooms. Remove the stems and save for another use. Microwave the sausage in a covered microwave-safe dish until crumbly. Combine the green onions, water chestnuts, ginger, soy sauce, egg and cracker crumbs. Spoon the filling into the fresh mushroom cups arranged on a baking sheet. Sprinkle with Parmesan cheese. Bake for 20 minutes. Yield: 25 to 50 servings.

Doris Ohe, Xi Tau Theta
Oakdale, California

PHILLY AND CRAB STUFFED MUSHROOMS

2 pounds medium mushrooms	2 ounces shredded mozzarella cheese
6 tablespoons margarine, softened	1/4 pound imitation crab meat
1 (8-ounce) package cream cheese, softened	1 tablespoon garlic powder

Preheat the oven to 400 degrees. Remove the mushroom stems and wash the mushrooms. Combine the margarine, cream cheese, mozzarella cheese, crab meat and garlic powder. Spoon the mixture by heaping teaspoons into the mushroom caps. Arrange on a nonstick baking sheet. Bake for 30 minutes or until lightly browned. Yield: 2 1/2 dozen.

Terry Merrill, Mu Iota
Sedalia, Missouri

REUBEN MUSHROOMS

20 fresh large mushrooms	1/4 cup shredded Swiss cheese
3 ounces thinly sliced corned beef, chopped	2 tablespoons crushed rye crackers
1/4 cup sauerkraut, rinsed and drained	2 tablespoons Thousand Island salad dressing

Clean the mushrooms and remove the stems. Arrange half the mushrooms hollow side up on a 10- or 12-inch microwave-safe plate, leaving the center of the plate empty. Cover with clear plastic wrap; vent by leaving a small area unsealed at the edge of the plate.

Microwave on High for 2 to 4 minutes or until the mushrooms are almost tender. Repeat with the remaining mushroom caps. Mix the remaining ingredients in a medium bowl. Spoon 1 rounded teaspoon of the corned beef filling into each mushroom cap. Arrange half the filled mushrooms on a plate, leaving the center of the plate empty. Microwave, uncovered, on High for 2 1/2 to 3 minutes. Repeat with the remaining filled mushrooms. Yield: 20 mushrooms.

Carla Morley, Laureate Gamma Tau
Jefferson City, Missouri

BACON STUFFED MUSHROOMS

30 medium mushrooms	1 teaspoon onion powder
1 (8-ounce) package cream cheese, softened	1 teaspoon garlic powder
2 teaspoons Worcestershire sauce	3 heaping tablespoons real bacon bits
1 teaspoon soy sauce	Paprika

Preheat the oven to 325 degrees. Wash and drain the mushrooms. Remove the stems from the caps and reserve the stems for another use. Combine the cream cheese, Worcestershire sauce, soy sauce, onion powder, garlic powder and bacon bits in a medium bowl. Stuff the mushroom caps with the cream cheese mixture. Arrange on a baking sheet. Heat in the oven until warm (or microwave on High for 3 to 5 minutes). Yield: 6 to 8 servings.

Beth Chamberlain
Tuscola, Illinois

COTTAGE STUFFED MUSHROOMS

12 fresh medium mushrooms	1/2 cup seasoned stuffing mix
2 tablespoons finely chopped green onion	1/3 cup small-curd cottage cheese
2 tablespoons finely chopped green pepper	Grated Parmesan cheese
3 tablespoons butter or margarine	

Preheat the broiler. Clean the mushrooms. Remove the stems. Finely chop the stems. Sauté the stems, green onion and green pepper in the butter until tender. Remove from heat. Stir in the stuffing mix, blending well. Add the cottage cheese; mix well. Stuff each mushroom abundantly and sprinkle with Parmesan cheese. Broil until brown on top, then turn off the broiler. Turn the oven on to 350 degrees and bake for about 10 minutes. Yield: 6 servings.

Betty J. Bowers, Beta Omicron Master
Fort Worth, Texas

STUFFED MUSHROOMS MOZZARELLA

16 ounces fresh mushrooms	**½ cup melted butter or margarine**
1 (6-ounce) package stovetop stuffing mix	**4 ounces shredded mozzarella cheese**
1 (10-ounce) can cream of mushroom soup	

Preheat the oven to 350 degrees. Clean the mushrooms and remove the stems. Chop the stems and sauté in a nonstick skillet until tender. Prepare the stuffing using package directions. Stir in the mushroom stems and cream of mushroom soup. Dip the mushroom caps in melted butter and arrange in a 9-by-13-inch baking dish. Stuff the mushrooms with the stuffing mixture. Sprinkle the cheese over the stuffed mushrooms. Bake for 15 minutes or until steaming and lightly browned. Yield: 8 servings.

Betty Whittinghill
Sellersburg, Indiana

CHEDDAR CHEESE BALL

This Cheese Ball keeps well when refrigerated for up to 7 days. After the first use, you can reshape it and serve it another time. Friends love receiving this Cheese Ball for Christmas.

1 (8-ounce) package cream cheese, softened	**1 tablespoon chopped green pepper**
¾ cup shredded Cheddar cheese	**½ teaspoon lemon juice**
Dash of Worcestershire sauce	**1 tablespoon sweet pickle relish**
	Chopped walnuts (optional)

Combine the cream cheese, Cheddar cheese, Worcestershire sauce, green pepper, lemon juice and pickle relish; mix well and form into a ball. Roll the ball in chopped walnuts if desired. Serve with crackers or celery sticks. Yield: 25 to 30 servings.

Caroline M. Vandean
St. Andrews, Manitoba, Canada

CHIPPED BEEF CHEESE BALL

1 (2½-ounce) package premium dried beef	**2 (8-ounce) packages cream cheese, softened**
1 small onion or 1 bunch green onions	**Triscuits**

Place the dried beef on a chopping board. Slice the beef lengthwise into thin strips; turn the chopping board ¼ turn and slice lengthwise again. Chop the onion in small pieces (if using green onion, use both white and green parts). Add the beef and the onion to the cream cheese; mix well with a fork. Shape into a ball. It is best if made 24 hours ahead of serving time. Chill, covered, until ready to serve. When ready to serve, place the ball on a serving dish; serve with crackers. Yield: 15 to 20 servings.

Donna Hoendorf, Laureate Gamma Upsilon
Gladstone, Missouri

CREAM CHEESE BALL

4 (8-ounce) packages cream cheese, softened	**1½ teaspoons seasoned salt**
3 tablespoons finely chopped green onion	**1 (20-ounce) can crushed pineapple, well drained**
3 tablespoons finely chopped green pepper	**¾ cup finely chopped walnuts, pecans, sunflower seeds or sesame seeds**
3 tablespoons chopped pimientos	

Combine the cream cheese, green onion, green pepper, pimientos, seasoned salt and pineapple in a bowl; mix well. Divide in half; make 2 cheese balls. Roll in the nuts or seeds. Chill for 8 to 10 hours before serving with your favorite crackers. Yield: 15 to 20 servings.

Virginia E. Johnson
The Dalles, Oregon

CHOCOLATE PEPPERMINT CHEESE BALL

This is an appetizer that is fun for parties around Christmastime. Serve with chocolate-flavored vanilla wafers or chocolate graham crackers.

1 (12-ounce) package semisweet chocolate chips	**2 cups pecans**
1 cup peppermint candies (36 candies)	**1 (8-ounce) package cream cheese, softened**

Process the chocolate chips, peppermint candies and pecans in a blender or food processor until finely ground. Place the mixture in airtight plastic bags until ready to use. There will be enough mixture to make several cheese balls. When ready to make a cheese ball, place the cream cheese in a bowl. Remove ½ cup of the ground candy-nut mixture from its bag and mix into the cream cheese. Shape into a ball and wrap in plastic wrap. Refrigerate for at least 2 or 3 hours or until firm. Yield: 20 to 30 servings.

Jane Harlan, Xi Iota Pi
Amarillo, Texas

❖ BAKED BRIE WITH CRUDITES

Serve with assorted crudités (such as zucchini rounds, broccoli and cauliflower florets, carrot and bell pepper sticks) or cubed bread. This is a great appetizer with a nice bottle of red wine. Slice the bread shell and toast it later for a "cheese sandwich."

2 tablespoons unsalted butter or margarine	2 teaspoons fresh lemon juice
1 large onion, chopped	2 teaspoons light brown sugar
2 tablespoons minced garlic	1 teaspoon Worcestershire sauce
8 ounces Brie cheese, peeled	1 (18-ounce) round sourdough bread loaf
1 (8-ounce) package cream cheese	Paprika
3/4 cup sour cream	

Melt the butter in a heavy medium skillet over medium heat. Add the onion and garlic and sauté until the onion is golden brown, about 10 minutes. Set aside. Cut the Brie and the cream cheese into pieces; place both in a large microwave-safe bowl. Microwave on Medium just until melted, about 2 minutes. Whisk in the onion mixture, sour cream, lemon juice, brown sugar and Worcestershire sauce. Cut off the top of the bread loaf. Scoop out the center of the loaf, leaving a 3/4-inch shell of bread. Spoon the cheese mixture into the loaf. Cover with the bread "lid." Wrap in foil. (It can be prepared a day ahead and kept in the refrigerator. Let stand for 2 hours at room temperature before continuing.) Preheat the oven to 400 degrees. Bake the loaf for 1 hour. Unwrap and place on a platter. Remove the bread lid. Sprinkle cheese mixture with paprika. Yield: 12 to 15 servings.

Peggy Ascherl, Preceptor Laureate Gamma Theta
Bellaire, Texas

CHILI BRIE IN SOURDOUGH

1 teaspoon sugar	1 round loaf sourdough bread
1 tablespoon chili powder	1 tablespoon soft butter or margarine
1 teaspoon dry ground mustard	1 (16-ounce) round Brie cheese, well chilled
1 teaspoon garlic powder	

Preheat the oven to 350 degrees. Combine the sugar, chili powder, mustard and garlic powder; set aside. Cut off the top of the bread and hollow out the bread to make room for the Brie. Butter the outside of the bread; sprinkle with half the spice mixture. Make vertical cuts in the top edge of the bread shell 2 inches down, 1 inch apart—all the way around.

Remove the rind from the Brie and place the Brie in the bread; sprinkle with the rest of the spice mixture. Replace the top of the bread and bake on a baking sheet for 20 to 30 minutes. Use the top of the bread and the pieces from the inside to dip into the hot cheese. Yield: 20 to 25 servings.

Debbie Cain
The Woodlands, Texas

JALAPENO CORN DIP

2 (11-ounce) cans Mexicorn	2 cups shredded Cheddar cheese
1 (8-ounce) jar mayonnaise	2 chopped jalapeño peppers
1 (8-ounce) container sour cream	1 bunch green onions, chopped
1 (4-ounce) can chopped green chiles	Pinch of sugar

Mix the Mexicorn, mayonnaise, sour cream, green chiles, Cheddar cheese, jalapeño peppers, green onions and sugar. Chill for 2 hours. Serve with corn chips. Yield: 25 to 30 servings.

Betsy Blake
Sweeny, Texas

CRAB DIP

2 (8-ounce) packages cream cheese, softened	Pinch of garlic powder
10 tablespoons Worcestershire sauce	1/3 cup onion flakes
	1 (12-ounce) bottle chili sauce
8 tablespoons mayonnaise	1 (8-ounce) can crab meat, drained
	Parsley

Mix the cream cheese, Worcestershire sauce, mayonnaise, garlic powder and onion flakes with an electric mixer; mixture does not have to be smooth. Spread in a 9-by-11-inch glass baking dish. Cover with the chili sauce. Spread the crab meat over the chili sauce. Sprinkle with parsley. Refrigerate for 2 hours. Serve with corn chips or crackers. Yield: 15 to 20 servings.

Brenda Yates
Tyler, Texas

Elizabeth Brennan, Beta, Clive, Iowa, spreads a pie pastry on a shallow baking pan and makes Pesto Pie by covering the pastry with pesto sauce, sprinkling with 3/4 cup shredded pepper Jack cheese, topping with a second pie pastry, and sealing the edges. After baking in a preheated 450-degree oven for about 10 minutes, cut into pieces and serve warm.

CRAB RANGOON DIP

2 (16-ounce) packages
  cream cheese,
  softened
2 (6-ounce) cans crab
  meat, drained
1/2 cup sour cream
4 green onions, chopped

1 1/2 teaspoons
  Worcestershire sauce
5 tablespoons grated
  Parmesan cheese
1/4 teaspoon garlic
  powder

Preheat the oven to 350 degrees. Combine the cream cheese, crab meat, sour cream, green onions, Worcestershire sauce, Parmesan cheese and garlic powder in a bowl; beat with an electric mixer. Pour into a greased 9-by-13-inch pan. Bake for 30 minutes. Serve with crackers or fried won ton skins. Note: This recipe does not work well with low-fat ingredients. Yield: 15 to 20 servings.

Judi Westendorf, Preceptor Delta Delta
Lenexa, Kansas

GREEN CHILE CHEESE DIP

1 (4-ounce) can
  California green
  chiles
1 (8-ounce) package
  cream cheese,
  softened

1 cup sour cream
1/2 medium onion,
  chopped fine
Half-and-half

Wearing protective gloves, split the green chiles, remove the seeds and finely chop. Combine the cream cheese, sour cream and chopped onion in a bowl; beat with an electric mixer until well blended, adding enough half-and-half to make a good dipping consistency. Chill, covered, in the refrigerator for 2 to 3 hours to blend the flavors. Yield: 15 to 20 servings.

Judy Weinmaster, Preceptor Xi
Albany, Oregon

MARGARITA GUACAMOLE

2 ripe avocados, peeled,
  chopped
3 tablespoons lime juice
1 tablespoon tequila
2 fresh jalapeño peppers,
  seeded, minced

6 green onions, chopped
1 tablespoon fresh
  chopped cilantro
1 clove of garlic, minced
1/4 teaspoon salt

Mash the avocados with a fork, add the lime juice and stir well; mixture will be lumpy. Add the tequila, jalapeño peppers, green onions, cilantro, garlic and salt, stirring until well blended. Chill until ready to serve. Yield: 2 cups.

Deborah A. Miller
Hutchinson, Kansas

HOT KIELBASA DIP

1 (8-ounce) package
  cream cheese
1/3 cup sour cream
1/3 cup milk
1 tablespoon
  mayonnaise or salad
  dressing
1/2 teaspoon
  Worcestershire
  sauce

8 ounces smoked
  kielbasa, finely
  chopped
1/2 cup sliced green
  onions
1/4 cup grated Parmesan
  cheese
Fresh raw vegetable
  dippers
Assorted crackers

Microwave the cream cheese, uncovered, in a 1 1/2-quart microwave-safe baking dish on High for about 1 minute or until soft. Stir in the sour cream, milk, mayonnaise and Worcestershire sauce. Add the kielbasa, half the sliced green onions and Parmesan cheese; stir. Cook uncovered on High for 2 to 4 minutes or until heated through, stirring once. Sprinkle with the remaining sliced green onions. Serve with vegetables and crackers. Yield: 2 1/2 cups.

Gladys Weems, Laureate Eta Iota
Highland, California

LAS VEGAS BROCCOLI CHEESE DIP

2 (10-ounce) packages
  frozen chopped
  broccoli
10 to 15 fresh
  mushrooms, chopped
1 chopped onion
1 cup butter or
  margarine

Garlic salt to taste
Onion salt to taste
1 (10-ounce) can cream
  of celery soup
16 ounces process
  cheese, chopped

Cook the frozen broccoli according to package directions. Drain and set aside. Sauté the mushrooms and onion in the butter for about 10 minutes or until tender; stir in the garlic salt and onion salt. Add the soup and the process cheese. Cook over low heat, stirring occasionally, until the cheese is melted. Stir in the broccoli. Place in a slow cooker on low heat to keep the dip warm. Serve with crackers or chips. Yield: 3 cups.

Susan Jones, Xi Delta Tau
Princeton, Missouri

Jane Richards of Sault Ste. Marie, Ontario, Canada, makes a delightful Curry Butter for crackers or Melba toast by mixing 1 cup butter, 1 1/2 tablespoons curry powder, 1 tablespoon lemon juice, and 1/2 teaspoon ginger. Mix well, shape into logs, and chill for about 2 hours before serving.

SLOW-COOKER MEXICAN DIP

Vary the spiciness of this dip by using mild or hot green chiles and mild or hot enchilada sauce.

1 (32-ounce) package
  process cheese, cubed
3 pounds ground beef,
  browned, drained
1 tablespoon dry minced
  onion

1 (4-ounce) can chopped
  green chiles
1 (10-ounce) can mild
  enchilada sauce
Tostito chips

Melt the cheese in a slow cooker on High. Stir in the ground beef, minced onion, green chiles and enchilada sauce. After the mixture is hot, turn the heat to Low to keep the dip warm. Use traditional Tostito chips for dipping. Yield: 30 to 60 servings.

Lois Stessman
Manning, Iowa

EASY LAYERED MEXICAN BEAN DIP

To cut the fat content, you can use fat-free cream cheese and fat-free shredded sharp cheese. Two cans of chicken may be substituted for the ground beef.

2 small cloves of garlic,
  minced
1/2 cup chopped onion
2 tablespoons vegetable
  oil
1 pound ground beef
Salt and pepper to taste
1 (16-ounce) can refried
  beans

1 (8-ounce) package
  cream cheese
1 (8-ounce) jar chunky
  salsa
1 (8-ounce) package
  shredded sharp
  Cheddar cheese

Preheat the oven to 375 degrees. Sauté the garlic and onion in the oil. Add the ground beef, salt and pepper and brown until crumbly. Drain and set aside. Layer the refried beans, cream cheese, ground beef mixture, salsa and shredded cheese in a 9-by-13-inch baking dish. Bake for 30 minutes or until bubbly. Serve warm with corn chips. Yield: 6 to 8 servings.

Camille Burt, Alpha Rho Nu
Huffman, Texas

Kimberly Peterson, Beta Delta, Havre, Montana, wows her guests with Watermelon Margaritas. She processes 1/2 cup freshly squeezed lime juice, 1 tablespoon sugar, 1/2 cup tequila, and 2 tablespoons orange-flavored liqueur in a blender at high speed, then gradually adds 4 cups watermelon chunks that have been frozen overnight. Rub the glass rims with lime wedges and dip in coarse salt.

HOT MEXICAN TACO DIP

1 cup shredded
  Monterey Jack cheese
1 cup shredded Cheddar
  cheese
1 (16-ounce) can refried
  beans
1 (8-ounce) package
  cream cheese,
  softened

1 cup sour cream
4 or 5 green onions,
  sliced
10 dashes hot pepper
  sauce
1 package taco
  seasoning mix
Taco chips

Preheat the oven to 350 degrees. Combine the Monterey Jack cheese and the Cheddar cheese. Mix the refried beans, cream cheese, sour cream, green onion, hot pepper sauce, taco seasoning mix and half the cheese mixture; pour into a large 9-inch pie plate. Bake for 20 minutes. Cover with the remaining cheese mixture; bake for 5 minutes longer or until the cheese is melted. Serve with taco chips. Yield: 12 servings.

Beverly S. Demers
Colorado Springs, Colorado

MEXICAN "GARBAGE"

Serve with tortilla chips.

2 (4-ounce) cans
  chopped black olives
2 (4-ounce) cans
  chopped green chile
  peppers
4 scallions, chopped
2 medium tomatoes,
  chopped

5 tablespoons vegetable
  oil
3 tablespoons white
  vinegar
1 tablespoon chopped
  garlic
1 tablespoon lime juice
Salt and pepper to taste

Combine the olives, chile peppers, scallions, tomatoes, oil, vinegar, garlic, lime juice, salt and pepper; mix well. Chill, covered, in the refrigerator for 8 to 10 hours, stirring occasionally. Drain well before serving. Yield: 6 servings.

Carol B. Keaton
Rex, Georgia

Camellia Kliewer, Cordell, Oklahoma, makes a delicious Peach Tea Mix that is a new twist on the old standby Friendship Tea. She mixes 1 1/2 cups sugar with 1/2 cup instant tea mix, one 3-ounce package of apricot gelatin, 3 packages of peach gelatin, 1/2 cup Tang, and a 5-ounce package of sweetened lemonade mix. Store in an airtight container and use 3 heaping teaspoonfuls of the mix in each cup of boiling water.

ORIENTAL LAYERED APPETIZER

Double the cream cheese and the milk to make a thicker base layer. A combination of water chestnuts and nuts may be used in the topping.

³/₄ cup chopped cooked chicken	1 clove of garlic, minced
½ cup shredded carrots	2 tablespoons soy sauce
½ cup chopped unsalted cashews, peanuts or water chestnuts	¼ teaspoon ground ginger
3 tablespoons sliced green onions	1 (8-ounce) package cream cheese, softened
1 tablespoon chopped fresh parsley	1 tablespoon milk
	Sweet and Sour Sauce

Combine the chicken, carrots, cashews, green onions, parsley, garlic, soy sauce and ginger in a small bowl; mix well. Refrigerate, covered, for several hours or overnight to blend flavors. Combine the cream cheese and milk in a small bowl; beat until smooth and fluffy. Spread the cream cheese mixture over the bottom of a 10-inch round serving dish. Spoon the chicken mixture evenly over the cream cheese. Drizzle with ¼ to ½ cup Sweet and Sour Sauce. Yield: 40 servings.

SWEET AND SOUR SAUCE

¼ cup packed light brown sugar	2 tablespoons vinegar
2 teaspoons cornstarch	1 tablespoon Worcestershire sauce
1 cup water	3 drops hot pepper sauce
¼ cup catsup	

Combine the brown sugar and cornstarch in a small saucepan; mix well. Add the water, catsup, vinegar, Worcestershire sauce and hot pepper sauce, stirring well. Cook over medium heat for 5 minutes, stirring frequently until the mixture thickens. Let cool.

Lillian Vannett
Minot, North Dakota

TANGY FRUIT SALSA WITH CINNAMON CHIPS

1 tablespoon sugar	2 kiwi fruit, peeled, sliced
¼ teaspoon cinnamon	1 teaspoon lime juice
4 (7-inch) flour tortillas	1 teaspoon sugar
1 cup frozen raspberries, thawed	
2 peaches, peeled, chopped	

Preheat the oven to 400 degrees. Combine the tablespoon of sugar and the cinnamon. Spray the tortillas with water. Sprinkle the dampened tortillas with the cinnamon mixture. Cut each tortilla into 8 wedges with a pizza cutter. Place the wedges in a single layer on a flat baking sheet. Bake for 8 to 10 minutes or until crisp. Let cool. Combine the raspberries, peaches, kiwi fruit, lime juice and 1 teaspoon sugar in a bowl. Serve the fruit salsa with the cinnamon chips. Yield: 16 servings.

Ronett M. Jones, Alpha Beta Chi
Clinton, Missouri

PICADILLO

2 pounds ground beef or venison	2 (6-ounce) cans tomato paste
2 (15-ounce) cans tomatoes, diced	1 cup raisins
6 green onions, finely chopped	2 jalapeño peppers, seeded, chopped
4 potatoes, diced	2 (15-ounce) cans beef consommé
1 cup diced pimientos	1 (6-ounce) can mushrooms (pieces and stems)
2 bottles cocktail onions, drained	
1 (6-ounce) can black olives, chopped	Salt, cayenne pepper, paprika, cumin, oregano and Worcestershire sauce to taste
1 green pepper, chopped	
2 (3-ounce) packages slivered almonds	
2 cloves of garlic	

Brown the beef in a large skillet until crumbly and cooked through. Add the tomatoes, green onion, potatoes, pimientos, cocktail onions, olives, green pepper, almonds, garlic, tomato paste, raisins, jalapeño peppers, beef consommé and mushrooms; stir well. Season with salt, cayenne pepper, paprika, cumin, oregano and Worcestershire sauce. Simmer over medium heat until the potatoes are tender, about 20 minutes. Serve as a hot dip with chips. Yield: 40 servings.

Diann Manning, Preceptor Eta
Lake Charles, Louisiana

CINDY'S "RED HOT MAMA" SALSA

4 (15-ounce) cans stewed tomatoes, drained, juice reserved	2 medium onions, finely chopped
¼ cup chopped parsley	2 (15-ounce) cans tomato sauce "with bits"
½ cup finely chopped green pepper	1 (12-ounce) jar sliced jalapeños, drained, juice reserved
1 clove of garlic, finely chopped	

Mash the stewed tomatoes in a very large bowl. Add the parsley, green pepper, garlic and onions; stir in the tomato sauce. Stir in the jalapeños and jalapeño juice to taste. Thin to desired consistency with juice from the stewed tomatoes. Yield: 10 to 12 cups.

Karli Carlile, Phi Theta Gamma
Stephenville, Texas

SENSATIONAL GREEN OLIVE SALSA

This is a tasty, delicious, change-of-pace salsa. The recipe makes a large amount, but it will disappear quickly. Put it in jars and give as gifts with bags of corn chips.

6 to 8 large ripe tomatoes
1 (20-ounce) can green salad olives, drained
2 (4-ounce) cans chopped green chiles
2 bunches green onions, finely chopped

2 to 3 teaspoons garlic salt
2 teaspoons lemon pepper
3 tablespoons olive oil
Red wine vinegar

Peel, core and finely chop the tomatoes. Chop the green olives in a food processor fitted with a steel blade. Combine the tomatoes, green olives, chiles, green onions, garlic salt, lemon pepper, olive oil and enough red wine vinegar to cover the ingredients. Place in an airtight container and store in the refrigerator. It will keep about a month. Serve with corn chips. Yield: 15 to 20 servings.

Patsy A. Hoff, Gamma Delta
Edmond, Oklahoma

COWBOY CAVIAR

You can make this appetizer into a salad when you stir in 2 cups finely shredded cabbage.

2 tablespoons red wine vinegar
1½ to 2 teaspoons hot pepper sauce
1½ teaspoons vegetable oil
1 clove garlic, minced
⅛ teaspoon pepper
1 large firm-ripe avocado (about 10 ounces)
1 (15-ounce) can black-eyed peas, drained, rinsed

1 (11-ounce) can corn kernels, drained, rinsed
⅔ cup thinly sliced green onion
⅔ cup chopped fresh cilantro
½ pound Roma tomatoes, coarsely chopped
½ teaspoon salt or to taste
1 (6-ounce) bag tortilla chips

Mix the vinegar, hot pepper sauce, oil, garlic and pepper in a large bowl. Peel, pit and cut the avocado into ½-inch cubes; add to the vinegar mixture, stir-ring gently to coat. Add the black-eyed peas, corn, green onion, cilantro and tomatoes to the avocado mixture; mix gently to coat. Add the salt. Serve with tortilla chips. Yield: 10 to 12 appetizers.

Helen Fisk, Xi Chi Nu
Escondido, California

TEXAS CAVIAR

This odd combination of foods will win over those who are not crazy about black-eyed peas.

2 (14-ounce) cans black-eyed peas, drained
1 (15-ounce) can white hominy, drained
2 medium tomatoes, chopped
4 green onions, chopped
2 cloves of garlic, minced

1 medium green pepper, chopped
1 jalapeño pepper, chopped
½ cup chopped onion
½ cup chopped parsley
8 ounces Italian salad dressing

Combine the black-eyed peas, hominy, tomatoes, green onions, garlic, green pepper, jalapeño, onion and parsley in a large bowl; mix well. Pour the salad dressing over the mixture. Marinate, covered, in the refrigerator for at least 2 hours, preferably overnight. Drain a little before serving with chips. Yield: 6½ cups.

Rose Ann Munn, Xi Psi Xi
League City, Texas

HOT BEEF TACO DIP

1 (8-ounce) package cream cheese, softened
1 (8-ounce) carton sour cream
1 cup mayonnaise-type salad dressing
1½ pounds lean ground beef

1 package taco seasoning mix
1 (8-ounce) can tomato sauce
1 ripe tomato, chopped
1 green pepper, chopped
1 cup (4 ounces) Cheddar cheese, cubed
1 bag bite-size Tostitos

Preheat the oven to 350 degrees. Beat the cream cheese, sour cream and mayonnaise-type salad dressing together. Spread in the bottom of a 9-by-13-inch pan. Chill, covered, for 15 minutes. Brown the ground beef until crumbly and cooked through; add the taco seasoning mix and tomato sauce. Pour over the chilled cream cheese mixture. Spread the tomato, green pepper and Cheddar cheese over the beef mixture. Heat in the oven for 30 minutes. Let cool for 4 to 5 minutes. Serve with Tostitos. Yield: 8 servings.

Marilyn Stewart
Miramichi, New Brunswick, Canada

TEX-MEX HOT DIP

1 (8-ounce) package
  cream cheese,
  softened
1 (10-ounce) can chili,
  no beans

1 cup shredded Colby
  cheese
Tortilla chips

Preheat the oven to 200 degrees. Spread the cream cheese over the bottom of an 8-by-8-inch glass baking dish. Pour the chili over the cream cheese. Top with the Colby cheese. Bake for 25 minutes. Serve with tortilla chips. Yield: 8 to 10 servings.

Pat Thibodeaux
Metairie, Louisiana

ROSA'S GREEN CHILE DIP

Everyone loves this dip. Be sure to double the recipe.

2 tomatoes, chopped
3 green onions, sliced
1 (4-ounce) can chopped
  green chiles
1 (4-ounce) can chopped
  black olives
1 teaspoon salt

1 teaspoon black pepper
1 teaspoon garlic
  powder
1½ tablespoons vinegar
  (any kind)
3 tablespoons vegetable
  oil

Mix the tomatoes, green onions, green chiles, olives, salt, pepper, garlic powder, vinegar and oil in a bowl. Chill, covered, in the refrigerator for 8 to 10 hours. Serve with tortilla chips. Yield: 1 cup.

Carolyn Tegeler, Preceptor Iota Omicron
San Angelo, Texas

SPICY PUMPKIN DIP

4 cups confectioners'
  sugar
2 (8-ounce) packages
  cream cheese,
  softened
1 (30-ounce) can
  pumpkin

2 teaspoons cinnamon
1 teaspoon ground
  ginger
Pumpkin, hollowed
Gingersnaps

Combine the confectioners' sugar and cream cheese in a bowl; beat until well blended. Add the canned pumpkin, cinnamon and ginger; mix well. Serve in a hollowed-out pumpkin with gingersnaps for dipping. Store in the refrigerator. Yield: 6 to 8 cups.

Ann Doucet, Laureate Zeta Gamma
Deer Park, Texas

FIESTA SHRIMP DIP

1 (4-ounce) can small
  shrimp
1 (3-ounce) package
  cream cheese,
  softened
½ cup Thousand Island
  dressing

¼ cup mayonnaise
⅓ cup picante sauce
2 tablespoons chopped
  green onion
1 teaspoon horseradish
  sauce
Tortilla chips

Chop the shrimp into small pieces. Combine the shrimp, cream cheese, salad dressing, mayonnaise, picante sauce, green onion and horseradish sauce in a bowl; mix well. Chill, covered, in the refrigerator for 8 to 10 hours. Serve with tortilla chips. Yield: 2 cups.

Jaylene Roberts
Othello, Washington

SHRIMP DIP MOLD

1 envelope unflavored
  gelatin
1 tablespoon water
1 (10-ounce) can tomato
  soup
¼ cup water
1 (8-ounce) package
  cream cheese,
  softened

½ cup diced onion
½ cup diced celery
1 cup mayonnaise
28 ounces fresh shrimp,
  steamed, shelled,
  deveined, chopped
Crackers or raw
  vegetables

Dissolve the gelatin in 1 tablespoon of water. Lightly coat a 6-cup mold with vegetable oil. Heat the soup in ¼ cup water in a saucepan over medium heat. Stir in the cream cheese and gelatin until blended. Remove from heat. Beat the mixture with an electric mixer until smooth. Add the onion, celery and mayonnaise; stir until blended. Stir in the shrimp. Pour into the prepared mold. Chill, covered, for 8 to 10 hours. Serve with crackers or vegetables.
Yield: 15 to 20 servings.

Marie Umbriac
Tamaqua, Pennsylvania

Lynn Schwehr, Quesnel, British Columbia, Canada, sends us Lemon Apple Sparkle, a punch she loved as a child. Simmer 3 cups apple juice with 8 inches of stick cinnamon, 24 whole cloves, and 3 whole allspice for 15 minutes and strain. Add four 6-ounce cans frozen lemonade concentrate and 9 cups apple juice. Chill and add ice cubes, two 28-ounce bottles of chilled ginger ale, and yellow food coloring if desired. Garnish with lemon slices.

TABOULI

½ cup medium cracked wheat	*1 bunch scallions, finely chopped*
¼ cup water	*¼ cup crushed dried mint*
4 bunches parsley, washed, dried, finely chopped	*¼ cup lemon juice*
½ to 1 green pepper, finely chopped	*¼ cup olive or other vegetable oil*
3 fresh tomatoes, sliced	*Romaine lettuce*

Soak the cracked wheat in the water until water is absorbed, about ½ hour or longer. Add the parsley, green pepper, tomatoes, scallions, mint, lemon juice and oil; mix well. Serve the with romaine lettuce for scooping. Yield: 6 servings.

Patricia Sahagian
Toluca Lake, California

SPINACH DIP

1 loaf round bread, hollowed	*½ cup sour cream*
1 (10-ounce) package frozen spinach, thawed, drained	*1 box vegetable soup mix*
1 (8-ounce) package cream cheese, softened	*1 (8-ounce) can water chestnuts, drained, chopped*
½ cup mayonnaise	*½ small onion, chopped*
	1 cup shredded Cheddar cheese

Preheat the oven to 350 degrees. Fill the hollowed-out bread with a mixture of the spinach, cream cheese, mayonnaise, sour cream, vegetable soup mix, water chestnuts, onion and Cheddar cheese. Bake for 1 hour on a baking sheet. Serve hot with crackers and pieces of bread. Yield: 12 to 15 servings.

Donna Fraser, Preceptor Beta
Calgary, Ontario, Canada

SPINACH CREAM CHEESE DIP

2 (8-ounce) packages cream cheese, softened	*1 medium tomato, chopped*
1 (10-ounce) package frozen chopped spinach, thawed, squeezed	*4 green onions, chopped*
	1 (4-ounce) can small green chiles
	2 teaspoons garlic
4 to 5 jalapeño peppers, chopped	*1 tablespoon milk*
	1 (10-count) package small flour tortillas

Preheat the oven to 350 degrees. Combine the cream cheese, spinach, jalapeño peppers, tomato, green onions, green chiles, garlic and milk in a baking dish; mix well. Bake for about 30 minutes or until steaming hot. Warm the tortillas, cut them in pie-shaped wedges for dipping and serve with the dip.
Yield: 15 to 20 servings.

Carrie Nelson, Xi Delta Rho
Smyrna, Tennessee

BAKED FRENCH BRIE

Serve this heavenly appetizer with Carr's wafer crackers or Waverly wafers. Use leftovers on English muffins for breakfast.

16-ounce wedge French Brie cheese	*2 or 3 small cloves of garlic, pressed*
¼ cup sliced almonds	
¼ cup butter or margarine	

Preheat the oven to 350 degrees. Place the wedge of Brie in a small baking dish with sides. Sauté the almonds in the butter until the almonds start to brown. Squeeze in the garlic cloves. Sauté over low heat for 1 minute. Spoon the almond mixture over the Brie. Bake for 3 to 5 minutes or until the sides of the Brie begin to ooze. Yield: 20 to 25 servings.

Alice Wright, Xi Gamma
Pierre, South Dakota

BASIL BRIE IN PASTRY SHELL

2 tablespoons grated Parmesan cheese	*1 (14-ounce) round Brie cheese*
2 tablespoons finely chopped fresh basil or 2 teaspoons dried basil	*½ (17-ounce) package frozen puff pastry, thawed*
	Assorted crackers or fruit

Preheat the oven to 400 degrees. Mix the Parmesan cheese and the basil. Cut the round of Brie horizontally into 2 layers. Sprinkle the basil mixture over the cut surface. Reassemble the cheese round. Roll the puff pastry into a 10-by-12-inch rectangle on a lightly floured surface. Cut out one 10-inch circle. Place the cheese in the center of the pastry circle. Bring the pastry up and over the cheese, pressing to make it smooth and even. Brush the pastry lightly with water and press gently to seal. Place seam side down on a baking sheet. Cut decorations from the remaining pastry if desired; moisten with water to attach to the Brie-filled pastry. Bake for 25 minutes or until golden brown. Place the baking sheet on a wire rack to cool for 30 minutes. Serve with assorted crackers or fruit. Yield: 20 to 25 servings.

Sherry Lynn Bowden, Preceptor Delta Delta
Lenexa, Kansas

CRAB MAXINE

2 (3-ounce) packages
  cream cheese,
  softened
1/2 pound fresh crab
  meat, boned, or 1 (4-
  ounce) can crab meat
1 teaspoon horseradish
1/2 teaspoon hot pepper
  sauce

1 teaspoon dry mustard
Dash of garlic salt
1/3 cup mayonnaise
1/2 cup (2 ounces)
  shredded sharp
  Cheddar cheese
English muffins

Preheat the oven to 350 degrees. Mash the cream cheese with a fork. Fold in the crab meat, horseradish, hot pepper sauce, mustard, garlic salt, mayonnaise and Cheddar cheese. Spread the mixture on English muffins. Bake for 5 to 10 minutes. Yield: 12 to 20 servings.

Stella Trumbly
Tacoma, Washington

CRABBY SANDWICH APPETIZER

8 ounces imitation crab
  meat
1/3 cup mayonnaise
1/4 cup sour cream
1/4 cup chopped green
  onion
1/4 cup finely chopped
  celery

1 tablespoon fresh
  lemon juice
1 hard-cooked egg,
  chopped
1/2 teaspoon dill seed
1/4 teaspoon black
  pepper

Combine the crab meat, mayonnaise, sour cream, green onion, celery, lemon juice, hard-cooked egg, dill seed and pepper; mix well. Chill until serving time. Serve on toast points, biscuit halves, crackers or puff pastry. Yield: 8 servings.

Darice Hostetler
Burlington, Colorado

GOTTA GET A GOUDA

1 large wheel Gouda
  cheese
French mustard

1 (4-count) package
  refrigerated crescent
  rolls

Preheat the oven to 375 degrees. Preheat a baking sheet in the oven. Peel the wax off the Gouda cheese. Cover the cheese with French mustard. Encase the cheese with the unbaked crescent dinner rolls, overlapping the dough and pinching together so the cheese is completely covered. Place on aluminum foil on the preheated baking sheet. Bake for 20 minutes. Serve on a plate surrounded with your favorite crackers. Yield: variable.

Donna Farrell
Cincinnati, Ohio

FROSTED PATE

1 pound liverwurst
1/2 teaspoon minced
  garlic
1/2 teaspoon Italian
  seasoning
3 tablespoons dried
  minced onion
1 (8-ounce) package
  cream cheese,
  softened

1 tablespoon
  mayonnaise
1/2 teaspoon minced
  garlic
1/8 teaspoon hot pepper
  sauce
Paprika
Parsley

Mash the liverwurst in a bowl; add 1/2 teaspoon minced garlic, Italian seasoning and minced onion. Mix well. Form into a ball or loaf on a plate. Chill, covered, for 1 hour. To make the frosting, combine the cream cheese, mayonnaise, 1/2 teaspoon minced garlic and hot pepper sauce; mix well. Spread the cream cheese frosting over the liverwurst. Garnish with paprika or parsley. Yield: 20 to 25 servings.

Susan Firestone
Sarasota, Florida

❖ PORTOBELLO PATE

Be sure to use the fabulous portobellos or an equally flavorful mushroom for this recipe. Don't use plain button mushrooms! This paté can also be used as a stuffing for vegetables or tart shells.

1/4 cup butter or
  margarine
1 cup chopped onion
16 ounces finely chopped
  portobello
  mushrooms
1 cup bread crumbs
1 clove of garlic, peeled
Juice of 1/2 lemon
1/3 cup sherry
2 tablespoons fresh
  chopped parsley

1 tablespoon cornstarch
1/2 cup heavy cream
1 teaspoon sea salt
Fresh ground pepper to
  taste
1 (4-ounce) package
  cream cheese
Healthy pinch of mace
Small pinch of thyme

Melt the butter in a skillet. Sauté the onion in the butter over medium-low heat until light brown. Add the chopped mushrooms. Cook until the liquid has evaporated. Stir in the bread crumbs. Place the garlic, lemon juice, sherry and parsley in the container of a blender or food processor; process until smooth. Add the garlic mixture to the mushroom purée in the skillet; cook for 5 minutes longer. Mix the cornstarch and cream in a small bowl; stir into the mushroom purée to thicken. Simmer for 5 minutes, stirring constantly. Season with sea salt and pepper and allow to cool. Combine the mushroom purée and cream cheese in a bowl; mix well. Add the mace and thyme; mix well. Chill, covered, in the refrigerator for 2 hours. Serve on individual serving plates or in a bowl surrounded by breads and vegetables. Yield: 10 or more servings.

Sally Ruscitti, Xi Alpha
Albuquerque, New Mexico

JAZZABELLE

This spread keeps for a long time.

1 (18-ounce) jar pineapple or apricot preserves	¼ cup horseradish
1 (18-ounce) jar apple jelly	1 tablespoon pepper (optional)
6 teaspoons dry mustard	Crackers
	Cream cheese

Combine the pineapple preserves, apple jelly, dry mustard, horseradish and pepper in a bowl; beat well. Chill, covered, until ready to serve. Serve over crackers spread with cream cheese.
Yield: 36 servings.

Judy W. Anderson, Xi Epsilon Alpha
Paonia, Colorado

REUBEN SPREAD

Serve warm on party-size rye bread, bagels, or crackers. This spread can be reheated in the microwave on Low.

1 (16-ounce) can sauerkraut, drained, chopped	1 cup shredded American cheese
1 cup mayonnaise	1 cup shredded Swiss cheese
8 ounces deli corned beef, chopped	

Preheat the oven to 350 degrees. Combine the sauerkraut, mayonnaise, corned beef, American cheese and Swiss cheese. Place in an 8-by-12-inch baking dish. Bake for 30 minutes. Yield: 6 cups.

Naomi E. Golden, Alpha Nu Master
Van Buren, Ohio

SHRIMP APPETIZER PIE

1 (8-ounce) package cream cheese, softened	1 medium red onion, chopped
1 cup catsup	1 green pepper, chopped
2 tablespoons prepared horseradish	1 fresh tomato, chopped
3 cloves of garlic, minced	2 to 3 ounces shredded sharp Cheddar cheese
2 (4½-ounce) cans baby shrimp	

Mix the cream cheese, catsup, horseradish and garlic in a bowl. Place the mixture in a pie plate or quiche pan. Top with the shrimp. Sprinkle the red onion, green pepper and tomato over the shrimp. Top with the Cheddar cheese. Chill, covered, until ready to serve. Serve with crackers. Yield: 15 to 20 servings.

Anne G. Heck, Xi Gamma Upsilon
Queensbury, New York

CANNONBALL SHRIMP SPREAD

This appetizer stays hot for a really long time wrapped in the foil—good for taking to a party!

1 medium cannonball bread loaf	1 teaspoon seasoning salt
12 ounces cream cheese	3 tablespoons cocktail sauce (optional)
8 ounces sour cream	
8 ounces shredded Cheddar cheese, medium or sharp	¾ pound cocktail shrimp, excess liquid squeezed out
1 bunch green onions, chopped	1 or 2 loaves baguette bread, sliced

Preheat the oven to 325 degrees. Slice off the top of the bread loaf. Hollow out the loaf, leaving the bottom and sides intact. Combine the cream cheese and sour cream in a bowl. Add the Cheddar cheese, green onion, seasoning salt and cocktail sauce; mix well. Stir in the shrimp. Fill the bread loaf with the shrimp mixture. Put the bread slice back on top of the loaf. Wrap the loaf with heavy-duty foil so it looks like a big candy kiss. Bake for 1 hour. Serve with sliced baguette bread. When the hollow loaf is empty, it may be eaten. Yield: 15 to 20 servings.

Paula M. Seeley
Vancouver, Washington

AMBROSIA PUNCH

2½ quarts orange juice	3 cups ginger ale or lemon-lime soda
2 cups pineapple juice	3 cups vanilla ice cream
1 cup cream of coconut	½ cup toasted flaked coconut (optional)
2 small oranges, halved, thinly sliced	

Chill all the ingredients before making the punch. Combine the orange juice, pineapple juice and cream of coconut in a punch bowl. Cut a slit halfway through each orange slice and perch the slices around the rim of the punch bowl. Stir in the ginger ale. Float scoops of vanilla ice cream in the punch. Sprinkle with coconut. Yield: 4 quarts.

M. "Jo" Bent, Epsilon Master
Kansas City, Missouri

CREAMY HOLIDAY EGGNOG

2 dozen eggs, separated
1 pint whipping cream
1 pint coffee cream
2 cups sugar
1/2 teaspoon salt

2 cups bourbon
1 cup rum
1/2 gallon vanilla ice
    cream, softened
Nutmeg

Beat the egg whites until stiff. Beat the egg yolks; set aside. Whip the whipping cream until very thick, adding the coffee cream gradually. Beat the egg yolks on low speed until thick, adding the sugar and salt gradually. Stir the bourbon and rum into the egg yolk mixture, stirring very slowly so as not to "cook" the eggs. Fold the egg yolk mixture into the egg whites. Stir in the cream mixture (you can start sampling now!). Add the ice cream, ladling the eggnog over the ice cream until blended. Garnish each serving with a sprinkle of nutmeg. Yield: 2 gallons.

Myra L. Williams, Eta
Orlando, Florida

MOCHA PUNCH

1 1/2 quarts water
1/2 (8-ounce) container
    instant chocolate
    drink mix
1/2 cup sugar
1/4 cup instant coffee
    granules
1/2 gallon vanilla ice
    cream

1/2 gallon chocolate ice
    cream
1 cup whipping cream,
    whipped
Chocolate curls
    (optional)

Bring the water to a boil in a large saucepan. Remove from heat. Add the chocolate drink mix, sugar and coffee granules; stir until dissolved. Chill, covered, in the refrigerator for 4 hours or overnight. About 30 minutes before serving, pour into a punch bowl. Add scoops of the ice cream; stir until partially melted. Garnish with dollops of whipped cream and chocolate curls. Yield: 20 to 25 servings (about 5 quarts).

Shelley Lewis, Xi Epsilon Alpha
Hereford, Texas

GOLDEN PHEASANTS

1 egg
1/3 cup sugar
6 shots gin

6 shots lemon juice
White cream soda

Blend the egg and sugar in a blender; add the gin and lemon juice and blend. Fill a glass 3/4 full of the cream soda. Add one shot of the gin mixture.
Yield: 12 servings.

Dawn Sweeney, Kappa Omicron
Arnold, Missouri

ACAPULCO MARGARITAS

Add a sprinkle of artificial sweetener for sweetness.

3/4 cup tequila
3/4 cup Triple Sec

1/2 cup fresh-squeezed
    lime juice

Fill the blender container with ice. Pour in the tequila, Triple Sec and lime juice. Blend well, at least 1 minute. Yield: 4 servings.

Sheron Lamberth, Xi Alpha Gamma Kappa
Houston, Texas

APPLE PUNCH

6 cups apple cider or
    apple juice
3 cups orange juice

3/4 cup lemon juice
3/4 cup sugar
6 cups ginger ale

Mix the apple cider, orange juice, lemon juice and sugar at least 8 to 10 hours before serving; chill. Add the ginger ale just before serving. Yield: 25 servings.

Frances Brillian, Preceptor Alpha Rho
Rochester, New York

BANANA PUNCH

4 cups sugar
6 cups water
1 (12-ounce) can frozen
    orange juice
    concentrate
1 (12-ounce) can water
1 (6-ounce) can frozen
    lemonade concentrate

1 (6-ounce) can water
1 (46-ounce) can
    pineapple juice
5 large bananas, mashed
1 quart non-diet lemon-
    lime soda for each
    container

Bring the sugar and the 6 cups of water to a boil; boil for 3 minutes. Let cool. Mix the orange juice concentrate, 12-ounce can of water, lemonade concentrate, 6-ounce can of water, pineapple juice and bananas. Add the sugar mixture to the juice mixture; stir well. Divide into six 1-quart containers and freeze. When ready to serve, remove a container from the freezer and let stand at room temperature for 15 minutes. Pour into a punch bowl. Mash the frozen juice and add 1 quart non-diet lemon-lime soda, stirring well. Yield: 2 quarts each serving time.

Milissa A. Duffey, Theta
Vincennes, Indiana

Lettie Loveleen Turner, Preceptor Zeta Tau, Orange Park, Florida, makes Peppermint Punch by pouring a quart of milk over a pint of peppermint ice cream that has been cut into 1-inch chunks. Add 40 ounces of chilled lemon-lime soda.

FESTIVE PUNCH

This recipe can be doubled or even tripled.

**1 (46-ounce) can
    pineapple juice,
    chilled**
**1 (6-ounce) can frozen
    limeade concentrate,
    thawed**

**1 quart ginger ale,
    chilled**
1 pint strawberry sorbet

Stir the pineapple juice and limeade concentrate together in a punch bowl until well blended. Add the ginger ale and sorbet. Serve immediately. Yield: 10 to 12 servings.

*Sandi Davison, Laureate Gamma Upsilon
Kansas City, Missouri*

GOLDEN SORORITY PUNCH

I have served this at sorority functions for 25 years.

**1 (46-ounce) can
    pineapple juice,
    chilled**
**1 (46-ounce) can apricot
    juice, chilled**

**1 (2-liter) bottle ginger
    ale or lemon-lime
    soda, chilled**
**1 quart pineapple
    sherbet**

Pour the pineapple juice, apricot juice and ginger ale into a large punch bowl. Spoon the sherbet into the liquids; stir and serve immediately. The sherbet will melt, and the punch will be a creamy golden color. Yield: 36 servings.

*Carolyn Livingston, Laureate Alpha Xi
Danville, Indiana*

NATURAL JUICE PUNCH

To make this an alcoholic punch, substitute champagne for the lemon-lime soda.

**1 (12-ounce) can frozen
    orange juice
    concentrate, thawed**
**1 (12-ounce) can frozen
    pink lemonade
    concentrate,
    thawed**

**1 (6-ounce) can frozen
    grape juice
    concentrate, thawed**
**1 (2-liter) bottle soda
    water**
**1 (2-liter) bottle lemon-
    lime soda**

Combine the orange juice concentrate, pink lemonade concentrate and grape juice concentrate in a 2-quart pitcher; fill the pitcher the rest of the way with water. Pour the juice mixture into a large punch bowl; stir in the soda water and lemon-lime soda. Yield: 4 quarts.

*Christie Rivas, Xi Alpha Pi
Tualatin, Oregon*

PARTY PUNCH

2 cups water
1½ cups sugar
**1 (46-ounce) can
    pineapple juice**

6 cups orange juice
3 cups lemon juice
**7 (12-ounce) cans lemon-
    lime soda**

Mix the water, sugar, pineapple juice, orange juice and lemon juice in a large covered container; refrigerate. Just before serving, add the lemon-lime soda; stir until all ingredients are well blended. Serve over ice. Yield: 2 gallons.

*Victoria Tornetto, Xi Master
St. Louis, Missouri*

TEEN'S CHOICE PUNCH

Teenagers love this, especially my son's football team. They choose this over soft drinks every time I make it. Be sure the frozen mix is dissolved, and add cold ginger ale. If you make an ice ring, make it out of ginger ale so it won't dilute the punch.

**1 can Bacardi Mixers
    (nonalcoholic)
    daiquiri mix**

**2 (2-liter) bottles ginger
    ale**

Combine the daiquiri mix with the ginger ale in a punch bowl. Stir until the daiquiri mix is dissolved. Yield: 20 servings.

*Helyn E. Brooks
Dahlonega, Georgia*

HOT CIDER PUNCH

4 cups water
4 cups apple juice
**1 package sugar-free
    cherry Kool-Aid mix
    (to make 2 quarts)**

¼ teaspoon cinnamon
⅛ teaspoon nutmeg
⅛ teaspoon cloves
**Lemon slices or
    cinnamon sticks**

Mix the water, apple juice, Kool-Aid mix, cinnamon, nutmeg and cloves in a large kettle; bring to a boil. Reduce the heat and simmer. Serve hot. Garnish with lemon slices or cinnamon sticks. Yield: 16 servings.

*Shari Joos, Mu Chi
Newton, Iowa*

Linda Lewis, Alpha Alpha Chi, Ft. Myers, Florida, served Anniversary Punch for her parents' sixtieth anniversary. Chill 48 ounces of apple juice, 24 ounces of white grape juice, 12 ounces frozen lemonade concentrate, and 34 ounces of club soda before mixing in a punch bowl and adding a decorative ice ring or fruit garnish.

HOT CRANBERRY PUNCH

4 cups cranberry juice
4 cups apple juice
2 cinnamon sticks
8 whole cloves
Juice of 2 oranges,
  strained
2 tablespoons sugar

Pour cranberry juice, apple juice, cinnamon sticks, cloves, orange juice and sugar into a large kettle; stir and heat slowly. When ready to serve, strain out the cloves and cinnamon sticks. Serve in clear punch cups. Yield: 8 to 12 servings.

Barbara Phillips, Preceptor Beta Delta
Poplar Bluff, Missouri

AMARETTO SLUSH

2 cups sugar
1 quart boiling water
1 (46-ounce) can
  unsweetened
  pineapple juice
1 (12-ounce) can frozen
  orange juice
  concentrate, thawed
1 (6-ounce) can frozen
  lemonade
  concentrate, thawed
2 quarts water
2 cups amaretto or
  almond liqueur
2 tablespoons vanilla
  extract
1 tablespoon almond
  extract

Dissolve the sugar in the boiling water. Stir in the pineapple juice, orange juice concentrate, lemonade concentrate, water, amaretto, vanilla extract and almond extract. Divide the mixture evenly among 6 heavy-duty quart-size sealable plastic bags; freeze. Remove a bag from the freezer as needed. Let stand at room temperature until the mixture is slushy. Yield: 6 quarts.

Karen McMillin, Beta Sigma
Lexington, Kentucky

APRICOT BRANDY SLUSH

7 cups water
2 cups sugar
3 tea bags
2 cups water
1 (12-ounce) can frozen
  lemonade
  concentrate, thawed
1 (12-ounce) can frozen
  orange juice
  concentrate, thawed
12 ounces apricot
  brandy
2 quarts club soda

Heat the 7 cups of water and 2 cups sugar in a skillet over medium heat until clear. Steep the tea bags in the two cups of water in a large 10-quart bowl. Remove the tea bags. Mix the sugar, water, tea, lemonade concentrate, orange juice concentrate and brandy. Freeze. When ready to serve, remove from the freezer. Fill a glass ³/₄ full of the slush; fill the rest of the glass with club soda. Yield: 24 servings.

Kimberly Collins
Belleville, Illinois

BRANDY SLUSH

7 cups water
2 cups sugar
1 (12-ounce) can frozen
  orange juice
  concentrate, thawed
1 (12-ounce) can frozen
  lemonade
  concentrate, thawed
1 pint brandy
1 liter lemon-lime soda
Maraschino cherries
  (optional)
Orange wedges
  (optional)

Bring the water and sugar to a boil. Remove from heat. Add the orange juice concentrate and lemonade concentrate; stir. Add the brandy, stirring again. Place in a large freezer container and freeze for 48 hours. When ready to serve, mix 2 scoops of the Brandy Slush with lemon-lime soda to taste. Top with a maraschino cherry and orange wedge. Yield: Variable.

Melody Sublette-Peyton, Omicron Chi
Spirit Lake, Iowa

FROSTY FRUIT SLUSH

2 (6-ounce) cans frozen
  orange juice
  concentrate, thawed
1 (6-ounce) can frozen
  lemon juice, thawed
1 (46-ounce) can
  pineapple juice
1 (12-ounce) can peach
  nectar
1 teaspoon almond
  extract
Sugar to taste
2 quarts ginger ale

Reconstitute the frozen juices in a large bowl as directed on the cans. Stir in the pineapple juice, peach nectar and almond extract. Add sugar to taste. Freeze in a freezer container. Remove from the freezer about 2 hours before serving. Slip the mixture from the carton; chip with a fork until flaky. Add the ginger ale. Yield: 50 servings.

Juanita W. Gray
Bluefield, West Virginia

Margaret Carey of Grand Blanc, Michigan, makes an unusual Pumpkin Party Punch by blending 6 cups apple juice with a 30-ounce can of pumpkin pie mix and 4 cups of softened vanilla ice cream, and stirring in a liter of lemon-lime soda.

Sensational Soups and Salads

Take a trip to the local produce market—and enjoy the season's best vegetables in a crisp, fresh salad or a hearty, flavorful soup! Soups and salads—whether they're served as the main meal or a side dish—bring out the ingenuity of any chef, allowing you to experiment with a wide variety of flavors and textures. Full of healthy ingredients, they're nutritious, satisfying, and great to eat any time of the year. Choose soups and salads that complement one another, and serve them in interesting combinations. Add a homemade loaf or muffin from our Bountiful Breads section to complete your meal in minutes!

CABBAGE AND GARLIC SOUP

3 tablespoons minced
  garlic
8 cups chicken
  broth
1 cup long grain white
  rice
6 cups shredded savoy
  cabbage

Kosher salt to taste
  (optional)
1 teaspoon freshly
  ground pepper
  (optional)
12 large croutons
2 tablespoons minced
  parsley

Combine the garlic, 2 cups of the chicken broth and rice in a medium saucepan; bring to a boil over moderate heat. Reduce heat; simmer, covered, for 20 minutes. Transfer to a blender container. Add 4 cups of the chicken broth. Process until smooth, blending in batches if necessary. Return to the saucepan. Stir in the cabbage and remaining chicken broth. Simmer for 15 minutes over moderately low heat. Stir in the kosher salt and pepper. Ladle the soup over croutons placed in individual soup bowls. Garnish with parsley. Serve immediately. Yield: 6 to 8 servings.

Lois L. Clark, Laureate Gamma Tau
Arleta, California

CREAM OF CARROT SOUP

1 tablespoon chopped
  onion
3 tablespoons butter or
  margarine
4 tablespoons all-
  purpose flour
1 teaspoon salt

Dash of pepper
3 cups milk
3 cups shredded carrots
1/3 cup light cream
Paprika
Chopped parsley

Sauté the onion in the butter in a large saucepan until soft. Whisk in the flour, salt and pepper. Add the milk slowly, stirring constantly, and cook until thickened. Cook the carrots in salted water to cover for 10 minutes over medium heat. Add the carrots to the milk mixture. Stir in the cream just before serving. Garnish with paprika and parsley. Yield: 6 servings.

Rose Lawson, Preceptor Laureate Phi
Temple, Texas

Barbara Appleton, Xi Gamma Beta, Paris, Arkansas, makes Ten-Can Soup with a pound of ground beef that she cooks and drains and then combines with two 15-ounce cans ranch-style beans, three 15-ounce cans minestrone, one 15-ounce can tomatoes with green chiles, one 15-ounce can tomatoes, one 15-ounce can mixed vegetables, and two vegetable cans of water. Simmer until hot.

CHEESE BEER SOUP

If a recipe requires several chopped vegetables, try chopping them all at once in the food processor. It's efficient and it blends their natural juices.

2/3 cup shredded carrots
1/4 cup chopped onion
1/4 cup margarine
1/4 cup all-purpose flour
Dash of salt
Dash of white pepper
1 cup chicken broth
1 1/2 cups milk

1/4 teaspoon hot pepper
  sauce
2 teaspoons
  Worcestershire sauce
2 cups shredded process
  cheese
1/2 cup beer

Sauté the carrots and onion in the margarine in a skillet over medium-low heat until tender. Stir in the flour, salt and white pepper gradually; cook, stirring constantly, until thickened. Stir in the broth, milk and sauces. Add cheese, reduce heat and stir until cheese melts. Stir in the beer. Heat through, but do not boil. Yield: 4 to 6 servings.

Carol Lintner, Preceptor Xi
Raleigh, North Carolina

GARLIC SOUP

4 large cloves of garlic
4 cups beef broth
4 slices day-old bread
1 to 1 1/2 tablespoons
  grated Parmesan
  cheese

1 to 1 1/2 tablespoons
  shredded mozzarella
  cheese
3 tablespoons butter or
  margarine, softened
1/2 cup sherry (optional)

Simmer the garlic in the beef broth in a kettle over medium heat for 30 minutes. Remove the garlic and set it aside. Preheat the broiler. Cut the bread with a round cookie cutter or glass. Broil the bread circles until light brown on one side. Let cool. Mix the Parmesan and mozzarella cheeses. Mash the garlic cloves with 1 tablespoon of the butter. Butter the untoasted side of the bread circles, spread with the garlic butter, then cover with the cheese. Broil until browned and bubbly, about 30 to 60 seconds. Stir the sherry into the hot garlic broth. Serve the broth topped with toasted bread. Yield: 4 servings.

Barbara McIntyre, Epsilon Rho
Colorado Springs, Colorado

Susan Wilson, Eta Iota, Brookfield, Missouri, heats 2 cans Mexican-style tomatoes, 1 can drained whole kernel corn, 2 tablespoons taco seasoning, and 1/2 cup water, tops with shredded cheese, and serves with corn chips to make Taco Soup.

GAZPACHO BLANCO

Serve this refreshing summer soup with French bread or crackers and a good dry wine. You may vary the amounts of the ingredients and spices to suit your taste.

1 medium red bell pepper, seeded, chopped	1 teaspoon cumin
	White pepper to taste
	Salt to taste
1 medium green pepper, seeded, chopped	1 teaspoon cayenne pepper
1 medium yellow pepper, seeded, chopped	1 teaspoon oregano
	1 teaspoon coriander
	Fresh basil, parsley, dillweed to taste
3 medium cucumbers, peeled, seeded, chopped	4 or 5 green onions
	1 quart sour cream
1 small red onion, chopped	Sprinkle of cayenne pepper

Mix the red bell pepper, green pepper and yellow pepper; set aside ½ cup of the mixture. Place the cucumbers in a blender container; process for a few seconds. Add the portion of the bell pepper mixture that was not set aside, the onion, cumin, white pepper, salt, cayenne pepper, oregano, coriander and fresh herbs, processing after each addition. When the mixture is blended completely, add color by adding the ½ cup mixed chopped peppers, pulsing for 1 second. Add the green onions; pulse for 1 second. Stir the sour cream into the soup. Serve in bowls and top with the cayenne pepper. Yield: 4 servings.

Pamela Smith, Xi Alpha
Albuquerque, New Mexico

MUSHROOM BARLEY SOUP

A mixture of different kinds of mushrooms makes this soup taste even better. I buy a bag of frozen mixed mushrooms from a local store.

1½ cups chopped onions	6 cups chicken broth
1 cup chopped carrots	1 teaspoon pepper
1 cup chopped celery	¼ teaspoon nutmeg
2 teaspoons minced garlic	1 teaspoon thyme
3 tablespoons butter or margarine	1 cup pearl barley, uncooked
16 ounces mushrooms, sliced	1 cup water
	Parsley

Sauté the onions, carrots, celery and garlic in the butter in a large kettle over medium-low heat for 5 to 10 minutes or until tender. Add the mushrooms; cook for 5 to 10 minutes or until soft. Stir in the chicken broth, pepper, nutmeg, thyme, barley and water.

Bring to a boil. Reduce heat and simmer, partially covered, for 2 hours. Serve topped with parsley. Yield: 6 to 8 servings.

Wendy Bennett, Xi Pi Rho
Napa, California

BROCCOLI MUSHROOM CHOWDER

1 pound fresh broccoli, cleaned, cut in half-inch pieces	8 ounces fresh mushrooms, cleaned, sliced
½ cup water	1 teaspoon salt
½ cup butter or margarine	¼ teaspoon white pepper
1 cup all-purpose flour	¼ teaspoon crushed tarragon
1 quart chicken broth	
1 quart half-and-half	

Steam the broccoli in the water until tender. Set aside undrained. Melt the butter in a saucepan over medium heat. Add the flour to make a roux; cook, stirring constantly for 2 to 4 minutes. Add the chicken broth, stirring with a wire whisk while bringing to a boil. Reduce the heat to low. Stir in the broccoli, half-and-half, mushrooms, salt, white pepper and tarragon. Heat completely through, but do not boil. Yield: 8 to 10 servings.

Joyce B. DeCrocker
Kalamazoo, Michigan

GRAMMA LAGER'S HOMEMADE POTATO SOUP

No water is drained from the cooked vegetables, which allows all the rich vitamins to remain.

3 large potatoes, peeled, diced	1 (5-ounce) can evaporated milk
1 medium carrot, peeled, chopped	1 teaspoon salt
	½ teaspoon garlic powder (optional)
1 medium rib celery, chopped	Dash of pepper
1 (¼-inch) slice of onion	
¼ cup butter or margarine	

Place the potatoes, carrot, celery and onion in a 2-quart heavy saucepan. Add enough water to cover the vegetables. Bring to a boil. Reduce heat to low. Cook until the vegetables begin to soften, stirring occasionally. The starch in the potatoes will thicken the soup. Stir in the remaining ingredients. Simmer for 10 to 15 minutes. Yield: 4 servings.

Mercedes T. Lager, Gamma Rho
Maryville, Missouri

HOT OR COLD POTATO SOUP

4 cups diced peeled
 potatoes
1/2 cup chopped onion
1 teaspoon chicken
 bouillon granules

2 cups milk
8 ounces sour cream
2 tablespoons chopped
 chives (optional)
Salt and pepper to taste

Place the potatoes in a large kettle. Add enough water to cover the potatoes. Bring to a boil. Reduce heat, then cook slowly until almost done, about 15 minutes. Do not drain. Add the chopped onion, chicken bouillon granules and 1 cup of the milk. Simmer for 20 minutes, stirring often. Stir in the remaining 1 cup milk, sour cream and chives. Add salt and pepper. Yield: 6 servings.

Loretta Smith, Xi Alpha Gamma Kappa
Houston, Texas

POTATO KNAPFLA SOUP

I grow my dill and freeze it for winter use.

2 cups peeled potatoes
 cut in 3/4-inch chunks
3 cups water
1 tablespoon chicken
 soup base
1/4 cup chopped fresh
 dillweed or 1
 tablespoon dried dill
1 cup sliced celery
1 cup coarsely chopped
 onion
1 teaspoon minced
 garlic

2 tablespoons butter or
 margarine
1 large egg
2 tablespoons milk
1/2 teaspoon salt
3/4 cup all-purpose flour
1 cup reduced-fat milk
1/2 teaspoon salt
Pepper to taste
1 (16-ounce) can green
 beans, undrained

Place the potatoes, water, chicken soup base and dillweed in a large saucepan over medium-low heat and cook until the potatoes are almost tender, about 15 minutes. Sauté the celery, onion and garlic in the butter in a medium skillet over medium-low heat until the onions are translucent, about 10 minutes. Stir the celery mixture into the potato mixture. Combine the egg, milk, salt and flour to make a thick dough. Drop small amounts of the dough, about 1/2 teaspoon, into the soup from a teaspoon dipped in the soup each time. Boil gently for 3 minutes. Stir in the 1 cup milk, salt, pepper and green beans. Yield: 8 servings.

Darleen A. Hicks, Beta Master
Deadwood, South Dakota

SHERRIED POTATO SOUP

1 medium onion,
 chopped
3 ribs celery, chopped
1/2 cup butter or
 margarine
2 carrots, grated
2 (14-ounce) cans
 chicken broth
3 (10-ounce) cans cream
 of potato soup

8 ounces Colby cheese,
 shredded
8 ounces sour cream
3 tablespoons sherry
Hot pepper sauce
 (optional)
Parsley (optional)
Salt and pepper to taste

Sauté the onion and celery in the butter for 3 minutes in a large saucepan over medium heat. Stir in the carrots and the chicken broth. Cook, stirring, until very hot. Add the cream of potato soup, cheese, sour cream and sherry. Continue to heat. Do not boil. Add the hot pepper sauce, parsley, salt and pepper. Yield: 8 servings.

Chris Nickey, Xi Lambda Tau
Bowling Green, Ohio

SLOW-COOKER SPINACH POTATO SOUP

3 (10-ounce) cans potato
 soup
1 (14-ounce) can chicken
 broth
1 quart heavy cream

1 (10-ounce) package
 frozen chopped
 spinach, thawed,
 drained

Combine the potato soup, chicken broth, heavy cream and spinach in a slow cooker. Heat on Low for 4 hours. Be sure not to let the soup boil. Yield: 12 servings.

Nancy Wahl, Epsilon Master
Cinnaminson, New Jersey

SPINACH SOUP WITH ROQUEFORT CHEESE

3 tablespoons butter or
 margarine
1 medium onion,
 chopped
2 cups chicken broth
3 ounces Roquefort
 cheese

2 cups chopped fresh
 spinach
2 plum tomatoes,
 skinned, chopped
1 teaspoon fresh thyme
6 tablespoons cream
Salt and pepper to taste

Melt 2 tablespoons of the butter in a heavy skillet. Add the onion and cook over medium heat until golden. Add the chicken broth. Stir in the cheese. Bring to a boil. Boil, stirring, until the cheese is melted and mixture is slightly reduced. Remove from heat. Pour into a blender container and process until smooth. Return the mixture to the skillet. Melt the remaining 1 tablespoon butter in a medium skillet over medium heat. Sauté the spinach, tomatoes and thyme in the butter for 2 minutes. Remove from heat. Stir in the cream. Add the spinach mixture to the soup; blend well. Add salt and pepper if necessary. Yield: 4 servings.

Joan MacDonald
Delta, British Columbia, Canada

STRAWBERRY SOUP

1/3 cup water	Zest of 1/2 lemon
1/2 teaspoon unflavored gelatin	16 ounces fresh strawberries, cleaned, hulled
1/4 cup sugar	
1/2 stalk lemongrass, chopped	Zest of 1/2 lime

Combine the water, gelatin, sugar, lemongrass and lemon zest in a saucepan; bring to a boil. Place the strawberries in a large bowl. Strain the boiling liquid over the strawberries. Stir in the lime zest. Chill, covered, in the refrigerator for 8 to 10 hours. Yield: 4 servings.

Ann-Joy Hardy, Xi Zeta Iota
Winter Haven, Florida

AUSTRIAN VEGETABLE SOUP

A cup of evaporated milk plus a cup of whole milk may be substituted for the whipping cream.

8 to 10 slices bacon, chopped	4 cups chicken broth
2 medium potatoes, peeled	2 cups whipping cream
1 medium onion	2 tablespoons cornstarch
1 medium leek, white only	Worcestershire sauce to taste
1 carrot, peeled	Hot pepper sauce to taste
2 or 3 ribs celery	
1/4 bunch parsley	Salt and pepper to taste

Sauté the bacon pieces in a large skillet; drain the fat. Cut the potatoes, onion, leek, carrot, celery and parsley into large chunks and process in the food processor, 1 vegetable at a time, until smooth. Add the vegetables to the bacon in the skillet. Cook, stirring, over medium-low heat until tender, about 10 minutes. Stir in the chicken broth. Simmer, covered, for 20 to 30 minutes. Stir in the whipping cream. Dissolve the cornstarch in 1/4 cup water. Pour into the skillet, stirring, until the soup is creamy but not thick. Season the soup with Worcestershire sauce, hot pepper sauce, salt and pepper. Yield: 6 to 8 servings.

Arliss Barnes, Preceptor Delta Gamma
Indianapolis, Indiana

TOMATO VEGETABLE SOUP

To reheat this soup, microwave on High for 4 to 5 minutes.

1 (28-ounce) can tomato juice	1 cup cooked small seashell macaroni
1 (28-ounce) can vegetable juice cocktail	1 (15-ounce) can mixed vegetables or 1 cup frozen mixed vegetables
1 (6-ounce) can sliced mushrooms	
1 (16-ounce) can kidney beans or chick-peas, drained	1 tablespoon celery salt
	1 teaspoon pepper
	1 teaspoon oregano

Combine the tomato juice, vegetable juice cocktail, mushrooms, beans, macaroni, mixed vegetables, celery salt, pepper and oregano in a large skillet; mix well. Adjust the seasoning to taste. Bring to a boil. Serve. Yield: 12 servings.

Carlyn MacDonald, Xi Master
Sudbury, Ontario, Canada

GRIFF'S HEARTY CABBAGE SOUP

2 pounds ground beef	1 (10-ounce) can of water
3 cloves garlic, minced	
2 large onions, chopped	1 envelope Italian salad dressing mix
1 small head of cabbage, chopped	1 (16-ounce) can red beans
1 (15-ounce) can diced tomatoes	
1 (15-ounce) can stewed tomatoes	2 tablespoons dried parsley
3/4 cup chopped celery	1 tablespoon Everglades seasoning
1 (15-ounce) can tomato sauce	1 teaspoon garlic salt
1 (10-ounce) can tomato purée	1 teaspoon seasoned salt
3 (15-ounce) cans of water	

Brown the ground beef with the garlic and onions in a large saucepan over medium-low heat, stirring until the meat is crumbly; drain. Stir in the cabbage, diced tomatoes, stewed tomatoes, celery, tomato sauce, tomato purée, water, salad dressing mix, red beans, parsley, Everglades seasoning, garlic salt and seasoned salt. Bring to a boil. Reduce heat to a simmer. Simmer for 45 to 50 minutes or until cabbage is tender. Serve with corn bread. Yield: 12 to 14 servings.

Griff Jappé, Laureate Delta Xi
Lehigh Acres, Florida

BROCCOLI AND CAULIFLOWER CHEESE SOUP WITH SAUSAGE

2 tablespoons butter or
   margarine
4 ounces smoked beef
   sausage or kielbasa,
   quartered lengthwise,
   sliced crosswise
1 medium onion,
   chopped
1/2 teaspoon caraway
   seeds, crushed
Freshly ground pepper
   to taste
1 pound russet potatoes,
   peeled, sliced

2 (15-ounce) cans
   chicken broth
1 bay leaf
1 1/2 cups bite-size
   broccoli florets
1 1/2 cups bite-size
   cauliflower florets
1/4 cup whipping cream
3 ounces shredded sharp
   Cheddar cheese
Salt to taste

Melt the butter in a heavy medium-size saucepan over medium heat. Add the sausage and cook until brown, about 4 minutes. Remove the sausage with a slotted spoon. Add the onion, caraway seeds and pepper. Reduce heat to medium-low and cook for 4 minutes, stirring occasionally. Stir in the potatoes, chicken broth and bay leaf. Simmer until the potatoes are tender, stirring occasionally and breaking potatoes with the spoon, about 25 minutes. Stir in the broccoli and cauliflower and simmer just until tender, about 10 minutes. Stir in the cream and sausage; cook until heated through. Add the cheese, stirring until it is melted. Season with salt and pepper. Discard the bay leaf. Ladle into bowls. Yield: 10 servings.

Fran Bogar, Preceptor Zeta Phi
St. Charles, Missouri

❖ FOUR BEAN SALSA SOUP

Substitute garbanzo beans for the white beans if you like. Use mild, medium, or hot salsa according to your taste.

1/2 to 3/4 pound smoked
   sausage, cut in bite-
   size pieces
1 (15-ounce) can chili
   beans, undrained
1 (15-ounce) can black
   beans, undrained
1 (15-ounce) can white
   beans, undrained

1 (15-ounce) can kidney
   beans, undrained
2 (15-ounce) cans salsa
Chopped cilantro
Shredded Monterey Jack
   and Cheddar cheese
   for garnish (optional)

Sauté the sausage until cooked through, about 3 to 5 minutes. Drain off the excess fat. Add the chili beans, black beans, white beans, kidney beans, salsa, and cilantro; mix well. Bring to a boil; reduce the heat.

Simmer, covered, for 5 to 10 minutes, stirring occasionally. Garnish with the Monterey Jack and Cheddar cheese. Yield: 6 servings.

Arlene Burton
Manchester, Washington

SAUERKRAUT SOUP

1 pound Polish sausage
5 medium potatoes,
   diced
2 medium onions,
   chopped
2 carrots, chopped
3 (15-ounce) cans
   chicken broth

1 (32-ounce) can
   sauerkraut, rinsed,
   drained
1 (8-ounce) can tomato
   sauce
1 teaspoon sugar

Slice the sausage in 1/4-inch slices into a 1-quart saucepan. Add the potatoes, onions, carrots and chicken broth; simmer for 30 minutes. Add the sauerkraut, tomato sauce and sugar; simmer for 45 minutes to 1 hour longer. Yield: 10 to 12 servings.

Nancy Youtzy
Palm Bay, Florida

❖ CHICKEN VEGGIE CHEESE SOUP

4 cups chicken broth
1 cup chopped onions
1 cup shredded carrots
1 (16-ounce) bag frozen
   broccoli-cauliflower
   mix
3 cups diced potatoes

2 cups chopped cooked
   chicken
1 (16-ounce) package
   process cheese, cubed
2 (10-ounce) cans cream
   of chicken soup

Combine the chicken broth, onions and carrots in a 4-quart kettle; simmer for about 10 minutes. Add the broccoli-cauliflower mix and potatoes; simmer until tender, about 15 minutes. Add the chicken, process cheese and cream of chicken soup; cook slowly until the cheese melts. Yield: 8 servings.

Beth Johnson, Lambda Upsilon
Pleasant Hill, Missouri

EGG DROP SOUP

1 tablespoon cornstarch
2 tablespoons cold
   water
3 cups chicken broth
1 teaspoon salt

1 egg, lightly beaten
1 scallion, finely
   chopped, including
   tops

Dissolve the cornstarch in the cold water; set aside. Bring the chicken broth to a boil in a 2-quart saucepan over high heat. Add the salt. Give the cornstarch a stir and add to the chicken broth, stirring for a few seconds until the broth thickens slightly and becomes clear. Pour in the egg slowly and stir gently once. Remove from heat. Garnish with the chopped scallion and serve at once. Yield: 4 to 6 servings.

Traci Lewis, Xi Alpha Gamma
Beckley, West Virginia

CHICKEN CHEESE SOUP

5 potatoes, peeled	1 (16-ounce) package
4 carrots	process cheese
4 chicken bouillon cubes	1 (10-ounce) package
1 quart water	frozen chopped
1/4 to 1/2 onion, minced	broccoli, cooked,
4 ribs celery, chopped	diced
2 (10-ounce) cans cream	
of chicken soup	

Cut up the potatoes and carrots. Cook them together in water to cover over medium heat until soft; mash by hand. Combine the chicken bouillon cubes, water, onion and celery in a large saucepan over medium heat; simmer for about 20 minutes. Stir in the mashed potato mixture, cream of chicken soup, process cheese and broccoli. Leave in the pan over low heat until ready to serve or keep warm in a slow cooker. Yield: 10 servings.

Christine Lathan
Savannah, Missouri

CHICKEN AND SAUSAGE GUMBO

1 1/2 gallons water	1 1/4 cups vegetable oil
1 (2- to 3-pound)	1 1/2 cups all-purpose
chicken, cut up	flour
5 parsley sprigs	1 tablespoon salt
3 cloves of garlic,	1 teaspoon ground red
minced	pepper
1 pound smoked	1 teaspoon black pepper
sausage, diced	1 bunch green onions,
1 medium onion	chopped
1 1/2 teaspoons celery salt	1/2 teaspoon filé powder
4 chicken bouillon cubes	Hot cooked rice

Combine the water, chicken, parsley and garlic in a large kettle; bring to a boil. Cover, reduce heat and simmer for 1 hour. Remove the chicken, allowing the broth to remain in the kettle. Skin and bone the chicken; chop coarsely. Set aside. Add the sausage, onion, celery salt and chicken bouillon cubes to the broth; simmer for 1 hour. Heat the oil in a skillet over medium heat; gradually add the flour to make a roux, stirring constantly for 20 minutes or until the roux is a dark or caramel color, being careful not to burn it. Stir the roux into the sausage mixture; simmer for 1 hour. Stir in the chicken, salt, red pepper

and black pepper; simmer for 45 minutes. Stir in the green onions; simmer for about 5 minutes. Stir in the filé powder. Serve over the rice. Yield: 4 1/2 quarts.

Cindy Praesel, Nu Delta
Hutto, Texas

TORTILLA SOUP

Be sure to add the tortillas just before serving or they will become soggy.

3 (15-ounce) cans	2 green onions, sliced
chicken broth	2 to 3 large soft flour
2 to 3 whole chicken	tortillas
breasts, cooked,	1 cup shredded Cheddar
boned, chopped	cheese
2 carrots, chopped	
1 (15-ounce) can chunky	
salsa	

Pour the chicken broth into a slow cooker. Stir in the chicken, carrots, salsa and green onions. Cook on Low for about 6 hours. Use a pizza cutter to slice the tortillas in the shape of wide egg noodles. Stir in the cheese and the tortilla strips just before serving. Yield: 8 to 10 servings.

Kelly Gerke and Karen Frohwein, Nu Beta
State Center, Iowa

CREAMY TORTILLA CHICKEN SOUP

4 to 5 boneless, skinless,	6 corn tortillas, cut into
preseasoned fajita	strips
chicken breasts	Vegetable oil for frying
1 (10-ounce) can diced	1 cup shredded Cheddar
tomatoes	cheese
1 (10-ounce) can cream	Sour cream and avocado
of chicken soup	for garnish
1 (16-ounce) package	
process cheese, cut	
into chunks	

Boil the chicken breasts in water until tender. Remove the fat and cut into bite-size pieces. Strain the water (now chicken broth) to remove any leftover pieces of chicken or fat. Return the bite-size chicken pieces to the broth. Stir in the tomatoes, cream of chicken soup and process cheese. Simmer, stirring, until smoothly blended. Fry the corn tortilla strips in the oil until crispy. Lay tortilla strips in the bottom of each bowl; sprinkle with the cheese, then ladle in the soup. Garnish with sour cream and avocado. Yield: 6 servings.

Deane Novosad and Charlotte Knesek, Iota Omicron
Gonzales, Texas

EASTON'S BOUILLABAISSE

I suggest this makes 6 servings because everyone is going to want more than one bowl! You can make the bouillabaisse stock in advance and freeze it. Then just add the seafood and finish cooking. There's no need to follow the ingredient list precisely. Sometimes I just put in our "catch of the day."

1/4 cup olive oil
1/2 cup thinly sliced celery
1 cup chopped onion
3 cloves of garlic, minced
1 teaspoon saffron
1 (49-ounce) can clam juice
1 cup chopped leeks, white part only
6 garden-ripe tomatoes (about 1 1/2 pounds), blanched, skinned, chopped
1/2 green pepper, finely chopped
1 cup julienned fresh carrots
6 sprigs parsley, coarsely chopped
1 bay leaf
1/2 teaspoon thyme
1 teaspoon paprika
1 tablespoon salt
1/8 teaspoon cayenne pepper

1 cup chablis
1 cup dry sherry
1 or 2 lobster tails, cut in 1-inch pieces
3/4 pound halibut, cut in 1-inch pieces
1 pound Ling cod, cut in 2-inch pieces
1 pound red snapper, cut in 2-inch pieces
16 scallops (about 1/2 pound)
16 large fresh shrimp (about 1 pound), shelled, deveined
1 pound Alaskan king crab, cut in 2-inch pieces, or Dungeness crab, uncut
15 small hard-shelled clams, removed from shells
1/2 cup sliced green onions
Chopped parsley, small amount to garnish

Heat the oil in an 8- to 10-quart stockpot over medium heat. Add the celery, onion, garlic and saffron; sauté until tender but not brown, about 5 minutes. Stir in the clam juice, leeks, tomatoes, green pepper, carrots and parsley. Bring to a boil; reduce heat and simmer for 5 minutes. Add the bay leaf, thyme, paprika, salt and cayenne pepper; simmer, uncovered, for 20 minutes. Stir in the chablis and sherry; cook for about 5 to 8 minutes longer. Taste and correct the seasoning (it may need more salt). Remove the bay leaf. Set the bouillabaisse stock aside. Shortly before you plan to eat, bring the bouillabaisse stock to a boil. Layer the lobster tails, halibut, cod, red snapper, scallops and shrimp in the stock. Simmer, covered, for 10 minutes. Add the crab meat, clams and green onions. Simmer, covered, for 5 to 8 minutes or until seafood is done. Be sure not to overcook the seafood! Remove the fish, shrimp and other large pieces and arrange them in large soup bowls. Pour the hot cooking juices over the pieces and garnish with parsley. Serve with buttered garlic bread. Yield: 6 to 8 servings.

Helen Easton, Laureate Zeta Beta
Yreka, California

CIOPPINO (ITALIAN BOUILLABAISSE)

1 1/2 teaspoons minced garlic
3 tablespoons olive oil
3 cups canned plum tomatoes, drained, 2 cups juice reserved
3 tablespoons parsley flakes
1 1/2 teaspoons oregano

1 1/2 teaspoons salt
12 to 16 littleneck clams
12 jumbo shrimp
2 lobster tails, cut in large pieces
2 to 3 crab legs
1/2 pound whitefish, cut in chunks

Sauté the garlic in the olive oil for 2 to 3 minutes. Add the tomatoes, juice from the tomatoes, parsley flakes, oregano and salt. Bring to a boil; reduce heat and simmer for 30 minutes. Add the clams, shrimp, lobster tails, crab legs and fish; simmer slowly for 20 minutes. Serve in bowls alongside fresh Italian or French bread. Yield: 4 servings.

Arlene Weed, Laureate Epsilon Delta
Camarillo, California

SHE-CRAB SOUP

After a day of "crabbing" on Chesapeake Bay, our teenage son cooks up the fresh crabs in this tantalizing soup. The soup should be served immediately, but any leftovers can be refrigerated and reheated the next day.

3 cups milk
1 cup heavy cream
1/2 cup butter or margarine
2 (10-ounce) cans cream of celery soup
2 hard-cooked eggs, chopped
1/4 teaspoon garlic salt

1/2 teaspoon Old Bay seafood seasoning
1/2 teaspoon Worcestershire sauce
1/2 teaspoon white pepper
1 cup crab meat, drained, flaked
1/4 cup dry sherry

Combine the milk, cream, butter, cream of celery soup, hard-cooked eggs, garlic salt, seafood seasoning, Worcestershire sauce, white pepper, crab meat and sherry in a large saucepan. Cook over low heat for 5 minutes. Do not boil. Serve immediately. Yield: 6 to 8 servings.

DeeDee Patrick, Xi Alpha Phi
Yorktown, Virginia

SPICY SEAFOOD SOUP

Cajun Power Garlic Sauce contains garlic, cayenne pepper, and tomatoes. If the sauce is too spicy for your taste, use less.

2 large potatoes, peeled, diced	1 (8-ounce) can whole kernel corn, drained
6 medium carrots, coarsely chopped	1 (4-ounce) can crab meat, drained
1 medium onion, coarsely chopped	1½ cups peeled baby shrimp
6 ribs celery, coarsely chopped	2 tablespoons Schilling Salt and Spice
1 large red bell pepper, coarsely chopped	1 tablespoon Cajun Power Garlic Sauce
1 (14-ounce) can stewed tomatoes	

Combine the potatoes, carrots, onion, celery, red bell pepper, stewed tomatoes, corn, crab meat, shrimp, Schilling Salt and Spice and Cajun Power Garlic Sauce in a 4-quart glass microwave-safe kettle. Cover the kettle. Microwave on Medium for 30 minutes. Continue microwaving and stirring, in 15-minute intervals until the vegetables are tender. Serve with garlic bread. Yield: 6 generous servings.

Barbara Vogel, Laureate Rho
Mesa, Arizona

OYSTER CLAM SOUP

2 (10-ounce) cans chunky cream of mushroom soup	8 ounces oysters
	6½ ounces clams
3 potatoes, peeled, diced	2 tablespoons sherry

Combine the cream of mushroom soup and potatoes in a large saucepan over medium heat. Simmer for 10 minutes. Stir in the oysters, clams and sherry. Simmer until the potatoes are tender, about 10 minutes longer. Yield: 4 to 6 servings.

Susan M. Schrepper, Xi Zeta Epsilon
Kalamazoo, Michigan

Carol A. Johannigmeier, Laureate Mu, Ft. Collins, Colorado, serves a delightfully refreshing summer Frosty Minted Soup by combining 4 cans of condensed green pea soup, 1 cup whipping cream, 4 cups milk, and 1/3 cup finely chopped fresh mint leaves in a large bowl and beating until smooth and creamy. Chill thoroughly and serve in chilled soup cups.

SUPER SALMON CHOWDER

This makes a good Lenten meal.

1 (7-ounce) can salmon	2 cups chicken broth
1 clove of garlic, minced	1 teaspoon salt
½ cup chopped onion	½ teaspoon pepper
½ cup chopped green pepper	½ teaspoon thyme
½ cup chopped celery	½ cup frozen peas
3 tablespoons butter or margarine	1 (8-ounce) can cream-style corn
1 cup diced potatoes	1 (12-ounce) can evaporated skim milk
1 cup chopped carrots	

Sauté the garlic, onion, green pepper and celery in the butter. Stir in the potatoes, carrots, reserved salmon liquid, chicken broth, salt, pepper and thyme. Simmer, covered, for 20 minutes or until the vegetables are nearly tender. Add the peas; simmer for 5 minutes. Stir in the corn, evaporated milk and salmon. Cook until heated through.
Yield: 4 to 5 servings.

Pat Howell
Bourbonnais, Illinois

SCALLOP AND VEGETABLE SOUP

1 clove of garlic, minced	2 medium tomatoes, seeded, diced
1 medium onion, sliced	
2 medium carrots, cut into thin strips	1 cup sliced mushrooms
	8 ounces fresh or frozen scallops
2 ribs celery, cut into thin strips	1 teaspoon basil
2 tablespoons melted margarine or vegetable oil	¼ teaspoon pepper
	1 tablespoon lemon juice
2½ cups chicken broth	

Sauté the garlic, onion, carrots and celery in the margarine in a large saucepan until tender. Add the chicken broth. Bring to a boil; reduce heat and simmer for 5 minutes. Stir in the tomatoes, mushrooms, scallops, basil, pepper and lemon juice. Simmer for 5 minutes or until scallops are tender. Yield: 6 servings.

Sherry MacFarlane
Dartmouth, Nova Scotia, Canada

Gena Farrin, Pocahontas, Arkansas, makes Homemade Clam Chowder by combining 3 cans of clam chowder, 2 cans of homestyle potato soup, 1 can of cream of celery soup, ½ cup butter, and 2 cups half-and-half and simmering in a saucepan or heating in a slow cooker.

BANANA SALAD

2 eggs
1/2 cup sugar
1 (16-ounce) can
 pineapple chunks,
 drained, liquid
 reserved
1/2 cup butter or
 margarine

2 tablespoons all-
 purpose flour
Pinch of salt
6 to 8 bananas, sliced
8 ounces process cheese,
 cubed

Beat the eggs in a large saucepan. Add the sugar, pineapple liquid, butter, flour and salt; cook over medium-low heat until the mixture thickens, about 5 to 10 minutes. Layer the bananas, alternating with pineapple chunks and cheese chunks in a 2-quart glass dish. Just before serving, pour the cooked mixture, either hot or cold, over the bananas, cheese and pineapple. Yield: 8 to 10 servings.

Pamela Ollie
Hot Springs, Arkansas

BUTTERSCOTCH SALAD

Before I first made this salad, I thought it could not possibly be good. I was very surprised; it was really good and my family loved it.

1 (8-ounce) container
 whipped topping,
 thawed
1 (4-ounce) package
 instant butterscotch
 pudding mix
1 (8-ounce) can crushed
 pineapple in own
 juice, undrained

3 cups diced apples
1 cup dry roasted nuts
1 cup miniature
 marshmallows

Combine the whipped topping, butterscotch pudding mix and pineapple. Stir in the apples, nuts and marshmallows. Chill, covered, in the refrigerator for 1 to 2 hours or until ready to serve.
Yield: 4 to 6 servings.

Patricia Kyle Vance
Lebanon, Tennessee

CHAMPAGNE DESSERT SALAD

1 (8-ounce) package
 cream cheese,
 softened
3/4 cup sugar
2 bananas, sliced
1 (10-ounce) package
 frozen strawberries,
 thawed, undrained

1 (15-ounce) can
 pineapple tidbits,
 drained
1 (8-ounce) container
 whipped topping
1/2 cup chopped walnuts
 or pecans

Beat the cream cheese and sugar together in a large bowl until light and fluffy. Combine the bananas, strawberries, pineapple tidbits and whipped topping in a separate bowl; stir in the nuts. Stir the banana mixture into the cream cheese mixture; blend well. Pour into a loaf pan and freeze, covered, for at least 8 to 10 hours. It will keep well in the freezer for a week. Yield: 10 servings.

Beverly Wellman, Laureate Omicron
Terre Haute, Indiana

CHERRY COLA SALAD

3/4 cup water
3/4 cup sugar
1 (21-ounce) can cherry
 pie filling
1 (6-ounce) package
 cherry gelatin mix
1 tablespoon lemon
 juice

1 (15-ounce) can crushed
 pineapple in juice,
 undrained
1 cup Pepsi Cola
1/2 cup walnuts or
 pecans (optional)

Combine the water and sugar in a saucepan and bring to a boil. Add the cherry pie filling; bring to a boil again. Place the contents of the cherry gelatin package in a bowl. Pour the hot liquid over the gelatin mix. Stir in the lemon juice, pineapple, Pepsi Cola and nuts. Chill, covered, in the refrigerator until set. Yield: 10 to 12 servings.

Karen Lading, Preceptor Beta Mu
Indianapolis, Indiana

CRANBERRY SOUR CREAM SALAD

This special Christmas-season salad can double as a dessert.

1 (6-ounce) package
 raspberry gelatin mix
1 1/2 cups boiling water
1 (16-ounce) can whole
 cranberry sauce (or
 make your own)

1 (20-ounce) can crushed
 pineapple
1 cup sour cream
1 1/2 cups seedless red
 grapes, halved
1/4 cup slivered almonds

Dissolve the gelatin mix in the boiling water in a large bowl. Stir in the cranberry sauce and pineapple. Chill, covered, in the refrigerator for 30 minutes. Use a wire whisk to stir the sour cream gently into the gelatin mixture. Add the grapes. Pour into a beautiful glass bowl. Sprinkle with the almonds. Chill, covered, in the refrigerator for 2 to 4 hours or until ready to serve. Yield: 8 servings.

Marion Tufford, Iota Master
St. Thomas, Ontario, Canada

CRANBERRY PINEAPPLE SALAD

This salad looks wonderful when chilled and served in a clear glass bowl.

1 (16-ounce) package fresh cranberries, minced	**¼ cup chopped pecans or walnuts**
1 cup minced apples	**1 (3-ounce) package cherry gelatin mix**
1 cup crushed pineapple	**¾ cup sugar**
1 cup pineapple juice	**1 cup boiling water**
2 tablespoons lemon juice	

Combine the cranberries, apples, pineapple, pineapple juice, lemon juice and nuts in a bowl. Set aside. Combine the gelatin mix and sugar in a separate bowl; add the boiling water and stir well. Stir the gelatin mixture into the cranberry mixture. Chill for 8 to 10 hours before serving. Yield: 6 to 8 servings.

Beverly Wolfe, Delta Omega
Danville, Kentucky

CRANBERRY NUT SALAD

2 cups ground cranberries	**2 cups crushed pineapple, drained**
2 cups sugar	**2 cups finely chopped celery**
2 (3-ounce) packages lemon gelatin mix	**1 cup chopped walnuts or pecans**
2 cups hot water	
2 cups pineapple juice	

Combine the cranberries and sugar in a bowl; set aside. Dissolve the gelatin mix in the hot water; stir in the pineapple juice. Chill until partially set, about 30 minutes. Stir in the cranberry mixture, crushed pineapple, celery and nuts. Pour into a large ring mold or a 9-by-13-inch pan. Chill, covered, in the refrigerator until ready to serve, at least 2 hours. Yield: 10 to 12 servings.

Edna M. Mays, Preceptor Psi
Wilmington, Ohio

EASY FRUIT SALAD

1 (15-ounce) can fruit cocktail, undrained	**1 (4-ounce) package instant lemon pudding mix**
1 (26-ounce) jar tropical fruit salad, drained	**Coconut for garnish (optional)**
3 bananas, sliced	
Marshmallows as desired	

Combine the fruit cocktail, tropical fruit salad, bananas and marshmallows in a large bowl. Sprinkle the lemon pudding mix over the fruit; stir in to make

a fruit glaze. Sprinkle coconut over the top. Yield: 8 servings.

Elsena Bender, Theta Masters
Great Bend, Kansas

EASY ORANGE FRUIT SALAD

1 small banana, sliced	**1 medium apple, unpeeled, diced**
1 medium orange, peeled, sectioned	**¼ cup frozen orange juice concentrate**
1 (8-ounce) can pineapple chunks, drained	**Lettuce leaves**

Combine the banana, orange, pineapple chunks and apple in a bowl; stir gently. Add the orange juice concentrate; toss gently. Chill, covered, in the refrigerator until serving time. Serve on lettuce leaves. Yield: 4 to 6 servings.

Joyce Bielfeldt, Laureate Gamma Sigma
Abilene, Texas

FROZEN FRUIT COCKTAIL SALAD

1 cup mayonnaise-type salad dressing	**2 cups fruit cocktail, drained**
1 (8-ounce) package cream cheese	**2 cups colored miniature marshmallows**
½ cup sugar	**2 drops red food coloring**
½ cup maraschino cherries, chopped	

Combine the mayonnaise-type salad dressing, cream cheese and sugar; mix well. Stir in the maraschino cherries, fruit cocktail and marshmallows. Add the food coloring; blend well. Freeze for 8 hours. Cut into 3-inch squares. Yield: 9 servings.

Marlys A. Montz
Marshalltown, Iowa

LAZY DAY FRUIT SALAD

1 (15-ounce) can crushed pineapple, undrained	**1 (3-ounce) package instant vanilla pudding mix**
1 (28-ounce) can fruit cocktail, drained	**1 (8-ounce) container whipped topping**
1 (3-ounce) package instant lemon pudding mix	

Combine the pineapple, fruit cocktail, lemon pudding mix and vanilla pudding mix in a large bowl; stir well. Fold in the whipped topping. Spoon into a 9-by-13-inch baking dish. Chill, covered, in the refrigerator for at least 2 hours. Yield: 12 servings.

Susan Wheeler, Preceptor Phi
Barboursville, West Virginia

MANDARIN ORANGE SALAD

60 butter crackers, crushed	1 (12-ounce) can evaporated milk
1/2 cup melted margarine	1 (8-ounce) container whipped topping
1/4 cup sugar	
1 (6-ounce) can frozen orange juice concentrate, thawed	4 (11-ounce) cans mandarin oranges, drained

Combine the crushed crackers, margarine and sugar; press in the bottom of a 9-by-13-inch baking dish, reserving some of the crumbs for a topping. Gently blend the orange juice concentrate, evaporated milk and whipped topping. Stir in the mandarin oranges. Spread the mixture over the cracker crumb crust. Sprinkle reserved crumbs over the top. Chill, covered, in the refrigerator for at least 4 hours or until ready to serve. Yield: 8 to 10 servings.

Krista Gusler, Delta Zeta
Traverse City, Michigan

SPRING SALAD

1 (6-ounce) package orange pineapple gelatin mix	1 (29-ounce) can sliced cling peaches, undrained
2 cups boiling water	15 lettuce leaves
1 (21-ounce) can lemon pie filling	

Dissolve the gelatin mix in the boiling water. Whip in the pie filling. Add the peaches, stirring until well blended. Spread in a 9-by-13-inch baking dish. Chill for at least 3 hours. Cut into squares; serve each square on a lettuce leaf. Yield: 15 servings.

Cheryl Krzmarzick, Lambda Rho
Manson, Iowa

SUSAN'S PINEAPPLE SALAD

1 envelope unflavored gelatin	1 cup chopped walnuts or pecans
1/2 cup water	2 cups shredded Cheddar cheese
1 (15-ounce) can crushed pineapple, undrained	3/4 cup mayonnaise
3/4 cup sugar	Dash of salt
1 cup chopped celery	

Dissolve the gelatin in the water; set aside. Combine the pineapple and sugar in a saucepan over medium-low heat; cook for 3 minutes. Remove from heat. Combine the celery, nuts and cheese in a large bowl. Add the mayonnaise, salt, gelatin mixture and pineapple mixture; mix well. Pour into a 9-by-13-inch glass baking dish or your choice of a fancy bowl.

Chill, covered, in the refrigerator until set. Cut in squares to serve. Yield: 10 servings.

MarthaJo Dick
Harrison, Arkansas

RED WHITE AND BLUE SALAD

This is a great dish for a 4th of July picnic!

2 (3-ounce) packages raspberry gelatin mix	1 (8-ounce) package cream cheese, softened
2 cups hot water	1 (3-ounce) package raspberry gelatin mix
1 envelope unflavored gelatin	1 cup hot water
1/2 cup cold water	1 (21-ounce) can blueberry pie filling
1 cup half-and-half	
1 cup sugar	
1 teaspoon vanilla extract	

Stir the 2 packages raspberry gelatin mix into the 2 cups hot water; pour into a 9-by-13-inch baking dish and chill until firm. Combine the unflavored gelatin and cold water in a small bowl; set aside. Heat the half-and-half and sugar in a saucepan over medium heat until hot, not boiling. Combine the unflavored gelatin mixture, sugar mixture, vanilla and cream cheese in a bowl; stir until smooth. Pour over the chilled raspberry layer in the baking dish. Chill until firm. Blend the remaining package of raspberry gelatin mix and the 1 cup hot water; stir in the blueberry pie filling. Pour over the second chilled layer. Chill until firm. Yield: 15 servings.

Tracy Kelly, Xi Gamma Rho
Forest Grove, Oregon

SHOPPING DAY ASIAN SALAD

You may substitute thinly sliced chuck-eye steak for the New York strip steak.

1 1/2 pounds New York strip steak	6 tablespoons soy sauce
3/4 teaspoon garlic powder	3 tablespoons sesame oil
1 1/2 tablespoons olive oil	6 tablespoons rice wine vinegar
6 cups cooked spaghetti	1 tablespoon sugar
3/4 teaspoon garlic powder	1/4 teaspoon pepper
6 tablespoons chunky peanut butter	6 green onions, chopped
	1 red bell pepper, chopped (optional)

The day before serving, partially freeze the steak, trim off the fat and thinly slice. Rub with 3/4 teaspoon garlic powder and refrigerate for 8 to 10 hours. 30 minutes before serving time, brown the meat in the olive oil in a large skillet over medium-high heat.

Remove from heat. Cook the spaghetti as on package directions; keep warm. Whisk together the remaining 3/4 teaspoon garlic powder, peanut butter, soy sauce, sesame oil, rice wine vinegar, sugar and pepper. Pour over the warm spaghetti. Arrange the meat strips on top. Sprinkle with the green onions and garnish with the red bell pepper. Yield: 4 servings.

Eleanor Patricia Clark, Preceptor Alpha Epsilon
Jasper, Alabama

HAM JAM

3/4 cup cold water	3/4 cup honey
1 envelope unflavored gelatin	10 ounces boneless ham, cubed
1/2 cup orange juice	Chopped fresh mint and additional grated orange zest for garnish
1 teaspoon grated orange zest	
1/4 cup lemon juice	
1 teaspoon grated lemon zest	

Combine the water and gelatin in a small microwave-safe bowl; allow to soften for 5 minutes. Microwave on High for 1 to 2 minutes or until the mixture boils and gelatin is completely dissolved. Place the hot gelatin mixture, orange juice, orange zest, lemon juice, lemon zest, honey and ham in a food processor fitted with a metal blade; process until all ingredients are puréed. Pour into a 3-cup mold or decorative bowl. Chill until firm. Garnish with mint and orange zest. Serve with hot biscuits, crusty rolls or assorted crackers. Yield: 2 1/2 cups.

Natalie N. Sekavec, Theta Master
Brownell, Kansas

SALAD BOWL PUFF

This salad is a great conversation piece!

1/4 cup margarine	4 eggs
2/3 cup water	Ham or chicken salad
1 cup baking mix	

Preheat the oven to 400 degrees. Grease a 9-inch pie plate heavily with the margarine. Heat the water in a 2-quart saucepan over medium heat. Add the baking mix all at once. Stir over the heat until it forms a ball. Remove from heat. Beat in the eggs 1 at a time until mixture is smooth. Spread over the bottom of the pie plate. Bake for 35 to 40 minutes or until puffed and dry. Let cool. Just before serving, fill with your choice of ham or chicken salad. Yield: 6 servings.

Karol Johnson, Laureate Alpha Rho
Columbus, Ohio

ALMOND CHICKEN SALAD

3 boneless chicken breasts, cooked, thinly sliced	3 to 6 green onions, diagonally sliced
1-inch piece fresh ginger, peeled, pulverized	1/4 cup sesame seeds, lightly toasted
2 cloves of garlic, minced	1 cup pea pods, microwaved 2 minutes
1/2 cup vegetable oil	1 small package sliced almonds, lightly toasted
4 tablespoons sugar	
4 tablespoons vinegar	
2 tablespoons soy sauce	Chow mein noodles for garnish
1/2 teaspoon pepper	
1 head lettuce, shredded	

Stir-fry the chicken, ginger and garlic in 1 tablespoon of the oil. Set aside. Dissolve the sugar in the vinegar and soy sauce in a small saucepan over low heat, stirring; add the pepper. Let cool. Stir in the remaining oil. Toss the vinegar mixture with the lettuce, green onions, sesame seeds, pea pods and chicken mixture in a large bowl. Garnish with the almonds and chow mein noodles. Yield: 12 servings.

Linda Johnson, Xi Alpha Alpha
Midland, Michigan

AMARETTO CHICKEN SALAD

1/2 cup slivered almonds	1/2 cup mayonnaise
1/4 cup butter or margarine	1 teaspoon salt
4 cups cooked chopped chicken	1/4 cup amaretto
1 (15-ounce) can crushed pineapple, drained	1 cup mayonnaise
1 cup chopped celery	1 (15-ounce) can pineapple slices
	Lettuce leaves

Sauté the almonds in the butter until golden brown. Drain well. Combine half the almonds with the chicken, crushed pineapple, celery, 1/2 cup mayonnaise and salt; mix well. Chill, covered, for 8 to 10 hours. Blend the amaretto with 1 cup mayonnaise and chill. Place a pineapple slice on a lettuce leaf and top with chicken salad. Spoon dressing over the salad. Sprinkle with the remaining almonds. Yield: 6 to 8 servings.

Karen Britting
Abilene, Texas

Betty Fagan, Preceptor Alpha Alpha, Cumberland, Maryland, shakes 2/3 cup oil with 1/3 cup raspberry vinegar and 1 tablespoon honey to make Raspberry Vinaigrette.

HOT CHICKEN ASPARAGUS SALAD

1 medium apple, cored,
   peeled, sliced
1 teaspoon lemon juice
2 green onions, sliced
1 rib celery, chopped
Salt and pepper to taste
2 boneless half chicken
   breasts, cooked
2 medium tomatoes,
   cored, halved, sliced
1 endive, separated into
   leaves

2 bunches fresh
   asparagus, cooked
2 tablespoons
   mayonnaise
2 tablespoons heavy
   cream
2 fresh mint leaves,
   chopped
4 tablespoons chopped
   nuts
Fresh fruit slices for
   garnish

Place the apple in a large bowl; toss with the lemon juice. Stir in the green onions and celery. Season with salt and pepper. Slice the chicken breasts into large strips and add to the apple mixture. Stir in the tomatoes and the endive. Cut the asparagus into thirds and add to mixture. Stir in the mayonnaise and cream. Add the mint and more salt and pepper if necessary; mix well. Toss in the nuts. Serve garnished with fruit slices. Yield: 4 servings.

Kay Poling, Xi Eta Nu
College Station, Texas

BLUE RIBBON CHICKEN SALAD PLATE

5 pounds potatoes,
   peeled, boiled, diced
2 medium Delicious
   apples, diced
8 small sweet pickles,
   diced
1 (15-ounce) can
   pineapple tidbits,
   drained
1 medium onion,
   chopped

1 cup celery, chopped
2 or 3 whole chicken
   breasts, skinned,
   cooked, diced small
Fat-free mayonnaise for
   desired consistency
Fat-free sour cream for
   desired consistency
Lettuce leaves
Sliced oranges for
   garnish

Mix the potatoes, apples, pickles, pineapple tidbits, onion, celery, chicken, mayonnaise and sour cream in a large bowl. Chill, covered, in the refrigerator. Serve over lettuce leaves. Garnish with orange slices. Yield: 6 to 8 servings.

Faye Siler, Alpha Alpha Theta
Sanford, Florida

Gerry Hurd, Laureate Delta Alpha, Jacksonville, Florida, makes Poppy Seed Dressing for fruit or green salads by beating 1/3 cup thawed lemonade concentrate with 5 tablespoons honey, 1/2 cup salad oil, 2 tablespoons lemon juice, and 1 teaspoon poppy seeds.

LISA'S CHICKEN SALAD ROLLUPS

1 (5-ounce) can white
   chicken meat
1/2 cup minced celery
1/2 cup minced white
   onion
1/2 cup halved green
   grapes
1/4 cup chopped pecans

1/4 cup dried cranberries
1/4 cup low-fat
   mayonnaise or
   yogurt
1/4 teaspoon pepper
6 to 8 large flour
   tortillas

Combine the chicken, celery, onion, grapes, pecans, cranberries, mayonnaise and pepper in a large bowl; beat until well blended. Spread the tortillas with the chicken salad and roll up, securing with toothpicks. Serve with carrot and celery sticks. Yield: 4 to 6 servings.

Lisa Ross, Xi Beta Psi
Morrisville, North Carolina

CHINESE CHICKEN SALAD

Using diced frozen chicken or canned chicken saves a lot of time.

1 to 2 tablespoons soy
   sauce
3 whole chicken breasts,
   skinned, cooked,
   diced
2 cups shredded lettuce
1 cup bean spouts, fresh
   or canned (drained)
1 cup cherry tomatoes
1 cup salted cocktail
   peanuts

1 bunch green onions,
   sliced
1/4 pound mushrooms,
   sliced
1/4 cup sesame seeds,
   toasted
Chinese Mustard
   Dressing
6 ounces chow mein
   noodles

Sprinkle soy sauce on the chicken to marinate while the rest of the dish is being prepared. Lightly mix the chicken with the lettuce, bean sprouts, tomatoes, peanuts, green onions, mushrooms and sesame seeds in a large bowl. Toss with the Chinese Mustard Dressing. Chill until serving time. Stir in the chow mein noodles just before serving. Yield: 6 to 8 servings.

CHINESE MUSTARD DRESSING

If you don't have Chinese mustard, substitute regular mustard mixed with a bit of horseradish.

1 teaspoon Chinese
   mustard
2 teaspoons sugar
2 teaspoons grated
   lemon zest
2 tablespoons lemon
   juice

4 teaspoons soy sauce
6 tablespoons vegetable
   oil
2 tablespoons sesame
   oil
1 tablespoon peanut
   butter

Mix the Chinese mustard, sugar, lemon zest, lemon juice, soy sauce, vegetable oil, sesame oil and peanut butter in a small bowl.

Susan Hinkhouse, Iota Psi
Burlington, Colorado

CHINESE CHICKEN SLAW

3/4 head cabbage, shredded	**3 tablespoons sesame seeds**
1 (11-ounce) can mandarin oranges, drained	**1/2 cup slivered almonds**
	1 (3-ounce) package ramen noodles, Oriental flavor
3 whole chicken breasts, grilled, cubed	**1/4 to 1/2 cup margarine**
1 bunch green onions, chopped	**3/4 cup vegetable oil**
	5 tablespoons sugar
1 small green pepper, chopped	**5 tablespoons vinegar**
	1 teaspoon pepper

Mix the cabbage, oranges, chicken, green onions and green pepper in a large bowl. Sauté the sesame seeds, almonds and ramen noodles (without flavoring packet) in the margarine in a medium skillet over medium heat until browned. Set aside. To make the dressing, mix the flavoring packet from the ramen noodles, oil, sugar, vinegar and pepper in a small bowl. Combine dressing with salad just before serving. Yield: 8 to 10 servings.

Karen Meinardhis, Alpha Pi Master
El Campo, Texas

CURRIED CHICKEN SALAD

Try substituting chopped dates for raisins.

3 cups cold chopped cooked chicken	**1/4 cup chopped celery**
1/2 cup chopped cashews or almonds	**3 tablespoons chopped chutney**
1/2 cup chopped green onions	**2 teaspoons curry powder**
1 small tart apple, cored, diced	**2 teaspoons lemon juice**
	1 cup mayonnaise
2 tablespoons raisins (optional)	**Salt to taste**
	Lettuce leaves
	Paprika

Combine the chicken, nuts, green onions, apple, raisins and celery in a large bowl. To make the dressing, blend the chutney, curry powder, lemon juice and mayonnaise in a separate bowl. Add the dressing to the chicken salad; mix well. Season with salt. To serve, scoop a portion onto a lettuce leaf and sprinkle with paprika. Yield: 4 servings.

Ethel M. Bausman
Ajo, Arizona

CHICKEN FAJITA SALAD

This recipe came from a desperate situation. I had completely forgotten it was potluck hostess night, and with only 25 minutes before meeting time, I panicked! Fortunately I remembered a beef taco salad recipe, and I made this variation using ingredients in the house. It was ready to go in 12 minutes.

1 (32-ounce) package frozen fully cooked chicken strips, thawed	**1 envelope taco seasoning**
	1 (24-ounce) jar Thousand Island dressing
2 cups shredded Cheddar cheese	**1 (7-ounce) bag of Doritos, crushed**
1 large onion, chopped	
1 head lettuce, chopped	

Toss the chicken strips, cheese, onion and lettuce. Add the taco seasoning to the Thousand Island dressing; mix well. Add the dressing to the salad; toss to coat the salad. Just before serving, add the Doritos; mix well. Yield: 10 to 12 servings.

Cathy Robb, Xi Preceptor Alpha Beta
Harvey, Louisiana

CHICKEN AND FRUIT SALAD

3 cups chopped cooked chicken	**1 1/2 cups purple seedless grapes**
3 tablespoons lemon juice	**1 cup pineapple tidbits, drained**
1 cup mayonnaise	**1/2 cup pecans**
1 teaspoon salt	**1/4 cup diced water chestnuts**
1 teaspoon dry mustard	
1 teaspoon curry powder	**Lettuce leaves**

Sprinkle the chicken with the lemon juice; chill, covered, in the refrigerator for 1 hour. Combine the next 4 ingredients in a bowl. Combine the chicken with the grapes, pineapple, pecans and water chestnuts. Add the dressing; stir to combine. Serve on lettuce leaves. Yield: 6 to 8 servings.

Lisa Gentry
Paducah, Texas

Hazel Ivey, Brackettville, Texas, makes Jicama Salad by mixing 8 ounces peeled jicama cut into julienne strips with the sections of 1 orange, 1/2 cup sliced green onions, 1/2 cup chopped red bell pepper, and a dressing made of 3/4 cup orange juice, 2 tablespoons fresh lime juice, 1 teaspoon chili powder, and 1 teaspoon salt. Chill, covered, for 4 hours to overnight, stirring occasionally, and serve on butter lettuce.

TROPICAL CHICKEN SALAD

2 whole chicken breasts
1 medium apple, cored, cubed
1 cup seedless grapes, halved
1/4 cup crushed pineapple
1/2 medium avocado, peeled, cubed
1 green onion, chopped
1 tablespoons raisins
1 tablespoon walnuts
1 tablespoon almonds
1/4 cup mayonnaise
Salt and pepper to taste
4 whole wheat pitas

Place the chicken in a small saucepan with just enough water to cover. Bring to a very gentle boil. Simmer for about 15 minutes; drain. Remove and discard the skin and bones; chop into small pieces. Refrigerate until ready to use. Combine the chicken, apple, grapes, pineapple, avocado, green onion, raisins, walnuts, almonds, mayonnaise, salt and pepper in a large bowl. Mix gently but thoroughly. Serve stuffed inside whole wheat pita bread. Yield: 4 servings.

Elizabeth Maguire
Barrie, Ontario, Canada

GRILLED CHICKEN CAESAR SALAD

4 chicken breasts
Italian dressing
1/2 cup olive oil
1/4 cup red wine vinegar
4 cloves of garlic
2 inches of anchovy paste
Dash of Worcestershire sauce
1 container Egg Beaters
Juice of 1 lemon
Salt and pepper to taste
Grated Parmesan cheese
Head of green leaf lettuce, washed, torn in bite-size pieces
Caesar-style croutons

Marinate the chicken breasts in the Italian dressing for 4 hours; 8 to 10 hours is best. Preheat the broiler. Broil or grill the chicken until blackened. Combine the next 10 ingredients. Cut the chicken into bite-size pieces; combine with the lettuce. Add the dressing; mix well. Add the croutons. Yield: 16 servings.

Jennifer Stammers
Atchison, Kansas

LIGHT CHICKEN SALAD

1 (5-ounce) can of chicken
2 heaping tablespoons mayonnaise-type salad dressing
2 tablespoons chopped celery
2 heaping tablespoons crushed pineapple
2 tablespoons chopped cashews
2 tablespoons slivered almonds
Pinch of salt
Party bread

Combine the chicken, mayonnaise-type salad dressing, celery and pineapple in a medium bowl. Chill, covered, for 1 hour. Stir in the cashews, almonds and salt just before serving. Serve on party bread or place in a bowl in the middle of a serving plate and surround with party bread. Yield: 2 to 4 servings.

Lrenda Dinsmore
Bixby, Oklahoma

LAYERED CHICKEN SALAD

Serve this delicious chicken salad alongside sliced cantaloupe, sliced honeydew, and a strawberry.

6 cups shredded lettuce
4 ounces bean sprouts
1 (8-ounce) can water chestnuts, drained
1 cup thinly sliced green onions
1 medium cucumber, thinly sliced
8 ounces fresh pea pods
4 cups sliced cooked chicken breasts
2 cups mayonnaise
1 teaspoon curry
1 tablespoon sugar
1/2 teaspoon ginger
1/2 cup Spanish peanuts
Cherry tomatoes to garnish

Layer the first 6 ingredients in a large bowl. Cover with the chicken. Combine the mayonnaise, curry, sugar and ginger; mix well. "Frost" the salad with the dressing. Chill, covered, for 8 to 10 hours. Sprinkle with Spanish peanuts and garnish with cherry tomatoes. Yield: 8 to 10 servings.

Donna E. Tischbirek, Xi Gamma Tau
Citrus Heights, California

Milena E. Verret, Preceptor Xi Beta, Clovis, California, gives Broccoli Slaw a Southwest flavor by adding a can of drained whole kernel corn and 1 can of black beans to a package of broccoli slaw, some chopped red and green bell peppers, red onion, 2 tablespoons chopped cilantro, and shredded Cheddar cheese. Complete the salad by adding a dressing of 3/4 cup ranch dressing, 1 tablespoon lime juice and 1 teaspoon cumin.

Lavada Harrison, Preceptor Beta Delta, Poplar Bluff, Missouri, makes a variation on a seven-layer salad by layering torn lettuce, chopped green bell pepper, red onion, water chestnuts, carrot, pineapple tidbits, and mushrooms. Blend 3/4 cup each mayonnaise and sour cream with 2 1/2 tablespoons sugar; spread over layers. Chill, covered, for 8 to 10 hours. Just before serving sprinkle shredded Cheddar cheese and crisp-fried bacon on top. Call it Frosted Polynesian Salad.

DILL CHICKEN SALAD

Serve as a sandwich or with party breads and crackers in a lettuce leaf bowl.

1 (12-ounce) can chicken
1/4 cup chopped onion
1/2 cup chopped celery
1 (8-ounce) package
   cream cheese,
   softened
1/2 teaspoon dillweed

1/8 teaspoon garlic
   powder
1/2 teaspoon salt
1 teaspoon chopped
   parsley
1/2 teaspoon paprika

Combine the chicken, onion, celery, cream cheese, dillweed, garlic powder, salt, parsley and paprika in a medium bowl; mix well. Chill for 1 hour or until time to serve. Yield: 4 servings.

Carol J. Harper
Lowry City, Missouri

WILD RICE CHICKEN SALAD

2 (6-ounce) packages
   wild rice
4 chicken breasts,
   cooked, cubed
1 cup mayonnaise
1 (6-ounce) jar
   marinated artichokes
1 1/2 cups chopped celery

1 (4-ounce) jar chopped
   pimiento, drained
1 green pepper, chopped
1 package Italian
   dressing mix
16 ounces fresh
   mushrooms
1 cup cashews

Prepare the wild rice using package directions, reducing the water by 1 cup for each package (i.e., 2 cups). Combine the rice, chicken and mayonnaise in a bowl. Chill, covered, for 8 to 10 hours. Mix the artichokes, celery, pimiento, green pepper and dry Italian dressing mix; chill, covered, for 8 to 10 hours. Before serving, combine both mixtures; stir in the mushrooms and cashews. Yield: 8 to 10 servings.

Rita Steffens
Hollywood, Florida

CHOPPED VEGETABLE SALAD

1 head romaine lettuce
   torn in bite-size
   pieces
1 (16-ounce) can kidney
   beans, drained, rinsed
1 (15-ounce) can
   garbanzo beans,
   drained, rinsed
1 bunch of beets, cooked,
   peeled, chopped
3 large carrots, chopped
3 ribs celery, chopped

3 fresh ears of corn,
   boiled, cut off cob
2 medium tomatoes,
   chopped
2 cups cooked chopped
   turkey
1 bunch scallions,
   chopped
1/2 cup pitted black
   olives (optional)
1 1/2 cups low-fat ranch
   dressing

Spread the lettuce on the bottom of a large glass bowl. Layer the kidney beans, garbanzo beans, beets, carrots, celery, corn, tomatoes, turkey, scallions and black olives over the lettuce. Add the dressing and toss well. Yield: 8 servings.

Natalie Sekavec, Theta Master
Brownell, Kansas

LAYERED TURKEY GREEN SALAD

4 cups torn mixed greens
1 (15-ounce) can
   garbanzo beans
1 cup cherry tomatoes,
   halved
1 cup sliced celery
1/2 cup chopped yellow
   bell pepper
1/2 cup chopped green
   pepper
1 cup chopped cooked
   turkey

1/4 cup thinly sliced
   green onions
2 tablespoons milk
1 cup reduced-calorie
   mayonnaise
1 teaspoon crushed
   fennel seed
1/8 teaspoon freshly
   ground pepper
3/4 cup shredded Cheddar
   cheese

Place the mixed greens in the bottom of a clear 2 1/2-quart salad bowl. Layer the garbanzo beans, tomatoes, celery, yellow bell pepper, green pepper, turkey and green onions over the greens. To make the dressing, stir together the milk, mayonnaise, fennel seed and pepper. Spread over the top of the salad to the edge of the bowl. Cover tightly with clear plastic wrap. Chill for 24 hours before serving. Sprinkle the cheese over the salad and serve.
Yield: 8 to 10 servings.

Bette Jane Felker, Laureate Eta Sigma
Salton City, California

SOUTHWEST TUNA SALAD

You may substitute ranch, French, or "jalapeño ranch" dressing for the Italian dressing.

1 bunch radishes, thinly
   sliced
4 ribs celery, chopped
1 green pepper, chopped
1/4 cup chopped fresh
   cilantro

6 green onions, chopped
1 large tomato, chopped
1 (6-ounce) can tuna
1/4 to 1/2 cup Italian
   dressing

Combine the radishes, celery, green pepper, cilantro, green onions, tomato, tuna and Italian dressing; mix well. Serve in a sandwich or as a salad.
Yield: 4 to 6 servings.

Anna Magoffin, Xi Psi
Douglas, Arizona

ASPARAGUS MOLD

1 (10-ounce) can cream
    of asparagus soup
1 (10-ounce) can water
1 (3-ounce) package
    lemon gelatin mix
1 (8-ounce) package
    cream cheese,
    softened
½ cup cold water

½ cup mayonnaise
¾ cup finely minced
    celery
½ cup finely minced
    green pepper
1 tablespoon grated
    onion
½ cup chopped pecans
    or walnuts

Bring the cream of asparagus soup and the 10-ounce can of water to a boil in a medium saucepan. Remove from heat. Add the gelatin mix, stirring until dissolved. Add the cream cheese, stirring until melted, using a mixer if desired. Stir in the ½ cup cold water, mayonnaise, celery, green pepper, onion and nuts. Turn into a gelatin mold or an 8-by-8-inch pan. Chill for 3 hours or until ready to serve. Yield: 6 servings.

Donita Balfour, Preceptor Alpha Beta
Oklahoma City, Oklahoma

BLACK BEAN AVOCADO SALAD

Drench the diced avocado in lemon juice to keep it from turning dark; drain well before adding to the salad. If you don't want to use canned beans, try cooking a whole bag of dried beans in the slow cooker and freeze them in meal-size portions.

2 tablespoons ranch
    dressing
2 tablespoons Italian
    dressing
3 cups cooked black
    beans

1 ripe avocado, diced
6 green onions, sliced
2 tablespoons chopped
    parsley, fresh or dried
½ teaspoon cumin
½ teaspoon oregano

Combine the ranch dressing and Italian dressing to make ¼ cup dressing. Combine the black beans, avocado, green onions, parsley, cumin, oregano and dressing in a bowl. Chill, covered, for 3 to 10 hours. Yield: 4 to 6 servings.

Nedra Schafer, Preceptor Gamma Rho
Greeley, Colorado

Nancy Robinson, Xi Alpha Delta Eta, Houston, Texas, makes New Potato and Asparagus Salad by cooking 6 new potatoes and a pound of asparagus until tender-crisp and cutting into bite-size pieces. Add half a slivered red bell pepper and a dressing of 1 tablespoon Dijon mustard, 1 tablespoon fresh lemon juice, ¼ cup olive oil, salt, and pepper whisked together.

TWO BEAN AND RICE SALAD

3 cups cold cooked rice
1 (15-ounce) can pinto
    beans, drained
1 (15-ounce) can black
    beans, drained
1 (10-ounce) package
    frozen peas, thawed
1 cup chopped celery
1 medium red onion,
    chopped

1 (4-ounce) can chopped
    green chile peppers,
    drained
¼ cup fresh cilantro or
    parsley
1 (8-ounce) bottle ranch
    or Italian salad
    dressing

Combine the rice, pinto beans, black beans, peas, celery, onion, chile peppers, cilantro and salad dressing; mix well. Chill for 24 hours before serving. Yield: 12 servings.

Mary A. Heck, Sigma Master
Westcliffe, Colorado

TASTY BEET GELATIN SALAD

1 (3-ounce) package red
    gelatin mix
1 cup boiling water
1 cup crushed pineapple,
    drained, juice
    reserved
1 tablespoon grated
    onion

1 tablespoon vinegar
2 (8-ounce) cans
    julienned beets
1 tablespoon
    horseradish or to
    taste
1 cup sour cream

Dissolve the gelatin mix in boiling water. Stir in 1 cup of the drained pineapple juice. Stir in the onion and vinegar. Add the pineapple and beets; stir well. Pour into an 8-by-12-inch glass dish. Chill, covered, in the refrigerator until set. Mix the horseradish and sour cream; cover the top of the salad with the sour cream mixture. Cut into squares; serve on lettuce leaves. Yield: 12 servings.

Rosemary Itrich, Alpha Tau Master
Garden Grover, California

ITALIAN SALAD

1 medium head
    cauliflower, cut into
    florets
3 stalks broccoli, cut
    into florets
1 cup diced green pepper
2 cups diced celery
2 medium zucchini,
    diced
1 medium cucumber,
    diced
1 (8-ounce) can black
    olives

1 (9-ounce) jar green
    olives
12 green onions,
    chopped
¼ teaspoon sugar or to
    taste
1 (6-ounce) jar Italian
    salad dressing
1 envelope Italian salad
    dressing mix

Combine the cauliflower, broccoli, green pepper, celery, zucchini, cucumber, black olives, green olives, green onions, sugar, salad dressing and salad dressing mix in a large bowl; mix well. Chill, covered, for 4 hours before serving. Yield: 20 servings.

Betty Jo Hardman
Edgewater, Florida

TASTY CAULIFLOWER SALAD

The pecans, mayonnaise, sugar and mustard may be combined and refrigerated the night before serving.

2 tablespoons chopped
** pecans**
1 cup mayonnaise
½ cup sugar
2 teaspoons mustard

1 head cauliflower,
** separated**
1 cup green grapes,
** halved**

Combine the pecans, mayonnaise, sugar and mustard. When ready to serve, stir in the cauliflower and grapes. Yield: 6 servings.

Pam Pertzborn, Xi Beta Pi
Des Moines, Iowa

CORN BREAD SALAD

1 (6-ounce) package corn
** bread mix**
1 envelope dry ranch
** dressing mix**
1 cup mayonnaise
1 (16-ounce) container
** sour cream**
2 medium tomatoes,
** chopped**
½ cup chopped green
** pepper**

¼ cup chopped green
** onions**
2 (15-ounce) cans black-
** eyed peas, drained**
1 (15-ounce) can whole
** kernel corn, drained**
¼ pound bacon, crisp-
** cooked, crumbled**
2 cups shredded Cheddar
** cheese**

Prepare and bake the corn bread using package directions. Combine the ranch dressing mix, mayonnaise and sour cream; set aside. Combine the tomatoes, green pepper and green onions; set aside. Crumble ½ pan of corn bread in a large salad bowl. Alternate layers of black-eyed peas, corn, tomato mixture, bacon, cheese and dressing mixture until all ingredients are used, ending with dressing. Decorate the top with bits of tomato and green pepper. Chill for at least 2 to 3 hours or overnight.
Yield: 15 or more servings.

Dana Lovins
Dexter, Missouri

BULGARIAN SALAD

Pipping (removing seeds from) the tomatoes keeps the juices down. Pipping the cucumbers is less expensive than buying English cucumbers. For a formal meal, place the salad on small salad dishes and sprinkle with feta cheese. For an informal meal, place the salad in an 8-by-8-inch glass dish and sprinkle with feta cheese. Give everyone a fork and share the common dish. A hearty bread like a crispy Italian loaf can be torn and shared.

6 tablespoons classic
** olive oil**
2 cloves of garlic, diced
Salt and pepper to taste
5 medium tomatoes,
** pipped, diced**
2 medium cucumbers,
** pipped, diced**

2 medium green peppers,
** diced**
2 medium yellow
** onions, diced**
2 to 3 ounces plain feta
** cheese, crumbled**

Combine the olive oil, garlic, salt and pepper in a small measuring cup; let stand while dicing other ingredients. Combine the tomatoes, cucumbers, green peppers and onions in a bowl. Pour the olive oil mixture over the vegetables; toss. Sprinkle with the feta cheese. Yield: 6 to 8 servings.

Sandra L. DeLeon
San Antonio, Texas

MIXED CUCUMBER TOMATO MINT SALAD

1 large (1-pound)
** European cucumber**
4 small (1-ounce) firm-
** ripe tomatoes**
4 small green onions,
** chopped**
⅓ cup minced fresh mint
** or 5 teaspoons dry**
** mint**

¼ cup lime juice
¼ cup olive or vegetable
** oil**
2 tablespoons white
** wine vinegar**

Cut the cucumber into ¼-inch slices; cut the tomatoes into ½-inch wedges. Place the cucumber and tomatoes in a large bowl. Add the green onions and mint. Combine the lime juice, olive oil and vinegar; pour over the vegetables. Stir gently. Cover and let stand at room temperature or in the refrigerator for 1 hour. If made ahead, it can be chilled for up to 4 hours. Yield: 4 to 6 servings.

Eileen Foster
Surrey, British Columbia, Canada

CABBAGE NOODLE SALAD

6 cups chopped cabbage
1/2 cup sunflower seeds
1/2 cup slivered almonds
1 (3-ounce) package
  ramen noodles,
  chicken flavor,
  uncooked, broken up

Green onions as desired,
  chopped
1/2 cup vegetable oil
3 tablespoons sugar
3 tablespoons vinegar
Flavor packet from
  ramen noodles

Combine the cabbage, sunflower seeds, almonds, noodles and green onions in a large bowl. Combine the oil, sugar, vinegar and flavor packet in a small bowl; mix well. Pour the mixture over the cabbage combination; stir well. Chill for 1 hour.
Yield: 10 servings.

Alice C. Hollingsworth
Lewisburg, West Virginia

CHINESE COLESLAW SALAD

1 bag coleslaw cabbage
1 small package
  sunflower seeds
1 small package
  almonds
2 (3-ounce) packages
  ramen noodles,
  Oriental flavor,
  uncooked, crushed

1 medium onion, finely
  chopped
1 flavor packet from
  ramen noodles
1/2 cup vegetable oil
1/4 cup sugar
1/3 cup vinegar

Mix the cabbage, sunflower seeds, almonds, noodles and onion in a large bowl; refrigerate. To make the dressing, combine the flavor packet, oil, sugar and vinegar; mix well. 1 hour before serving, pour the dressing over the cabbage mixture; stir well.
Yield: 15 to 20 servings.

Lois A. Carlson, Laureate Gamma
Spencer, Iowa

MEXICAN SLAW

1 medium head green
  cabbage, shredded
1/4 head red cabbage,
  shredded
1 carrot, julienned
1 red bell pepper,
  chopped
6 green onions, sliced
1/2 cup chopped fresh
  cilantro
1/2 cup chopped fresh
  parsley
1 medium jicama,
  julienned

1 cup Italian dressing
1 tablespoon chopped
  canned chipotle
  chiles
1 teaspoon ground
  coriander
1 teaspoon ground
  cumin
Juice of 1/2 lime
Dash of freshly ground
  black pepper

Toss the green cabbage with the red cabbage, carrot, red bell pepper, green onions, cilantro, parsley and jicama. To make the dressing, combine the Italian dressing, chipotle chiles, coriander, cumin, lime juice and pepper; toss with the cabbage mixture. Chill, covered, for at least 2 hours before serving.
Yield: 8 to 10 servings.

Marjorie Parks
Casa Grande, Arizona

TEXAS TWO-STEP SLAW

This recipe was a recent winner in a Pillsbury Bake-Off Contest.

4 cups shredded green
  cabbage
1 cup shredded red
  cabbage
1/4 cup chopped red
  onion
2 jalapeño peppers,
  seeded, finely
  chopped
2 tablespoons chopped
  fresh cilantro

1 (11-ounce) can
  Mexicorn, drained
4 ounces (1 cup)
  shredded Cheddar
  cheese
3/4 cup ranch salad
  dressing
1 tablespoon fresh lime
  juice
1 teaspoon cumin
Fresh cilantro sprigs

Combine the green cabbage, red cabbage, red onion, jalapeño peppers, cilantro, Mexicorn and cheese in a large bowl; mix well. Combine the ranch salad dressing, lime juice and cumin in a small bowl; blend well. Pour over the salad, tossing to coat. Serve immediately or refrigerate until serving time. Garnish with cilantro sprigs. Yield: 8 servings.

Juanita Lunn
Eustis, Florida

SPINACH SALAD

1 (3-ounce) package
  lemon gelatin mix
1/2 cup boiling water
1 tablespoon lemon
  juice
1 (10-ounce) package
  frozen spinach,
  thawed, drained
2 cups small-curd
  cottage cheese

1/2 cup finely chopped
  celery
1/2 cup finely chopped
  onion
1/2 cup mayonnaise
Pineapple rings,
  maraschino cherries
  (optional)

Dissolve the lemon gelatin mix in the boiling water. Stir in the lemon juice. Set aside. Use scissors if necessary to squeeze out the spinach liquid. Combine the spinach and cottage cheese. Add the celery, onion and mayonnaise; mix well. Pour into a 6-cup mold. Chill for 8 to 10 hours. After unmolding the salad, you may garnish the outside edges with half slices of

pineapple and maraschino cherry halves.
Yield: 6 to 8 servings.

Marjorie Biddlecom
Waukegan, Illinois

EASY SPINACH SALAD

1/3 cup vinegar	2 hard-cooked eggs,
3/4 cup sugar	shredded or sliced
1 teaspoon salt	3 slices bacon, crisp-
2 slices white onion	fried, crumbled
1 cup vegetable oil	2 slices red onion (rings)
1 teaspoon	Tomato wedges to taste
Worcestershire sauce	Grated Parmesan cheese
1 (10-ounce) bag washed	to taste
fresh spinach	Croutons to taste
1 cup sliced mushrooms	

Process the vinegar, sugar, salt, white onion slices, oil and Worcestershire sauce in a blender until smooth. Chill the dressing until ready to serve. Layer the spinach, mushrooms, hard-cooked eggs, bacon, red onion, tomato wedges, Parmesan cheese and croutons in a large salad bowl. Just before serving, shake the salad dressing and pour over the salad. Toss and serve. Yield: 6 to 8 servings.

Ann Sanders
Percy, Illinois

❖ SPINACH SALAD WITH DRIED TOMATO VINAIGRETTE

1 pound fresh spinach	1 medium sweet onion,
1 (14-ounce) can hearts	sliced, separated into
of palm, drained, cut	rings
into 1/2-inch slices	1/2 cup unsalted
16 ounces fresh	sunflower seeds
mushrooms, sliced	Dried Tomato
2 ripe avocados, cubed	Vinaigrette

Remove the stems from the spinach. Wash the leaves thoroughly and pat dry. Tear into bite-size pieces. Combine the spinach, hearts of palm, mushrooms, avocados, onion and sunflower seeds; toss with the Dried Tomato Vinaigrette. Serve immediately. Yield: 10 servings.

DRIED TOMATO VINAIGRETTE

1 (7-ounce) jar oil-	1 clove of garlic,
packed sun-dried	chopped
tomatoes	1/4 teaspoon salt
2/3 cup loosely packed	1/8 teaspoon pepper
fresh basil leaves	1/4 cup red wine vinegar
2 tablespoons chopped	Olive oil
shallots	

Drain the tomatoes, reserving the oil; set the oil aside. Place the tomatoes in a food processor fitted with a metal blade; pulse 3 or 4 times. Add the basil, shallots, garlic, salt, pepper and red wine vinegar; process until smooth, stopping once to scrape down the sides. Add enough olive oil to the oil reserved from the tomatoes to equal 1/2 cup. Pour the oil mixture through the food chute in a slow, steady stream, processing until blended.

Cindy Layton, Xi Epsilon Nu
Cape Girardeau, Missouri

STRAWBERRY SPINACH SALAD

2 bunches fresh spinach,	1/2 cup sugar
washed, dried, torn in	1 1/2 teaspoons minced
pieces	onion
1 pint fresh	1/4 teaspoon
strawberries, washed,	Worcestershire sauce
sliced	1 1/4 teaspoons paprika
2 tablespoons sesame	1/3 cup vegetable oil
seeds	1/4 cup cider vinegar

Place the spinach and strawberries in a large bowl. To make the dressing, combine the sesame seeds, sugar, onion, Worcestershire sauce, paprika, oil and vinegar. Just before serving, shake the dressing, pour over the salad and toss. Yield: 8 to 10 servings.

Kathy Conway, Preceptor Chi
Rawlins, Wyoming

TABOULI

One of my neighbors taught me to make this salad when I was living in Cyprus.

2 cups bulgur (cracked	2 teaspoons salt or to
wheat)	taste
8 cups boiling water	1 cup lemon or lime
1 cup chopped fresh	juice (about 8 fresh
parsley	lemons or limes)
3/4 cups chopped fresh	3/4 cup olive oil
mint	2 1/2 bunches scallions,
6 medium tomatoes,	chopped, including
chopped	2 inches of green

Pour the bulgur into a large bowl. Cover with the boiling water. Let stand, covered, for 2 to 3 hours or until bulgur is light and fluffy. Drain well; shake into a strainer until dry. Add the parsley, mint, tomatoes, salt, lemon juice, olive oil and scallions to the bulgur in a large bowl; mix thoroughly. Chill for at least 1 hour or overnight before serving. It will last a couple of weeks in the refrigerator. Yield: 24 servings.

Ginny Thomas, Preceptor Gamma Eta
Merritt Island, Florida

TOMATO SALAD

1 tablespoon vegetable oil	2 medium tomatoes, sliced
1 tablespoon lime juice	1 cup fresh or frozen yellow corn
1 tablespoon honey	
1/2 teaspoon cumin	1 small avocado, cut into wedges
1/4 teaspoon salt	
1/4 teaspoon pepper	1/4 cup chopped cilantro

Mix the oil, lime juice, honey, cumin, salt and pepper in a bowl. Layer the tomatoes, corn and avocado in a salad bowl. Drizzle the dressing over the vegetables. Garnish with the cilantro. Yield: 4 servings.

Ann Lovelace, Laureate Tau
Overland Park, Kansas

TOMATO SOUP SALAD

1 (3-ounce) package lemon gelatin	1 cup mayonnaise
	1/2 cup chopped celery
1 cup boiling water	1/4 cup chopped green pepper
1 (10-ounce) can tomato soup	
	1/4 cup chopped green onion
2 (3-ounce) packages cream cheese, softened	
	1 tablespoon vinegar

Dissolve the gelatin in boiling water; chill until partially set. Stir in the tomato soup, cream cheese and mayonnaise. Add the celery, green pepper, green onion and vinegar. Chill until set.
Yield: 10 to 12 servings.

Mildred Sharp, Kappa Master
McClave, Colorado

VEGETABLE SALAD MOLD

1 1/2 cups canned tomatoes, drained	1 medium cucumber, peeled, chopped
2 (4-ounce) packages lemon gelatin mix	1 cup chopped celery
	1 cup chopped green pepper
1 tablespoon lemon juice	
	1/2 cup chopped onion
1 tablespoon horseradish, drained	1/2 cup mayonnaise
	1/2 cup sour cream

Chop the tomatoes and place in a saucepan with the juice that appears when chopping. Bring to a boil. Stir in the gelatin mix; heat and stir until dissolved. Chill until the mixture is partially set, stirring often. Fold in the remaining ingredients. Pour into an oiled 1 1/2-quart mold; chill until set. Unmold on a bed of lettuce. Yield: 10 to 12 servings.

Florence Diotte, Xi Kappa
Miramichi City, New Brunswick, Canada

WATERCRESS SALAD

2 bunches watercress, washed, trimmed	1 cup sliced fresh mushrooms
	1/2 cup peanuts
1 large red grapefruit, peeled, sectioned	Poppy Seed Dressing

Toss the watercress, grapefruit, mushrooms and peanuts with Poppy Seed Dressing to taste.
Yield: 4 to 6 servings.

POPPY SEED DRESSING

1/3 cup vinegar (red wine or balsamic)	2 tablespoons chopped onion
3/4 cup sugar	1 tablespoon poppy seeds
1 teaspoon salt	
1 teaspoon mustard	1/2 cup olive oil

Pour the vinegar, sugar, salt, mustard, onion, poppy seeds and olive oil into a blender container and process until smooth.

Margaret Pappoulas
North Bay, Ontario, Canada

BLEU CHEESE DRESSING

1 quart mayonnaise	1/4 teaspoon salt
4 ounces bleu cheese	1/2 cup buttermilk
2 tablespoons lemon juice	1 teaspoon Worcestershire sauce
1/8 teaspoon garlic salt	1 tablespoon sugar

Combine the mayonnaise, bleu cheese, lemon juice, garlic salt, salt, buttermilk, Worcestershire sauce and sugar in a medium bowl, stirring just enough to blend. Store in a jar in the refrigerator.
Yield: 1 quart plus 1 cup.

Lois A. Carlson, Laureate Gamma
Spencer, Iowa

POPPY SEED PEANUT DRESSING

3/4 cup sugar	1 teaspoon grated onion (optional)
1 cup vegetable oil	
1 teaspoon prepared mustard	1/4 to 1/2 cup shredded mozzarella cheese
1 teaspoon poppy seeds	1/2 to 1 cup peanuts or cashews
1/2 teaspoon salt	

Mix the sugar, oil, mustard, poppy seeds, salt, onion, cheese and nuts. Just before serving, shake and pour over lettuce. Yield: 6 to 10 servings.

Shirley Jansen
Valley, Nebraska

Enticing Entrées

Whether you're celebrating
a special occasion or sharing a
quiet dinner with family,
make the entrée something
they'll really love. But by all means,
don't spend all day in the kitchen!
The entrées in this section—
whether poultry, beef, fish, or pork—are just right
for today's hectic life-styles. You'll find easy entrées
for family-style dining, some sophisticated yet
deceptively simple main dishes for entertaining,
a few quick casseroles everyone will enjoy,
and several updated classics.
In short, they're all "keepers"—
the recipes you'll return to
time and time again!

BARBECUED BEEF BRISKET

7 pounds beef brisket, trimmed	2 tablespoons Worcestershire sauce
2 teaspoons onion salt	1½ tablespoons liquid smoke
1 tablespoon celery salt	smoke
1 teaspoon garlic salt	Barbecue Sauce

Rub the brisket with the onion salt, celery salt and garlic salt; let stand for about 30 minutes. Place in a roaster. Pour the Worcestershire sauce and liquid smoke over the surface of the roast. Refrigerate, covered, for 3 to 4 hours. Preheat the oven to 300 degrees. Drain off the Worcestershire marinade. Wrap the brisket, fatty side up, in heavy-duty aluminum foil and seal. Bake for 5 hours. Allow to cool. Increase the oven temperature to 325 degrees. Slice the roast thinly across the grain and place in a baking dish. Cover with Barbecue Sauce; bake for 20 minutes. Yield: 6 to 8 servings.

BARBECUE SAUCE

½ cup butter or margarine	¼ cup sugar
¼ cup vinegar	2 cups catsup
¼ cup Worcestershire sauce	¼ cup lemon juice
	½ cup water

Combine the butter, vinegar, Worcestershire sauce, sugar, catsup, lemon juice and water in a saucepan. Simmer over medium heat for 15 minutes.

Sue Flower, Xi Delta Kappa
Scott City, Kansas

STUFFED BEEF TENDERLOIN

2 cups herb-seasoned stuffing	⅓ cup water
1 (1-pound) slice smoked ham, diced	¼ teaspoon pepper
	1 (7- to 7½-pound) beef tenderloin
1 cup finely chopped onion	Paprika
	6 slices bacon
1 (3-ounce) package sliced pepperoni, minced	1 cup water
	1 bay leaf
	4 whole cloves
2 eggs, beaten	1½ tablespoons cornstarch
½ teaspoon garlic powder	⅛ teaspoon pepper

Preheat the oven to 350 degrees. Combine the stuffing, smoked ham, onion, pepperoni, eggs, garlic powder, the ⅓ cup water and pepper. Remove 3 to 4 inches from the small end of the tenderloin, reserving it for another use. Cut a pocket lengthwise in the tenderloin to within ¼ inch of the opposite side. Spoon the stuffing mixture into the opening. Close the pocket over the stuffing. Tie at 3-inch intervals. Sprinkle paprika on all sides. Place on the rack of a roasting pan. Lay the bacon slices over the top of the tenderloin. Place the 1 cup water, bay leaf and cloves in the pan under the rack. Bake for 60 to 70 minutes to 140 degrees on a meat thermometer for a rare tenderloin, or to 160 degrees for a medium tenderloin. Remove the tenderloin from the rack. Reserve ¼ cup of the drippings. Remove the bay leaf and cloves. Add water to the reserved drippings to make 1½ cups liquid. Combine with the cornstarch in a medium saucepan; stir well. Cook over medium heat, stirring constantly, until thickened and bubbly. Stir in the pepper. Serve the tenderloin with the drippings sauce. Yield: 14 to 16 servings.

Sylvia Friday, Xi Lambda
Columbus, Mississippi

BEEF TENDERLOIN WITH MUSTARD SAUCE

1 (4- to 5-pound) beef tenderloin	2 tablespoons white wine
½ cup heavy cream	1 (8-ounce) container sour cream
4 teaspoons dry mustard	sour cream
2 teaspoons sugar	

Preheat the oven to 425 degrees. Place the tenderloin on a rack in a roasting pan. Bake for 50 minutes. While the tenderloin is baking, combine the cream, mustard, sugar and wine; stir in the sour cream. Chill until ready to serve. Remove the tenderloin from the oven. Place the chilled sauce in a gravy boat and serve with tenderloin slices. Yield: 10 to 15 servings.

Sharon Ann Heiman, Xi Rho Alpha
Trinidad, Texas

BRACIOLE

Braciole is pronounced BRA-zho-lee. Braciole meat can be bought from a butcher. It is sliced very thin so that it can be rolled around a stuffing.

½ pound bacon, crisp-fried, crumbled	1 tablespoon olive oil
3 hard-cooked eggs, chopped	1 (8-ounce) can sliced mushrooms
2 to 3 cups bread crumbs	2 small zucchini, diced
2 tablespoons parsley flakes	1 (24-ounce) jar spaghetti sauce
1 teaspoon oregano	Red wine
1 teaspoon garlic powder	Your favorite pasta
2 round steaks, tenderized	Salad

Preheat the oven to 350 degrees. Combine the bacon, eggs, bread crumbs, parsley flakes, oregano and garlic powder. Add a bit of olive oil if necessary to hold the mixture together. Cut each tenderized steak into 3 pieces. Place 1/6 of the bacon stuffing on each piece. Roll up the meat and secure with toothpicks. Sauté in the olive oil over medium heat until brown. Arrange in a 9-by-13-inch baking dish. Sprinkle with the mushrooms and zucchini. Barely cover with the spaghetti sauce. Splash red wine over the top. Bake for 1 hour. Serve with your favorite cooked pasta and a crisp salad. Yield: 4 to 6 servings.

Elaine Wilson, Xi Beta
Artesia, New Mexico

MOM'S CHICKEN-FRIED STEAK

For many years my mother owned and operated a restaurant that was well known in Wichita, Kansas. We always had a full house on Wednesday night, when my mother prepared her specialty, chicken-fried steak. Use the pan drippings to make a white gravy to serve with the steak.

3 cups all-purpose flour	*1 teaspoon salt*
3 teaspoons baking powder	*1 teaspoon pepper*
1 teaspoon chili powder	*3 eggs, beaten*
1 teaspoon garlic powder	*1 cup buttermilk*
1 teaspoon onion powder	*4 cube steaks*
	Vegetable oil for frying

Combine the first 7 ingredients in a medium bowl. Combine the eggs and buttermilk in a shallow pan. Dip each cube steak in the egg mixture; dredge in the flour mixture, coating well. Dip each in the egg mixture again, and coat again with the flour mixture. Lay on waxed paper for 10 minutes to air dry. Heat 1/2 inch of oil in a skillet. Fry the steaks for 10 minutes over low heat; turn and fry for 10 minutes. Serve the pan drippings over the steaks. Yield: 4 servings.

Marquetta Fouts, Xi Epsilon Xi
Stafford, Virginia

Deborah Evans, Cape Coral, Florida, does a Cherry Chuck Roast by marinating a 4-pound roast in a mixture of the juice from a can of dark pitted cherries, 1/3 cup vinegar, 1/2 cup packed brown sugar, and 1 tablespoon instant beef bouillon for several hours. Drain, reserving marinade. Sear roast on both sides and braise for 2 1/2 to 3 hours. Add the reserved marinade to the pan juices and thicken as desired. Stir in the cherries. Serve with the roast.

TEXAS LASAGNA

Serve this delectable dish with Spanish rice, lettuce, and tomatoes garnished with sour cream.

2 (8-ounce) portions filet mignon	*1 (16-ounce) container sour cream*
1 teaspoon cumin	*2 cups (8 ounces) shredded Mexican-blend cheese*
Salt to taste	
Freshly ground pepper to taste	*6 tortillas*
2 tablespoons unsalted butter or margarine	*2 (16-ounce) cans refried beans*
1 (14-ounce) can Mexican-style tomatoes	*1 (4-ounce) can sliced black olives*
1 (4-ounce) can green chiles	

Preheat the oven to 350 degrees. Cut the filets into thin strips; season with cumin, salt and pepper. Sauté the meat in the butter in a skillet over medium-low heat. Add the tomatoes and green chiles to the skillet. Mix the sour cream with the shredded cheese and set aside. Layer the tortillas, steak mixture, refried beans and cheese 1/2 at a time in a lightly greased 9-by-13-inch baking dish. Bake, uncovered, for 30 to 40 minutes or until bubbly. Sprinkle with the black olives. Cut into squares. Yield: 8 servings.

Gail McDowell, Laureate Sigma
Asheboro, North Carolina

STEAK AND SOUR CREAM

2 tablespoons all-purpose flour	*1/4 cup butter or margarine*
2 teaspoons dry mustard	*1 cup sliced mushrooms*
1 teaspoon salt	*1 onion, chopped*
1/4 teaspoon pepper	*1/2 cup water*
1 1/2 pounds round steak, cut in strips	*1/2 cup sour cream*
	Mashed potatoes

Combine the flour, mustard, salt and pepper on a plate. Dredge the steak strips in the flour mixture, coating well. Melt the butter in a large skillet. Brown the steak strips in the butter on all sides. Add the mushrooms, onion and water to the skillet. Simmer for 1 1/2 hours or until the steak is tender, stirring occasionally. Add more water if needed so that the moisture is like a gravy. When the steak is done, stir in the sour cream, stirring over low heat until hot. Serve with mashed potatoes. Yield: 4 servings.

Kim Adams
Danville, Kentucky

ORIENTAL STUFFED STEAKS

1 (6-ounce) package long
   grain and wild rice
   mix
1 egg, slightly beaten
¼ cup chopped green
   onion
6 beef strip steaks

¼ to ½ cup bottled
   teriyaki sauce
Mushrooms for garnish
   (optional)
Watercress for garnish
   (optional)

Prepare the rice mix using package directions. Cool slightly. Stir in the egg and green onion. Preheat the broiler for 5 minutes. Cut a pocket in each steak with a sharp knife. Stuff the pockets with the rice mixture. Broil the steaks 4 inches from the heat until desired doneness, brushing often with teriyaki sauce. Garnish with mushrooms and watercress.
Yield: 6 servings.

Nelda Dotray, Preceptor Delta Tau
Greenville, Illinois

SANTA FE STEW

This is a great spicy stew. For a milder stew, use mild tomatoes with green chiles. It may be adjusted for use in a slow cooker by browning the beef and onion in the oil in a skillet. Add the flour, salt, and pepper. Add with the remaining ingredients to a slow cooker.

2 tablespoons vegetable
   oil
3 tablespoons all-
   purpose flour
2 pounds beef stew
   cubes, cut in bite-size
   pieces
1 medium white onion,
   chopped
Salt and pepper
   to taste
3 pounds potatoes,
   peeled, cut in bite-
   size pieces

1 (8-ounce) package
   baby carrots, halved
1 (16-ounce) can whole
   kernel corn
1 (16-ounce) can cut
   green beans
1 (10-ounce) can HOT
   diced tomatoes with
   green chiles
1 (24-ounce) can chili
   with beans
½ cup brown gravy
   made from package
   of dry gravy mix

Heat the oil in a Dutch oven. Add the flour, beef stew cubes, onion, salt and pepper; stir over high heat until the meat is covered with flour and browned. Lower heat to medium. Add the potatoes and carrots; simmer for about 20 minutes. Add the corn, green beans and tomatoes with green chiles. Simmer, covered, for 2 hours or until meat is tender. Stir in the chili; heat until entire mixture is warm. Add the gravy mix, stirring over low heat until desired thickness. Yield: 6 servings.

Mariann Chance, Preceptor Zeta
Enid, Oklahoma

UNSANDWICH REUBEN CASSEROLE

2 (12-ounce) cans corned
   beef
2 (16-ounce) cans
   sauerkraut, drained
4 cups (16 ounces)
   shredded Swiss
   cheese
1 cup Thousand Island
   salad dressing

2 large tomatoes, sliced
2 cups pumpernickel
   bread crumbs
4 tablespoons butter or
   margarine
4 tablespoons caraway
   seeds

Preheat the oven to 350 degrees. Layer the corned beef, sauerkraut, cheese, salad dressing, tomatoes and bread crumbs in an 11-by-13-inch baking dish. Dot with butter and sprinkle with caraway seeds. Bake for 30 minutes. Let stand for 5 minutes before serving. Yield: 8 servings.

Betty Lail, Laureate Sigma
New London, North Carolina

HOT AND SWEET CORNED BEEF

3 pounds corned beef
4 cloves of garlic
10 peppercorns
6 whole cloves
2 bay leaves
2 teaspoons pickling
   spices

½ (10-ounce) bottle
   cherry syrup
Beer
½ to ¾ cup packed light
   brown sugar
Prepared mustard

Preheat the oven to 300 degrees. Place the corned beef in a roasting pan. Add the garlic, peppercorns, cloves, bay leaves, pickling spices and cherry syrup. Pour in enough beer so that the meat is covered with liquids. Roast, covered, for 3 to 4 hours until tender, turning several times. Drain and discard the liquid. Return the beef to the pan. Blend the brown sugar with enough mustard to make a paste; spoon over the meat. Bake for 20 minutes longer. Let stand for 5 minutes before slicing. Yield: 4 to 6 servings.

Marilyn Borras, Xi Epsilon Xi
Stafford, Virginia

SIMPLE VEAL FRANCESE

6 veal scallops (½
   pound) from leg
Salt and pepper to taste
1 egg, beaten well
All-purpose flour for
   dredging

6 tablespoons butter or
   margarine
1 cup dry white wine

Place veal scallops between 2 sheets of waxed paper. Pound with a mallet until veal is thin. Season with salt and pepper. Place the egg in a wide, shallow bowl. Spread the flour on a wide plate. Dip the veal in the egg; remove from the egg, allowing excess to drip off. Place in the flour, coating the veal lightly. Place 4 tablespoons of the butter in a frying pan large enough to hold the 6 veal scallops in a single layer. Melt the butter over medium-high heat; when it foams, add the veal. Sauté, turning once, until the veal is golden on the outside. Remove the veal scallops; let them rest in a single layer. Drain and discard the butter from the pan. Pour the white wine into the pan and cook over high heat until the wine is reduced to 1/2 cup. Reduce the heat to very low. Swirl in the remaining 2 tablespoons butter to thicken the sauce. Return the veal scallops to the pan, turning until they are coated with the sauce. Arrange the scallops on plates and pour the sauce from the pan over them. Serve immediately. Yield: 2 servings.

Mary Lou Couch, Preceptor Alpha Iota
Riverside, California

THE BEAN THING

I have varied this recipe so much that it is sometimes hard to remember the original recipe. The recipe is one step: just put everything in a kettle or slow cooker. What could be easier?

1 (15-ounce) can Great Northern beans	1 cup packed light brown sugar
1 (15-ounce) can pinto beans	1 small onion, chopped
1 (15-ounce) can kidney beans	1 cup catsup
1 (15-ounce) can black-eyed peas	2 tablespoons mustard or barbecue sauce
1 (15-ounce) can baby lima beans	1 pound ground beef, browned, crumbled (optional)
1 (2-ounce) can real bacon bits	

Preheat the oven to 350 degrees. Combine the Great Northern beans, pinto beans, kidney beans, black-eyed peas, lima beans, bacon bits, brown sugar, onion, catsup, mustard and beef in a 9-by-13-inch baking dish. Bake for 1 hour. To prepare in a slow cooker, combine the ingredients in the slow cooker and cook for 4 to 5 hours on Medium Low. Variations: Use Dijon mustard, honey mustard, or another flavored mustard. Add hot sauce for a hotter flavor. Serve over a salad to make a barbecue salad. Serve as a finger food with corn chip scoops.
Yield: 8 to 12 servings.

Gina Emerson, Zeta Eta
Salisbury, North Carolina

BARBECUED BEEF IN A PITA

Serve with a salad or French fries.

2/3 cup plus 1 tablespoon catsup	2 teaspoons cider vinegar
2 tablespoons water	2 teaspoons Worcestershire sauce
1 tablespoon light brown sugar	2 teaspoons lemon juice
2 teaspoons chili powder	Dash of hot pepper sauce
2 teaspoons honey	1 pound ground beef, browned, crumbled
2 teaspoons Dijon mustard	Pita bread

Combine the catsup, water, brown sugar, chili powder, honey, Dijon mustard, vinegar, Worcestershire sauce, lemon juice and hot pepper sauce in a medium saucepan. Cook over medium heat, stirring, until mixture is hot. Add the ground beef; cook for 4 to 5 minutes or until the beef is heated through, stirring occasionally. Fill pita halves with the beef mixture. Yield: 6 to 8 servings.

Jennifer Box, Gamma Psi
Mississauga, Ontario, Canada

MEXICAN SHEPHERD'S PIE

Serve with a green salad and your favorite cornbread.

6 large potatoes, peeled, chopped, cooked	1 (14-ounce) can stewed tomatoes
1/4 cup butter or margarine	1 envelope taco seasoning
1/2 cup low-fat sour cream	1 (14-ounce) can kidney beans, rinsed
1/4 cup milk	1 (10-ounce) can corn niblets, drained
2 pounds lean ground beef	1/2 cup medium salsa
1 medium onion, chopped	1 cup (4 ounces) shredded sharp Cheddar cheese
2 ribs celery, chopped	2 cups crushed taco chips
1 clove of garlic, minced	

Preheat the oven to 350 degrees. Mash the warm cooked potatoes with the butter and sour cream. Add the milk and mash again. Brown the ground beef with the onion, celery and garlic. Add the next 5 ingredients. Stir well and simmer for 15 minutes. Divide the meat mixture between two 9-by-9-inch baking pans. Spread the mashed potatoes evenly over the meat mixture. Sprinkle with the cheese, then sprinkle with the crushed taco chips. Bake for 20 minutes. Yield: 6 servings.

Brigitte Bellamy, Xi Alpha Phi
Spruce Grove, Alberta, Canada

SPINACH MEATBALL CASSEROLE

2 small onions
3 tablespoons vegetable
   oil
1 (10-ounce) package
   frozen spinach,
   cooked, drained,
   squeezed
1 pound ground beef
1/2 teaspoon salt

1/2 teaspoon pepper
1 egg
3 tablespoons shredded
   Cheddar cheese
All-purpose flour
1 (10-ounce) can
   mushroom soup
1/2 cup water

Preheat the oven to 350 degrees. Sauté the onions in the oil in a frying pan until golden. Mix the spinach and onions with the ground beef. Mix in the salt, pepper, egg and cheese. Form into 1-inch balls. Roll the meatballs lightly in the flour and brown in the oil left in the frying pan. Arrange in an ovenproof casserole dish. Dilute the mushroom soup with the 1/2 cup water and pour over the meatballs. Bake for 40 minutes. Yield: 4 servings.

Carmel Payton, Nu Master
Pacifica, California

BARBECUED MEATBALLS

3 pounds lean ground
   beef
1 (12-ounce) can
   evaporated milk
1 cup rolled oats
1 cup cracker crumbs
2 eggs
1/2 cup chopped onion
1/2 teaspoon garlic
   powder
2 teaspoons salt
1/2 teaspoon pepper

2 teaspoons chili
   powder
1 to 2 teaspoons liquid
   smoke
2 cups catsup
1 cup packed light
   brown sugar
2 to 3 teaspoons liquid
   smoke
1/2 teaspoon garlic
   powder
1/4 cup chopped onion

Preheat the oven to 400 degrees. Mix the ground beef, evaporated milk, oats, cracker crumbs, eggs, 1/2 cup onion, garlic powder, salt, pepper, chili powder and the 1 to 2 teaspoons liquid smoke in a large bowl. Shape the mixture into walnut-size meatballs. Bake in a large roasting pan for about 30 minutes. Combine the catsup, brown sugar, the 2 to 3 teaspoons liquid smoke, garlic powder and the remaining onion to make a sauce. Reduce oven heat to 300 degrees. Pour the sauce over the meatballs and bake for 30 minutes longer. Yield: 10 to 12 servings.

Deborah Creighton, Preceptor Xi Eta
Weldon, California

MEAT LOAF MEAL

1 pound ground round
1/2 pound ground pork
1 medium onion,
   chopped
1 large egg
Salt and pepper to taste
1/2 cup crushed
   cornflakes
2 tablespoons vegetable
   oil

2 (10-ounce) cans
   tomato soup
1 (10-ounce) can water
6 carrots, cleaned, cut in
   1 1/2-inch pieces
8 medium potatoes,
   peeled, quartered
Pepper to taste

Preheat a covered electric skillet to 350 degrees. Combine the ground round, ground pork, onion, egg, salt and pepper. Shape the mixture into a loaf; roll in the crushed cornflakes until all sides are coated. Pour the oil into the electric skillet. Brown the coated meat loaf on all sides. Pour the tomato soup and the can of water around and across the meat loaf. Add the carrots and potatoes. Sprinkle pepper over the vegetables. Cover the skillet and cook for 1 1/4 hours. Serve with warm bread. Yield: 4 servings.

Virginia Ann (Ginny) Thomas, Preceptor Gamma Eta
Merritt Island, Florida

MEAT LOAF SURPRISE

2/3 cup dry bread crumbs
1 cup milk
1 1/2 pounds ground beef
1/2 pound ground pork or
   veal
2 eggs, beaten
1/4 cup grated onion

1 teaspoon salt
1/3 teaspoon pepper
1/2 teaspoon ground sage
2 hard-cooked eggs,
   peeled
Piquant Sauce

Preheat the oven to 350 degrees. Soak the crumbs in the milk in a large bowl for 10 minutes. Add the ground beef, ground pork, eggs, onion, salt, pepper and sage; mix well. Spread half the meat mixture in a 5-by-9-inch loaf pan. Place the hard-cooked eggs end to end over the mixture. Add the rest of the meat mixture and press into a loaf shape. Cover with Piquant Sauce. Bake for 45 minutes. Yield: 8 servings.

PIQUANT SAUCE

1/4 cup catsup
3 tablespoons light
   brown sugar

1/4 teaspoon nutmeg
1 teaspoon dry mustard

Combine all the ingredients in a bowl; mix well.

Neoma Hoffmann, Xi Phi Sigma
Coleville, California

MARVELOUS MEAT LOAF

To make a glaze, combine 1 cup brown sugar, 1/3 cup catsup, and 3 tablespoons Worcestershire sauce. Spread the glaze over the meat loaf before cooking. For a lower-fat version, use a special meat loaf pan that has drainage holes. The meat loaf still tastes great!

2 extra-large eggs, beaten	1 teaspoon basil
3/4 cup vegetable juice cocktail	1 teaspoon oregano
1 medium onion, chopped	1 teaspoon seasoned salt
1/4 cup chopped carrots	1 tablespoon Worcestershire sauce
1 cup old-fashioned rolled oats	1 pound ground beef
	1/4 pound ground Italian sausage

Preheat the oven to 375 degrees. Combine the eggs with the vegetable juice cocktail in a large bowl. Add the onion, carrots, rolled oats, basil, oregano, seasoned salt and Worcestershire sauce; mix well. Stir in the ground beef and sausage. Pat into a 5-by-9-inch loaf pan. Bake for 1 hour. Let stand for 45 minutes before slicing. Yield: 6 to 8 servings.

Shelia DeSantis, Xi Zeta Nu
Westchester, Ohio

FROSTED MEAT LOAF

1 1/2 pounds ground beef	1 egg, slightly beaten
1 (10-ounce) can golden mushroom soup	Generous dash of pepper
1 cup small bread cubes	1/2 teaspoon salt
1/4 cup finely chopped onion	2 cups mashed potatoes
	1/4 cup water

Preheat the oven to 350 degrees. Combine the ground beef, half the golden mushroom soup, bread cubes, onion, egg, pepper and salt in a large bowl; mix thoroughly. Shape firmly into a loaf; place in a shallow loaf pan. Bake for 1 hour. Drain the meat loaf, reserving 1 to 2 tablespoons of the drippings. Frost the loaf with the mashed potatoes, covering completely. Bake for 15 minutes longer. Blend the remaining half can of soup with the water and the reserved drippings in a small saucepan. Heat to serving temperature, stirring occasionally and serve over the meat loaf. Yield: 4 to 6 servings.

Patricia A. Astle, Preceptor Chi
Baraboo, Wisconsin

CRAZY CRUST PIZZA

2 cups all-purpose flour	1/4 cup chopped onion
1 teaspoon salt	1 (4-ounce) can mushrooms, drained
1 1/2 teaspoons oregano	Pizza Sauce or 1 cup store-bought pizza sauce
1/4 teaspoon pepper	
4 eggs	
1 1/2 cups milk	1 cup (4 ounces) shredded mozzarella cheese
1 1/2 pounds ground beef or sausage, browned, crumbled, drained, seasoned to taste	1 or 2 green peppers, chopped
Pepperoni and Canadian bacon	

Preheat the oven to 425 degrees. Lightly grease and flour a baking sheet that has shallow edges. Prepare the batter by combining the flour, salt, oregano, pepper, eggs and milk, mixing until smooth. Pour the batter over the baking sheet, tilting to evenly coat the sheet. Arrange the ground beef, pepperoni, Canadian bacon, onion and mushrooms over the batter. Bake for 25 to 30 minutes. Remove from the oven and drizzle with the Pizza Sauce. Sprinkle with the cheese and green peppers. Return to the oven for 10 to 15 minutes longer. Yield: 6 servings.

PIZZA SAUCE

1 cup tomato sauce	1/4 teaspoon black pepper
1 to 2 teaspoons leaf oregano	

Combine all the ingredients in a bowl; mix well.

Cheri Friedrich
Wooldridge, Missouri

KIMA

1 small onion, chopped	2 or 3 medium potatoes, diced
2 or 3 cloves of garlic, crushed	2 or 3 Roma tomatoes, diced
2 teaspoons butter or margarine	3/4 (16-ounce) package frozen peas, broken apart
1 pound ground beef	
Curry powder to taste	
Pepper to taste	Coconut to taste

Preheat an electric skillet to 300 to 350 degrees. Sauté the onion and garlic in butter in the skillet until onion is tender. Add the ground beef. Cook until brown and crumbly. Add the next 5 ingredients. Cook until the potatoes are tender. Reduce heat to 250 degrees if necessary to avoid burning. Serve sprinkled with coconut. Yield: 4 to 6 servings.

Barbara Rudy, Xi Kappa Pi
Fairview Heights, Illinois

QUICK PIZZA

*1 envelope dry active
 yeast*
1/4 cup warm water
1 egg
1/4 cup tomato sauce
*3 tablespoons melted
 shortening*
1 tablespoon sugar

1 teaspoon salt
*1/2 teaspoon chili
 powder*
2 cups all-purpose flour
Ground Beef Topping
*1 cup shredded
 mozzarella cheese*

Preheat the oven to 400 degrees. Soften the yeast in the water for 5 minutes. Add the egg, tomato sauce, shortening, sugar, salt and chili powder; blend well. Gradually stir in the flour. Knead on a well-floured board for 2 minutes. Roll out the dough and place in a lightly greased pizza pan. Pour the Ground Beef Topping over the crust. Sprinkle the cheese over the top. Bake for 15 to 18 minutes. Yield: 6 servings.

GROUND BEEF TOPPING

1 pound ground beef
1/4 cup chopped onion
*1/2 teaspoon chili
 powder*

3/4 cup tomato sauce
1/2 teaspoon salt
1/4 teaspoon pepper

Cook the ground beef with the onion in a large skillet until brown and crumbly. Stir in the remaning ingredients.

*Jane F. McDonald, Laureate Delta Delta
Fort Worth, Texas*

KILLER BURRITO

This recipe is quick, easy, and inexpensive to make. Use your imagination—the variations can be endless. I call it the Killer Burrito because it's tempting to eat a little too much—which can be deadly.

*1 pound process cheese,
 cubed*
*1 (15-ounce) can diced
 tomatoes*
*Hot pepper sauce to
 taste*
1 pound ground beef
1 small onion, chopped

*1 or 2 cloves of garlic,
 chopped*
*1 (10-ounce) can cream
 of mushroom soup*
*1 (16-ounce) can refried
 beans*
*1 (12-count) package
 flour burrito shells*

Combine the cheese and tomatoes in the top of a double boiler. Heat over boiling water until the cheese melts, stirring occasionally. Add a few drops of hot pepper sauce for a spicier cheese sauce. Brown the ground beef in a large skillet, stirring until crumbly; drain. Add the onion and garlic to the ground beef; simmer for 10 to 15 minutes. Stir in the cream of mushroom soup and refried beans. Simmer, stirring, until heated through. Cover and set aside. Micro-

wave a burrito shell on a plate for 10 to 15 seconds or until slightly warm. Place about 3/4 cup of the meat mixture in the center of the burrito. Fold the four sides toward the center of the burrito and turn over with the folded side down. Spoon about 1/3 cup of the cheese sauce over the burrito. Repeat the procedure to form more burritos. Yield: 12 servings.

*Pamela S. Kane
Kingsville, Missouri*

SOUR CREAM ENCHILADAS

1 1/2 pounds ground beef
*1 envelope taco
 seasoning*
1 pint sour cream
*2 (10-ounce) cans cream
 of chicken soup*
*1 (4-ounce) can chopped
 green chiles*

*1 bunch green onions,
 chopped*
*3 cups (12 ounces)
 shredded mozzarella
 cheese*
*1 (12-count) package
 flour tortillas*

Preheat the oven to 350 degrees. Brown the ground beef in a skillet, stirring until the ground beef is crumbly; drain. Stir in the taco seasoning. Heat until mixture is warm. Lightly grease a 9-by-13-inch baking pan. Mix the sour cream, cream of chicken soup, green chiles, green onions, and 2 cups of the mozzarella cheese by hand. Place 1 tablespoon of the ground beef mixture and 1 tablespoon of the sour cream mixture in the center of each tortilla and roll up the tortilla. Place the rolled tortillas in the prepared baking dish. Spread the remaining ground beef mixture and sour cream mixture over the tortillas. Sprinkle with the remaining 1 cup mozzarella cheese. Bake, covered, for 20 minutes. Bake, uncovered, for 10 minutes longer. Yield: 8 to 10 servings.

*Michelle Fisketjon, Xi Omega
Worland, Wyoming*

MEXI-TACO HASH BROWNS

1 pound ground beef
1/2 cup chopped onions
*1/2 teaspoon minced
 garlic*
*1 (8-ounce) can tomato
 sauce*
1 teaspoon chili powder
3/4 teaspoon salt
*1 tablespoon butter or
 margarine*

*1 tablespoon vegetable
 oil*
*1/2 (26-ounce) package
 (4 1/2 cups) frozen hash
 browns, thawed*
4 large tomato slices
*1 cup (4 ounces)
 shredded Cheddar
 cheese*

Brown the ground beef with the onions and garlic in a large skillet; drain. Stir in the tomato sauce, chili powder and 1/2 teaspoon of the salt; bring to a boil.

Reduce heat. Simmer, uncovered, for 10 minutes or until most of the liquid is absorbed, stirring occasionally. Combine the butter and oil in a 10-inch nonstick ovenproof skillet. Heat over medium-high heat until sizzling. Add the hash browns, pressing into one layer. Sprinkle with the remaining 1/4 teaspoon salt. Cook for 5 minutes or until hash browns are golden brown. Preheat the broiler. Spoon the meat mixture over the hash browns; top with tomato slices and cheese. Broil 3 to 4 inches from the heat source for 2 to 3 minutes. Yield: 4 servings.

Teri Farney
Derby, Kansas

TASTY TACO PIE

1 pound ground beef	1 cup shredded lettuce
2 (8-ounce) cans tomato sauce	1/2 cup chopped tomatoes
1 envelope taco seasoning	1/4 cup olives, pitted and sliced
1 (8-ounce) can crescent rolls	Sour cream (optional)
1/2 pound Mexican process cheese, cubed	

Preheat the oven to 375 degrees. Brown the ground beef in a skillet, stirring until crumbly; drain. Stir in the tomato sauce and taco seasoning. Simmer for 5 minutes. Unroll the crescent roll dough and press into the bottom and sides of an ungreased 12-inch pizza pan. Prick the dough all over with a fork. Bake for 10 to 12 minutes or until golden brown. Cover the dough crust with the meat mixture. Sprinkle the cheese over the meat. Return to the oven and bake for 1 to 3 minutes or until the cheese begins to melt. Remove from the oven. Cover the pizza with the lettuce, tomatoes and olives. Serve with sour cream. Yield: 6 servings.

Kris Vessels, Mu Phi
Evansville, Indiana

TACO RING

3/4 pound ground beef	1 medium green pepper
1 envelope taco seasoning	1 cup salsa
1 cup (4 ounces) shredded Cheddar cheese	3 cups shredded lettuce
2 tablespoons water	1 medium tomato, seeded, chopped
2 (8-ounce) cans refrigerator crescent rolls	1/4 cup chopped onion
	1/2 cup sliced pitted ripe olives
	Sour cream for garnish

Preheat the oven to 375 degrees. Brown the ground beef in a medium skillet over medium heat, stirring until crumbly; drain. Stir in the taco seasoning, cheese and water; set aside. Unroll the crescent roll dough; separate into triangles. Arrange the triangles in a circle on a greased 14-inch pizza pan. The corners of the wide ends of the triangles should overlap in a circle; points should face the outside rim of the pan. (Leave a 5-inch-diameter opening in the center.) Scoop the meat mixture evenly onto the wide end of each triangle. Bring the outside point of the triangle down over the filling, tucking under the wide end of the dough at the center. The filling will not be completely covered. Bake for 20 to 25 minutes or until golden brown. Cut the top off the green pepper in a zigzag pattern. Place the green pepper in the center of the pizza pan. Fill with salsa. Mound the lettuce, tomato, onion and olives over the ring. Serve garnished with sour cream. Yield: 8 servings.

Judy Ann Evans, Laureate Xi
Fairmont, West Virginia

DEER PATTIES

1 pound ground deer meat	1 to 2 cups seasoned bread crumbs
1 medium onion, chopped	2 tablespoons chopped parsley
2 or 3 cloves of garlic, finely chopped	1 tablespoon ginger
2 eggs, beaten	2 tablespoons basil
1 cup (4 ounces) shredded Cheddar cheese	1 tablespoon olive oil
	Deer Patty Gravy

Mix the deer meat, onion, garlic, eggs, cheese, bread crumbs, parsley, ginger, basil and olive oil in a bowl. Roll into patties. Sauté in a 10- to 12-inch frying pan until brown on both sides. Serve with Deer Patty Gravy. Yield: 4 to 6 servings.

DEER PATTY GRAVY

1 cup water	2 ounces shredded Gouda cheese
2 tablespoons cornstarch	

Combine the water and the cornstarch; pour into the pan that was used to fry the deer patties. Cook over medium-low heat, stirring with a fork, until the sauce thickens. Add the Gouda cheese; stir until melted.

Judith A. Brehm
Strongsville, Ohio

GREEK LAMB BURGERS WITH LEMON YOGURT CUCUMBER SAUCE

¼ cup plain yogurt
⅛ cup chopped cucumber
¼ cup mayonnaise
1 scallion, chopped
1 teaspoon lemon juice
½ teaspoon grated lemon zest
⅛ teaspoon salt
1 tablespoon olive oil
2 cloves of garlic, minced
1 pound ground lamb

¼ cup plain dry bread crumbs
1 egg
1 teaspoon dried oregano
¼ teaspoon dried rosemary, crumbled
⅛ teaspoon pepper
½ teaspoon salt
2 large pita breads, halved
Tomato slices and lettuce for garnish

Combine the yogurt, cucumber, mayonnaise, scallion, lemon juice, lemon zest and the ⅛ teaspoon salt to make the yogurt sauce. Refrigerate until ready to serve. Heat the olive oil in a skillet over medium heat. Sauté the garlic in the oil for 1 minute. Combine the garlic, lamb, bread crumbs, egg, oregano, rosemary, pepper and the ½ teaspoon salt. Form into 4 burgers. Cook the burgers in the same skillet over medium heat, turning once, until done, about 15 minutes. Place in pita with tomato slices, lettuce and yogurt sauce. Yield: 4 servings.

Sandra Robbins, Mu Master
Weirton, West Virginia

ROAST PORK WITH FRUIT SAUCE

My grandmother always served this roast with homemade noodles and baby lima beans. It was a wonderful combination.

1 (3- to 4-pound) pork loin roast, bone in
1 (8- to 10-ounce) jar apple jelly
1 cup (8 ounces) apple juice

½ teaspoon ground cardamom
¾ cup chopped dried apricots
1 tablespoon cornstarch
2 tablespoons water

Preheat the oven to 350 degrees. Bake the roast, uncovered, in a shallow roasting pan for 1½ hours. Combine the apple jelly, apple juice and cardamom in a saucepan; cook, stirring, over medium heat until smooth and heated through. Set aside ½ cup of the apple jelly sauce. Brush some of the remaining sauce over the roast. Bake for 40 to 60 minutes longer or to 165 degrees on a meat thermometer, brushing with apple jelly sauce every 20 minutes. Remove the roast to a serving platter and cover loosely with foil. Pour the pan drippings into a medium saucepan. Stir in the apricots and the reserved ½ cup apple jelly

sauce. Cook over medium heat for about 5 minutes or until the apricots are softened. Combine the cornstarch and water; add to the apricot mixture. Bring to a boil. Serve with the roast. Yield: 10 servings.

Al Smit-Briggs
Cameron, Missouri

PORK ROAST WITH FRUIT STUFFING

Purchase celery and onions already chopped from the deli counter, buy chopped apricots, use canned chicken broth and bottled lemon juice to save time.

2 tablespoons margarine
1 cup chopped onion
1 cup chopped celery
1 (7-ounce) package sage-onion stuffing mix
½ cup chopped dried apricots

½ cup dried cranberries
1½ cups chicken broth
1 (2- to 3-pound) boneless pork loin roast
Salt and pepper to taste
Apricot Glaze

Preheat the oven to 325 degrees. Melt the margarine in a large skillet. Sauté the onion and celery until tender, about 5 minutes. Add the stuffing mix, apricots, cranberries and chicken broth, stirring until all liquid is absorbed. Spoon the stuffing mixture into a 2-quart baking dish that has been sprayed with nonstick cooking spray. Sprinkle the roast with salt and pepper; place it over the stuffing. Bake, uncovered, for 1 hour. Brush ½ cup of the Apricot Glaze over the roast. Bake for 1½ hours to 155 degrees on a meat thermometer. Cover with aluminum foil and let stand for 15 minutes before slicing. Heat the remaining Apricot Glaze and serve with the sliced roast. Yield: 6 to 8 servings.

APRICOT GLAZE

1 (12-ounce) jar apricot preserves
1 tablespoon lemon juice

1 tablespoon soy sauce
¼ teaspoon ground ginger

Combine the apricot preserves, lemon juice, soy sauce and ginger in a small bowl. Yield: 1½ cups.

Esther Hess, Xi Iota Sigma
Harrisonville, Missouri

Lisa Quinn, Xi Beta Xi, Dublin, Georgia, cooks 4 to 6 pork chops, 4 peeled and sliced tart green apples, and a can of chicken broth mixed with ½ cup spicy mustard, salt, and pepper to taste in a slow cooker for 8 hours to make All-Day Pork Chops.

TERIYAKI ROAST PORK

When she comes home to this slow-cooker roast, a working woman can have dinner ready in 20 minutes, adding only quick-cooking rice and a package of frozen stir-fry vegetables to the meal.

1 (3- to 6-pound) pork roast	1 teaspoon ground ginger
3/4 cup apple juice	1/4 teaspoon garlic powder
2 tablespoons sugar	1/8 teaspoon pepper
2 tablespoons soy sauce	3 tablespoons cornstarch
1 tablespoon vinegar	

Place the pork roast in a slow cooker. Combine the apple juice, sugar, soy sauce, vinegar, ginger, garlic powder and pepper; pour over the roast. Cook for 3 1/2 hours on High or for 7 to 8 hours on Low. Remove the roast to a platter for carving. Pour the juices into a small saucepan. Add the cornstarch to the juices and cook over medium low heat until thickened, stirring constantly. Yield: 4 to 8 servings.

Janet Price, Xi Alpha Phi
Clarina, Iowa

❖ PORK SAINT TAMMANY

2 (6-ounce) packages long grain and wild rice mix	1/4 cup chopped fresh parsley
1/2 cup boiling water	1/4 teaspoon salt
1/2 cup chopped dried apricots	1/4 teaspoon garlic powder
1/2 cup chopped fresh mushrooms	1/4 teaspoon ground red pepper
1/2 cup chopped green pepper	1/4 teaspoon black pepper
3 green onions, finely chopped	4 (3/4-pound) pork tenderloins
2 tablespoons melted butter or margarine	1/2 cup apricot preserves, melted
2/3 cup chopped pecans, toasted	2 tablespoons honey
	8 slices bacon

Preheat the oven to 375 degrees. Prepare the rice using package directions. Set aside. Pour the boiling water over the apricots; let stand for 20 minutes to soften. Drain the apricots and set aside. Sauté the mushrooms, green pepper and green onions in the butter in a large skillet over medium heat, stirring constantly, until the vegetables are tender. Add the cooked rice, apricots, pecans, parsley, salt, garlic powder, red pepper and black pepper; stir well. Cut a lengthwise slit into the top of each tenderloin toward, but not through, the bottom. Spoon 1 cup of the rice mixture into the opening of 1 tenderloin. Place the cut side of a second tenderloin over the rice mixture. Bring the sides of the meat together, and tie the tenderloins at 3-inch intervals with heavy string. Place on a rack in a roasting pan lined with aluminum foil. Repeat the procedure with the 2 remaining tenderloins and 1 cup of rice. Set the remaining rice mixture aside and keep warm. Combine the apricot preserves and honey; brush the mixture lightly over the tenderloins. Cover the tenderloins with foil and bake for 25 minutes. Uncover the tenderloins and remove the string. Crisscross the bacon slices over the tops of the tenderloins; secure the bacon at the base of each with wooden picks. Brush with the preserves mixture. Bake, uncovered, for 35 to 40 minutes or to 160 degrees on a meat thermometer, basting often with the preserves mixture. Remove from oven and let stand for 5 minutes before slicing. Serve with the reserved rice mixture. Yield: 10 to 12 servings.

Sandy Howell, Laureate Beta
Kelso, Washington

GRILLED PORK TENDERLOINS

1/2 cup teriyaki sauce	1/2 teaspoon ground ginger
1/2 cup soy sauce	1/2 teaspoon pepper
3 tablespoons light brown sugar	1 tablespoon vegetable oil
2 green onions, chopped	3 (1 1/2-pound) pork tenderloins
1 clove of garlic, pressed	
1 tablespoon sesame seeds	

Combine the teriyaki sauce, soy sauce, brown sugar, green onions, garlic, sesame seeds, ginger, pepper and oil in a shallow dish. Dredge the tenderloins in the teriyaki mixture, turning to coat. Chill, covered, in the refrigerator for 2 to 4 hours. Prepare medium-hot coals (350 to 400 degrees) in a barbecue grill. Grill the tenderloins, covered with a grill lid, for 20 minutes to 160 degrees on a meat thermometer, turning once. Yield: 12 to 16 servings.

Jenny Poole, Preceptor Mu
Lexington, Kentucky

Nancy Walton, Kerrville, Texas, prepares Absolutely Fabulous Pork Tenderloin by butterflying 3 pounds tenderloin and packing with a stuffing made of a chopped tomato, 2 or 3 chopped jalapeños, a bunch of cilantro, juice of 1 lime, and salt to taste. Roll up the tenderloin, secure with string, and grill over hot coals for about 25 minutes.

HONEY GRILLED TENDERLOINS

This is a great dish to serve when you have company. The brief grilling time allows more time for socializing.

2 (³/4-pound) pork tenderloins	2 tablespoons light brown sugar
⅓ cup soy sauce	3 tablespoons honey
½ teaspoon ground ginger	2 teaspoons vegetable oil
5 cloves of garlic, halved	

Prepare medium-hot coals (350 to 400 degrees) in a barbecue grill. Trim the fat from the tenderloins and butterfly by making a lengthwise cut in each. Place them in a shallow container or in a large heavy-duty reclosable plastic bag. Combine the soy sauce, ginger and garlic; pour over the tenderloins. Cover or seal. Refrigerate for 4 hours, turning occasionally. Remove the tenderloins from the marinade; discard the marinade. Combine the brown sugar, honey and oil in a small saucepan. Cook over low heat until the sugar dissolves. Coat a barbecue grill with nonstick cooking spray. Arrange the tenderloins on the grill over the coals and brush them with the honey marinade. Grill for 20 minutes or to 160 degrees on a meat thermometer, basting frequently. Yield: 6 to 8 servings.

Dorothy Hay
Blairsville, Georgia

PORK TENDERLOIN PARMIGIANA

This great recipe for company can be made earlier in the day and refrigerated; just increase the baking time. Prepare a salad early as well—then all you'll have to do at serving time is put the tenderloin in the oven and cook some pasta.

1 egg, beaten	1 (14- to 26-ounce) jar spaghetti sauce
½ teaspoon seasoned salt	¼ cup grated Parmesan cheese
⅛ teaspoon pepper	½ cup (4 ounces) shredded mozzarella cheese
1 (2-pound) pork tenderloin	
½ cup bread crumbs	
2 tablespoons vegetable oil	

Preheat the oven to 350 degrees. Combine the egg, salt and pepper in a shallow bowl. Place the bread crumbs in a separate shallow bowl. Dip the tenderloin into the egg mixture, then into the bread crumbs. Heat the oil in a large skillet. Brown the tenderloin on all sides. Place in a 9-by-12-inch baking dish. Pour the spaghetti sauce over the tenderloin. Sprinkle with the Parmesan cheese. Cover with foil and bake for 30 minutes. Remove the foil. Sprinkle the tenderloin with mozzarella cheese. Bake for 10 minutes or to 170 degrees on a meat thermometer. Yield: 4 to 6 servings.

Cherie Moye, Eta Omicron
Rogers, Arkansas

PORK CHOPS WITH CABBAGE AND DUMPLINGS

Large head cabbage, sliced	Salt and pepper to taste
½ teaspoon salt	¼ cup sugar
5 lean pork chops	¼ cup vinegar
Vegetable oil for browning	Dumplings, homemade or made from baking mix
¼ cup all-purpose flour	⅔ cup milk

Place the cabbage with enough water to cover in a large saucepan. Add the ½ teaspoon salt and bring to a boil; simmer for 10 minutes or until cabbage is tender. Drain, reserving 1 cup of the liquid. Brown the pork chops in a small amount of vegetable oil in a large iron skillet or electric frying pan. Remove the pork chops from the pan and set aside. Add the flour with the salt and pepper to taste to the drippings in the pan; stir until the flour is absorbed. Add the reserved 1 cup of liquid from the cooked cabbage, stirring until smooth. Stir in the sugar and vinegar. Return the pork chops to the pan. Add the cabbage to the pan. Allow to simmer, uncovered, while preparing the dumplings; use a dumpling recipe or directions on the baking mix package. Drop the dumplings over the cabbage. Simmer, uncovered, for 10 minutes. Cover and simmer for 10 minutes longer. Yield: 3 to 4 servings.

Marilyn Ramunno
Steamboat Springs, Colorado

SPICY PORK CHOPS

½ cup all-purpose flour	⅛ teaspoon ground oregano
1½ teaspoons garlic powder	⅛ teaspoon salt
1½ teaspoons ground mustard	4 (³/4-inch) pork chops
1½ teaspoons paprika	2 tablespoons olive oil
½ teaspoon celery salt	1 cup chili sauce
¼ teaspoon ground ginger	1 cup water
⅛ teaspoon dried basil	¼ cup firmly packed light brown sugar
	1 cup chopped onion

Preheat the oven to 350 degrees. Combine the flour, garlic powder, mustard, paprika, celery salt, ginger, basil, oregano and salt in a shallow bowl. Dredge both sides of the pork chops in the flour mixture.

Heat the olive oil in a skillet over high heat. Brown the pork chops on both sides in the oil. Place the chops in a greased 9-by-13-inch baking dish. Combine the chili sauce, water and brown sugar. Spread the onions over the pork chops; pour the chili sauce mixture over the onions. Bake for 1 hour or until chops are tender. Yield: 4 servings.

Vergie Stockton, Beta Omicron Master
Fort Worth, Texas

TASTY VEGGIE SLOW-COOKER PORK CHOPS

4 lean pork chops, ½ inch thick
½ teaspoon salt
⅛ teaspoon pepper
2 medium onions, chopped
2 ribs celery, chopped
½ cup sliced fresh mushrooms
1 (15-ounce) can stewed tomatoes
1 beef bouillon cube

½ cup catsup
2 tablespoons red wine vinegar
2 tablespoons light brown sugar
2 tablespoons teriyaki sauce
2 tablespoons cornstarch
2 tablespoons water
Cooked rice (optional)

Place the chops in the bottom of a slow cooker. Sprinkle with the salt and pepper. Add the onions, celery, mushrooms and tomatoes. Dissolve the bouillon cube in a small amount of hot water and combine with the catsup, vinegar, brown sugar, teriyaki sauce and bouillon cube; pour the mixture over the vegetables in the slow cooker. Cover and cook on Low for 5 to 6 hours. Mix the cornstarch and water until smooth; stir into the liquid in the slow cooker. Cover and cook on High for 30 minutes or until thickened. Serve over rice. Yield: 4 servings.

Joan Grabber, Chi Nu
Englewood, Florida

SIMPLE CHOP SUEY

1 (15-ounce) can Oriental vegetables, drained, liquid reserved
½ to ¾ cup precooked instant rice
2 tablespoons cornstarch
2 tablespoons cold water

Leftover fully cooked pork, chicken or roast beef, cut in bite-size pieces
1 (10-ounce) bottle sweet and sour sauce
1 to 2 tablespoons soy sauce
Chow mein noodles (optional)

Measure ½ to ¾ cup of the reserved vegetable liquid. Pour into a saucepan and bring to a boil. Add rice in an amount equal to that of the liquid. Cover and remove from heat. Heat the remaining vegetable liquid in a medium saucepan. Combine the cornstarch and water and add to the vegetable liquid. Simmer, stirring, until the liquid is thickened and clear. Add the cooked meat to the liquid. Add sweet and sour sauce and soy sauce to taste. Stir in the vegetables. Cover and turn off heat. Allow to stand for 10 to 20 minutes. Serve over the rice. Sprinkle with the chow mein noodles. Yield: 4 servings.

Carol Zack, Preceptor Gamma Rho
Kankakee, Illinois

HAWAIIAN SPARERIBS

1 (1- to 2-pound) package country-style spareribs
2 (8-ounce) cans tomato sauce
1 (15-ounce) can pineapple tidbits

1 onion, chopped
½ cup light brown sugar
⅓ cup vinegar
1 tablespoon Worcestershire sauce
½ teaspoon dry mustard

Preheat the oven to 250 degrees. Brown the spareribs in a large pan in the oven for 1 hour. Combine the remaining ingredients; pour over the spareribs. Increase oven temperature to 275 degrees. Bake for 2 hours longer, basting often so ribs remain covered with the sauce. Yield: 4 to 6 servings.

M. Gloria Dimmick, Xi Gamma Iota
Orlando, Florida

MAPLE COUNTRY RIBS

3 pounds country-style pork ribs
1 cup pure maple syrup
½ cup applesauce
¼ cup catsup
3 tablespoons lemon juice

¼ teaspoon salt
¼ teaspoon pepper
¼ teaspoon paprika
¼ teaspoon garlic powder
¼ teaspoon cinnamon

Preheat the oven to 325 degrees. Place the ribs in a large kettle. Cover with water; bring to a boil. Reduce the heat and simmer for 10 minutes. Drain. Place the ribs in a greased 9-by-13-inch baking dish. Combine the maple syrup, applesauce, catsup, lemon juice, salt, pepper, paprika, garlic powder and cinnamon; pour half the mixture over the ribs. Bake, uncovered, for 1½ hours or until meat is tender, basting often with the remaining maple syrup sauce.
Yield: 4 servings.

Judy K. Herning, Zeta Zeta
Pine, Arizona

SPARERIBS AND SAUERKRAUT

Boil the ribs ahead of time and bake when ready to serve. Boiling removes some of the fat so the ribs are low-fat and tasty. These ribs are good served with mashed potatoes.

1 rack pork spareribs	**½ teaspoon salt**
3 bay leaves	**1 (16-ounce) package**
2 cloves of garlic	**sauerkraut**
1 teaspoon seasoned	**¼ cup firmly packed**
salt	**light brown sugar**
½ teaspoon pepper	**(optional)**

Preheat the oven to 350 degrees. Place the ribs in a large kettle and cover ribs with water. Add the bay leaves, garlic, seasoned salt, pepper and salt. Bring to a boil; boil until the ribs are tender. Pour off the water. Place the ribs in a 9-by-13-inch baking dish. Combine the sauerkraut with the brown sugar; cover ribs with sauerkraut. Bake for 30 to 40 minutes, lifting and turning ribs several times to allow more even browning. Yield: 2 to 4 servings.

Patricia Taylor
Garden Grove, California

POTATO BALLS

Have the bacon chopped and slowly frying while you are preparing the potatoes. Have the water boiling—add each potato ball right after you form it.

1 pound bacon, finely	**3 cups dry curd cottage**
chopped	**cheese**
8 medium potatoes,	**¼ cup butter or**
peeled, grated	**margarine**
½ to ¾ cup all-purpose	**¼ teaspoon pepper**
flour	**Salt to taste**
1 teaspoon salt	

Preheat the oven to 350 degrees. Slowly fry the bacon over medium heat until crisp; drain well. Strain the potatoes in a sieve or cheesecloth. Add enough flour to the potatoes to allow the forming of a firm ball. Add the 1 teaspoon salt, mixing well. Form 1-teaspoon balls and drop them into a large kettle of boiling water. Boil for about 30 minutes or until potato balls are cooked through. Drain well. Place in a 2-quart casserole dish. Add the cottage cheese, butter, pepper, salt and bacon; mix well. Bake, covered, for 30 minutes. Yield: 6 to 8 large servings.

Kelly MacDonald
Abbotsford, British Columbia, Canada

HAM LOAF WITH MUSTARD SAUCE

2 pounds ground fresh	**1 cup milk**
pork	**2 eggs**
1 pound ground smoked	**1 teaspoon prepared**
ham	**mustard**
3 cups crushed	**Mustard Sauce**
cornflakes	

Preheat the oven to 350 degrees. Combine the pork, ham, cornflakes, milk, eggs and mustard. Form into a loaf and place in a small roasting pan. Bake for 1½ hours. Serve with warm Mustard Sauce.
Yield: 6 to 8 servings.

MUSTARD SAUCE

⅓ cup brown sugar	**1 teaspoon all-purpose**
⅓ cup cider vinegar	**flour**
⅓ cup hot water	**1 egg, well beaten**
1 teaspoon prepared	**1 tablespoon butter or**
mustard	**margarine**

Mix the first 5 ingredients in a small saucepan; bring to a boil. Remove from heat. Stir in the egg. Return to heat and cook slowly until thick. Stir in the butter; serve warm. Yield: 6 to 8 servings.

Clema Rhoades
Warsaw, Missouri

HAM AND EGGS CRESCENT BRUNCH PIZZA

1 (8-ounce) can	**1 (10-ounce) package**
refrigerated crescent	**frozen broccoli,**
rolls	**thawed, drained**
4 eggs	**1 (4-ounce) jar sliced**
½ teaspoon dry Italian	**mushrooms**
dressing mix	**2 tablespoons chopped**
½ teaspoon salt	**green pepper**
1¼ cups cubed cooked	**1 large tomato, peeled,**
ham	**seeded, diced**
1¼ cups shredded	**2 tablespoons grated**
mozzarella cheese	**Parmesan cheese**

Preheat the oven to 350 degrees. Press the crescent dough triangles evenly on the bottom and ½ inch up the sides of an ungreased pizza pan or 9-by-13-inch baking dish. Seal the perforations. Beat the eggs with the Italian dressing mix and salt; pour into the dough-lined pan. Spread the ham, mozzarella cheese, broccoli, mushrooms, green pepper and tomato over the eggs. Sprinkle with the Parmesan cheese. Bake for 30 to 40 minutes or until eggs are set.
Yield: 6 to 8 servings.

Mary M. Fronczak, Laureate Gamma Nu
Oviedo, Florida

HAWKEYE EGGS

8 hard-cooked eggs,
  halved lengthwise
1/4 cup melted butter or
  margarine
1/2 teaspoon
  Worcestershire sauce
1/4 teaspoon prepared
  mustard
1/2 teaspoon minced
  parsley

1 tablespoon grated
  onion
1/3 cup chopped boiled
  ham
Béchamel Sauce
1 cup shredded
  American cheese

Preheat the oven to 325 degrees. Remove the yolks from the eggs and mash them with the butter, Worcestershire sauce, mustard, parsley, onion and ham in a small bowl. Stuff the egg whites with the yolk mixture. Arrange in a greased 9-by-9-inch baking dish. Pour Béchamel Sauce over the eggs. Bake for 20 minutes. Remove from the oven, sprinkle with the cheese and bake for 5 minutes longer.
Yield: 6 to 8 servings.

BECHAMEL SAUCE

3 tablespoons melted
  butter or margarine
1/4 cup all-purpose flour
1 cup boiling water
1 teaspoon beef bouillon
  granules

Salt and pepper to taste
Paprika to taste
3/4 cup light cream or
  half-and-half

Blend the melted butter and flour in a medium saucepan. Stir in the boiling water and beef bouillon granules. Season with salt, pepper and paprika. Add the light cream. Cook over medium-low heat, stirring, until thick and smooth.

Tamra Wulff, Alpha Tau
Reno, Nevada

HASH BROWN QUICHE

3 cups frozen loose-pack
  shredded hash brown
  potatoes, thawed
1/3 cup melted butter or
  margarine
1 cup diced cooked ham
1 cup shredded Cheddar
  cheese

1/4 cup chopped green
  pepper
2 eggs
1/2 cup milk
1/2 teaspoon salt
1/4 teaspoon pepper

Preheat the oven to 425 degrees. Press the hash brown potatoes between paper towels to remove excess moisture. Press into the bottom and up the sides of an ungreased 9-inch pie plate. Drizzle with the butter. Bake for 25 minutes. Remove from oven and reduce oven heat to 350 degrees. Combine the

ham, cheese and green pepper; spoon over the potato crust. Beat the eggs with the milk, salt and pepper in a small bowl. Pour over the ham mixture. Bake for 25 to 30 minutes. Yield: 6 servings.

Debbie Cargile, Epsilon Pi
Searcy, Arizona

HAM SWISS QUICHE

1 cup (4 ounces)
  shredded Swiss
  cheese
1 (3-ounce) package
  thin-sliced ham,
  julienned
2 green onions

1 unbaked (9-inch) pie
  shell
2 eggs
1 1/4 cups half-and-half
1/2 teaspoon salt
Dash of cayenne pepper
1/8 to 1/4 teaspoon nutmeg

Preheat the oven to 350 degrees. Layer the cheese, ham and green onions in the pie shell. Beat the eggs with the half-and-half, salt, cayenne pepper and nutmeg in a bowl; pour over the onion layer in the pie shell. Bake on the lowest oven rack for 40 minutes or until inserted knife comes out clean. Let stand for 10 minutes before serving. Yield: 6 to 8 servings.

Michelle Cooper, Xi Alpha Mu
Ottumwa, Iowa

❖ IRRESISTIBLE SCAMBOLI

2 loaves Rhodes frozen
  bread dough, thawed
2 eggs
1/2 cup vegetable oil
1/2 teaspoon oregano
1/2 teaspoon garlic
  powder
1/2 teaspoon salt
1/2 teaspoon pepper
1/2 teaspoon basil
1/2 pound pepperoni,
  chopped

1 pound ham, finely
  diced
1 pound sausage or
  ground beef, browned
  until crumbly,
  drained
2 to 3 cups (8 to 12
  ounces) shredded
  mozzarella cheese
Spaghetti sauce
  (optional)

Preheat the oven to 350 degrees. Allow the bread dough to rise. Combine the eggs, oil, oregano, garlic powder, salt, pepper and basil in a small bowl. Combine the pepperoni, ham, sausage and cheese in a separate bowl. Roll the risen bread dough into 2 rectangles. Layer the egg mixture and the pepperoni mixture over the dough. Roll up like a jelly roll, tucking the ends and placing seam side down on a jelly roll pan. Bake for 25 to 30 minutes. Slice and serve with warm spaghetti sauce poured over the slices. Yield: 8 to 10 servings.

Teresa Richter, Beta Sigma
Nicholasville, Kentucky

SPAGHETTI SQUASH CARBONARA

This dish is colorful, light, and tasty. Be sure not to undercook the squash or it will be crunchy.

1 (2½- to 3-pound) spaghetti squash, halved lengthwise	1 clove of minced garlic
2 tablespoons vegetable oil	1 cup fresh snow peas, julienned
1 tablespoon butter or margarine	¼ cup diced red bell pepper
4 ounces smoked ham, julienned	3 large eggs
¼ cup chopped onion	¼ cup grated Parmesan cheese
	Freshly ground black pepper (optional)

Preheat the oven to 350 degrees. Scoop the seeds from the squash. Place the halves cut side down in ½ inch of water in a 9-by-13-inch baking dish. Bake for 35 to 40 minutes or until squash is tender. Heat the oil and butter in a medium skillet over medium heat; sauté the ham, onion and garlic until the onion is soft. Add the snow peas and red bell pepper; sauté for 2 minutes, stirring occasionally. Remove from heat. Beat the eggs with the cheese in a large bowl. Turn the cooked squash halves cut side up; pull out "strands" of the squash with a fork, working carefully so as not to tear the squash shell. Add the hot squash to the egg mixture; toss well. Add the warm ham-vegetable mixture; toss well. Spoon the squash mixture into the shells. Serve with black pepper. Yield: 2 servings.

Marie Bray, Laureate Gamma Nu
Orlando, Florida

CABBAGE AND KIELBASA

I entered this recipe in a local restaurant's recipe contest and won. It's wonderful!

6 slices bacon	1 teaspoon minced garlic
1 medium head cabbage, cut up	1 teaspoon seasoned salt
½ medium onion, chopped	1 pound kielbasa sausage, cut in bite-size pieces
2 tablespoons sugar	
¼ cup water	

Fry the bacon in a large skillet until crisp. Remove the bacon, leaving the drippings in the skillet. Add the next 6 ingredients to the bacon drippings. Cook, covered, over medium heat for 30 to 45 minutes or until cabbage is tender. Stir in the kielbasa; cook for 10 to 15 minutes. Crumble the bacon; sprinkle over the top of the cabbage mixture. Yield: 6 to 8 servings.

Holly Crowell, Zeta Kappa
Red Oak, Iowa

SAUSAGE CASSOULET

12 ounces fully cooked kielbasa sausage	1 (16-ounce) can pork and beans in tomato sauce, undrained
2 tablespoons vegetable oil	1 (15-ounce) can Great Northern beans, drained
1 small onion, chopped	½ teaspoon thyme
1 clove of garlic, minced	⅛ teaspoon pepper
¼ cup white wine	

Split the kielbasa lengthwise, then cut in 3-inch pieces. Heat the oil in an electric skillet. Brown the sausage with the onion and garlic in the hot oil; cook until the sausage is lightly brown and onion is tender. Add the wine (watch for steam!). Reduce the temperature; simmer for 2 to 3 minutes. Stir in the pork and beans, Great Northern beans, thyme and pepper. Simmer, uncovered, for about 10 minutes until beans are heated through. Yield: 4 servings.

Gale Bull, Preceptor Beta Beta
Lakewood, California

CREAM CAN COOKOUT

For a social extravaganza you won't soon forget, try a Cream Can Cookout. It is a recipe for success at an outdoor party. You will need a milk can for the cooking food and a barrel to hold the milk can in place. Cut out the bottom of an old barrel, and place 2 steel bars across it to make it secure when cooking. After simmering the ingredients for about an hour and 45 minutes, the mouth-watering cookout feast can begin!

1 stick margarine	15 to 20 white sweet onions, halved
3 dozen ears of corn, unhusked	40 Polish sausage
1 (10-pound) bag potatoes, washed, cut in half	3 medium heads of cabbage, quartered
8 to 10 pounds carrots, uncut	6-pack beer
	1 (20-pound) bag charcoal

Tightly pack the food items into a milk can in the following manner: Grease the inside of the milk can with the stick of margarine. Place any remaining margarine in the bottom of the milk can. Place the corn, standing on end, at the bottom of the can. Place the potatoes, standing on end, over the corn. Place the carrots, standing on end, over the potatoes. Place the onions over the carrots. Place the sausage, standing on end, over the onions. Place the cabbage on top. Can will be very full, so press down the food items. Pour the beer over the top of the food. Wire the lid tightly to the can. Put the charcoal across the bars in the bottom of the barrel, then place the milk can on top of the charcoal. The can will begin to steam after about 1 hour. After the can begins to steam, allow to cook for 45 minutes longer. Yield: about 22 servings.

Cheryl Punteney, Laureate Beta Phi
Council Bluff, Iowa

SAUSAGE FRUIT BAKE

1 pound pork sausage	**1 (16-ounce) can sliced**
3 tart cooking apples,	**peaches, drained**
peeled, cored	**2 tablespoons melted**
1 (16-ounce) can sweet	**butter or margarine**
potatoes, drained,	**1/4 cup firmly packed**
sliced	**light brown sugar**

Preheat the oven to 375 degrees. Panfry the sausage over medium heat, stirring until crumbly, for 15 to 20 minutes or until cooked through. Drain off excess fat. Cut the cooking apples into eighths. Layer the sausage, sweet potatoes, peaches and apples in a greased 2-quart casserole dish. Pour the melted butter over the top. Sprinkle with the brown sugar. Bake, covered, for 20 minutes. Remove cover; bake for 15 minutes longer or until apples are tender. Yield: 6 servings.

Lucille A. Buckley
Palaika, Florida

SAVORY SANDWICH RING

This is great for Super Bowl parties and lazy Sunday afternoons.

2 (1-pound) loaves	**2 cups chopped lettuce**
refrigerated French	**6 tablespoons Italian**
bread dough	**dressing**
3 cloves of garlic,	**1 medium onion, thinly**
pressed	**sliced**
1/2 teaspoon dried	**1 medium green pepper,**
oregano leaves	**thinly sliced**
1/2 teaspoon dried basil	**1 medium tomato,**
8 ounces thinly sliced	**thinly sliced**
deli meat	**1/2 cup pitted ripe olives,**
4 ounces thinly sliced	**sliced**
Cheddar or Swiss	
cheese	

Preheat the oven to 350 degrees. Place the 2 loaves of bread dough, seam sides down, on a 15-inch round baking stone. Join the ends of the loaves together to form a large ring. Cut 6 to 8 diagonal slashes, 1/2 inch deep, on the top of the dough with a serrated bread knife. Rub the garlic evenly over the dough. Sprinkle with the oregano and basil. Bake for 26 to 30 minutes or until deep golden brown. Remove immediately

from the stone; cool completely. To assemble the sandwich ring, cut the bread ring in half horizontally with a serrated bread knife. Arrange the deli meat and cheese over the lower bread half; cover with the lettuce. Drizzle 2 tablespoons of the dressing over the lettuce. Cover with the onion, green pepper, tomato and olives. Brush the cut side of the top bread half with the remaining salad dressing and place it over the bottom half. Cut into wedges and serve. Yield: 8 servings.

Gari Luttrell
Iberia, Missouri

ROAST LEG OF LAMB WITH POTATO AND TOMATO GRATIN

1 clove of garlic, halved	**2 teaspoons fresh thyme**
2 pounds baking	**leaves**
potatoes, peeled,	**6 cloves of garlic, finely**
sliced	**chopped**
2 large onions, thinly	**2/3 cup dry white wine**
sliced	**1/3 cup extra-virgin olive**
5 large ripe tomatoes,	**oil**
sliced	**1 (6- to 7-pound) leg of**
Coarse salt and fresh	**lamb**
pepper to taste	**Salt and pepper to taste**

Preheat the oven to 400 degrees. Rub the inside of a large (10-by-16-inch) oval roasting pan with the garlic halves. Layer the potatoes, onions and tomatoes in the pan, seasoning each layer with the coarse salt, pepper and 1/3 of the thyme and chopped garlic. Add the wine and olive oil. Trim the thicker portions of the fat from the leg of lamb; season with salt and pepper. Place the pan in the oven and lay a sturdy cake rack over the top of the pan. Set the lamb on the rack so that juices will drip into the gratin. Roast, uncovered, for 1 3/4 hours. (Do not turn the lamb as it cooks.) Remove the lamb from the oven; let stand for 20 minutes before carving. Leave the gratin in the turned-off oven with the door ajar. Carve the lamb into slices; serve on warmed plates or a warmed platter, accompanied by the gratin. Yield: 8 to 10 servings.

Georgina Wilson, Beta Tau
Windsor, Ontario, Canada

Carol Brinkman, Batesville, Indiana, mixes 3 cups shredded lettuce, 1 1/2 cups chopped tomatoes, a 3-ounce jar of bacon bits or 12 slices of crumbled crisp-cooked bacon, 1/3 cup mayonnaise, and pepper to taste. Wrap the mixture in warm flour tortillas (especially flavored tortillas such as Southwestern chile or sun-dried tomato) to make BLT Burritos.

BAKED GOLDEN HONEYED CHICKEN

Sit back and enjoy the compliments.

1 (2- to 3-pound) chicken	**1 cup milk**
Salt and pepper to taste	**½ cup honey**
All-purpose flour	**½ cup sliced mushrooms**
4 tablespoons melted butter or margarine	**(optional)**

Preheat the oven to 400 degrees. Rinse the chicken and pat dry. Season the chicken with salt and pepper and dredge in flour until lightly dusted. Arrange in a 9-by-13-inch baking dish. Pour the melted butter over the chicken. Bake, uncovered, for 30 minutes. Reduce heat to 350 degrees. Combine the milk and honey, stirring until well blended. Pour over the chicken. Bake, uncovered, for 45 minutes to 1 hour longer. Add the mushrooms 15 minutes before chicken will be removed from oven. Yield: 4 to 6 servings.

Diana Payne Peterson
Rio Grande City, Texas

CHICKEN BOLA GAI

If preparing this dish for a large crowd, the chicken may be browned in a large roasting pan in the oven.

2 (2- to 3-pound) chickens, cut into pieces	**4 tablespoons butter or margarine**
½ cup all-purpose flour	**1 (20-ounce) can pineapple chunks in syrup, drained, syrup reserved**
1 teaspoon salt	
1 teaspoon celery salt	
¼ teaspoon garlic salt	**½ cup soy sauce**
¼ teaspoon nutmeg	**2 tablespoons sugar**

Preheat the oven to 350 degrees. Rinse the chicken and pat dry. Place the flour, salt, celery salt, garlic salt and nutmeg in a paper bag. Shake to mix. Shake the chicken in the bag, a few pieces at a time, to lightly coat with the flour mixture. Melt the butter in a skillet. Brown the chicken evenly in the butter, adding more butter if necessary. Place the chicken in a 3-quart baking dish. Combine the pineapple syrup, soy sauce and sugar; pour over the chicken. Bake, covered, for 1 hour, basting with the juices 2 or 3 times. Uncover shortly before the baking is finished and add the pineapple chunks. Yield: 6 to 8 servings.

Sara Louise Brebrick, Preceptor Phi
Las Vegas, Nevada

CHEESY CITRUS CHICKEN

1 (2- to 3-pound) chicken, cut in bite-size pieces	**¼ cup chopped onions**
	1 (10-ounce) can cream of mushroom soup
2 tablespoons melted butter or margarine	**2 cups shredded mozzarella cheese**
Salt and pepper to taste	**Hot cooked rice**
¾ cup orange juice	**⅓ cup toasted almonds**

Preheat the oven to 375 degrees. Rinse the chicken and pat dry. Place the chicken in a 9-by-13-inch baking dish. Brush with the butter; sprinkle with salt and pepper. Bake for 45 minutes; remove from oven. Mix the orange juice, onions, cream of mushroom soup and cheese in a medium bowl. Pour over the chicken. Return to the oven and bake for 15 minutes longer or until chicken is completely cooked. Arrange the chicken over hot rice; spoon the sauce over the chicken. Sprinkle with the almonds. Yield: 6 servings.

Linda Anderson, Preceptor Alpha Phi
Greely, Ontario, Canada

CHICKEN AND CABBAGE CASSEROLE

1 (2- to 3-pound) chicken, cut up	**1 (8-ounce) can tomato sauce**
⅓ cup all-purpose flour	**2 teaspoons caraway seeds**
½ teaspoon seasoned salt	
½ teaspoon celery seed	**¼ teaspoon salt**
¼ cup vegetable oil	**1 teaspoon sugar**
⅔ cup chopped onions	**4 cups shredded cabbage**
1 (15-ounce) can tomatoes	**4 cups shredded mozzarella cheese**

Preheat the oven to 350 degrees. Rinse the chicken and pat dry. Combine the flour, seasoned salt and celery seed in a plastic bag. Shake the chicken in the bag, a few pieces at a time, to lightly coat with the flour mixture. Heat the oil in a skillet over medium heat. Cook the chicken in the oil, turning, for about 10 minutes or until brown on all sides. Remove the chicken from the skillet and place in a 9-by-13-inch baking dish. Sauté the onions for about 3 minutes in the same skillet. Stir in the tomatoes, tomato sauce, caraway seeds, salt and sugar. Bring to a boil. Add the cabbage, stirring to combine well. Spoon the mixture over the chicken, lifting the chicken pieces to allow some cabbage mixture to run underneath. Cover with aluminum foil and bake for about 1 hour. Remove the foil. Sprinkle the cheese over the chicken. Return to the oven to bake for 1 minute longer. Yield: 4 servings.

Barbara Sherstone
Nanaimo, British Columbia, Canada

CHICKEN AND DUMPLINGS

1 (2- to 3-pound) whole chicken	8 to 12 pearl onions
1 medium onion, coarsely chopped	3 medium carrots, peeled, sliced
1/3 lemon	1 small head cabbage, cut up
2 (10-ounce) cans vegetable broth	1 tablespoon sugar
1 tablespoon seasoned salt	2 cups all-purpose flour
	2 teaspoons baking powder

Rinse the chicken and pat it dry. Mix chicken, onion, lemon, 1 can of the vegetable broth, seasoned salt and enough water to cover in a large Dutch oven over medium-high heat. Boil for about 45 minutes or until the juices run clear when the chicken is pierced with a fork. Remove from heat. Remove the chicken to a cooling plate, allowing broth to remain in the Dutch oven. Discard the lemon. When chicken is cool enough to handle, remove skin and bones. Return the chicken meat to the broth with the pearl onions, carrots, cabbage and sugar. Add the remaining vegetable broth and enough water to bring the liquid level almost to the top of the Dutch oven. Simmer for about 30 minutes. Combine the flour and baking powder. Add enough water to make a dough that is soft but not sticky. Roll very thinly on a floured surface. Cut into strips. Bring the chicken mixture to a rapid boil; add the dumplings 1 at a time. Cook until the dumplings rise to the surface. Yield: 6 servings.

Lynne Wiggins, Xi Alpha
Honolulu, Hawaii

HUNGARIAN CHICKEN PAPRIKASH

My great-grandmother, who came over to the States from Hungary during World War II, always made this meal for us when we visited her in Ohio. Serve it over rice or noodles.

1 (4- to 5-pound) chicken, cut in pieces	4 tablespoons paprika
1 onion, sliced	1 teaspoon pepper
4 tablespoons shortening	2 tablespoons salt
	2 1/2 cups water
	1 cup sour cream

Rinse the chicken and pat dry. Sauté the onion in the shortening in a large skillet over medium heat for 3 to 4 minutes. Add the seasonings and chicken; sauté 10 minutes longer. Add the water. Simmer slowly, covered, until chicken is tender. Remove the chicken. Add the sour cream to the pan drippings; mix well. Return the chicken to the pan. Yield: 6 servings.

Rebecca Danford
Brazoria, Texas

ARROZ CON POLLO (CHICKEN AND RICE)

1 (3-pound) chicken, cut in 6 to 8 serving pieces	1/4 teaspoon cayenne pepper
1/4 cup olive oil	1 bay leaf
1 large onion, chopped	1/2 teaspoon paprika
3 cloves of garlic, minced	1/4 teaspoon ground saffron or turmeric
1 green pepper, seeded, deribbed, chopped	2 cups water
1 1/4 cups peeled, seeded, chopped tomatoes	1 1/2 cups white wine
1/2 teaspoon salt	1 (10-ounce) package frozen green peas
1/4 teaspoon freshly ground black pepper	2 cups long grain white rice
	Roasted red bell pepper strips for garnish

Rinse the chicken and pat dry. Heat the oil in a large skillet over medium heat. Sauté the chicken pieces in the oil, a few at a time, until lightly browned on all sides. Set the chicken aside on paper towels. Drain all but 1 tablespoon of the fat from the skillet. Sauté the onion, garlic and green pepper for 3 to 5 minutes, until the onion is translucent but not brown. Add the tomatoes, salt, black pepper, cayenne pepper, bay leaf, paprika, saffron and water. Cover and bring to a boil. Add the chicken. Simmer, covered, over medium-low heat for 30 minutes. Stir in the wine, peas and rice. Simmer, covered, for 20 minutes longer. Transfer to a large serving platter. Garnish with roasted red pepper strips and serve hot. Yield: 6 to 8 servings.

Mirtha Grayaon
Pahokee, Florida

CHICKEN AND BRIE CROQUE

1/2 prepared rotisserie chicken	1/3 pound Brie cheese, thinly sliced
8 slices sturdy bread	2 eggs
8 tablespoons whole-berry cranberry sauce	2/3 cup milk
	Grated rind of 1 orange

Preheat the oven to 400 degrees. Bone the chicken and cut the meat into thin slices. Place 4 slices of the bread on a work surface. Spread 2 tablespoons of the cranberry sauce on each bread slice. Top with the chicken slices. Top with Brie slices. Cover with the remaining slices of bread. Beat the eggs, milk and orange rind together in a shallow bowl. Dip the sandwiches into the egg mixture, coating both sides. Arrange on a baking sheet. Bake for 15 to 20 minutes, turning once. Yield: 4 servings.

Esther-Lee Powers, Psi Mu
North Miami Beach, Florida

CHEESE STUFFED CHICKEN

4 boneless skinless
chicken breast halves
1/2 cup (2 ounces)
shredded Monterey
Jack cheese
1/2 cup (2 ounces)
shredded Cheddar
cheese
2 tablespoons unsalted
butter or margarine,
softened
2 tablespoons chopped
parsley

1/4 teaspoon dried
tarragon or 2
teaspoons chopped
fresh tarragon
1/2 teaspoon pepper
1/4 teaspoon salt
Salt and pepper to
season chicken
8 sheets phyllo dough
4 tablespoons melted
unsalted butter or
margarine

Preheat the oven to 350 degrees. Rinse the chicken and pat dry. Place the Monterey Jack cheese, Cheddar cheese, the 2 tablespoons softened butter, parsley, tarragon, pepper and salt in a bowl. Beat and mash the ingredients together until they form a stiff paste, using your fingers or a big wooden spoon. Divide the mixture into 4 finger-shaped logs, each about 3 inches long. Set aside. Flatten each chicken breast by placing it between 2 sheets of plastic wrap or waxed paper and pounding with a mallet or rolling pin until roughly 1/4 inch thick and 5 to 6 inches across. Season lightly with salt and pepper. Place a cheese log in the center of each breast, then roll and fold the chicken around the cheese to enclose it completely. Place a sheet of phyllo dough on your work surface. Top with a second sheet and brush lightly with melted butter. Place a chicken breast in the center of one of the narrower ends; roll it up in the phyllo, tucking the ends of the dough under to enclose the chicken in a neat package. Repeat the process with the remaining chicken breasts. Place the packages folds down in a 9-by-13-inch baking dish. Brush with the remaining melted butter. Bake for about 40 minutes to 170 degrees on a meat thermometer, or until sizzling and well browned. Yield: 4 servings.

Susan Nilson, Xi Pi Gamma
Rohnert Park, California

CHICKEN ANGELIS

3 whole chicken breasts,
split, boned, skinned
Salt and pepper to taste
1/2 cup melted butter or
margarine
1 tablespoon parsley
1 teaspoon marjoram
1/2 teaspoon thyme

8 ounces sliced
mozzarella cheese
2 cups all-purpose flour
3 eggs, beaten
2 cups seasoned
breadcrumbs
1/2 cup white wine

Preheat the oven to 350 degrees. Rinse the chicken and pat dry. Lay the chicken breasts on waxed paper. Sprinkle with salt and pepper. Spoon a little melted butter on each breast. Add the parsley, marjoram and thyme to the remaining butter; combine and set aside. Lay a slice of cheese on each chicken breast. Roll up each breast. Dredge each roll in the flour, dip in the eggs and roll in the breadcrumbs. Arrange in a greased 9-by-13-inch baking pan. Drizzle with the butter-herb mixture. Bake for 25 minutes. Pour the wine over the chicken and bake for 15 to 20 minutes longer, basting occasionally. Yield: 4 servings.

Nikki Angelis, Tau Omega
Parma, Ohio

ARTICHOKE CHICKEN BREASTS

3 chicken breasts,
halved
1/2 teaspoon minced
garlic
2 tablespoons butter or
margarine
1 (10-ounce) can cream
of chicken soup
1 (8-ounce) carton sour
cream

1/2 cup shredded Cheddar
cheese
1/4 cup chicken broth
2 tablespoons grated
Parmesan cheese
1 (6-ounce) jar
marinated artichoke
hearts, drained
Cooked noodles

Rinse the chicken and pat dry. Brown the chicken and garlic in the butter in a skillet over medium heat. Combine the cream of chicken soup, sour cream, Cheddar cheese, chicken broth and Parmesan cheese in a bowl; stir into the chicken. Simmer, covered, for 5 to 7 minutes or until chicken is tender. Remove the chicken; add the artichoke hearts. Simmer for 1 to 2 minutes. Return the chicken to the skillet. Serve over noodles. Yield: 6 servings.

Vickie Thomas
Weiser, Idaho

Georgine Wasley, Preceptor Nu Delta, Nevada City, California, makes Pollo Rellenos by pounding boneless skinless chicken breasts flat, placing peeled seeded green chiles and Monterey Jack cheese on the chicken, spinkling with red pepper and cilantro, and rolling up. Dip each in beaten eggs, roll in a mixture of 1/2 cup cornmeal and 1/2 envelope taco seasoning mix, and place in a greased shallow baking pan. After sprinkling with any remaining cornmeal mix, additional cilantro and cheese, bake in a preheated 400-degree oven for 40 to 50 minutes and serve with guacamole and salsa.

CHICKEN WITH CREAMY DIJON MUSTARD SAUCE

4 medium boneless
   chicken breast halves
16 ounces medium-size
   mushrooms, thinly
   sliced
1 large onion, diced
2 tablespoons butter or
   margarine
2 teaspoons vegetable
   oil

½ teaspoon salt
1 (9-ounce) package
   frozen artichoke
   hearts
½ cup water
1 cup half-and-half
¼ cup Dijon mustard
Cooked rice or noodles
1 tablespoon parsley for
   garnish

Rinse the chicken and pat dry. Sauté the mushrooms and onion in the butter in a 12-inch skillet over medium-high heat. Remove the mushrooms and onion; set aside in a bowl. Add the oil to the skillet; cook the chicken in the oil over medium heat for 10 to 12 minutes or until the chicken is golden. Stir in the mushrooms, onion, salt, artichoke hearts and water. Bring to a boil. Reduce heat to medium; cook for 5 minutes longer. Reduce heat to low; stir in the half-and-half and Dijon mustard. Heat completely. Serve over rice or noodles. Garnish with parsley. Yield: 4 servings.

Krista Fry
Salem, Oregon

CHICKEN BREAST JUBILEE

You can vary this recipe by trying different salad dressings and different fruit pie fillings such as peach or apricot. For even quicker cooking, use frozen pre-cooked chicken breasts and shorten the cooking time in the oven or use the microwave.

6 to 8 boneless skinless
   chicken breast halves
1 teaspoon salt
¼ teaspoon pepper
¼ cup melted margarine
2 tablespoons dried
   minced onion
½ cup chili sauce

1 (8-ounce) bottle
   Russian salad
   dressing or sweet-
   and-sour salad
   dressing
1 (21-ounce) can black
   cherry pie filling
Hot cooked rice

Rinse the chicken and pat dry. Sprinkle the chicken breasts with the salt and pepper. Sauté in the margarine in a skillet over medium heat until brown, or drizzle with the margarine and broil until brown. Combine the next 4 ingredients. Spoon over the browned chicken breasts in a 9-by-13-inch baking dish. Bake for 1 hour or until chicken is tender. Serve over rice. Yield: 6 to 8 servings.

Joyce Horvath, Preceptor Epsilon Lambda
Wellington, Ohio

NITA'S MACADAMIA CHICKEN

6 boneless skinless
   chicken breast halves
¼ teaspoon salt
⅛ teaspoon pepper
½ cup finely ground
   macadamia nuts

½ cup all-purpose flour
2 tablespoons butter or
   margarine
2 cups heavy cream

Rinse the chicken and pat dry. Sprinkle the chicken breasts with the salt and pepper. Place in a 9-by-13-inch glass baking dish that has been sprayed with nonstick cooking spray or greased. Combine the nuts and flour; sprinkle over the chicken breasts. Place 1 teaspoon of butter on each breast. Pour the cream over the chicken. Chill for 8 to 10 hours. Preheat the oven to 400 degrees. Bake, uncovered, for 15 minutes. Reduce oven heat to 350 degrees. Bake, covered, for 30 to 45 minutes longer or until chicken is cooked through. Yield: 6 servings.

Nita Price, Preceptor Delta Eta
Arlington, Texas

CHICKEN MARBELLA

This dish keeps well for several days in the refrigerator. It is good served hot or at room temperature.

3 to 4 pounds boneless
   chicken breasts
1 clove of garlic, peeled,
   finely puréed
¼ cup dried oregano
Salt and pepper to taste
½ cup red wine vinegar
½ cup olive oil
½ cup Spanish green
   olives

1 cup pitted prunes
½ cup capers with a bit
   of juice
6 bay leaves
1 cup packed light
   brown sugar
1 cup white wine
½ cup chopped fresh
   parsley or cilantro

Rinse the chicken and pat dry. Combine the chicken and the next 10 ingredients in a large bowl. Marinate, covered, in the refrigerator for 8 to 10 hours. Preheat the oven to 350 degrees. Arrange the chicken breasts in a single layer in an 11-by-13-inch baking pan. Spoon the marinade evenly over the chicken. Sprinkle the brown sugar over and pour the wine around the chicken. Bake, uncovered, for 50 minutes to 1 hour, basting often with the pan juices. Remove the chicken, prunes and olives from the pan with a slotted spoon, arranging them on a serving platter. Moisten the chicken with some of the pan juices and sprinkle with the parsley. Serve accompanied by the remaining pan juices in a gravy boat.
Yield: 8 to 10 servings.

Valerie McPherson, Preceptor Alpha Theta
Kelowna, British Columbia, Canada

BASIL GRILLED CHICKEN

4 chicken breast halves,
 skinned
3/4 teaspoon coarsely
 ground black pepper
1/3 cup melted butter or
 margarine
1/4 cup chopped fresh
 basil
1/2 cup butter or
 margarine, softened

2 tablespoons minced
 fresh basil
1 tablespoon grated
 Parmesan cheese
1/4 teaspoon garlic
 powder
1/8 teaspoon salt
1/8 teaspoon pepper
Fresh sprigs of basil
 (optional)

Prepare charcoal for grilling or preheat a gas grill. Rinse the chicken and pat dry. Press the 3/4 teaspoon ground black pepper into the meaty sides of the chicken breast halves. Combine the 1/3 cup melted butter with the 1/4 cup chopped basil in a small bowl; stir well. Brush the chicken lightly with the melted butter mixture. Combine the 1/2 cup softened butter, the 2 tablespoons minced basil, Parmesan cheese, garlic powder, salt and pepper in a small bowl; beat with an electric mixer on low speed until well blended and smooth. Transfer to a small serving bowl; set aside. Grill the chicken over medium coals for 10 minutes on each side, basting frequently with remaining melted butter mixture. Serve with the butter-garlic mixture. Garnish with basil sprigs. Yield: 4 servings.

Syble Ann Shoults, Xi Alpha Xi
Bessemer, Alabama

GRILLED CHICKEN PIZZA

This is one of those good recipes that came from having leftover grilled chicken. It makes a wonderful complete meal that has bread, meat, and vegetables.

2 (10-ounce) cans
 refrigerated crescent
 rolls
1/4 cup chopped green
 onions
8 ounces mushrooms,
 sliced
1 red bell pepper,
 roasted, peeled,
 chopped
3 tablespoons margarine
1/4 cup port wine

1/2 cup whole kernel
 corn, drained
1/4 cup Dijon honey
 barbecue sauce
2 boneless skinless
 chicken breasts,
 grilled, cut into bite-
 size pieces
1/2 cup shredded
 mozzarella or
 Cheddar cheese

Preheat the oven to 425 degrees. Spray a baking sheet with nonstick cooking spray. Unroll the crescent roll dough and pat into the baking sheet. Bake the dough for 6 minutes. Sauté the green onions, mushrooms and red bell pepper in the margarine until vegetables are tender, for 5 to 10 minutes. Add the wine; cook over medium heat until liquid is slightly reduced. Add the corn, barbecue sauce and chicken; cook over medium-low heat until heated through, stirring constantly. Spread the chicken mixture over the baked dough. Sprinkle with the cheese. Bake for 6 minutes. Yield: 4 servings.

Merline McCoy, Alpha Psi Master
Village Mills, Texas

HERBED CHICKEN A LA FRANCAISE

4 boneless skinless
 chicken breast halves
2 green onions, chopped
1/2 teaspoon dried
 crushed tarragon
1 tablespoon butter or
 margarine
Salt and pepper to taste

1/2 cup white wine or
 chicken broth
1 egg white
1 tablespoon grated
 Parmesan cheese
1 tablespoon snipped
 parsley for garnish

Preheat the oven to 350 degrees. Rinse the chicken and pat dry. Arrange the chicken breast halves in an 8-by-12-inch baking dish. Sprinkle with the green onions and tarragon. Dot with butter. Season with salt and pepper. Pour the wine into the baking dish. Bake, uncovered, for 30 minutes. Remove from oven. Beat the egg white in a mixer bowl until stiff peaks form. Spoon the egg white over the chicken breasts. Sprinkle with the Parmesan cheese. Return to oven. Bake, uncovered, for 12 to 15 minutes. Sprinkle the chicken with parsley. Yield: 4 servings.

Rose Kinczel
Twinsburg, Ohio

HERBED CHICKEN EN CASSEROLE

This chicken dish may be served over rice or noodles.

6 chicken breast halves
Salt and pepper to taste
1/4 cup butter or
 margarine
1 (10-ounce) can cream
 of mushroom soup
3/4 cup sauterne
2 tablespoons chopped
 green pepper

1 (5-ounce) can water
 chestnuts
1 (3-ounce) can sliced
 mushrooms, drained
1/4 teaspoon crushed
 thyme

Preheat the oven to 350 degrees. Rinse the chicken and pat dry. Lightly season the chicken with salt and pepper. Brown slowly in the butter in a skillet over medium-low heat. Remove to a 9-by-12-inch baking dish. Add the cream of mushroom soup to the drippings in the skillet over medium-low heat to make the sauce. Add the sauterne slowly, stirring until smooth. Stir in the green pepper, water chestnuts, mushrooms and thyme. Pour over the chicken. Bake uncovered for 40 to 45 minutes. Yield: 6 servings.

Frances McMullen
Hilltop Lakes, Texas

MAPLE WALNUT CHICKEN

4 (8-ounce) boneless skinless chicken breast halves	**1⅓ cups chopped walnuts**
1 egg, lightly beaten with 1 teaspoon water	**8 tablespoons maple syrup**
1 cup finely crushed butter crackers	**4 tablespoons melted butter or margarine**

Preheat the oven to 450 degrees. Rinse the chicken and pat dry. Dip the chicken in the egg wash, then dredge through the cracker crumbs. Place chicken in a foil-lined 9-by-12-inch baking dish. Press ¼ of the walnuts into each breast. Pour 1 tablespoon syrup over each breast; drizzle 1 tablespoon melted butter over each. Bake for 10 to 12 minutes until the nuts darken and crust is golden. Drizzle another 1 tablespoon maple syrup over each breast. Serve hot. Yield: 4 servings.

Marjorie A. Bailey, Epsilon Master
Kittery Point, Maine

CHICKEN IN WINE SAUCE

This chicken dish is good served with rice pilaf, fruit or vegetable salad, buttered rolls, and asparagus or broccoli.

8 boneless skinless chicken breast halves	**1 (6-ounce) can sliced mushrooms**
1 cup all-purpose flour	**1 medium onion, finely chopped**
⅛ teaspoon thyme	**1 tablespoon dried parsley flakes**
2 teaspoons salt	
½ teaspoon pepper	**1 (8-ounce) can sliced water chestnuts, drained**
6 tablespoons butter or margarine	
2 (10-ounce) cans cream of chicken soup	**1 teaspoon garlic powder**
1 cup dry sherry	

Preheat the oven to 350 degrees. Rinse the chicken and pat dry. Combine the flour, thyme, salt and pepper in a plastic bag. Shake the chicken in the bag until coated. Melt the butter in a heavy skillet; brown the chicken in the butter. Remove chicken to a 9-by-13-inch glass baking dish. Make a sauce by stirring the cream of chicken soup, sherry, mushrooms, onion, parsley, water chestnuts and garlic powder into the butter remaining in the skillet. Heat over medium-low heat. Pour evenly over the chicken breasts in the baking dish. Bake, covered, for 1 hour. Yield: 4 to 6 servings.

Nedra J. Murphy, Xi Phi Iota
Victorville, California

COQ AU VIN BLANC

4 chicken breast halves	**½ cup white wine**
5 tablespoons all-purpose flour	**½ cup boiling water**
	2 chicken bouillon cubes
¼ teaspoon salt	**¼ teaspoon thyme**
¼ teaspoon paprika	**¼ teaspoon garlic salt**
⅛ teaspoon pepper	**½ bay leaf**
¼ cup butter or margarine	**Fluffy cooked rice**

Rinse the chicken and pat dry. Measure the flour, salt, paprika and pepper into a strong paper bag; shake to mix. Add the chicken breasts and shake to coat. Cook the chicken in the butter in a medium-large skillet over medium heat until golden brown. Remove the chicken to a holding plate. Add the remaining flour mixture to the skillet, stirring into the butter. Combine the wine, water, bouillon cubes, thyme, garlic salt and bay leaf; stir into the butter-flour mixture. Heat, stirring constantly, until the mixture is boiling gently. Reduce the heat. Return the chicken to the skillet. Simmer, covered, for 1¼ hours. Serve over rice. Yield: 4 servings.

Linda Alkema, Xi Gamma Xi
Elmvale, Ontario, Canada

CHICKEN VERMOUTH

4 chicken breast halves	**1 cup sliced mushrooms**
1 tablespoon olive oil	**½ cup vermouth**
2 cloves of garlic, minced	**Salt and pepper to taste**

Rinse the chicken and pat dry. Heat the olive oil in a skillet over medium-low heat. Add the garlic; cook for 2 minutes. Brown the chicken on both sides in the olive oil. Stir in the mushrooms; cook for 1 or 2 minutes. Remove chicken from skillet. Add the vermouth, stirring and scraping the bottom of the skillet. Cook until the vermouth is reduced to a sauce consistency. Return the chicken to the pan and stir to coat with the sauce. Yield: 4 servings.

Gloria Guericke, Beta Alpha
Pierre, South Dakota

CHICKEN ROLLUPS

My husband and I raise poultry for a living. We love chicken, and this is a very tasty dish! Low-fat or reduced-fat products may be used in this recipe.

2 (8-count) cans
  refrigerated biscuits
4 chicken breast halves
  or leg quarters,
  cooked, cooled, boned
1 cup milk
1 (10-ounce) can cream
  of chicken soup

1 to 1½ cups chicken
  broth
Salt and pepper to taste
½ to 1 stick butter or
  margarine

Preheat the oven to 375 degrees. Flatten the refrigerated biscuit dough. Place chicken meat in the center of each flattened biscuit and roll up jelly roll style. Arrange the rolled biscuits in a 9-by-13-inch baking dish. Combine the milk, cream of chicken soup and broth; pour over the rolled biscuits. Season with salt and pepper. Dot with butter. Bake for 30 to 40 minutes. Yield: 8 to 10 servings.

Phyllis G. Moore, Epsilon Eta
Jonesboro, Louisiana

VANILLA WAFER CHICKEN

4 boneless skinless
  chicken breast halves
¼ cup all-purpose flour
1 egg, beaten
1 cup crushed vanilla
  wafers
4 tablespoons butter or
  margarine
1 teaspoon minced
  ginger

1 clove of garlic, minced
1 cup chicken broth
1 medium red bell
  pepper, sliced
2 tablespoons sherry
2 tablespoons white
  vinegar
2 tablespoons soy sauce
1 tablespoon sugar

Rinse the chicken and pat dry. Dredge the chicken breasts in the flour until lightly coated; dip in the egg. Roll in the vanilla wafer crumbs; reserve remaining crumbs. Brown chicken in 3 tablespoons of the butter in a skillet over medium heat. Reduce heat. Cook for 15 to 20 minutes or until chicken tests done. Remove from skillet to a serving plate. Add the remaining 1 tablespoon butter, ginger and garlic to the skillet; sauté for 1 minute. Add the red bell pepper; sauté for 2 to 3 minutes. Stir in the sherry, vinegar, soy sauce, sugar and the reserved vanilla wafer crumbs. Spoon over the chicken.
Yield: 4 servings.

Denise Ladenburg, Xi Tau
Havre, Montana

❖ CHICKEN BREASTS IN PHYLLO DOUGH

This delicious recipe is best if made early in the day to allow plenty of time for the chicken to marinate in the refrigerator. Another type of baking pan can be used if a jelly roll pan is not available. Be sure to keep unused phyllo dough covered—it will dry out very quickly. Butter-flavored cooking spray may be substituted for the melted butter, but do not use margarine as a substitute.

8 boneless skinless
  chicken breast halves
1 cup mayonnaise
⅔ cup chopped green
  onions
3½ tablespoons lemon
  juice
1 small clove of garlic,
  mined
¾ teaspoon dried
  tarragon

¼ teaspoon salt
⅛ teaspoon pepper
16 sheets frozen phyllo
  dough, thawed
½ cup melted butter, or
  butter-flavored
  cooking spray
3½ tablespoons grated
  Parmesan cheese

Preheat the oven to 350 degrees. Rinse the chicken and pat dry. Combine the next 5 ingredients in a small bowl. Sprinkle the chicken with the salt and pepper. Place 1 sheet of phyllo dough on a sheet of plastic wrap. Brush butter evenly over the phyllo, using enough butter to lightly coat. Place a second sheet of phyllo over the first and brush with butter. Spread about 3 tablespoons of the mayonnaise mixture on both sides of a chicken breast half. Place the chicken diagonally across 1 corner of the buttered phyllo. Fold the end and sides of the phyllo dough inward; carefully roll up the dough. Place seam side down on an ungreased jelly roll pan. Repeat with the rest of the chicken and phyllo. Spread more melted butter over the top and sprinkle with the Parmesan cheese. Bake for 40 to 45 minutes. Yield: 8 servings.

Connie A. Flaugher, Xi Gamma Rho
Petersburg, West Virginia

Judy Ramer, Xi Beta Theta, North Little Rock, Arkansas, makes Quick Chicken and Dumplings by boiling 4 to 6 chicken breasts in water to cover. Cut the chicken into bite-size pieces and dissolve 3 or 4 chicken bouillon cubes in the broth. Return the chicken to the broth, pinch 2 cans of refrigerated biscuits into small pieces, and drop into boiling broth. Boil for 5 minutes, stirring occasionally. Add a can of cream of chicken soup, reduce heat, and simmer for 10 to 15 minutes, stirring occasionally.

CHICKEN, BROCCOLI AND STUFFING CASSEROLE

4 cups herb-seasoned stuffing cubes
1¼ cups boiling water
½ cup melted margarine
16 ounces frozen broccoli pieces, cooked
4 to 6 whole boneless skinless chicken breasts, cooked, cut into bite-size pieces
4 ounces cream cheese, softened
1 (10-ounce) can cream of mushroom soup
1 cup mayonnaise
¼ cup milk
1 teaspoon garlic powder
1 cup (4 ounces) shredded Cheddar cheese
1 (6-ounce) package butter crackers, crumbled

Preheat the oven to 400 degrees. Spray a 9-by-13-inch baking dish with nonstick cooking spray. Combine the stuffing cubes with the boiling water and 4 table-spoons of the melted margarine. Spoon the stuffing into the baking dish to make an even layer. Combine the broccoli and chicken; spread over the stuffing, then mash into the stuffing. Combine the cream cheese and cream of mushroom soup in a medium bowl. Stir in the mayonnaise; mix well. Stir in the milk, garlic powder and Cheddar cheese. Pour the cream cheese-soup mixture over the chicken and broccoli. Combine the remaining 4 tablespoons melted margarine with the crumbled butter crackers; spread over the top of the casserole. Bake for 30 minutes. Yield: 6 to 8 servings.

Shelly Brandom, Gamma Omicron
Carrollton, Texas

BAKED SUPER BOWL WHITE CHILI

1 medium onion, chopped
1 clove of garlic, chopped
Cumin to taste
1 tablespoon vegetable oil
2 large whole boneless skinless chicken breasts, cut into 1-inch cubes
1 (16-ounce) can white kidney beans, drained
1 (16-ounce) can garbanzo beans, drained
1 (16-ounce) can white navy beans, drained
2 (4-ounce) cans chopped green chiles, drained
1 (12-ounce) can white corn, drained
2 chicken bouillon cubes
1½ cups water
Hot pepper sauce to taste
1 cup shredded Monterey Jack cheese
Parsley sprigs

Preheat the oven to 350 degrees. Sauté the onion, garlic and cumin in the oil in a medium skillet over medium-low heat until onion is tender but not brown. Combine onion mixture with the chicken, kidney beans, garbanzo beans, navy beans, green chiles and corn in a large bowl. Dissolve the bouillon cubes in the water; stir into the chicken mixture. Spoon into a lightly greased 2½-quart casserole dish. Bake, covered, for 50 to 60 minutes or until chicken is cooked through and tender. Add the hot pepper sauce. Sprinkle with the cheese. Garnish with parsley sprigs. Yield: 8 servings.

Betty Dyer, Zeta Master
Rome, New York

BAKED MEXICAN CHICKEN

8 ounces thin egg noodles
4 cooked boneless skinless chicken breast halves
¼ cup vegetable oil
½ cup chopped onions
¾ cup green or red bell pepper
6 ounces plain yogurt
1 teaspoon garlic salt
½ teaspoon chili powder
½ teaspoon cumin
6 eggs
¾ cup shredded Monterey Jack cheese
1 cup diced green chile peppers
3 ounces tortilla chips, crushed

Preheat the oven to 350 degrees. Cook the noodles in boiling water until barely tender, about 2 to 4 minutes. Drain, rinse and turn into a large bowl. Cut the chicken into strips. Heat the oil in a skillet over medium heat. Sauté the chicken, onions and bell pepper until onion is translucent. Combine the yogurt, garlic salt, chili powder, cumin and eggs in a blender container; process until smooth. Add this mixture to the noodles; mix well. Stir in the cheese and chile peppers. Spread in a 9-by-13-inch baking dish that has been sprayed with nonstick cooking spray. Spread the chicken mixture over the noodles. Cover with the tortilla chips. Bake, covered, for 45 to 55 minutes. Uncover and bake for 5 to 10 minutes. Let stand for 5 minutes before serving. Yield: 8 servings.

Walda Weaver, Xi Gamma Omicron
Pryor, Oklahoma

Linda Wilson, Xi Nu Zeta, Jacksonville, Florida, makes a Hot Curried Chicken Casserole by mixing 5 cups chopped cooked chicken with a 12-ounce bottle of coleslaw dressing, ¼ cup mayonnaise, 2 teaspoons curry powder, 1 cup grapes, and a small can of drained mandarin oranges. Pour into an ungreased 9-by-13-inch baking dish and bake in a preheated 350-degree oven for 30 minutes.

CHICKEN OLE

3 whole boneless
    skinless chicken
    breasts, cooked,
    cubed
1 medium onion,
    chopped
1 (10-ounce) can
    tomatoes with green
    chiles
1 (10-ounce) can cream
    of mushroom soup

2 tablespoons dry
    tapioca
8 (8-inch) soft flour
    tortillas, moistened
    and torn up
2 cups (8 ounces)
    shredded Cheddar
    cheese

Preheat the oven to 350 degrees. Combine the chicken, onion, tomatoes with green chiles, cream of mushroom soup and tapioca. Grease a 3-quart deep casserole dish, or spray with nonstick cooking spray. Layer 4 of the tortillas, half the chicken mixture and half the cheese in the dish; repeat the layers. Bake, covered, for 30 to 45 minutes. Yield: 6 servings.

Conni Blessing, Tau Delta
La Grange, Missouri

BEST CHICKEN NOODLE CASSEROLE

To cut down on fat content, use the low-fat versions of the soup, sour cream, and cream cheese. You can also use no-yolk noodles and skinless chicken.

3 (1-pound) whole
    chicken breasts
1 (8-ounce) package
    noodles
2 (10-ounce) cans cream
    of mushroom soup
1 cup sour cream
1 (8-ounce) package
    cream cheese,
    softened

1 small onion, finely
    chopped
Salt and pepper to taste
Garlic salt to taste
1 cup fine bread crumbs
1/2 cup melted butter or
    margarine

Preheat the oven to 350 degrees. Cover the chicken with water in a medium saucepan. Bring to a boil; simmer until chicken is tender and cooked through. Remove the chicken, retaining the broth in the pan. Cook the noodles in the chicken broth using package directions. Bone the chicken while the noodles are cooking; cut into bite-size pieces. Combine the next 4 ingredients in a large bowl. Stir in the chicken and noodles. Season with salt, pepper and garlic salt. Spread in a greased 9-by-13-inch baking dish. Combine the bread crumbs with the butter; sprinkle over the noodle mixture. Bake for 45 to 50 minutes or until bubbly. Yield: 6 to 8 servings.

Linda Thiele, Preceptor Kappa
Delaware, Ohio

MEXICAN CHICKEN CASSEROLE

1 (10-ounce) can cream
    of mushroom soup
1 (10-ounce) can cream
    of chicken soup
1 cup milk
1 (4-ounce) can chopped
    green chiles
1 medium onion,
    chopped
1 (7-ounce) jar green
    chile salsa

6 boneless skinless
    chicken breast halves,
    cooked, sliced
1 (12-count) package
    corn tortillas, torn or
    cut in strips
4 cups (16 ounces)
    shredded sharp
    Cheddar cheese

Preheat the oven to 325 degrees. Combine the cream of mushroom soup, cream of chicken soup, milk, green chiles, onion and chile salsa in a bowl; mix well. Layer the chicken, soup mixture, tortilla strips and cheese in a 9-by-13-inch baking dish. Bake for 25 to 30 minutes. Yield: 6 to 8 servings.

Shirley Moran
Templeton, California

CHICKEN ARTICHOKE ENCHILADAS

3 whole boneless
    skinless chicken
    breasts
4 green onions, thinly
    sliced
1 (4-ounce) can chopped
    green chiles
1 (2-ounce) can sliced
    black olives, drained
2 cups (8 ounces)
    shredded garlic Jack
    cheese

8 (10-inch) flour
    tortillas
1 (14-ounce) can
    artichoke bottoms,
    drained
1 (10-ounce) can cream
    of mushroom soup
1 cup sour cream
3/4 cup chicken broth
2 cups (8 ounces)
    shredded garlic Jack
    cheese

Preheat the oven to 350 degrees. Boil the chicken breasts in a kettle for 20 minutes. Remove the chicken from the kettle, reserving the liquid. Chop the chicken. Combine the chicken with the green onions, green chiles, black olives and the first 2 cups shredded cheese; mix well. Place 8 equal portions of the chicken mixture over the 8 tortillas; roll up tortillas and place in a 9-by-13-inch baking dish. Place the artichoke bottoms in the container of a blender or food processor; process until smooth. Add the cream of mushroom soup and sour cream to the container; process until blended. Add the chicken broth slowly, processing until well blended. Pour over the chicken-stuffed tortillas. Cover with the second 2 cups shredded cheese. Bake for 30 minutes or until the cheese melts and is hot and bubbly. Yield: 8 servings.

Virginia Chase, Xi Mu Delta
Merced, California

CHICKEN MUSHROOM ENCHILADAS

If you would like the dish to be more moist, use more sour cream and more cream of mushroom soup.

8 frozen boneless
   skinless chicken
   breast halves
1 pint sour cream
2 (10-ounce) cans cream
   of mushroom soup
8 (10-inch) soft flour
   tortillas
3 cups (12 ounces)
   shredded Cheddar
   cheese

1 (4-ounce) can chopped
   green chiles
1 (4-ounce) can chopped
   black olives
1 (4-ounce) can sliced
   mushrooms
Onions and green
   peppers (optional)

Preheat the oven to 350 degrees. Boil the frozen chicken breasts until they rise to the top of the water. Cool and cut into bite-size pieces. Combine the sour cream and cream of mushroom soup. Spread 1/3 to 1/2 of the sour cream mixture in 2 dishes: 1 (9-by-13-inch) glass baking dish and 1 (9-by-9-inch) glass baking dish. Place the tortillas on a work surface. Divide the chicken pieces evenly among the tortillas. Spread a soup-spoonful of the cheese over the chicken on each tortilla. Combine the green chiles, black olives and mushrooms; place equal portions of the mixture over the cheese-chicken mixture on each tortilla. Roll up the tortillas, without tucking the ends, and arrange in the baking dishes. Pour the remaining sour cream mixture over the top. Sprinkle with the remaining cheese. Bake for 35 to 40 minutes. Garnish with onions and green peppers.
Yield: 8 to 10 servings.

Margie C. Warren, Laureate Kappa
Vancouver, Washington

SOUR CREAM CHICKEN ENCHILADAS

1 pint sour cream
2 (10-ounce) cans cream
   of chicken soup
1 (7-ounce) can diced
   green chiles
2 bunches green onions,
   chopped
1 (12-count) package
   corn tortillas

3 to 4 cooked whole
   chicken breasts,
   skinned, boned,
   chopped
1 1/2 pounds Cheddar
   cheese, shredded

Preheat the oven to 350 degrees. Combine the sour cream, cream of chicken soup, green chiles and green onions. Spread a tablespoon of the mixture over each tortilla. Spoon the chicken and 2/3 of the cheese over the sour cream mixture. Roll up tortillas and place in a greased 9-by-13-inch baking pan. Spread the remaining sour cream mixture over the rolled tortillas. Bake for 40 minutes. Remove from oven. Sprinkle the remaining cheese over the top. Bake until cheese is melted. Yield: 8 to 12 servings.

VaLynn Mednansky, Lambda
Belle Fourche, South Dakota

CHICKEN CHALUPAS

6 boneless skinless
   chicken breast halves,
   cut in bite-size pieces
2 (10-ounce) cans cream
   of chicken soup
1 (4-ounce) can chopped
   green chiles
1 pint sour cream
3 cups (12 ounces)
   shredded Monterey
   Jack cheese

3 cups (12 ounces)
   shredded sharp
   Cheddar cheese
Tops of 2 bunches green
   onions, chopped
1 (4-ounce) can sliced
   black olives
2 tablespoons butter or
   margarine
1 dozen (8-inch) flour
   tortillas

Preheat the oven to 350 degrees. Rinse the chicken and pat dry. Combine the cream of chicken soup, green chiles, sour cream, Monterey Jack cheese, Cheddar cheese, green onion tops and black olives in a large bowl. Remove 1 1/2 cups of the mixture to a small bowl. Sauté the chicken in the butter in a skillet over medium heat until chicken is cooked through. Combine the chicken with the sour cream mixture in the large bowl. Place 3 tablespoons of the chicken mixture over each tortilla. Fold tortillas and place seam side down in a greased 11-by-13-inch baking dish. Pour the remaining sour cream mixture over the top. Bake for 45 minutes. Yield: 10 servings.

Gladys Jester, Laureate Beta Kappa
Springfield, Missouri

RITZ CHICKEN

4 to 6 cooked chicken
   breast halves
8 ounces sour cream
1 (10-ounce) can cream
   of chicken soup

40 butter crackers,
   crushed
1/2 cup melted margarine
2 teaspoons poppy seeds

Preheat the oven to 350 degrees. Tear the chicken into bite-size pieces and place in a greased 8-by-8-inch baking dish. Combine the sour cream and cream of chicken soup and pour over the chicken. Toss the butter crackers with the margarine and sprinkle over the chicken. Sprinkle with the poppy seeds. Bake for 30 minutes or until bubbly. Yield: 4 to 6 servings.

Robin Sanderson, Zeta Iota
Aurora, Nebraska

CHINESE CHICKEN PIZZA

1 package frozen pizza dough, thawed	3/4 cup vegetable oil
5 small boneless skinless chicken breasts	2 cups (8 ounces) shredded Gruyère cheese
2 cloves of garlic, coarsely chopped	1 cup (4 ounces) shredded mozzarella cheese
2 teaspoons crushed red chile pepper	1/4 cup chopped green onions
1/2 cup soy sauce	Cornmeal (if using pizza pan)
5 tablespoons honey	1/4 cup sesame seeds, toasted
1 1/2 cups rice wine vinegar	

Roll the dough to fit the pizza stone. Set aside the dough. Place the stone in a 500-degree oven and preheat for 1 hour. If using a pizza pan, simply preheat the oven to 500 degrees. Rinse the chicken and pat dry; cut into bite-size pieces. Combine the garlic, red chile pepper, soy sauce, honey and vinegar in a small bowl; set aside. Heat 1/4 cup of the oil in a large skillet over medium-high heat; sauté the chicken in the oil until opaque. Remove with a slotted spoon. Pour the garlic mixture into the skillet. Cook, stirring frequently, until the sauce is reduced to a syrupy consistency. Return the chicken to the skillet and cook, stirring constantly, until the pieces are lightly glazed, about 2 minutes. Brush the pizza dough with the remaining 1/2 cup oil. Layer the Gruyère cheese, mozzarella cheese and glazed chicken over the dough, leaving a 1/2-inch border along the edges. Sprinkle with the green onions. If using a pizza pan, sprinkle the pan with cornmeal. Place the pizza on the preheated pizza stone or the pizza pan. Bake until the crust is golden, 8 to 10 minutes. Remove from the oven and sprinkle with the sesame seeds. Serve immediately. Yield: 4 to 6 servings.

Janis Vogel
Goderich, Ontario, Canada

Rita C. Steffens, Hollywood, Florida, says World's Fair Chicken is great if your company is late—it only gets better when held at 200 degrees. She cuts three 2 1/2-pound chickens into pieces, sprinkles with salt, pepper, and butter, and bakes in a preheated 425-degree oven for 15 minutes. Simmer 1 1/4 cups orange juice, 1/2 cup raisins, 1/4 cup chutney, 1/2 cup split almonds, 1/2 teaspoon each cinnamon and curry powder, and a dash of thyme for 10 minutes and pour over the chicken. Bake at 350 degrees for 1 hour. Serve with rice garnished with mandarin oranges.

CHICKEN LIVERS AND THREE PEPPERS

Serve with French bread and a salad.

2 pounds chicken livers, rinsed	1 1/2 teaspoons paprika
Seasoned flour for coating chicken livers	1 each large green, yellow and red bell pepper, chopped
2 tablespoons olive oil	16 ounces fresh mushrooms
1 large yellow onion, chopped	1 1/2 to 2 cups red wine
3 cloves of garlic, minced	16 ounces wide egg noodles, cooked

Dredge the chicken livers in enough seasoned flour to lightly coat. Heat the olive oil in a large skillet and brown the chicken livers in the oil. Drain on paper towels. Place the onion, garlic, paprika, green pepper, yellow bell pepper, red bell pepper and mushrooms in the skillet; cook over medium-low heat for 7 to 10 minutes or until the vegetables are tender. Add the wine; simmer for 7 to 10 minutes. Return the chicken livers to the skillet and heat through. Serve over the egg noodles. Yield: 6 servings.

Robin LaFerrara, Kappa Kappa
Slidell, Louisiana

JAMAICAN JERK CHICKEN

1 1/2 cups white vinegar	1/2 cup soy sauce
1/2 cup olive oil	2 tablespoons salt
3 small onions, chopped	2 tablespoons ground thyme
2 cloves of garlic, minced	1 tablespoon ground sage
Grated zest of 2 limes	1 teaspoon ground allspice
2 tablespoons sugar	12 whole chicken breasts
1 cup orange juice	
3 jalapeño peppers, seeded, diced	

Combine the vinegar, olive oil, onions, garlic, lime zest, sugar, orange juice, jalapeño peppers, soy sauce, salt, thyme, sage and allspice in a large nonaluminum pan. Pierce each chicken piece 4 to 5 times with a fork. Place the chicken in the mixture in the pan; spoon the mixture over the chicken. Refrigerate, covered, for at least 4 hours; the longer it is marinated, the better it will be. Remove the chicken from the marinade. Preheat the broiler or grill. Broil or grill, basting frequently with the remaining marinade, until the chicken is no longer pink near the bone. Yield: 12 servings.

Linda M. McAndrews
Prattville, Alabama

CHICKEN ASPARAGUS STROGANOFF

**1 (10-ounce) can cream
  of chicken soup**
1/4 cup sour cream
1/4 cup milk
**2 cups sliced cooked
  asparagus**
**1 cup chopped cooked
  chicken**
1/4 teaspoon rosemary
**1/4 cup shredded Cheddar
  cheese**
Cooked noodles or rice

Preheat the oven to 350 degrees. Spray a 1-quart casserole dish lightly with nonstick cooking spray. Combine the cream of chicken soup, sour cream and milk. Pour half the soup mixture into the casserole dish. Layer the asparagus, chicken and rosemary over the mixture. Pour the remaining soup mixture over the chicken layer. Sprinkle with the cheese. Bake for 30 minutes. Serve with noodles or rice. Yield: 4 servings.

*Meloni Soll, Xi Pi
Riverton, Wyoming*

CHICKEN AND BROCCOLI CASSEROLE

**2 cups broccoli
  florets**
**2 cups chopped cooked
  chicken**
**1 (10-ounce) cream of
  chicken soup**
1/2 cup mayonnaise
**1/2 cup grated Parmesan
  cheese**
**1/2 teaspoon curry
  powder**
1 cup cubed fresh bread
**2 tablespoons melted
  butter or margarine**

Preheat the oven to 350 degrees. Cook the broccoli in water in a covered saucepan until crisp-tender; drain. Spread in a greased 7-by-11-inch baking dish; set aside. Combine the chicken, chicken soup, mayonnaise, Parmesan cheese and curry powder; spoon over the broccoli. Sprinkle with the bread cubes and drizzle with the butter. Bake uncovered for 25 to 30 minutes or until heated through. Yield: 6 servings.

*Mildred K. Loe, Laureate Delta Gamma
Houston, Texas*

CHICKEN BROCCOLI SUPREME

**1 (16-ounce) package
  frozen broccoli,
  thawed**
Salt and pepper to taste
2 teaspoons sugar
8 slices process cheese
**1 (10-ounce) can cream
  of chicken soup**
1/2 cup sour cream
**3 cups chopped cooked
  chicken**
**3 tablespoons chicken
  broth**
**1 (6-ounce) package
  chicken-flavored
  stove-top stuffing mix**

Preheat the oven to 350 degrees. Spread the broccoli over the bottom of a greased 9-by-13-inch pan. Sprinkle with the salt, pepper and sugar. Place the cheese slices over the broccoli. Combine the chicken soup and sour cream; spread over the cheese layer. Sprinkle the chicken over the soup layer. Drizzle the broth over the chicken. Prepare the stuffing using package directions; spread over the mixture in the pan. Bake for 45 minutes. Yield: 12 to 15 servings.

*Marilyn Person, Laureate Nu
Pierre, South Dakota*

CHICKEN CORN BREAD CASSEROLE

**1 (2 1/2- to 3-pound)
  chicken**
**1 1/2 cups corn bread
  crumbs**
1 cup light bread crumbs
**3 hard-cooked eggs,
  chopped**
1 small onion, chopped
1 1/2 cups chicken broth
Chicken giblets
1 tablespoon salt
1/2 teaspoon pepper
**1 (10-ounce) can cream
  of chicken soup**

Simmer the chicken in salted water until tender. Remove the meat from the bones. Preheat the oven to 350 degrees. Combine the corn bread crumbs, light bread crumbs, half the eggs, onion, the chicken broth, giblets, salt and pepper in a large bowl. Pour the mixture into a greased 11-by-13-inch baking dish. Layer the chicken and remaining eggs over the mixture. Pour the cream of chicken soup over the top. Bake about 20 minutes. Yield: 6 servings.

*Iris R. Flowe, Xi Beta Epsilon
Ninety Six, South Carolina*

CHICKEN ENCHILADAS

1 large onion, chopped
2 tablespoons margarine
**2 (4-ounce) cans
  chopped green chiles,
  drained**
**1 (10-ounce) can
  tomatoes with green
  chiles, drained**
**1 (2- to 3-pound)
  chicken, cooked,
  boned, chopped**
**1 (12-count) package
  corn tortillas**
**Hot vegetable oil to
  soften tortillas**
**10 ounces Monterey Jack
  cheese, shredded**
1 1/2 cups sour cream
Milk

Preheat the oven to 350 degrees. Sauté the onion in the margarine until tender. Stir in the green chiles, tomatoes with green chiles and chicken. Fry tortillas in hot oil to soften. Place about 2 tablespoons of the chicken mixture in the center of each tortilla and roll up. Melt the cheese in the top of a double boiler or microwave until melted. Stir in the sour cream and enough milk to make the mixture pourable. Pour the mixture over the enchiladas. Bake 30 minutes. Yield: 8 servings.

*Sandra Sparkman
Kerrville, Texas*

CHICKEN A LA KING WITH BAKING POWDER BISCUITS

I made this recipe as low-fat as possible without changing the texture.

3 tablespoons margarine	1/2 cup sautéed
3 tablespoons all-purpose flour	mushrooms
1 1/2 cups low-fat chicken stock	1/4 cup diced pimientos
	1/2 cup frozen peas (optional)
1 cup chopped cooked chicken	Baking Powder Biscuits

Melt the margarine in a skillet over medium-low heat. Add the flour; cook, stirring, until smooth. Add the chicken stock gradually, stirring; cook for 1 minute. Stir in the chicken, mushrooms, pimientos and peas. Serve over Baking Powder Biscuits. Yield: 4 servings.

BAKING POWDER BISCUITS

2 cups all-purpose flour	1/2 teaspoon salt
2 1/2 teaspoons baking powder	1/4 cup margarine
	3/4 cup skim milk

Preheat the oven to 450 degrees. Sift the flour, baking powder and salt into a bowl. Cut in the margarine until crumbly. Stir in the milk quickly. Knead 10 to 12 times on a floured cloth. Pat into a circle 1/4- to 1/2-inch thick. Cut with a 2-inch biscuit cutter. Place on a greased baking sheet. Bake for 12 to 15 minutes or until lightly browned.

Esther Westfall
Grand Island, New York

CHICKEN MEXICALE CASSEROLE

You can save time by using roasted chicken purchased at the deli counter.

1 medium onion, chopped	1 cup frozen white corn
1 tablespoon vegetable oil	3 cups (12 ounces) shredded Monterey Jack cheese
1 (12-ounce) jar salsa verde	1 cup light sour cream
1 (12-count) package corn tortillas	1/4 cup shredded Cheddar cheese
1 store-bought roasted chicken, skinned, boned, hand shredded	

Preheat the oven to 350 degrees. Sauté the onion in the oil until tender but not brown. Pour 1/4 cup of the salsa over the bottom of a deep 8-inch-round soufflé dish. Cover the salsa with 3 or 4 tortillas. Layer 1/4 cup salsa, 1/3 of the chicken, a sprinkle of sautéed onions, 1/3 of the corn, 1 cup of the Monterey Jack cheese and 1/3 of the sour cream over the tortillas. Repeat the layers twice. Top with the remaining tortillas; pour the remaining salsa over the top. Sprinkle with the Cheddar cheese. Cover with foil. Bake for 30 minutes. Remove the foil and bake for 15 minutes. Yield: 6 servings.

Mary Ann Poulos, Delta Lambda Rho
Los Altos, California

POPPY SEED CHICKEN CASSEROLE

When adding salt to the casserole, remember that the saltines will also add salt.

1 (4-pound) chicken, boiled, boned	1/2 cup slivered almonds
	Salt and pepper to taste
1 (8-ounce) carton sour cream	1 stick butter or margarine
1 (10-ounce) can cream of celery soup	4 ounces saltines, crushed
1 (10-ounce) can cream of mushroom soup	2 tablespoons poppy seeds

Preheat the oven to 350 degrees. Combine the first 5 ingredients in a medium bowl. Stir in the salt and pepper. Pour the mixture into a greased 9-by-13-inch baking dish. Melt the butter in a small skillet; stir in the saltine crumbs and poppy seeds. Sprinkle over the chicken mixture. Bake for 30 minutes. Yield: 8 to 12 servings.

Margie Pongetti, Xi Iota
Florence, Alabama

BECKY'S CHICKEN POT PIE

1 cup chopped cooked chicken	3/4 cup melted butter or margarine
1 (10-ounce) can cream of chicken soup	1 1/2 cups milk
3 cups chicken broth	1 1/2 teaspoons baking powder
1/2 (10-ounce) package frozen peas	1 1/2 cups self-rising flour
4 or 5 medium carrots, thinly sliced	

Preheat the oven to 425 degrees. Combine the chicken, cream of chicken soup, chicken broth, peas and carrots in a bowl. Pour into a greased 9-by-13-inch baking pan. Combine the butter, milk, baking powder and flour; pour over the chicken mixture. Bake for 45 minutes or until crust is brown and carrots are cooked. Yield: 10 servings.

Leta Homan
Mount Carmel, Illinois

ROCK CORNISH GAME HENS

When carrying a pan of sauce from stove to table, I slipped. The sauce slid out of the pan and hit the ceiling. I caught it as it came down, right in the pan. That saved my dinner . . . but we had to paint the ceiling after that incident!

2 medium white onions, sliced	1 mango, peeled, sliced
1 medium cucumber, peeled, sliced	1 (15-ounce) can pitted black cherries, drained, juice reserved
1/2 pound butter or margarine	3 ounces brandy
2 ounces light brown sugar	1 piece crystallized ginger, or 1 cup ground ginger
4 ounces white, tarragon, or red wine vinegar	1 (20-ounce) can water-packed pineapple chunks
2/3 ounce rum	2 teaspoons arrowroot
2/3 ounce chicken stock or bouillon	5 large or 10 small roasted Cornish game hens
2/3 ounce soy sauce	
2 or 3 medium bananas, peeled, sliced	

Preheat the oven to 350 degrees. Brown the onions and cucumber in a few tablespoons of the butter in a small skillet over medium-low heat. Stir in the brown sugar and vinegar. Combine the rum, chicken stock and soy sauce in a large saucepan over medium-low heat. Sear the bananas in a few tablespoons of the butter in a medium skillet over medium heat; stir in the mango and black cherries. Cook until lightly browned. Pour the brandy over the fruit and light with a match. The alcohol will burn off. Combine the reserved black cherry juice, ginger, pineapple chunks and arrowroot in a saucepan over medium-low heat. When the contents of all pans are hot, combine all in the large saucepan with the chicken stock mixture. Pour over the roasted hens. Yield: 10 servings.

Doris M. Pelrine
Andover, Massachusetts

CORNISH HENS WITH PECAN DRESSING

1/4 cup raisins	Dash of ground pepper
1/2 cup white grape juice	1/4 teaspoon poultry seasoning
1/4 cup butter or margarine	2 eggs
1/4 cup chopped onions	3/4 cup chopped pecans
2 cups crumbled cornmeal muffins	4 Cornish game hens
1/2 teaspoon salt	Parsley for garnish
	Cooked wild rice

Soak the raisins in the grape juice in the refrigerator for 8 to 10 hours. Preheat the oven to 350 degrees. Melt the butter in a small skillet over medium-low heat; sauté the onions in the butter until tender. Place the crumbled muffins in a large bowl. Stir in the onions, raisin mixture, salt, pepper, poultry seasoning, eggs and pecans; mix well. Stuff the hens with the mixture. Arrange in a 9-by-12-inch baking dish. Bake for 11/4 to 11/2 hours. Garnish with parsley. Serve with wild rice. Yield: 4 servings.

Twyla Folk, Laureate Eta
Huron, South Dakota

ALMOND CORNISH HENS

2 Cornish game hens	1 cup water
Salt and pepper to taste	1 chicken bouillon cube
2 tablespoons slivered almonds	1/2 teaspoon salt
3 tablespoons butter or margarine	1 teaspoon lemon juice
2 tablespoons chopped onion	1 (3-ounce) can mushrooms, drained
1/2 cup uncooked long grain white rice	Melted butter or margarine to glaze

Preheat the oven to 400 degrees. Season the hens with the salt and pepper. Combine the almonds, the 3 tablespoons butter, onion and rice in a saucepan over medium-low heat; sauté for 5 to 10 minutes. Stir in the water, bouillon cube, salt and lemon juice. Bring to a boil, stirring to dissolve the bouillon. Reduce heat. Cook, covered, for 20 to 25 minutes or until liquid is absorbed and rice is fluffy. Stir in the mushrooms. Lightly stuff the hens with the mixture from the saucepan. Place breast side up in a roasting pan. Brush lightly with melted butter. Bake, covered, for 30 minutes. Uncover and bake for 1 hour longer or until drumstick is loose. Yield: 2 servings.

Maureen Armstrong, Xi Gamma
Auburn, Maine

Elaine Steele, Quesnel, British Columbia, Canada, prepares a delicious Cucumber Sauce for Broiled Salmon by combining 1 cup chopped onion, 1/2 cup vinegar, 4 cloves of garlic, minced, 2 teaspoons of minced fresh gingerroot, and 1 teaspoon soy sauce. Cook over medium-high heat for 3 minutes, stirring constantly. Add a thinly sliced cucumber and set aside. Broil salmon fillets brushed with olive oil about 6 inches from the heat source for 4 to 5 minutes on each side, and serve on a bed of rice with the sauce.

FRENCH STUFFED CORNISH GAME HENS

4 Cornish game hens	*1 clove of garlic, crushed*
¼ pound ground lamb	*Salt and pepper to taste*
¼ pound ground beef	*2 French rolls, crumbled,*
4 pork sausages	*soaked in ½ cup hot*
1 egg	*wine*
1 (10-ounce) can onion	*Melted butter, salt,*
soup	*pepper and wine for*
½ cup white wine	*outside of hens*
4 fresh mushrooms	*Wine for basting*
4 green onions, chopped	*1 teaspoon Kitchen*
½ teaspoon basil	*Bouquet*
½ teaspoon oregano	*Watercress or chicory*
1 teaspoon sage	*lettuce*
1 tablespoon butter or	
margarine	

Preheat the oven to 325 degrees. Rinse the hens and pat dry. Combine the ground lamb, ground beef and pork sausages in a large bowl. Stir in the egg, onion soup and white wine; mix well. Sauté the mushrooms with green onions, basil, oregano and sage in the butter in a medium skillet over medium-low heat until vegetables are soft. Add the garlic. Add the mushroom mixture, salt and pepper to the meat mixture; mix well. Add the wine-soaked rolls; mix well. Stuff the hens, brushing the outside of the hens with melted butter, salt, pepper and wine. Bake for 1½ hours, basting frequently with wine. Add the Kitchen Bouquet to the pan juices at serving time. Serve the game hens on watercress or chicory lettuce au jus. Yield: 4 servings.

Audrey Polk, Alpha Upsilon Master
San Lorenzo, California

OSTRICH IN PUFF PASTRY

This recipe seems much more difficult than it really is. After you make it the first time, it's a snap to put together.

1 sheet frozen puff	*½ small roasted red bell*
pastry, thawed for 1	*pepper*
hour or until pliable	*1 (12-ounce) ostrich*
8 ounces mushrooms,	*steak*
finely chopped	*1 (10-ounce) package*
¼ cup minced shallots	*frozen chopped*
2 teaspoons butter or	*spinach, thawed,*
margarine	*thoroughly squeezed*
¼ teaspoon dried thyme	*dry*
¼ teaspoon rosemary	*Salt and pepper to taste*

While the pastry is thawing, sauté the mushrooms and shallots in the butter in a medium skillet over low heat until soft, adding the thyme and rosemary during the last few minutes. Cool and set aside. Slice the roasted red bell pepper into long, thin strips. Pound the ostrich steak until ¼ to ½ inch thick and about 9 by 12 inches in area. If more than 1 steak is used, overlap the steaks slightly to create 1 large piece. Make sure the meat grain runs horizontally the long way so when slices of the meal roll are cut, they are being cut against the grain. Spread a thin layer of spinach over the ostrich. There may be leftover spinach; reserve for another use. Add a thin layer of cooked mushrooms, strips of red bell pepper, salt and pepper, pressing the ingredients firmly into the steak. Beginning at the long edge, roll up jelly roll style. Roll out the puff pastry gently to a size slightly larger than the meat. Wrap the meat "log" with the pastry, pinching to seal the seams. Place in the freezer for 45 minutes to 1 hour. Preheat the oven to 400 degrees. Place the ostrich roll seam side down on a baking sheet. Bake until the pastry is golden, about 30 minutes. Remove and let cool for 5 to 10 minutes. Slice into 1-inch pieces with a serrated knife and arrange several slices on each plate, allowing them to slightly overlap. Yield: 4 servings.

Penny Rae Fine, Laureate Phi
Kennewick, Washington

BIRDS OF MIDWESTERN SKIES

My husband hunts only a few times a year, and we always want to make the feast extra-special. Serve with wild rice with almonds. Other birds may be substituted for those in this recipe.

Melted butter or	*1 prairie chicken, boned*
margarine	*3 dove breasts, boned*
1 pheasant, boned	*½ pound smoked bacon*

Preheat the oven to 350 degrees. Dip a 9-by-9-inch square of cheesecloth in the melted butter. Lay it flat on the work surface. Lay the pheasant on the cheesecloth, back side down. Place a layer of bacon over the pheasant. Lay the prairie chicken over the bacon, back side down; cover with a layer of bacon. Lay the dove breasts over the bacon. Bring all 4 corners of the cheesecloth together, tucking the corners under the meat "package." Tie the package together and place in a small roasting pan. Bake, covered, for 40 minutes. Remove from the oven and allow to stand for 10 minutes before slicing. Yield: 4 to 6 large servings.

Laura Hannan
Hays, Kansas

PHEASANT SAUTE SUPREME

Chicken can be used in this recipe if pheasant is not available.

2 pheasants	1 tablespoon butter or
Garlic powder and	margarine
pepper to taste	1/2 cup white wine
1/4 cup all-purpose flour	2 ounces capers
2 tablespoons olive oil	1/2 (10-ounce) can
8 ounces mushrooms,	chicken broth
sliced	

Filet the pheasant breasts and thighs. Pound the pheasant pieces lightly. Season both sides of pheasant pieces with garlic powder and pepper. Dredge in the flour. Brown in the olive oil in a skillet over medium heat, cooking for 1 minute on each side. Remove from the skillet. Sauté the mushrooms in the butter in a large skillet until tender. Stir in the wine, capers and chicken broth; simmer for 5 minutes. Add the pheasant pieces to the mushroom mixture; simmer for 10 minutes. Yield: 4 to 6 servings.

Jeanine Newell, Laureate Alpha Rho
Fremont, California

ZESTY FISH

This is a strange-sounding recipe, but it is delicious—equally good whether preparing salmon or white fish.

1 1/4 teaspoons salt	4 medium leeks, white
1 teaspoon dried	and pale green parts,
tarragon	cut into matchsticks,
1 teaspoon grated lemon	or 10 green onions
zest	1/4 cup chicken broth
1/2 teaspoon pepper	3 tablespoons white
4 fish fillets or 1 1/2	wine or chicken broth
pounds salmon	1 tablespoons lemon
2 tablespoons butter or	juice
margarine	8 ounces radishes
2 tablespoons olive oil	(about 12), sliced

Combine 3/4 teaspoon of the salt, tarragon, lemon zest and 1/4 teaspoon of the pepper; sprinkle over the fish. Heat 1 tablespoon of the butter with 1 tablespoon of the olive oil in a large skillet over medium heat. Cook the fish in the skillet for 4 to 5 minutes or until fish flakes easily with a fork. Remove the fish from the skillet; keep warm. Heat the remaining 1 tablespoon butter and remaining 1 tablespoon olive oil in the same skillet; sauté the leeks in the skillet until slightly soft, about 3 minutes. Stir in the chicken broth, wine, lemon juice and remaining 1/2 teaspoon salt and 1/4 teaspoon pepper. Cook, covered, until leeks are tender, about 6 minutes. Stir in the radishes;

cook until slightly soft, 2 to 3 minutes. Serve the sauce over the fish. Yield: 4 servings.

Frances Deaver
Gurley, Nebraska

SPICY BROILED FISH FILLETS

2 pounds skinless fish	2 tablespoons soy sauce
fillets	1 teaspoon paprika
1 (4-ounce) can chopped	1/2 teaspoon chili
green chiles	powder
2 tablespoons vegetable	1/2 teaspoon garlic
oil	powder
2 tablespoons	Dash of hot pepper
Worcestershire sauce	sauce

Preheat the broiler. Cut the fillets into service-size portions; arrange in a single layer in a well-greased 9-by-13-inch baking dish. Combine the green chiles, oil, Worcestershire sauce, soy sauce, paprika, chili powder, garlic powder and hot pepper sauce; pour over the fillets. Broil 4 inches from heat source for 5 minutes or until fish is opaque, basting once with the natural juices during broiling. Yield: 6 servings.

Kathleen Plake
Fort Wayne, Indiana

ORANGE ROUGHY WITH PARSLEY SAUCE

2 tablespoons olive oil	Salt and pepper to taste
1 1/2 pounds orange	Finely chopped fresh
roughy	parsley
Seasoned salt to taste	Small red potatoes,
1 1/2 cups two-percent	unpeeled, scrubbed
milk	Fresh or canned green
4 tablespoons	beans
all-purpose flour	

Heat the olive oil in a large skillet over medium heat. Sprinkle the fish with the seasoned salt. Sauté in the olive oil, turning once, until done, about 6 to 7 minutes. Mix the milk, flour, salt and pepper in a bowl. Pour into a small kettle; bring to a boil. Stir in the parsley. Cook over low heat for about 5 minutes, stirring constantly. Boil the potatoes in salted water to cover in a medium saucepan, stirring constantly, for about 20 minutes or until potatoes are tender. Cook fresh green beans in boiling salted water for about 15 minutes or until tender; simply heat canned green beans. Serve the orange roughy with the potatoes and green beans on a plate. Spoon the parsley sauce over the fish and potatoes. Yield: 4 to 6 servings.

Aleksandra Stolley, Delta Gamma
Corpus Christi, Texas

BAKED FLOUNDER RICOTTA

2 tablespoons butter or
  margarine
1 clove of garlic, crushed
1 large green onion,
  chopped
Pinch of ground thyme
Salt and pepper to taste
6 ounces ricotta cheese
1½ tablespoons lightly
  beaten egg
1½ teaspoons finely
  chopped parsley

1 pound flounder fillets,
  cut into 8 pieces
8 (¼-inch) tomato slices
2 tablespoons melted
  butter or margarine
Salt and pepper to taste
Juice of ¼ lemon
1 or 2 tablespoons water
3 cups (12 ounces)
  shredded mozzarella
  cheese

Melt the 2 tablespoons butter in a small skillet; sauté the garlic and onion in the butter until softened. Season with the thyme, salt and pepper. Combine the ricotta cheese, egg, parsley and onion-garlic mixture in a small bowl; mix until smooth. Chill, covered, for 1 hour in the refrigerator. Preheat the oven to 350 degrees. Lightly grease a 9-by-13-inch baking dish. Arrange half the fillets in a single layer in the dish. Spread the ricotta mixture evenly over the fillets. Cover with the remaining fillets, pressing the edges to enclose the ricotta filling. Lay a tomato slice over each fillet, brush with melted butter and sprinkle with salt and pepper. Squeeze the lemon juice over the top. Add the water to the baking dish so fish will stay moist while baking. Bake for about 15 minutes or until fish is almost cooked through. Sprinkle with the mozzarella cheese. Continue baking until cheese melts, about 5 minutes. Yield: 4 servings.

Amy Schenck, Xi Beta Tau
Pahokee, Florida

COTTAGE CHEESE AND SALMON PIE

You may substitute tuna for the salmon if salmon is not available.

8 ounces cottage cheese
1 egg, beaten
Salt and pepper to taste
1 (7-ounce) can red or
  pink salmon, drained,
  flaked

10 ounces puff pastry
Beaten egg for glaze
Tomatoes for garnish

Preheat the oven to 400 degrees. Combine the cottage cheese with the egg, salt and pepper in a bowl. Stir in the salmon. Roll pastry thinly into a 12-by-12-inch square; place on a baking sheet. Spoon the salmon filling into the center of the pastry square. Brush the edges of the pastry with beaten egg; draw the pastry edges toward the center to form an envelope shape. Press edges together well and flute the edges. Brush with beaten egg. Bake for about 30 minutes or until golden brown. Serve hot. Garnish with tomatoes. Yield: 4 servings.

Kay Davis, Xi Rho Sigma
Avila Beach, California

SALMON BARONOFF

For an elegant dinner, serve with rice and a vegetable.

1½ pounds fresh salmon
  fillets
Juice of ½ lemon
Garlic salt to taste
½ cup low-fat
  mayonnaise

½ cup low-fat sour
  cream
1 to 2 teaspoons
  paprika

Preheat the oven to 350 degrees. Place salmon skin side down in a 9-by-13-inch ovenproof baking pan. Squeeze the lemon over the fish; sprinkle with garlic salt. Combine the mayonnaise, sour cream and paprika in a small bowl. Mixture will be bright pink. Spread the mayonnaise mixture over the fish. Bake, covered with aluminum foil, for 30 minutes. Remove the foil and bake for 15 minutes longer or until salmon is cooked through. Yield: 4 servings.

Barbara Rodgers, Preceptor Beta Iota
Colorado Springs, Colorado

SALMON PIE

1 (15-ounce) can salmon,
  drained, liquid
  reserved
1 cup salmon liquid and
  milk
1 cup soft bread crumbs
3 eggs, slightly beaten
1 cup chopped celery
¼ cup chopped onion

2 tablespoons margarine
  or vegetable oil
2 tablespoons chopped
  parsley
1 tablespoon lemon
  juice
¼ teaspoon salt
1 unbaked (9-inch) pie
  shell

Preheat the oven to 400 degrees. Bone, skin and flake the salmon. Combine the salmon liquid and milk, bread crumbs and eggs; set aside. Sauté the celery and onion in the margarine in a small skillet over medium-low heat until celery is tender. Add the celery mixture, salmon, parsley, lemon juice and salt to egg mixture; mix well. Pour into the pie shell. Bake for 25 to 30 minutes or until salmon mixture is set. Let stand for 8 to 10 minutes before cutting. Yield: 6 servings.

Lois Burant
Milwaukee, Wisconsin

SALMON LOAF

1 (15-ounce) can pink salmon	Salt and pepper to taste
2 eggs	Minced onion as desired
20 soda crackers	3/4 cup milk
2 tablespoons baking mix	

Preheat the oven to 350 degrees. Combine the salmon, eggs, soda crackers, baking mix, salt, pepper, onion and milk. Press into a greased 5-by-9-inch loaf pan. Bake for 1 hour. Yield: 6 to 8 servings.

Maurine Glantz
Harvard, Nebraska

SOLE WITH GRAPES

1 pound sole fillets	1/4 cup mayonnaise
6 large mushrooms, sliced	Juice of 1/2 lemon
2 tablespoons butter or margarine	3 to 4 dozen seedless grapes, red, green or a combination
1/2 cup sour cream	

Preheat the oven to 350 degrees. Arrange the fish fillets in a single layer in a well-buttered 9-by-11-inch baking dish, folding the fillets in halves or thirds if necessary. Sauté the mushrooms in the butter in a small saucepan over medium-low heat until softened. Add the sour cream, mayonnaise and lemon juice; blend well. Blend in the grapes gently. Spoon over the fish. Make a foil tent over the dish. Bake until fish is flaky and sauce is heated through, about 20 minutes. Yield: 4 servings.

Doris G. Evans
Eureka, California

ORIENTAL GRILLED TUNA STEAKS

6 (4-ounce) Alaskan tuna steaks, 3/4 inch thick	1/4 cup plus 2 tablespoons low-sodium soy sauce
1 cup thinly sliced green onions	1 tablespoon sesame oil
1/4 cup plus 2 tablespoons rice wine vinegar	1 tablespoon grated peeled gingerroot
	1/4 teaspoon ground red pepper

Place the tuna steaks in a shallow dish. Combine the green onions, rice wine vinegar, soy sauce, sesame oil, gingerroot and red pepper in a small bowl, stirring well. Set aside 1/4 of the mixture. Pour the remaining mixture over the steaks. Refrigerate, covered, for 2 hours or longer. Preheat the grill, coating the rack with nonstick cooking spray. Grill fish for 4 minutes each side or until flaky, over medium coals, basting frequently with the reserved green onion mixture. Yield: 4 to 6 servings.

Marge Harrington
Scranton, Pennsylvania

BROCCOLI AND CRAB CASSEROLE

1 pound broccoli, washed, separated into pieces	2 tablespoons all-purpose flour
1 cup shredded Cheddar cheese	1/4 teaspoon curry
1/4 cup melted butter or margarine	1/2 teaspoon salt
	1 cup milk
2 tablespoons grated or chopped onions	1 tablespoon lemon juice
	1 to 2 cups crab meat
	1/2 cup bread crumbs

Preheat the oven to 350 degrees. Boil the broccoli for 2 minutes; drain. Arrange evenly in a 9-by-11-inch pan sprayed with nonstick cooking spray. Sprinkle the cheese over the broccoli. Combine the butter, onions, flour, curry, salt and milk in a small saucepan over medium heat. Cook, stirring constantly, until the mixture is thick, about 2 minutes. Remove from heat. Stir in the lemon juice and crab meat. Pour evenly over the broccoli and cheese. Sprinkle with the bread crumbs. Bake for 30 minutes or until bubbly. Yield: 8 servings.

Thelma Manning, Epsilon Master
Vancouver, Washington

HEATHER'S HEAVENLY CRAB QUICHE

8 ounces crab meat	1 cup (4 ounces) shredded Swiss cheese
1 bunch green onions, chopped	1 unbaked (10-inch) deep-dish pie shell
4 tablespoons butter or margarine	4 eggs, beaten
1 teaspoon salt	2 cups half-and-half
1/4 teaspoon nutmeg	
1/4 teaspoon pepper	

Preheat the oven to 425 degrees. Sauté the crab meat and green onions in the butter for 2 minutes in a skillet over medium heat. Stir in the salt, nutmeg and pepper. Remove from heat. Spread the cheese in the bottom of the pie shell. Beat the eggs with the half-and-half. Spread the crab mixture over the cheese. Pour the egg mixture over the crab. Bake for 15 minutes. Reduce oven heat to 300 degrees; bake for 40 minutes longer. Serve warm or at room temperature. Yield: 8 servings.

Heather Margaret Agazzi
Petaluma, California

SAVANNAH CRAB CAKES

1 pound cooked crab
    meat, picked over
1½ cups fresh bread
    crumbs
2 eggs, beaten
¼ cup milk
1 cup chopped green
    onions
½ teaspoon salt

⅛ teaspoon pepper
1 teaspoon
    Worcestershire sauce
1 tablespoon Dijon
    mustard
¼ cup vegetable oil for
    frying
Tartar sauce

Combine the crab meat and ¾ cup of the bread crumbs in a large bowl. Blend the eggs and milk in another bowl. Pour the egg-milk mixture over the crab. Stir in the onions, salt, pepper, Worcestershire sauce and Dijon mustard; mix lightly. Form into medium-size patties. Press each patty into the remaining bread crumbs. Heat the oil in a large skillet. Fry the crab cakes until lightly browned, about 5 minutes on each side. Serve hot with tartar sauce. Yield: 4 to 6 servings.

Susan L. Parsley
Savannah, Georgia

CRAB MEAT SUPREME

Serve this delectable crab over rice or noodles.

1 medium red onion,
    finely chopped
1 medium green pepper,
    finely chopped
¼ cup butter or
    margarine
½ teaspoon salt
Dash of black pepper
1 rounded teaspoon chili
    powder
2 tablespoons
    all-purpose flour

Dash of cayenne pepper
1½ cups milk
¾ cup mayonnaise
Dash of hot pepper
    sauce
2 cups Dungeness crab
    meat
3 tablespoons sherry
3 to 5 slices bread,
    cubed, sautéed in
    butter
Paprika

Preheat the oven to 350 degrees. Sauté the onion and green pepper in the butter in a medium saucepan over medium heat for a few minutes. Sprinkle in the salt, black pepper, chili powder, flour and cayenne pepper; blend well. Remove from heat. Stir in the milk slowly. Return to heat. Cook slowly for about 10 minutes, stirring occasionally. Blend in the mayonnaise and hot pepper sauce. Meanwhile, heat the crab meat and sherry in the top of a double boiler. Blend the crab mixture into the creamed mixture. Pour into a 1½-quart casserole dish. Spread the bread cubes over the top. Garnish with paprika. Yield: 4 to 6 servings.

Diana Schocker, Xi Phi Omicron
Willow Creek, California

HOT CRAB MEAT SANDWICH

1 (6-ounce) can crab
    meat
2 (3-ounce) packages
    cream cheese
3 tablespoons
    mayonnaise
1 tablespoon chopped
    green onions
½ teaspoon
    Worcestershire sauce

4 drops hot pepper sauce
Juice of ½ lemon
4 Holland rusks
4 slices tomato
Salt and pepper to taste
4 slices cooked bacon or
    Canadian bacon
4 slices sharp Cheddar
    cheese

Mix the crab meat, cream cheese, mayonnaise, green onions, Worcestershire sauce, hot pepper sauce and lemon juice in a large bowl. Chill, covered, for 8 to 10 hours. Preheat the oven to 300 degrees. Spread portions of crab meat mixture evenly over the Holland rusks. Cover each with a tomato slice. Season with the salt and pepper. Layer a slice of bacon and a slice of cheese over the top of each. Arrange on a baking sheet. Bake for 30 to 40 minutes. Yield: 4 servings.

Ann Bedgood, Xi Eta
Birmingham, Alabama

SMOTHERED CABBAGE WITH CRAWFISH

Instead of chopping vegetables, try using 1 or 2 packages of frozen mixed vegetables.

2 medium heads of
    cabbage, chopped
1 medium onion,
    chopped
1 medium green pepper,
    chopped
1 teaspoon vegetable oil

1 (10-ounce) can cream
    of mushroom soup
2 (10-ounce) cans water
2 pounds crawfish,
    cooked, peeled
Salt and pepper to taste

Sauté the cabbage, onion and green pepper in the oil in a large kettle. Stir in the cream of mushroom soup and water. Simmer until the cabbage is very limp, about 20 minutes. Stir in the crawfish. Cook for 10 minutes longer. Season with salt and pepper. Yield: 6 hearty servings.

Wendy C. Pepper, Laureate Mu
Baytown, Texas

Cathy Daddario, Upsilon, Voorhees, New Jersey, makes an All-Purpose Oriental Marinade for seafood, chicken, or beef with ¼ cup teriyaki or soy sauce, 2 tablespoons brown sugar, 2 tablespoons grated fresh gingerroot, and 2 chopped scallions. She also uses it as a sauce for stir-fry dishes.

CHAFING DISH SCALLOPS

1 pound scallops	1/4 teaspoon oregano
1 cup sliced unblanched almonds	1/8 teaspoon pepper
1/3 cup butter or margarine	3 tablespoons sherry
1 cup light cream	3 tablespoons cornstarch
1/3 cup chopped parsley	2 teaspoons lemon juice
1/2 teaspoon salt	Hot cooked rice
	Paprika

Wipe the scallops and cut the large ones in half. Sauté the almonds in the butter in a large skillet until lightly browned. Stir in the scallops. Cook gently, stirring, until the scallops lose their translucent look. Blend in the cream, parsley, salt, oregano and pepper. Combine the sherry with the cornstarch; stir into the scallop mixture. Cook gently until thickened. Blend in the lemon juice. Serve over hot rice with a sprinkle of paprika. Yield: 4 servings.

Margaret O'Neill
Victoria, British Columbia, Canada

SAVORY SHRIMP AND SCALLOPS

4 cups fat-free chicken broth	2 green onions, thinly sliced
1½ tablespoons low-sodium soy sauce	1 cup snow peas
1¼ teaspoons hot pepper sauce	1 small red bell pepper, cut in large chunks
1 teaspoon grated gingerroot	1/4 pound medium shrimp, peeled
2 cloves of garlic, halved	1/4 pound small scallops
	1½ cups cooked brown rice

Bring the chicken broth to a boil in a saucepan over medium-high heat. Stir in the soy sauce, hot pepper sauce, gingerroot, garlic and half the green onions. Return to a boil; simmer for 5 minutes. Discard the garlic. Stir in the snow peas and red bell pepper. Cook for about 4 minutes or until red bell pepper begins to become tender. Add the shrimp and scallops. Cook for 1 minute or until cooked through. Stir in the rice. Ladle the soup into bowls. Sprinkle with the remaining green onions. Yield: 3 servings.

Mary Ellen Cramer, Xi Zeta Psi
Stroudsburg, Pennsylvania

SHRIMP AND BACON

Serve over rice or pasta.

1 pound bacon, crisp-fried, crumbled	1 small onion, chopped
1 cup chopped celery	1 pound small shrimp, cleaned
3 large carrots, sliced	Salt and pepper to taste

Drain most of the bacon drippings from the skillet. Sauté the celery, carrots and onion in the remaining drippings until tender. Stir in the bacon and shrimp. Season with salt and pepper. Serve when mixture is heated through. Yield: 6 to 8 servings.

Joyce Homan
Abilene, Texas

SESAME SHRIMP AND ASPARAGUS

1 tablespoon sesame seeds	2 teaspoons vegetable oil
1 pound asparagus, cut in 2-inch pieces	4 teaspoons soy sauce
1 pound shrimp	Salt to taste
1 small onion, sliced	Hot cooked rice

Toast the sesame seeds in a skillet over medium heat. Remove the seeds; set aside. Stir-fry the asparagus, shrimp and onion in the oil in the same skillet over medium-high heat, for about 5 minutes, or until shrimp is pink and vegetables crisp. Stir in the sesame seeds and soy sauce. Add salt if necessary. Serve over rice. Yield: 4 servings.

Charlene Gonzalez, Xi Beta Lambda
Derby, Kansas

SHRIMP WITH CASHEWS

1 pound medium shrimp	1/2 each medium green and red bell pepper, cut into strips
1/8 teaspoon freshly ground black pepper	1/4 teaspoon salt
1 teaspoon cornstarch	1 tablespoons chopped garlic
3 tablespoons water	1½ teaspoons shredded fresh ginger
1 tablespoon oyster sauce	2 green onions, cut into 1-inch pieces
1 tablespoon soy sauce	1/2 cup roasted cashews
2 tablespoons vegetable oil	

Shell, devein, rinse and drain the shrimp. Combine the next 5 ingredients in a small bowl. Heat 1 tablespoon of the oil in a wok over high heat. Stir-fry the green pepper, red bell pepper and salt in the oil for 1 minute. Remove to a plate. Wipe the wok with paper towels. Heat the remaining 1 tablespoon oil in the wok. Stir-fry the garlic, ginger, shrimp and green onions for 1 or 2 minutes or until shrimp turns pink. Return the green pepper mixture to the wok. Stir the cornstarch mixture and pour into the wok. Cook, stirring, until thickened. Stir in the cashews and serve. Yield: 2 to 3 main-course servings.

Evalynn Christiansen, Laureate Eta Nu
Houston, Texas

CURRIED SHRIMP

1/4 cup butter or margarine	3 tablespoons catsup
1/4 cup all-purpose flour	1/4 cup cooking sherry
1 1/2 teaspoons curry powder	1 pound large shrimp, cooked, shelled
1/16 teaspoon paprika	1 to 1 1/2 cups raw rice, cooked
1 1/2 cups milk	Chutney (optional)

Blend the butter, flour, curry powder and paprika in a medium saucepan over low heat. Stir in the milk gradually. Cook until thickened and smooth, stirring constantly. Stir in the catsup, sherry and shrimp. Cook until right at the boiling point. Serve with hot rice and chutney. Yield: 4 servings.

Carmen Fisher
Newhall, California

SHRIMP MOSCA

1 cup melted butter or margarine	1/2 teaspoon black pepper
1 tablespoon olive oil	1/8 teaspoon cayenne pepper
3 teaspoons thyme	
Juice of 3 lemons	1 to 2 tablespoons rosemary
2 teaspoons seasoned salt	2 pounds peeled uncooked shrimp
1/2 teaspoon salt	
2 bay leaves	French bread
2 teaspoon minced garlic	

Preheat the broiler. Combine the butter, olive oil, thyme, lemon juice, seasoned salt, salt, bay leaves, garlic, black pepper, cayenne pepper and rosemary in a saucepan over medium heat. Arrange the shrimp on a broiling pan and drizzle with the butter mixture. Broil for 3 to 5 minutes to cook the shrimp. Serve with French bread for dipping. Yield: 6 to 8 servings.

Marjorie Kuhr, Preceptor Psi
Fremont, Nebraska

SHRIMP NEWBURG

1 small onion, sliced	5 tablespoons all-purpose flour
1 lemon, sliced	
1/2 teaspoon salt	3/4 teaspoon salt
1/4 teaspoon pepper	1/4 teaspoon pepper
1 clove of garlic, minced	2 cups cream
2 ribs celery with leaves, chopped	1/4 cup catsup
	1/4 cup dry sherry
1 quart boiling water	Hot cooked rice
2 pounds raw shrimp	
5 tablespoons butter or margarine	

Stir the onion, lemon, salt, pepper, garlic and celery into the boiling water. Simmer for 15 minutes. Add the shrimp; simmer for 15 minutes longer. Remove from heat; drain and rinse with cool water. Shell and devein the shrimp. Pat dry with paper towels. Melt the butter in a skillet. Stir in the flour, salt and pepper. Add the cream. Cook, stirring constantly, over medium-high heat until the sauce boils, about 2 minutes. Stir in the catsup. Remove from heat. Stir in the sherry and shrimp. Serve immediately over rice. Yield: 2 to 4 servings.

Rena Heinz
San Angelo, Texas

SHRIMP-STUFFED MIRLITONS

A mirliton is a vegetable that is similar to a squash and is sometimes called a vegetable pear.

6 to 8 mirlitons, washed, halved lengthwise	1 pound fresh medium shrimp, washed, deheaded, peeled, deveined
4 strips bacon	
2 tablespoons butter or margarine	1/2 teaspoon dillweed
	Salt and pepper to taste
1 large white onion	Up to 2 cups Italian bread crumbs
4 cloves of garlic	

Preheat the oven to 325 degrees. Parboil the mirlitons by dropping them in boiling water for about 5 minutes or until fork tender. Drain, cool and remove seeds. Scoop out the pulp, leaving the skin intact. Panfry the bacon until crisp. Stir in the butter, onion and garlic; sauté for a few minutes. Add the shrimp; sauté for no more than 3 to 4 minutes longer. Stir in the dillweed, salt, pepper and bread crumbs. Fill the mirlitons with the mixture. Bake, uncovered, until the tops are golden brown, about 30 minutes. Yield: 6 servings.

Lisa Ann Carter, Gamma Gamma
Pensacola, Florida

Kelly Layfield, Richland, Washington, makes this Salmon and Artichoke Quiche that is similar to one she enjoyed on her honeymoon. She flakes a 15-ounce can of salmon, cuts marinated artichokes from a 6-ounce jar into pieces, and layers salmon and artichokes in an unbaked pie shell. Process 4 eggs, 8 ounces of cream cheese, and enough milk to make 2 1/4 cups of the mixture in a blender, pour it into the pie shell, and add a sprinkle of paprika. Bake in a preheated 375-degree oven for 45 minutes. Let stand for 5 minutes before serving.

Vegetarian Delights

Many people today are
turning to a vegetarian cuisine
in keeping with a healthier
style of living. But can meals
minus-the-meat be interesting . . .
inviting . . . even exciting to eat? You bet!
Our Vegetarian Delights section proves that
meatless meals don't have to be bland and boring—
or leave you hungry an hour after you've eaten.
Vegetarian cooking relies on fresh, natural ingredients
and a variety of aromatic herbs that will surprise you
with their flavor. And an abundance of
beans, fruits, vegetables and grains
makes many of these meals as
delicious and filling as
their meat-filled cousins!

BAKED ITALIAN BEANS

2 cups coarsely chopped
    carrots
2 ribs celery, coarsely
    chopped
1 onion, coarsely
    chopped
1 green pepper, chopped
2 tablespoons vegetable
    oil
1 (28-ounce) can stewed
    tomatoes
1 (6-ounce) can tomato
    paste
1 (6-ounce) can of water
1 teaspoon oregano

1 teaspoon basil
Pinch of hot pepper
    flakes
Pinch of sugar
1/2 cup Parmesan cheese
1 (16-ounce) can white
    kidney beans, drained
1 (16-ounce) can chick-
    peas, drained
1 1/2 cups shredded
    mozzarella cheese
1 cup fresh bread crumbs
1/4 cup chopped parsley
2 tablespoons melted
    butter or margarine

Preheat the oven to 375 degrees. Sauté the carrots, celery, onion and green pepper in the oil in a large saucepan for about 7 minutes. Stir in the tomatoes, tomato paste, water, oregano, basil, hot pepper flakes, sugar and 2 tablespoons of the Parmesan cheese. Bring to a boil. Reduce the heat and simmer, uncovered, stirring often, for 20 minutes. Stir in the white kidney beans and chick-peas; simmer, uncovered, stirring occasionally, for 15 minutes. Pour into a greased 9-by-13-inch baking dish. Sprinkle with the mozzarella cheese. Combine the remaining Parmesan cheese, bread crumbs, parsley and butter; sprinkle the mixture over the mozzarella. Bake for 20 to 30 minutes or until bubbly. Yield: 4 to 6 servings.

Elizabeth Gourlay, Laureate Delta Epsilon
Toronto, Ontario, Canada

BONZO BURGERS

1 (15-ounce) can
    garbanzo beans,
    drained
2 cloves of garlic
1 egg
1 cup brown rice, cooked
1/4 cup wheat germ

1/3 cup ground sunflower
    seeds
1/2 cup grated carrot
1 small onion, minced
Salt and pepper to taste
Vegetable oil

Place 1/4 cup of the garbanzo beans, the garlic and the egg in a food processor container; process until smooth. Mash the remaining beans in a large bowl; stir in the rice, wheat germ, sunflower seeds, carrot, onion, salt and pepper. Add the processed mixture and stir well. Form into 8 patties. Panfry in a small amount of vegetable oil until golden brown. Yield: 8 servings.

Vicki Pochodylo, Xi Lambda Omega
Lee's Summit, Missouri

CASHEW CASSEROLE

1 cup chopped celery
1 large onion, chopped
1 cup cashews
1 cup chow mein
    noodles

1 cup uncooked fine egg
    noodles
1 (10-ounce) can
    mushroom soup

Preheat the oven to 350 degrees. Combine the celery, onion, cashews, chow mein noodles and egg noodles in a large bowl; mix well. Add the mushroom soup, mixing gently to evenly coat the dry mixture. Spray an ovenproof casserole dish with nonstick cooking spray. Spread the cashew mixture in the dish. Bake for 30 minutes or until lightly browned. Yield: 6 servings.

Jody Prokupek, Xi Epsilon
Auburn, Indiana

SLOW-COOKER VEGETABLE CHILI

If you like a spicy chili, use a can of tomatoes with green chiles.

1 (15-ounce) can
    garbanzo beans,
    undrained
2 (15-ounce) cans kidney
    beans, undrained
1 (15-ounce) can whole
    peeled tomatoes,
    undrained
2 medium onions,
    chopped

4 green peppers, chopped
2 ribs celery, chopped
4 teaspoons pepper
4 teaspoons salt
2 teaspoons chili
    powder
1 teaspoon basil
2 tablespoons vegetable
    oil
1 clove of garlic

Combine the garbanzo beans, kidney beans, tomatoes, onions, peppers, celery, pepper, salt, chili powder, basil, oil and garlic in a slow cooker. Simmer for 2 hours on low to medium heat. Yield: 10 servings.

Brenda Daniels
Williston, North Dakota

THREE-CHEESE ENCHILADAS

1 1/2 cups (6 ounces)
    shredded Monterey
    Jack cheese
1 1/2 cups (6 ounces)
    shredded Cheddar
    cheese
1 (3-ounce) package
    cream cheese,
    softened
1 cup picante sauce
1 medium red or green
    bell pepper, chopped

1/2 cup sliced green
    onions
1 teaspoon crushed
    cumin
8 (7- to 8-inch) flour
    tortillas
Shredded lettuce
Chopped tomato
Sliced black olives
    (optional)

Preheat the oven to 350 degrees. Mix 1 cup of the shredded Monterey Jack cheese, 1 cup of the shredded Cheddar cheese, cream cheese, 1/4 cup of the picante sauce, red bell pepper, green onions and cumin. Spoon 1/4 cup of the cheese mixture down the center of each tortilla. Roll and place, seam side down, in a 9-by-13-inch baking dish. Spoon the remaining 3/4 cup picante sauce evenly over the enchiladas. Cover with the remaining Monterey Jack cheese and the remaining Cheddar cheese. Bake for 20 minutes or until hot. To serve, top with shredded lettuce, tomato and black olives. Serve with additional picante sauce if desired. Yield: 4 servings.

Janice Burnside
Hale, Missouri

BLACK BEAN AND VEGETABLE TACOS

This has become a regular meal for my son's river rafting trips. No cooking is necessary, and the taco shells may be heated on the campfire.

8 taco shells
2 tablespoons olive oil
2 tablespoons fresh lime juice
1 teaspoon ground cumin
1 teaspoon minced garlic
1 teaspoon ground red pepper
1 (16-ounce) can black beans, drained, rinsed
1/2 cup chopped celery
1 (7-ounce) can whole kernel corn, drained
1/2 cup coarsely chopped carrots
1/3 cup chopped red onion
2 cups shredded iceberg lettuce
1/4 cup sour cream
4 ounces coarsely shredded Cheddar cheese

Preheat the oven to 250 degrees. Separate the taco shells; heat them in the oven while preparing the filling. Whisk the next 5 ingredients in a large bowl until blended. Add the black beans, corn, carrots, celery and onion; mix well. Place a spoonful of lettuce in each taco shell; add a spoonful of the vegetable mixture. Add more lettuce, a spoonful of sour cream and some Cheddar cheese. Yield: 4 servings.

Nancy Blair, Xi Tau
Ely, Nevada

Terri Stewart, Beta Gamma, Severna Park, Maryland, makes That Bean Thing by mashing two 15-ounce cans of drained black beans with 1/3 cup water and an envelope of taco seasoning mix, simmering for 5 minutes, and spooning into taco shells. Add shredded lettuce, cheese, and salsa.

❖ DELICIOUS PORTOBELLO MUSHROOM DELIGHT

4 portobello mushroom caps
4 tablespoons olive oil
4 slices mozzarella cheese
1 loaf French bread
1 medium onion, sliced
6 ounces mushrooms, sliced
1 red bell pepper, julienned
1 green pepper, julienned
4 tablespoons butter
Parsley

Preheat the broiler. Brush each portobello mushroom cap with olive oil. Broil for 1 or 2 minutes on each side. Lay one slice of cheese on each cap; allow the cheese to melt. Slice the bread in 2-inch pieces; broil both sides of each piece a few minutes or until golden brown. Sauté the onion, sliced mushrooms, red bell pepper and green pepper in the remaining olive oil and butter. Arrange the bread pieces on a plate. Cover with the portobello mushrooms. Smother with the sautéed mushroom mixture. Garnish with parsley. Yield: 4 servings.

Joyce M. Gough
Lakewood, California

LENTIL LOAF

This vegetarian substitute for meat loaf is also enjoyed by non-vegetarians.

2 cups lentils, cooked, drained
2 cups shredded Cheddar cheese
1 small onion, finely chopped
1/2 teaspoon pepper
1/2 teaspoon thyme
1 egg
1 cup toasted bread crumbs
1 tablespoon melted margarine or vegetable oil
Salt to taste
Dijon mustard (optional)
Honey (optional)

Preheat the oven to 350 degrees. Mash the lentils in a large bowl. Stir in the cheese and onion. Add the pepper, thyme, egg, bread crumbs, margarine and salt; mix well. Press into a 5-by-7-inch loaf pan. Bake for 45 minutes. Top with Dijon mustard and honey and bake for 5 minutes longer. Yield: 6 to 8 servings.

Sarah Stephens, Tau Master
Austin, Texas

Carolyn Spencer, Laureate Alpha Lambda, Manhattan, Kansas, sends a hint for Vegetable Pizza—make it more nutritious with a whole wheat crust and quicker by preparing the vegetables the night before.

VEGETABLE LOAF WITH CHEESE

1 cup cooked brown rice
2 cups (8 ounces)
    shredded Cheddar
    cheese
1 cup wheat germ
1 cup chopped walnuts
1 cup chopped
    mushrooms
1 large onion, chopped
1/2 cup finely chopped
    green pepper
1/2 cup finely shredded
    carrots
5 eggs
2 tablespoons soy sauce
2 tablespoons prepared
    mustard
1/2 teaspoon pepper
1/2 teaspoon thyme
1/2 teaspoon marjoram
1/2 teaspoon sage

Preheat the oven to 350 degrees. Mix the ingredients in a bowl. Pat firmly into a greased 5-by-9-inch loaf pan. Bake for 55 minutes or until browned. Let stand for 10 minutes before slicing. Yield: 6 servings.

Janet Gosack
Salmon, Idaho

CONFETTI VEGETABLE PANCAKES

1 cup finely shredded
    peeled russet or
    Idaho potatoes
1 cup finely shredded
    zucchini
1 cup finely shredded
    carrots
1 large onion, finely
    chopped
2 eggs, beaten
1/4 cup all-purpose flour
1/2 teaspoon poultry
    seasoning
Few drops of
    Worcestershire sauce
1/2 teaspoon salt
2 or 3 dashes of cayenne
    pepper
2 tablespoons vegetable
    oil
Applesauce or sour
    cream

Combine the potatoes, zucchini, carrots and onion in a large bowl. Combine the eggs, flour, poultry seasoning, Worcestershire sauce, salt and cayenne pepper in a separate bowl; add to the potato mixture; mix well. Heat the oil in a large skillet. Use 1/4 cup of the vegetable mixture to form each pancake. Fry the pancakes for 8 to 10 minutes or until golden on both sides, flattening with a spatula. Serve with applesauce or sour cream. Yield: 4 servings (8 pancakes).

Carole Stokes, Xi Zeta Epsilon
Portage, Michigan

Mary Jane Davis, Zeta Beta, Timberon, New Mexico, reminds us that New Mexico-Style Enchiladas are not rolled but stacked 3 or 4 tortillas high after dipping in red enchilada sauce, with chopped onions and mixed Cheddar and Jack cheese between the layers. Bake until heated through and top with a fried egg.

VEGETABLE CHEESE PIE

If desired, mix some cheese or a small amount of white sauce into the vegetables to hold them together.

1 cup broccoli florets
1 cup cauliflower florets
1 cup fresh peas
1 cup sliced carrots
1 (8-inch) whole wheat
    pastry shell,
    uncooked
1 large tomato,
    quartered
1 medium onion,
    chopped
1 clove of garlic, minced
1 1/2 cups shredded
    Cheddar cheese
1 tablespoon butter or
    margarine

Preheat the oven to 350 degrees. Steam the broccoli, cauliflower, peas and carrots for about 5 minutes or until tender-crisp. Drain the vegetables and place in the pastry shell. Add the tomato. Sprinkle with the chopped onion and garlic. Cover with the shredded cheese. Dot with butter. Bake for 30 minutes or until the cheese is melted and the crust is brown. Yield: 6 to 8 servings.

Ann Miles
Meriden, Kansas

ARTICHOKE AND RED PEPPER PIZZA

1 (10-ounce) can
    refrigerated pizza
    dough
4 cloves of garlic,
    minced
3 tablespoons olive oil
2 red bell peppers, cut
    into 1/4-inch strips
1 (12-ounce) package
    shredded mozzarella
    cheese
1 (4-ounce) jar sliced
    mushrooms
1 teaspoon dried basil
1 (6-ounce) jar
    marinated
    artichokes, drained,
    chopped

Preheat the oven to 425 degrees. Unroll the pizza dough and press into a lightly greased 15-inch pizza pan (or use a pizza stone). Bake for 6 to 8 minutes until lightly browned. Combine the garlic and 2 tablespoons of the olive oil; blend well. Spread the garlic mixture over the partially baked crust. Heat the remaining tablespoon of olive oil in a medium skillet. Add the red bell peppers; sauté until tender, about 5 minutes. Layer 1/2 of the cheese, the red bell peppers, the mushrooms, basil and artichokes over the crust. Top with the remaining cheese. Bake for 10 minutes or until the crust is golden brown and the cheese is melted. Yield: 8 to 10 servings.

Jeirenne McCraney, Xi Beta Xi
Dublin, Georgia

VEGETABLE BEAN STEW

1/4 cup olive oil	1/2 cup water
1 large onion, chopped	1 1/2 cups vegetable juice
1 large red bell pepper, chopped	cocktail (optional)
1 large green pepper, chopped	2 medium sweet potatoes, peeled, cut into 1/2-inch cubes
2 ribs celery, chopped	4 medium white potatoes, cooked, cubed
4 cloves of garlic, chopped	
1 1/2 teaspoons coriander	2 cups cooked chick-peas or 1 (16-ounce) can chick-peas
1/2 teaspoon cinnamon	
1/2 teaspoon turmeric	
4 large tomatoes, chopped	Salt to taste
	Hot Pepper Sauce

Heat the olive oil in a 5-quart kettle or frying pan over medium heat. Add the onion, red bell pepper, green pepper, celery, garlic, coriander, cinnamon and turmeric. Cook, stirring occasionally, until the onions are soft, about 5 minutes. Stir in the tomatoes, water and vegetable juice cocktail; cook for 2 minutes. Add the sweet potatoes, white potatoes, chick-peas and salt. Cover, reduce heat and simmer for 10 minutes or until the sweet potatoes are tender. Serve with Hot Pepper Sauce. Yield: 6 to 8 servings.

HOT PEPPER SAUCE

3/4 cup olive oil	2 cloves of garlic, minced
5 teaspoons ground red pepper	1/2 teaspoon salt
3 teaspoons cumin	

Combine the olive oil, red pepper, cumin, garlic and salt in a small saucepan. Cook over medium heat, stirring, about 5 minutes. Serve warm or room temperature.

Donna Terry, Preceptor Alpha Mu
Burnaby, British Columbia, Canada

❖ FRESH TOMATO BASIL TART

2 cups all-purpose flour	1/2 teaspoon dried basil or 2 teaspoons fresh basil
1/4 teaspoon salt	
2 tablespoons sugar	
4 teaspoons baking powder	1 cup mayonnaise
1/3 cup shortening	1 cup shredded Swiss cheese
3/4 cup buttermilk	
5 or 6 medium tomatoes, peeled, diced into 1-inch cubes	1 cup shredded sharp Cheddar cheese
1/2 teaspoon salt	2 tablespoons Parmesan cheese

Preheat the oven to 450 degrees. Combine the flour, the 1/4 teaspoon salt, sugar and baking powder in a large bowl. Cut the shortening into the flour mixture. Add the buttermilk, stirring just until ingredients are moistened. Let the dough rest for 1/2 hour. Meanwhile, combine the tomatoes, the 1/2 teaspoon salt and basil in a medium bowl. Combine the mayonnaise, Swiss cheese, Cheddar cheese and Parmesan cheese in a separate bowl. When time to assemble, press the dough into the bottom of a 9-inch springform pan. Bake for 10 minutes or until golden brown. Remove from the oven. Reduce the oven temperature to 400 degrees. Scatter the tomato mixture over the top of the crust. Cover with the cheese mixture. Bake for 15 minutes or until bubbly and browned. Yield: 6 to 8 servings.

Barbara T. Coates, Preceptor Beta Alpha
Portland, Oregon

PEACH BREAKFAST PUDDING

1/2 cup packed light brown sugar	1 1/4 cups milk
	1 teaspoon vanilla extract
2 tablespoons light corn syrup	Dash of nutmeg
2 tablespoons margarine	8 to 10 (1/2-inch) slices Italian, French or raisin bread, crusts removed
1/3 cup pecan pieces	
1 (12-ounce) package frozen sliced peaches, thawed, well drained	
	Whipped cream
3 eggs, beaten	

Combine the brown sugar, corn syrup and margarine in a saucepan over medium heat; bring to a boil, stirring. Remove from heat and pour into a greased 9-by-9-inch baking dish. Sprinkle with the pecans and half the peaches. Place the eggs, milk, vanilla and nutmeg in a medium bowl; whisk to combine. Cover the mixture in the baking dish with a layer of half the bread slices, trimming to fit. Cover with the remaining peaches; cover the peaches with the remaining bread. Pour the egg-milk mixture over the bread. Press down so the bread absorbs the liquid. Cover with plastic wrap and chill for 8 to 10 hours. Preheat the oven to 325 degrees. Remove the plastic wrap. Cover lightly with foil. Bake for 40 to 45 minutes or until a knife inserted in the center comes out clean. Remove from oven and run a knife around the edge. Let stand for 15 minutes. Slice into 3-by-3-inch squares. Carefully invert each serving so the pecans are on top. Serve with whipped cream. Yield: 9 servings.

Mary Elizabeth Reinhart, Gamma Master
Fox Point, Wisconsin

CHEESE TOMATO CASSEROLE

1 (16-ounce) can whole tomatoes	5 eggs, beaten
8 slices bread, crusts removed, cubed	Salt and pepper to taste
8 ounces shredded Cheddar cheese	2 tablespoons butter or margarine

Preheat the oven to 350 degrees. Drain the tomatoes, reserving the liquid. Layer the bread and cheese alternately in a greased 8-by-8-inch baking dish, ending with a layer of cheese. Combine the tomato liquid with the eggs, salt and pepper. Pour over the bread and cheese. Slice the tomatoes and arrange over the last cheese layer. Dot with butter. Bake for 45 minutes or until browned. Yield: 4 servings.

Margot H. Peverley, Preceptor Chi
Rawlins, Wyoming

CHILES RELLENOS SOUFFLE

Chiles rellenos made the old-fashioned way require a lot of time and are fried. This recipe gives you great rellenos without the hassle.

6 (4-ounce) cans whole green chiles, drained	1 (5-ounce) can evaporated milk
16 ounces shredded sharp Cheddar cheese	3 tablespoons all-purpose flour
16 ounces shredded Monterey Jack cheese	Salt and pepper to taste
2 large egg yolks, beaten	2 large egg whites
	Pinch of cream of tartar

Preheat the oven to 345 degrees. Layer the green chiles, Cheddar cheese and Monterey Jack cheese, 1/2 at a time, in a well-greased 9-by-13-inch baking dish. Combine the next 5 ingredients in a medium bowl. Beat the egg whites and cream of tartar to stiff peaks in another bowl. Fold the egg whites into the evaporated milk mixture. Spoon over the chiles and cheese. Bake for 45 minutes or until lightly browned. Yield: 8 to 10 servings.

Anna Magoffin, Xi Psi
Douglas, Arizona

COTTAGE CHEESE ROAST

4 cups Special-K cereal	1/2 cup finely chopped walnuts or pecans
1 large onion, finely chopped	1/2 cup milk
1/2 cup margarine or vegetable oil	5 eggs
2 (16-ounce) cartons cottage cheese	3 or 4 packets George Washington seasoning (golden)

Preheat the oven to 350 degrees. Combine the cereal, onion, margarine, cottage cheese, nuts, milk, eggs and seasoning in a bowl; mix well. Pour into a greased 9-by-13-inch baking dish. Bake for 1 to 1 1/2 hours or until golden brown. Yield: 6 to 8 servings.

Linda Anglin, Preceptor Theta
Reno, Nevada

MOCK CRAB CAKES

2 cups grated zucchini	2 eggs, beaten
1 cup seasoned bread crumbs	Salt and pepper to taste
1 tablespoon mayonnaise	1 medium onion, chopped
1 teaspoon Worcestershire sauce	3/4 cup shredded Cheddar cheese
1 teaspoon mustard	Vegetable oil for frying

Combine the zucchini, bread crumbs, mayonnaise, Worcestershire sauce, mustard, eggs, salt, pepper, onion and cheese in a medium bowl. Spoon the mixture into hot oil in a deep fryer. Cook until golden brown. Yield: 4 servings.

Margaret Beasley
Elkhorn, West Virginia

VEGETARIAN QUICHE

3 eggs	2 cups chopped vegetables such as cauliflower, broccoli, peas, parboiled carrots, drained canned mushrooms
1 1/2 cups evaporated milk	
2 tablespoons chopped onion	
1/2 cup chopped green pepper	
1/2 teaspoon salt	1 cup shredded Swiss or Cheddar cheese
1/2 teaspoon pepper	1 (9-inch) pastry shell

Preheat the oven to 375 degrees. Beat the eggs with the evaporated milk until well blended. Add the next 6 ingredients; blend well. Pour the mixture into the pastry shell. Bake for 40 minutes or until a knife inserted in the center comes out clean. Cool slightly and serve. Yield: 6 servings.

Elnora Teed
Livonia, New York

Phyllis Anne Ponn, Alpha Gamma, Manassas, Virginia, makes Baked Oatmeal by mixing 1/3 cup oil, 1/2 cup sugar, 1 egg, 2 cups quick-cooking oats, 1 1/2 teaspoons baking powder, 3/4 cup milk, and 1/2 teaspoon salt, pouring into a greased 6-by-9-inch pan, adding a sprinkle of cinnamon-sugar, and baking in a preheated 350-degree oven for 25 to 30 minutes. Serve with peaches and milk.

EASY CREAMY SOUFFLE

2 (16-ounce) cartons
  small-curd cottage
  cheese
6 eggs
1/2 cup melted butter or
  margarine
2 cups cubed process
  cheese

6 tablespoons all-
  purpose flour
1 (10-ounce) package
  frozen chopped
  spinach or broccoli,
  thawed, drained

Preheat the oven to 350 degrees. Beat the cottage cheese lightly with the eggs. Stir in the butter, process cheese, flour and spinach. Bake in a greased 11-by-13-inch pan for 1 hour. Yield: 12 servings.

Avos S. Klase, Laureate Pi
Bowie, Maryland

RICOTTA CHEESE BALLS (MEATLESS MEATBALLS)

This recipe came through Ellis Island from Italy in 1916. The dish was prepared on the Feast of Saint Joseph (March 19), which is celebrated all over Italy and the United States. Serve with macaroni or spaghetti for a meatless meal.

2 (16-ounce) cartons
  ricotta cheese
3 cups bread crumbs
2 teaspoons chopped
  parsley
1 teaspoon ground
  cloves

1 cup grated Romano
  cheese
6 eggs
Vegetable oil for frying

Combine the ricotta cheese, bread crumbs, parsley, cloves, Romano cheese and eggs in a bowl; mix well. Shape into balls using your hands, then flatten the balls. Fry in deep oil slowly until brown on both sides. Drain on paper towels. Yield: 3 dozen.

Joanne Morgan, Alpha Alpha Beta
Kansas City, Missouri

Ruth Siddens, Alpha Zeta, Mitchell, Indiana, makes Italian Stuffed Spaghetti Squash by cutting 2 medium squash in half, steaming for 15 minutes, and discarding the seeds. Loosen the squash pulp with a fork, pour off juices, and pat dry. Fill the squash with a mixture of 2 cups ricotta cheese, 1 cup shredded mozzarella cheese, 1/4 cup Parmesan cheese, and Italian seasoning and garlic powder to taste. Top with 2 cups tomato sauce and provolone or mozzarella slices and bake in a preheated 350-degree oven for 15 minutes.

SPANISH EGGS

2 cups uncooked
  medium noodles
1/2 cup chopped onions
1/2 cup chopped green
  pepper
3 tablespoons butter or
  margarine
1 (15-ounce) can sliced
  tomatoes, drained

1 cup shredded Cheddar
  cheese
1/4 cup butter or
  margarine
1/4 cup all-purpose flour
1/2 teaspoon salt
6 hard-cooked eggs

Preheat the oven to 350 degrees. Cook the noodles in boiling salted water until tender. Drain and set aside. Sauté the onions and green pepper in the 3 tablespoons butter in a medium saucepan until tender but not brown. Stir in the tomatoes. Simmer for 10 minutes. Stir in the cheese. Melt the 1/4 cup butter in a small saucepan; blend in the flour and salt. Stir the flour mixture into the tomato mixture. Cook, stirring, until thick. Place half the cooked noodles in a greased 2-quart ovenproof casserole dish. Slice 3 of the hard-cooked eggs over the noodles. Cover with half the tomato mixture. Repeat the layers. Bake for 25 minutes. Yield: 4 servings.

Marnie Tanner, Laureate Beta Mu
Kelowna, British Columbia, Canada

ARTICHOKE PASTA

This is a great recipe for a romantic dinner for two.

2 tablespoons butter or
  margarine
1 large clove garlic,
  minced
1 small onion, chopped
1 medium tomato,
  chopped
2 tablespoons sliced
  olives
1/2 cup dry white wine

1 tablespoon lemon
  juice
1 (6-ounce) jar
  marinated artichoke
  hearts, drained, sliced
6 ounces angel hair
  pasta
Grated Parmesan cheese
  to taste

Melt the butter in a wide frying pan over medium heat. Add the garlic and onion. Sauté, stirring occasionally, until the onion is translucent. Stir in the tomato, olives, wine, lemon juice and artichoke hearts. Bring to a boil. Continue to boil until the sauce is reduced by a third, about 5 to 10 minutes. Bring salted water to a boil in a 5- to 6-quart saucepan and cook the pasta until tender. Drain the pasta well. Place it in a warm bowl. Pour the sauce over the pasta. Mix well with 2 forks. Serve on plates and top with Parmesan cheese. Yield: 2 servings.

Michelle A. Worden, Chi
Laramie, Wyoming

ANGEL HAIR PASTA WITH GARLIC OIL

Serve this savory pasta with a green salad and crusty bread.

1/2 cup olive oil	24 ounces Angel hair
1 to 2 tablespoons chile	pasta
pepper seeds	Salt and pepper to taste
1 to 2 tablespoons dried	Grated Parmesan cheese
parsley flakes	
6 to 8 cloves of garlic,	
finely chopped	

Heat the olive oil for a couple of seconds in a large nonstick skillet over medium heat. Add the chile seeds, parsley and garlic. Sauté for a few minutes, stirring constantly, until the garlic is fragrant and lightly golden. Set aside. Boil the pasta until it is al dente; drain and add to the frying pan. Stir the pasta, coating it evenly with the olive oil and seasonings. Sprinkle with salt, pepper and Parmesan cheese. Serve immediately. Yield: 6 servings.

Mary Giuliano, Xi Delta Kappa
Fernie, British Columbia, Canada

❖ BLACK BEAN MANICOTTI

1/4 cup chopped onion	12 manicotti shells
1 clove of garlic, minced	2 eggs, beaten
1 tablespoon olive oil	2 1/2 cups 1-percent
2 3/4 cups cooked black	cottage cheese
beans	1 1/2 cups shredded
1 1/2 cups tomato sauce	mozzarella cheese
1 teaspoon ground	
oregano	

Preheat the oven to 350 degrees. Sauté the onion and garlic in the olive oil in a medium skillet. Stir in the black beans, tomato sauce and oregano. Heat thoroughly. Pour half the mixture into a 7 1/2-by-12-inch baking dish. Set aside. Cook the manicotti in boiling salted water for about 10 minutes or until tender. Drain and set aside. Mix the egg, cottage cheese and 1 cup of the mozzarella cheese in a bowl. Spoon about 1/4 cup of the cheese mixture into each manicotti shell. Arrange the stuffed shells over the bean mixture in the baking dish. Pour the remaining bean mixture over the stuffed shells. Cover with aluminum foil. Bake for 40 to 50 minutes. Remove the foil, sprinkle with the remaining 1/2 cup mozzarella cheese, return to the oven and bake for 3 minutes longer. Let stand for 5 minutes before serving. Yield: 6 servings.

Annora Bentley, Xi Gamma Iota
Alliance, Nebraska

PASTA WITH BLACK BEANS AND ARTICHOKE HEARTS

This dish is good even straight out of the refrigerator! Radiatore is a short, fat, rippled pasta.

1 tablespoon olive oil	2 (14-ounce) can low-
1 cup sliced green onions	sodium whole
3/4 teaspoon dried whole	tomatoes, undrained,
oregano	chopped
1/4 teaspoon salt	1 (15-ounce) can black
1/8 teaspoon crushed red	beans, drained
pepper	4 cups hot cooked
1/8 teaspoon black	radiatore
pepper	1 (14-ounce) can
1 clove of garlic,	artichoke hearts,
minced	drained, quartered

Heat the olive oil in a large nonstick skillet over medium heat. Add the green onions; sauté for 6 minutes. Stir in the oregano, salt, red pepper, black pepper, garlic and tomatoes. Simmer, covered, for 10 minutes. Add the black beans. Simmer, covered, for 5 minutes longer. Combine the bean mixture, radiatore and artichoke hearts in a large bowl. Toss to mix well. Serve warm or at room temperature. Yield: 6 servings.

Wyonne Metcalf, Xi Tau Tau
Santa Clarita, California

PASTA CECI

Healthy, inexpensive, and delicious, this is a meatless meal that children love. Serve with a tossed salad.

2 tablespoons olive oil	1 (16-ounce) can chick-
1 whole head of garlic	peas (ceci), undrained
cloves, peeled	Salt to taste
4 quarts water	Grated Parmesan cheese
1 (16-ounce) package	(optional)
ditalini pasta or	Crushed red pepper
elbow macaroni	(optional)

Heat the olive oil in a small skillet. Brown the garlic cloves in the oil just until golden brown. Set aside. Boil the water in a large kettle and add the pasta. Cook for 9 to 10 minutes or until the pasta is al dente. Pour off some of the water, leaving 1 to 1 1/2 inches of water covering the pasta in the kettle. Add the chickpeas, sautéed garlic and salt. Mix well and serve. Parmesan cheese and red pepper may be sprinkled on each individual serving. Yield: 4 hearty servings.

Gloria Giovelli
Winter Haven, Florida

BRIE, BASIL AND TOMATO PASTA

Yogurt cheese may be substituted for quark cheese.

12 ounces fettuccini
2 tablespoons olive oil
1/4 pound Brie cheese
3/4 cup quark cheese
2 cloves of garlic,
 minced

1 cup chopped fresh
 basil
1/2 teaspoon salt
1/4 teaspoon pepper
3 large tomatoes,
 seeded, chopped

Cook the fettuccini al dente in a large saucepan of boiling water. Combine the olive oil, Brie cheese, quark cheese, garlic, basil, salt and pepper; mix well. When the pasta is done, drain it and return it to the saucepan. Add the tomatoes and cheese mixture. Toss to blend. Serve immediately. Yield: 4 servings.

Yvonne Evans
Burton, New Brunswick, Canada

CHEESE STUFFED SHELLS

You may want to freeze half of the 2 dozen shells this recipe makes. After the shells are stuffed with cheese, place a dozen of them on a waxed-paper-lined baking sheet, cover, and place in the freezer until frozen, about 2 hours. Remove them from the sheet and place them in a freezer bag to store in the freezer until needed. Add 10 minutes to the baking time.

2 eggs, beaten
2 (15-ounce) containers
 part-skim ricotta
 cheese
2 cups shredded
 mozzarella cheese
3/4 cup grated Parmesan
 cheese
3/4 teaspoon oregano
1/2 cup chopped parsley
 or 1 tablespoon dried
 parsley

1/8 teaspoon pepper
12 ounces jumbo shell
 pasta, cooked,
 drained
3 cups prepared
 spaghetti sauce
Parmesan cheese for
 garnish

Preheat the oven to 350 degrees. Stir together the eggs, ricotta cheese, mozzarella cheese, the 3/4 cup Parmesan cheese, oregano, parsley and pepper in a medium bowl. Spoon 2 tablespoons of the mixture into each pasta shell. Spread a thin layer of spaghetti sauce in the bottom of a 9-by-13-inch glass baking dish. Arrange the shells in a single layer over the sauce. Spoon the remaining spaghetti sauce over the shells. Sprinkle with Parmesan cheese. Bake for 30 minutes or until heated through.
Yield: 5 or 6 servings.

Molly Golemo, Zeta Pi
Iowa City, Iowa

EGGPLANT SAUCE FOR PASTA

4 tablespoons butter or
 margarine
4 tablespoons olive oil
1 small onion, very
 thinly sliced
8 to 12 mushrooms,
 sliced
Parsley to taste
Oregano to taste

Onion salt to taste
1 small eggplant,
 chopped, bite-size
 pieces
1 to 4 cloves of garlic,
 chopped
1 medium tomato,
 peeled, chopped

Heat the butter and olive oil in a large skillet over medium-low heat. Add the onion; sauté until brown and limp. Add the mushrooms; sauté until very dark. Add the parsley, oregano and onion salt. Add the eggplant; sauté until very dark and very soft. Add the garlic and tomato. Sauté for 15 to 20 minutes to blend flavors, adding tomato juice or water if mixture gets too dry. Yield: 2 to 4 servings.

Julie DeMoss, Iota Chi
Salida, Colorado

LASAGNA ROLLUPS

2/3 (16-ounce) package
 lasagna noodles
1 tablespoon vegetable
 oil
1 (10-ounce) package
 frozen chopped
 broccoli, thawed,
 squeezed dry
2 tablespoons minced
 onion
1 (15-ounce) container
 ricotta cheese

1/4 cup grated Parmesan
 cheese
1/2 teaspoon salt
1 egg, beaten
1 (14-ounce) jar
 spaghetti sauce
1/2 cup water
1 (4-ounce) package
 shredded mozzarella
 cheese

Preheat the oven to 375 degrees. Cook the lasagna according to package directions. Heat the oil in a 2-quart saucepan over medium heat. Add the broccoli and onion; sauté until tender, about 5 minutes. Remove from heat. Stir in the ricotta cheese, Parmesan cheese, salt and egg. Drain the noodles; place them in a single layer on waxed paper. Spread some cheese mixture on each noodle; roll up like a jelly roll. Mix the spaghetti sauce with the water in a bowl. Spoon about 3/4 of the diluted sauce into a 7-by-11-inch baking dish. Arrange the noodles seam side down over the sauce. Cover with the remaining sauce and the mozzarella cheese. Cover loosely with foil. Bake for 30 minutes or until hot and bubbly and the cheese is melted. Yield: 10 to 12 servings.

Dee Carter
Wooster, Ohio

HOME-STYLE MUSHROOM LASAGNA

4 tablespoons butter or
  margarine
4 cups thickly sliced
  mushrooms
3 cups prepared tomato
  sauce
3 tablespoons all-
  purpose flour
2 cups milk
1/4 teaspoon nutmeg
1/2 teaspoon salt
2 cups Canadian ricotta
  cheese

1 tablespoon chopped
  fresh basil or 2
  teaspoons dried
  parsley
2 cups shredded
  Canadian mozzarella
  cheese
1/2 cup shredded
  Canadian Parmesan
  cheese
15 to 18 oven-ready
  lasagna noodles

Preheat the oven to 375 degrees. Melt 2 tablespoons of the butter in a large skillet. Add the mushrooms and cook over medium heat until tender. Drain. Combine the mushrooms and 1 cup of the tomato sauce. Set aside. To make a béchamel sauce, melt the remaining 2 tablespoons butter in a small saucepan. Add the flour, stirring to blend well. Add the milk, nutmeg and salt; cook, stirring, over medium heat until thick. Remove from heat; set aside. Combine the ricotta cheese, basil, 1 cup of the mozzarella cheese, 1/4 cup of the Parmesan cheese and 1 cup of the béchamel sauce in a bowl. Spread 1 cup of the tomato sauce over the bottom of a 9-by-13-inch baking dish. Layer 5 to 6 lasagna noodles over the sauce, overlapping the noodle slightly and allowing them to reach the edges of the dish. Spread the ricotta mixture evenly over the noodles. Layer the mushroom mixture and the rest of the lasagna noodles over the ricotta. Spread the remaining cup of tomato sauce over the noodles, covering them completely. Drizzle with the remaining béchamel sauce. Top with the remaining 1 cup mozzarella cheese and 1/4 cup Parmesan cheese. Cover the dish with foil. Bake for 35 minutes. Remove the foil. Return to the oven and bake for 10 minutes longer. Yield: 6 servings.

Irja Hansen
Ramore, Ontario, Canada

CORNY MACARONI AND CHEESE

This dish pleases everyone and is great for the working woman.

2 cups tricolor macaroni
  twists, cooked,
  drained
1 cup skim milk
1 cup 1-percent cottage
  cheese
1/2 cup Egg Beaters

1 (8-ounce) can whole
  kernel corn, drained
1/2 cup shredded Cheddar
  cheese
10 crackers, any variety,
  coarsely crushed

Preheat the oven to 350 degrees. Combine the macaroni twists, milk, cottage cheese, Egg Beaters, corn and 1/4 cup of the Cheddar cheese in a large bowl. Spoon the mixture into a 9-by-9-inch baking dish. Bake for 30 minutes. Toss the crushed crackers with the remaining 1/4 cup of cheese in a small bowl. Remove the lasagna from the oven and sprinkle with the cracker mixture. Return to oven. Bake for 30 minutes more or until browned and set. Yield: 6 servings.

Virginia Y. Bailey
Iaeger, West Virginia

THREE-CHEESE BAKED PENNE WITH VEGETABLES

This dish can be prepared, covered, and refrigerated for up to a day.

1 red bell pepper,
  chopped
1 yellow bell pepper,
  chopped
8 ounces mushrooms,
  quartered
2 zucchini, chopped
1 small eggplant, diced
2 cloves of garlic, minced
1/4 cup olive oil
Salt and pepper to taste

2 tablespoons basil
16 ounces penne pasta
1 (26-ounce) can
  meatless spaghetti
  sauce
8 ounces mozzarella
  cheese, shredded
8 ounces fontina cheese,
  shredded
1 cup grated Parmesan
  cheese

Preheat the oven to 500 degrees. Toss together the red bell pepper, yellow bell pepper, mushrooms, zucchini, eggplant, garlic and oil in a large shallow pan. Spread over a rimmed baking sheet. Bake for 20 minutes to soften. Remove to a greased 9-by-13-inch baking dish. Season with salt, pepper and basil. Cook the pasta in a large kettle of boiling salted water. Drain and rinse under cold water. Add the pasta, spaghetti sauce, mozzarella cheese and fontina cheese to the vegetables; toss to mix. Sprinkle with Parmesan cheese. Reduce oven heat to 375 degrees. Bake for 35 to 40 minutes. Yield: 8 servings.

Patricia Brooks
Oshawa, Ontario, Canada

Marie Franzen, Mt. View, California, says she loves Hawaiian Tofu Delight (invented by her native Hawaiian significant other) when served cold with Chinese food. Drain 16 ounces of tofu well and cut into 1-inch pieces. Sprinkle with 1 tablespoon shoyu and 1 teaspoon sesame oil. Top with 1 sliced scallion, 1 teaspoon sesame seeds, and a sprinkle of cayenne pepper or paprika.

SPICY PASTA

16 ounces rotini, cooked al dente, drained
4 to 6 tablespoons olive oil
2 tablespoons red vinegar
Dash of salt
1/4 teaspoon black pepper
1/4 teaspoon cayenne pepper
2/3 cup sliced black olives
1 1/2 cups chopped cucumber
1 1/2 cups chopped celery
4 to 6 green onions, thinly sliced
1/2 cup chopped sweet pickles
1/2 cup chopped pimiento
1/2 to 1 cup mayonnaise
1/2 to 1 cup grated Parmesan cheese

Toss lightly the rotini, olive oil, vinegar, salt, black pepper and cayenne pepper in a large bowl. Cool, covered, in the refrigerator for 1 hour. Combine the pasta mixture with the black olives, cucumber, celery, green onions, pickles and pimiento. Add the mayonnaise and Parmesan cheese; mix lightly. Chill for several hours before serving. Yield: 8 to 12 servings.

Mary Ellen Grossman, Preceptor Gamma Eta
Lawrenceburg, Indiana

CREAMY BROCCOLI PASTA

1 (10-ounce) can cream of mushroom soup
1 cup shredded Cheddar cheese
1/2 cup mayonnaise
1 tablespoon dried minced onions
1 teaspoon black pepper
8 ounces pasta shells, cooked, drained
1/2 cup sliced black olives
1 (10-ounce) package frozen broccoli pieces, cooked, drained
1 cup seasoned bread crumbs

Preheat the oven to 350 degrees. Mix the first 5 ingredients in a large bowl. Stir in the pasta shells, black olives and broccoli. Pour the mixture into a 9-by-13-inch glass baking dish. Cover with bread crumbs. Bake for 40 minutes. Yield: 8 servings.

Diane Heaphy, Preceptor Alpha Nu
Syracuse, New York

Dottie Inman, Laureate Alpha Pi, Sedona, Arizona, says the Quick Easy Way to Cook Spaghetti is to bring a large pot of water to a boil, add 12 ounces spaghetti, and stir to separate. Return to a boil. Turn off the burner, cover the pot, and let stand for 10 minutes; do not lift the lid to peek. The spaghetti will be just perfect and ready to drain and serve with your favorite sauce.

SPINACH MANICOTTI

1 (10-ounce) package frozen chopped spinach, cooked, drained
1 (5-ounce) can cooked chicken
1 (4-ounce) can mushroom pieces
1 egg
1/4 cup Parmesan cheese
1 (16-ounce) package manicotti noodles, cooked al dente, drained
2 tablespoons butter or margarine
2 tablespoons all-purpose flour
2 cans Milnot (nondairy canned milk)
1/4 teaspoon pepper
1/4 teaspoon nutmeg
1/2 cup Parmesan cheese

Preheat the oven to 350 degrees. Heat the cooked spinach in a medium saucepan over medium heat, stirring, for 1 minute. Add the chicken and mushroom pieces; cook, stirring, for 3 minutes longer. Combine with the egg and the 1/4 cup Parmesan cheese in a bowl. Stuff the pasta with the spinach mixture; arrange in a 9-by-13-inch baking dish. Melt the butter in a medium saucepan over medium-high heat. Add the flour and heat for 1 minute. Add the Milnot and bring to a boil. Stir in the pepper and nutmeg. Pour the hot Milnot mixture over the pasta. Sprinkle with 1/2 cup Parmesan cheese. Bake for 15 to 20 minutes or until bubbly. Yield: 10 to 12 servings.

Amillia I. Perrine, Xi Kappa Pi
Lebanon, Illinois

ITALIAN SQUASH AND PASTA

Serve this inexpensive main dish with a salad and bread.

1/2 onion, chopped
1/4 cup olive oil
3 yellow squash, sliced
2 zucchini, sliced
1 (15-ounce) can diced Italian tomatoes, undrained
8 ounces mushrooms, sliced
1 (8-ounce) can tomato sauce
1 (8-ounce) package angel hair pasta, cooked, drained

Sauté the onion in the olive oil in a deep kettle. Add the squash, zucchini, tomatoes, mushrooms and tomato sauce. Simmer over low heat until squash is tender, about 20 minutes. Serve the squash sauce over the pasta. Yield: 4 servings.

Sharon Toups, Pi Psi
Bryan, Texas

FRAN'S VEGETABLE MEDLEY OVER PASTA

I use this as a side dish when having a large number (fifty!) of people over for a buffet.

2 medium zucchini	1 cup dry white wine
2 medium yellow summer squash	1/2 teaspoon minced garlic
1 medium yellow onion	16 ounces vermicelli or angel hair pasta, cooked, drained
2 (15-ounce) cans diced tomatoes	2 tablespoons grated Parmesan cheese
1 1/2 teaspoons salt	
1/2 cup olive oil	
1 teaspoon dried sweet basil	

Peel and slice the zucchini and summer squash; place in a 3-quart microwave-safe casserole dish with a lid. Peel and slice the onion; separate into rings. Add the onion rings to the squash. Add the tomatoes, salt, olive oil, basil, wine and garlic; toss well. Cover and microwave on High for 30 minutes, stirring every 10 minutes. Serve over the cooked pasta. Sprinkle the cheese over the sauce. Yield: 6 servings.

Fran LaFrance-Proscino, Laureate Nu
Wallingford, Connecticut

VEGETABLE LASAGNA

This recipe takes time to prepare, but you can make it ahead of time and freeze. Then just thaw and bake for 20 to 30 minutes. It can be frozen in individual serving sizes as well—for a quick lunch, just take a serving out of the freezer and pop it in the microwave.

4 medium zucchini, coarsely chopped	2 tablespoons finely chopped parsley
1 large onion, chopped	2 teaspoons oregano
1 medium green pepper, chopped	1 teaspoon basil
1 carrot, finely chopped	1 teaspoon salt
1/2 cup celery, chopped	1/2 teaspoon thyme
2 cloves of garlic, minced	1/4 teaspoon pepper
1/4 cup olive oil	9 wide curly lasagna noodles, cooked, drained
2 (15-ounce) cans tomatoes in sauce	16 ounces (2 cups) part-skim ricotta cheese
1 (8-ounce) can tomato sauce	10 ounces (2 1/4 cups) shredded skim mozzarella cheese
1 (6-ounce) can tomato paste	1/2 cup grated Parmesan cheese
1/4 cup dry white wine	

Preheat the oven to 350 degrees. Cook the zucchini, onion, green pepper, carrot, celery and garlic in the olive oil in a large skillet over medium heat for 15 minutes, stirring frequently. Stir in the tomatoes, tomato sauce and tomato paste. Add the wine, parsley, oregano, basil, salt, thyme and pepper; bring to a boil, stirring to break up the tomatoes. Reduce heat to low. Simmer, covered, for 30 minutes. Uncover the skillet and bring to a boil. Boil until the sauce is reduced to about 5 cups. Spread 1/4 of the sauce over the bottom of a 9-by-11-inch baking dish. Arrange 3 noodles over the sauce; dot with 1/3 of the ricotta cheese; sprinkle with 1/4 of the mozzarella cheese and 1/4 of the Parmesan cheese. Repeat this procedure twice. Spread the remaining sauce over all; top with the remaining mozzarella cheese and Parmesan cheese. Bake for 30 to 40 minutes or until bubbly. Let stand for 5 minutes before serving. Yield: 8 servings.

Tammy E. Schlueter, Mu Sigma
Concordia, Missouri

RATATOUILLE STRUDEL

1/2 small eggplant	Basil, salt and pepper to taste
1/2 medium red onion	1/2 cup grated Parmesan cheese
1 small zucchini	
1 small yellow squash	1/2 cup ricotta cheese
1 small yellow pepper	8 sheets phyllo dough
3 cloves of garlic, minced	Melted butter or margarine
1 tablespoon olive oil	Basil for garnish
2 medium tomatoes, chopped	

Peel the eggplant and onion. Scrub the zucchini, squash and yellow pepper. Finely chop the vegetables. Chill, covered, in separate bowls in the refrigerator for 8 to 10 hours. Preheat the oven to 350 degrees. Sauté the onion and garlic in the olive oil in a medium skillet over medium-low heat for a few minutes. Add the eggplant, zucchini, squash and yellow pepper; sauté a few minutes longer. Stir in the tomatoes. Season with basil, salt and pepper. Pour into a medium bowl; cool slightly. Stir in the cheeses. Adjust seasoning. Alternate layers of phyllo and melted butter, ending with phyllo. Spread with the vegetable filling. Roll up like a jelly roll. Place the roll seam side down; cut it in 1-inch pieces at an angle. Arrange on a baking sheet. Bake for 10 to 15 minutes or until golden brown. Yield: 12 to 20 servings.

Julia Gatsos
New Albany, Indiana

Pleasing Pastas

Can you imagine a food
that boasts more variety and
versatility than pasta?
Smothered in a thick, hearty sauce,
it's the most satisfying of meals for
the long, cold days of winter.
Tossed with garden-fresh vegetables
and a simple dressing, it's a refreshing
light lunch for the porch or patio.
As a side dish, pasta makes the perfect stand-in
for a baked potato—or use it as an entrée and
enjoy a health-conscious alternative to meat.
Any way you fix it, pasta is
a no-fuss way to please
every member of the family!

❖ PASTA REFRESHER

To save even more time and to enhance flavor, try making this simple dish a day ahead. And don't be afraid to substitute any in-season fruit for the pineapple, melon, or grapes.

**3 cups (8 ounces)
uncooked rotini
1 (20-ounce) can
pineapple chunks,
drained
1 cup halved seedless
grapes**

**2 cups cubed melon
1 cup sliced celery
1 cup vanilla yogurt
1/4 cup mayonnaise
1/2 teaspoon ground
ginger**

Cook the rotini pasta in boiling water until tender; drain well. Set aside to cool. Prepare the fruit and celery. Combine the pasta, fruit and celery in a large bowl. Gently stir in the yogurt, mayonnaise and ginger; combine well. Chill, covered, in the refrigerator for at least 2 hours or overnight. Serve chilled. Yield: 6 to 10 servings.

*Dura A. Barbour
Uniontown, Ohio*

SPAGHETTI FRUIT SALAD

**1 cup confectioners'
sugar
2 eggs
1/2 cup lemon juice
1/2 teaspoon salt
8 ounces uncooked
spaghetti, broken
into 2-inch pieces
1 (20-ounce) can
pineapple tidbits**

**3 medium tart apples,
diced
1/4 cup chopped nuts
1/4 cup maraschino
cherries, halved
1 (8-ounce) carton
whipped topping**

Combine the confectioners' sugar, eggs, lemon juice and salt in a saucepan; cook over medium heat, stirring, for about 4 minutes or until the temperature reaches 160 degrees and mixture is thickened. Cool completely. Cook the spaghetti according to package directions; drain and rinse in cold water. Place in a large bowl. Drain the pineapple, reserving the juice; pour the reserved juice over the spaghetti; stir in the diced apples. Toss gently; drain. Stir in the egg mixture and the pineapple tidbits. Chill, covered, in the refrigerator for 8 to 10 hours. Stir in the nuts and cherries. Fold in the whipped topping. Yield: 12 to 14 servings.

*Doris L. Claypole, Alpha Gamma Alpha
Warsaw, Missouri*

ANTIPASTO SALAD

If you cut up all the ingredients ahead of time, you can simply toss them together at meal time.

**2 ounces sliced hard
salami
2 ounces sliced ham
2 ounces sliced
provolone
1 pound uncooked bow
tie pasta
6 cups torn romaine
lettuce or lettuce of
choice
1 cup thinly sliced celery**

**1 cup thinly sliced red
onion or green onion
1/2 cup pitted black
olives
1/4 cup sliced pimientos
(optional)
1/4 cup olive oil
3 tablespoons red wine
vinegar
1 1/2 teaspoons salt**

Cut the salami and ham into 1/4-inch-wide strips. Cut the provolone into 1/2-inch-wide strips. Cook the pasta according to package directions; drain. Place in a large bowl. Add the lettuce, celery, onion, salami, ham, cheese, olives and pimientos. Whisk together or shake in a jar the olive oil, vinegar and salt. Pour over the pasta; toss to coat. Yield: 12 servings.

*Debra Hinzman, Sigma
Rapid City, South Dakota*

BOW TIE PASTA SALAD

This is a fast, easy side dish. I buy ripe olives already halved.

**16 ounces uncooked bow
tie pasta
1 (16-ounce) bag frozen
mixed broccoli,
cauliflower and
carrots**

**1 cup light Italian
dressing
1 bunch green onions,
thinly sliced
1 cup pitted ripe olives,
halved**

Cook the pasta using package directions; drain. Cook the frozen vegetables according to package directions; drain. Combine the pasta and vegetables with the Italian dressing, green onions and olives in a large bowl. Chill, covered, in the refrigerator until serving time. Yield: 8 servings.

*Laura Best, Rho Alpha
Winfield, Kansas*

Annette Thivierge, Alpha Omicron, Lewiston, Idaho, makes a versatile Easy Pasta Salad with a package of pasta cooked and cooled, drained black olive halves, cherry tomato quarters, and ranch dressing. She frequently adds other fresh vegetables. Her daughter always picks out the "yucky" things and tries to get her brother to eat them.

MARINATED ITALIAN SALAD

1½ cups vegetable oil	1 small head
1 cup lemon juice	cauliflower, broken
1½ cups grated	up
Parmesan cheese	2 small stalks broccoli,
1 tablespoon dry Italian	broken up
dressing mix	2 stalks celery, chopped
1½ teaspoons sugar	1 (6-ounce) can ripe
⅛ teaspoon garlic	olives, sliced
powder	2 bunches green onions,
½ teaspoon parsley	chopped
½ teaspoon paprika	½ green pepper, chopped
½ teaspoon pepper	3 or 4 carrots, sliced
1 (16-ounce) package	8 ounces mushrooms,
tortellini	sliced

Put the oil, lemon juice, Parmesan cheese, dressing mix, sugar, garlic powder, parsley, paprika and pepper in a blender container; blend well. Put the tortellini, cauliflower, broccoli, celery, olives, green onions, green pepper, carrots and mushrooms in a large bowl. Pour the dressing over the vegetables and refrigerate for 8 to 10 hours. Mix and serve. Yield: 10 servings.

Paula Stark, Beta Delta
Waukesha, Wisconsin

PICKLED NOODLES

This dish is delicious with a sandwich! It keeps well in the refrigerator.

2 cups sugar	1 (16-ounce) package
2½ cups distilled or	rigatoni, cooked
cider vinegar	1 unpeeled cucumber,
¼ cup vegetable oil	finely chopped
1 teaspoon pepper	1 (2-ounce) jar
2 teaspoons prepared	pimientos
mustard	1 medium onion, finely
1 tablespoon salt	chopped
1 teaspoon garlic salt	1 medium unpeeled
(optional)	cucumber, finely
1 tablespoon parsley	chopped
flakes	1 (2-ounce) jar
1 onion, finely chopped	pimientos

Combine the sugar, vinegar, oil, pepper, mustard, salt, garlic salt and parsley flakes in a saucepan over medium heat to make the marinade. Bring just to a simmer; remove from heat. Place the onion, rigatoni, cucumber and pimientos in a large bowl. Pour the hot marinade over the pasta and vegetables. Cover and marinate for 24 hours in the refrigerator. Yield: 10 servings.

June Baysinger, Theta Master
Tucson, Arizona

RADIATORE CHEF'S SALAD

This is a great recipe for using the "special" vinegars you may receive as gifts.

12 ounces radiatore	1 bunch romaine lettuce,
pasta, cooked,	torn
drained	½ cup olive oil
3 medium tomatoes,	½ cup of your favorite
chopped	vinegar
1 red onion, sliced thin	2 cups croutons
16 ounces Gruyère	½ cup grated Parmesan
cheese, diced	cheese

Prepare the pasta, tomatoes, onion, Gruyère cheese and lettuce. Chill, covered, in a large bowl in the refrigerator until ready to serve. Mix the oil and vinegar, pour over the salad and toss. Top with the croutons and Parmesan cheese. Yield: 4 to 6 servings.

Sue Lieberman, Xi Rho Chi
Roseville, California

SPRINGTIME SALAD YEAR ROUND

You may substitute any kind of pasta for the macaroni. The recipe may be halved.

2 (8-ounce) packages	1 onion
large shell macaroni	2 cups real mayonnaise
1½ green peppers	1¼ cups sugar
1½ cucumbers	½ cup white vinegar
¼ pound radishes	1 teaspoon white pepper
2 ribs celery	1 scant teaspoon salt

Cook the shell macaroni according to package directions; drain and cool. Cut the green pepper into medium slices or chunks; quarter the cucumber and slice; slice the radishes; cut the celery into thin diagonal slices; thinly slice the onion. Add the vegetables to the macaroni; mix well. Add the mayonnaise, sugar, vinegar, white pepper and salt; mix well. Chill, covered, in the refrigerator for 8 to 10 hours. Mix well before serving. Yield: 10 servings.

Judy Flannery, Laureate Alpha Omega
Yukon, Oklahoma

Dixie Hickrod, Laureate Alpha Omega, Princeton, Indiana, marks special occasions with a hot or cold Pasta Specific by cooking 6 to 8 ounces of a special-shape and/or color pasta such as valentine hearts, Christmas trees, or college logos. She adds a can of water-pack tuna and ⅓ cup Italian salad dressing. Serve immediately or chill until serving time.

BROCCOLI AND CHICKEN PASTA SALAD

Add bread and dessert for a quick low-calorie meal.

3 cups raw chunked
    broccoli florets and
    peeled stems
1/2 cup chopped celery
1/4 cup chopped red bell
    pepper
1/4 cup chopped red
    onion
1 (10-ounce) package
    cheese tortellini,
    cooked, drained

2 cups chopped cooked
    chicken breasts,
    defatted
2/3 cup fat-free salad
    dressing of choice
1/2 cup fat-free croutons
    of choice

Mix the broccoli, celery, bell pepper, red onion, tortellini, chicken and salad dressing in a large bowl. Chill, covered, in the refrigerator for at least 1 hour or overnight to blend flavors. Sprinkle croutons over the top before serving. Yield: 6 servings.

Heather A. Barker
Fort Worth, Texas

SUMMER CHICKEN PASTA SALAD

Substitute or add any favorite in-season vegetables. Use green pepper if the red pepper is not in season. Much of this salad can be prepared in advance.

6 cups water
1 teaspoon salt
1 (3-pound) chicken
8 ounces spaghetti
    noodles
1 cruet Good Seasons
    Italian dressing
1 cup thinly sliced green
    scallions
1 sweet red pepper,
    chopped

1 (6-ounce) jar
    marinated artichoke
    hearts, cut up
4 ounces fresh
    mushrooms, sliced
1/2 cup sliced black
    olives
1 pint red cherry
    tomatoes, halved
1 ripe avocado, chunked

Bring the water and salt to a boil. Add the chicken, breast side up, and simmer for 25 minutes. Simmer back side up for 20 minutes longer. Chill chicken in broth, covered, in the refrigerator for 2 to 4 hours or overnight. Cook the spaghetti according to package directions; drain. Toss the spaghetti with 3/4 cup of the Italian dressing, reserving the remainder. Chill the spaghetti, covered, in the refrigerator for 2 to 4 hours or overnight. Remove the skin and bones from the chicken. Cut the meat into 1-inch pieces; set aside. Toss the spaghetti to separate the strands; add the chicken and toss again. Add the scallions, red pepper, artichoke hearts, mushrooms, olives, cherry tomatoes and avocado. Shake the remaining Italian dressing; sprinkle over the salad. Gently toss once more. Yield: 6 to 8 servings.

Jan Pochert, Xi Sigma Omicron
Browns Valley, California

FLORENTINE DITALI WITH MEAT SAUCE

1 tablespoon olive oil
1 pound ground beef
1 medium onion,
    chopped
2 cloves of garlic,
    minced
1 (15-ounce) can tomato
    sauce
1 (6-ounce) can tomato
    paste
1 1/2 cups water
1/2 cup dry red wine
2 tablespoons parsley
1 teaspoon oregano

3/4 teaspoon hot pepper
    sauce
1 1/4 teaspoons salt or
    salt to taste
1/4 teaspoon black
    pepper, or to taste
1 (10-ounce) package
    frozen spinach,
    thawed
3 cups uncooked ditali
    macaroni
1/2 cup grated Parmesan
    cheese

Preheat the oven to 375 degrees. Heat the olive oil in a 10-inch skillet; add the ground beef, onion and garlic; cook over medium-high heat until the meat is brown; drain and return to heat. Add the tomato sauce, tomato paste, water, wine, parsley, oregano, hot pepper sauce, salt and pepper; reduce heat and simmer for 30 minutes. Stir in the spinach. While the sauce is simmering, cook the macaroni according to package directions; drain. Combine the meat sauce, macaroni and 1/4 cup of the Parmesan cheese in a large bowl; pour into a 9-by-13-inch baking pan. Sprinkle the top with the remaining 1/4 cup Parmesan cheese. Bake, uncovered, for 25 to 30 minutes. Yield: 6 to 8 servings.

Sandy Casey, Xi Tau Psi
Highland Village, Texas

SPINACH AND ORZO PIE

1/2 pound ground beef
2 eggs, beaten
3 cups cooked orzo (1 1/2
    cups uncooked)
1 (15-ounce) jar chunky
    spaghetti sauce
1/3 cup grated Parmesan
    cheese

1 (10-ounce) package
    frozen chopped
    spinach
1/2 cup ricotta cheese
1/4 teaspoon nutmeg
1/2 cup shredded
    mozzarella cheese

Preheat the oven to 350 degrees. Brown the beef in a skillet; drain the fat. Combine the eggs, cooked orzo, 1/2 cup of the spaghetti sauce and Parmesan cheese in a medium bowl. Spread the mixture over the bottom and up the sides of a greased 9-inch pie plate, forming a shell. Cook the spinach according to package directions; drain well. Mix the ground beef, spinach, ricotta cheese and nutmeg in a medium bowl. Spoon over the pasta. Spread the remaining spaghetti sauce over the filling. Cover the edge of the pie with foil strips. Bake for 30 minutes. Remove from the oven. Top with the shredded cheese. Return to the oven and bake for 3 to 5 minutes longer or until the cheese is melted. Remove to a wire rack. Let stand for 5 minutes before serving. Yield: 6 servings.

Cynthia Hirst
Cardville, Maine

JOAN'S LASAGNA

2 pounds ground beef	1 (10-ounce) package
1/2 cup chopped onion	lasagna noodles
1/2 cup chopped celery	3 cups cottage cheese
1/2 cup chopped carrots	1/2 cup grated Parmesan
1 (16-ounce) can	cheese
tomatoes, cut up	2 eggs, beaten
1 (16-ounce) can tomato	2 tablespoons minced
purée	parsley
1 teaspoon salt	1/4 teaspoon pepper
1/2 teaspoon dried	16 ounces mozzarella
oregano, crushed	cheese, thinly sliced
1/4 teaspoon pepper	

Preheat the oven to 375 degrees. Cook the ground beef, onion, celery and carrots in a skillet sprayed with nonstick cooking spray over medium-low heat until the meat is lightly browned. Drain excess fat. Stir in the next 5 ingredients. Simmer, uncovered, for 30 minutes. Cook the lasagna noodles using package directions; drain. Combine the cottage cheese, Parmesan cheese, eggs, parsley and remaining pepper. Place half the noodles in a greased 9-by-13-inch baking dish. Spread with half the cottage cheese filling, half the mozzarella cheese and half the meat sauce. Repeat the layers. Bake, uncovered, for 30 minutes. Let stand for 10 to 15 minutes. Yield: 10 to 12 servings.

Claire Domning, Xi Gamma Xi
Logansport, Indiana

Rebecca Bough, Theta Lambda, Rogers, Arkansas, makes Lasagna by mixing a cup of spaghetti sauce, 1/2 cup cottage cheese, 3/4 cup shredded mozzarella cheese, and 1 1/2 cups wide noodles in a small casserole. Sprinkle with 2 tablespoons Parmesan cheese. In a preheated 375-degree oven it requires only 20 minutes to bake.

FETTUCCINI VERDE

3 tablespoons olive oil	1 medium tomato,
1 large onion, thinly	chopped
sliced	1 (8-ounce) package dry
8 ounces mushrooms,	green fettuccine
thinly sliced	1/2 cup whipping cream
1/4 teaspoon minced	1/2 cup chopped parsley
garlic	1/2 cup dry white wine or
1/4 cup butter or	dry sherry (optional)
margarine	1/8 teaspoon nutmeg
1 (3-ounce) package	Salt and pepper to taste
thinly sliced ham,	1/2 cup grated Parmesan
julienned	cheese
1 teaspoon dry basil	

Heat the olive oil in a large frying pan over medium-high heat. Add the onion. Cook, stirring often, for 6 to 8 minutes or until the onion is lightly browned. Add the mushrooms. Continue to cook, stirring, until the mushrooms are lightly browned. Add the garlic, butter, ham, basil and tomato. Bring to a gentle boil. Reduce heat and boil gently, uncovered, for 5 minutes. Cook fettuccine in 3 quarts boiling water in a 5- to 6-quart saucepan for 8 to 10 minutes or just until tender to bite. Drain well. While the fettuccine is cooking, add the cream, parsley, wine and nutmeg to the mushroom-ham mixture. Mix gently. Add the fettuccine and mix lightly, using 2 forks. Season with salt and pepper. Serve with Parmesan cheese. Yield: 4 servings.

Jean Mortensen, Epsilon Iota
Arlington, Nebraska

SMOKY TOMATO BASIL PASTA

16 ounces uncooked	1 (2- to 3-ounce)
pasta (fusilli, rotini	package fresh basil,
or other)	chopped
16 ounces fresh	1 tablespoon minced
mushrooms, sliced	garlic
1 large onion, chopped	2 (15-ounce) cans diced
1 to 2 tablespoons	tomatoes
butter or margarine	Grated fresh Parmesan
1 pound smoked bacon	cheese

Cook the pasta according to package directions. Sauté the mushrooms and onion in the butter until tender. Remove from the skillet and drain. Chop the bacon and cook it in the same skillet until crisp; drain the grease. Add the basil, garlic and tomatoes; bring to a simmer. Stir the mixture into the hot pasta. Serve immediately with Parmesan cheese. Yield: 6 to 8 servings.

Sharon Prunty
Rochester, Minnesota

PIZZA SPAGHETTI PIE

1 pound ground beef
½ cup chopped onion
½ cup fine dry bread
    crumbs
1 teaspoon salt
1 teaspoon pepper
⅔ cup evaporated milk
4 ounces spaghetti,
    cooked and drained
1 egg, beaten
¼ cup grated Parmesan
    cheese

2 tablespoons butter or
    margarine
½ teaspoon oregano
1 (14-ounce) jar pizza
    sauce
1 green pepper, cut into
    rings
1 cup shredded
    mozzarella cheese

Preheat the oven to 350 degrees. Combine the ground beef, onion, bread crumbs, salt, pepper and evaporated milk. Press the mixture firmly on the bottom and sides of a 9-inch pie pan. Bake for 35 to 40 minutes. Spoon off the drippings. Combine the spaghetti, egg, Parmesan cheese, butter and oregano. Spread the mixture in the baked meat shell. Top with the pizza sauce, green pepper rings and mozzarella cheese. Bake for 10 to 15 minutes longer or until the cheese is golden brown. Let stand for 5 minutes. Cut into wedges. Yield: 6 servings.

Marilyn Heinisch, Xi Gamma Alpha
Dubuque, Iowa

HOMEMADE CHILI NOODLES

I make several pounds of noodles at a time, divide into recipe-size portions, and freeze for several months. After thawing, the noodles are cooked just as if they are freshly made.

3⅔ cups all-purpose
    flour
1 envelope chili
    seasoning mix
4 eggs
2 tablespoons cold
    water
2 slices bacon

½ cup chopped mixed
    red and green bell
    peppers
½ cup chopped onion
9 tablespoons butter or
    margarine
1½ cups shredded sharp
    Cheddar cheese

Combine the flour and chili seasoning mix in a large bowl. Beat the eggs and the cold water together. Add to the flour mixture; mix well. Knead on a lightly floured surface for 3 minutes. Shape into a large ball. Roll very thin; let rest for 20 minutes. Roll up as if for a jelly roll. Cut into ¼- to ½-inch slices. Spread the cut noodles on a lightly floured surface. Let dry for 15 minutes. Cook the bacon in a skillet until slightly crisp; drain, chop and set aside. Discard the drippings. Sauté the bell peppers and onion in 1 tablespoon butter in the same skillet until tender-crisp; do not overcook. Bring a generous amount of water to a boil in a 6- to 8-quart stockpot. Add the noodles gradually. Boil for 4 minutes; drain and place in a large bowl. Add the remaining ½ cup butter and Cheddar cheese to the hot noodles; toss to mix. Top with the sautéed vegetables and the bacon. Serve immediately. Yield: 6 servings.

Helen Easton, Laureate Zeta Beta
Yreka, California

❖ ROTELLE WITH BACON AND SAUTEED WALNUTS OR PECANS

This is a favorite of mine that I prepare when my grandchild visits. It's fast, easy, and has everything needed for a balanced diet in one dish.

16 ounces uncooked
    rotelle pasta
1 teaspoon olive oil
½ pound sliced lean
    bacon, cut into 2-inch
    pieces
½ cup walnuts or
    pecans, halved

1 bunch broccoli florets
4 large carrots, thinly
    sliced
Salt and pepper to taste
Parmesan cheese
Butter or margarine

Cook the pasta in a large kettle of boiling salted water with the olive oil; cook for 12 minutes or until al dente. Drain and rinse quickly with cold water; set aside. Fry the bacon in a large skillet until brown and crisp. Remove from the skillet and drain on paper towels, leaving the bacon fat in the pan. Sauté the nuts in the same skillet over medium-high heat until the nuts begin to brown. Remove quickly from the pan; drain on paper towels. Add the broccoli and carrots to boiling salted water and cook for about 10 minutes or until al dente; drain. Combine the bacon, nuts, vegetables and pasta in a large bowl; toss. Add the salt, pepper, Parmesan cheese and butter to taste. Yield: 4 to 6 servings.

Diana O'Conor
Wallkill, New York

HOUND DOG ROLLS

12 lasagna noodles
2 (15-ounce) cans pizza
    sauce
½ teaspoon oregano
½ teaspoon salt
⅛ teaspoon pepper

12 hot dogs
1 (6-ounce) package
    sliced mozzarella
    cheese
½ cup grated Parmesan
    cheese

Preheat the oven to 350 degrees. Cook the lasagna noodles until tender as on package directions; rinse and drain well. Combine the pizza sauce, oregano, salt and pepper. Split the hot dogs lengthwise; do not cut all the way through. Stuff each hot dog with ⅓ slice mozzarella cheese; wrap each with 1 lasagna noodle. Secure the noodles with toothpicks. Place in a greased 9-by-13-inch pan. Pour the sauce over the top. Sprinkle with Parmesan cheese. Bake for 30 minutes. Yield: 6 servings.

Phyllis Paine, Laureate Beta Lambda
Mount Pleasant, Iowa

BAKED ANGEL HAIR SPAGHETTI

½ cup chopped green bell pepper	1 (15-ounce) can diced tomatoes
1 small red onion, chopped	1 (5-ounce) can lean ham, flaked
1 teaspoon minced garlic from a jar	1 envelope savory herb and garlic soup mix
1 tablespoon margarine	1 teaspoon parsley flakes
5 ounces mushrooms, halved, sliced	½ teaspoon dried basil
1 large zucchini	1½ teaspoons salad seasoning
4 ounces angel hair pasta, cooked	¼ cup fat-free Parmesan cheese
2 small yellow squash	

Preheat the oven to 400 degrees. Microwave the green pepper, onion and garlic in half the margarine in a microwave-safe dish just until tender. Add the mushrooms; microwave for 3 minutes. Remove mushroom mixture. Cut zucchini and squash in half lengthwise and slice. Place with remaining margarine in same dish. Microwave for 3 minutes. Drain tomatoes, reserving juice. Place the pasta in a 2-quart baking dish; add the mushroom mixture, zucchini, squash, tomatoes and ham. Combine the dry soup mix, reserved tomato juice and enough water to measure 1¾ cups. Pour over the pasta. Add the parsley flakes, basil and salad seasoning; toss to mix. Sprinkle with the Parmesan cheese. Bake for 30 minutes or until bubbly. Yield: 2 to 3 servings.

Barbara M. Harbath, Member at Large
Dalzell, South Carolina

PASTA WITH SAUSAGE CREAM SAUCE

12 ounces uncooked rigatoni or other large pasta	⅔ cup evaporated skim milk
8 ounces sweet Italian-style turkey sausage	1 tablespoon dried basil
6 ounces small fresh mushrooms, quartered (2 cups)	¼ teaspoon pepper
	1 (10-ounce) package frozen green peas, thawed
1 teaspoon Worcestershire sauce	¼ cup grated Parmesan cheese

Cook the pasta using package directions; drain. Brown the sausage in a medium skillet over medium heat; remove with a slotted spoon to a bowl. Cook the mushrooms in the drippings for 3 to 4 minutes or until lightly browned. Sprinkle with the Worcestershire sauce. Stir in the evaporated milk. Bring to a simmer. Add the basil and pepper. Simmer for 3 to 4 minutes or until slightly thickened. Add the peas and sausage. Heat thoroughly and add to the pasta and Parmesan cheese in a large bowl and serve. Yield: 4 servings.

Cindy Beavers, Theta Delta
Burlington, Colorado

STUFFED PASTA SHELLS

1 pound bulk Italian sausage	2 cups shredded Cheddar cheese
1 onion, chopped	1 cup cottage cheese
1 (10-ounce) package frozen chopped spinach, cooked, drained	¼ cup grated Parmesan cheese
	¼ teaspoon salt
1 (8-ounce) package cream cheese, softened	¼ teaspoon pepper
	20 jumbo pasta shells, cooked, drained
1 egg, beaten	Pasta Sauce
2 cups shredded mozzarella cheese	

Preheat the oven to 350 degrees. Brown the sausage and onion in skillet; drain. Remove to a large bowl. Stir in the spinach, cream cheese and egg. Add 1 cup of the mozzarella cheese, Cheddar cheese, cottage cheese and Parmesan cheese. Stir in the salt and pepper. Mix well. Stuff the shells with the cheese mixture. Arrange in a 9-by-13-inch baking dish that has been coated with nonstick cooking spray. Spoon the Pasta Sauce over the shells. Bake, covered, for 40 minutes. Uncover and sprinkle with the remaining 1 cup mozzarella cheese. Bake until the cheese melts. Yield: 12 servings.

PASTA SAUCE

1 (29-ounce) can tomato sauce	2 cloves of garlic, minced
1½ teaspoons dried basil	1 teaspoon sugar
	½ teaspoon salt
1½ teaspoons dried parsley flakes	1 teaspoon oregano
	¼ teaspoon pepper

Combine the tomato sauce, basil, parsley, garlic, sugar, salt, oregano and pepper; mix well.

Ginger Tyler, Xi Xi
Thomaston, Georgia

HOT CHERRY PEPPER AND CHICKEN PASTA

Serve this dish right from the pan, but warn your guests it is very hot!

1 pound boneless skinless chicken breast, cubed	1 (12-ounce) package fresh mushrooms, sliced
Salt and pepper to taste	1 large tomato, chopped
Parsley to taste	1 (1-quart) jar pickled hot cherry peppers, drained, juice reserved
1/2 cup all-purpose flour	
3 tablespoons olive oil	
2 cloves of garlic, minced	1 cup juice reserved from peppers
1/2 cup butter or margarine	1 pound penne, mezzani or ziti pasta
1 cup white table wine	Parmesan cheese
4 cups chicken broth	
1 (6-ounce) can black olives, sliced	

Season the chicken cubes with salt, pepper and parsley. Combine the flour and seasoned chicken in a plastic bag; toss to coat the chicken well. Heat the olive oil in a large skillet over medium to high heat. Brown the chicken in the oil; drain. Return the chicken to the skillet over medium heat. Add the garlic and the butter; heat until butter is melted. Stir in the white wine; mixture will begin to thicken. Add the chicken broth and heat thoroughly. Add the black olives, mushrooms and tomato; cook for 10 minutes. Carefully remove the seeds from the hot cherry peppers; slice. Stir the hot cherry pepper slices and juice into the chicken mixture; cook for 10 minutes. Cook the pasta using package directions; drain. Pour the cooked pasta into the skillet with the chicken mixture. Sprinkle with Parmesan cheese. Serve from the skillet. Yield: 4 servings.

Janice DiBeneditto, Laureate Iota
Waterbury, Connecticut

STUFFED CHICKEN BREASTS IN ALFREDO SAUCE

3/4 cup butter or margarine	4 boneless skinless chicken breast halves
2 cloves of garlic, minced	1 cup heavy cream
1/2 cup finely chopped onions	16 ounces fettuccini, cooked
2 cups coarsely chopped mushrooms	3/4 cup shredded Parmesan cheese
3/4 cup Italian bread crumbs	

Melt 1/2 cup of the butter in a small saucepan. Add the garlic, 1/4 cup of the onions and 1 1/2 cups of the mushrooms. Sauté for 5 to 8 minutes. Fold in the bread crumbs. Pound the chicken breast halves flat. Place 1 tablespoon stuffing in the center of each; fold and secure with a toothpick. Melt the remaining 1/4 cup butter in a deep skillet over medium heat. Add the chicken. Cook for 20 to 25 minutes, turning occasionally. Stir in the remaining 1/4 cup onions and the remaining 1/2 cup mushrooms; sauté for 5 minutes. Stir in the heavy cream; sauté for 5 to 8 minutes. Remove the toothpicks from the chicken. Serve over a bed of fettuccini. Sprinkle with the Parmesan cheese. Yield: 4 servings.

Ritté A. Bradshaw
Houston, Texas

CHICKEN BROCCOLI FETTUCCINI

1 clove of garlic, minced	1/4 cup Parmesan cheese
1 tablespoon margarine	1 1/2 cups cooked chicken strips
1 (10-ounce) can broccoli-cheese soup	3 cups cooked fettuccini (8 ounces dry)
1 cup milk	

Sauté the garlic in the margarine for about 2 minutes in a skillet over low heat. Stir in the soup, milk and Parmesan cheese. Bring to a boil. Add the chicken, reduce heat to low and cook for 5 minutes. Toss with the fettuccini. Yield: 4 servings.

Vernell A. Perry, Xi Beta Lambda
Chambersburg, Pennsylvania

SOUTH OF THE BORDER CHICKEN CACCIATORE

16 ounces uncooked pasta	1 green pepper, thinly sliced
4 chicken breasts (2 1/2 pounds)	1 (14-ounce) jar pizza sauce
1/8 teaspoon salt	1 (10-ounce) can taco sauce
1/8 teaspoon pepper	1/2 cup water
2 tablespoons olive oil	2 teaspoons chopped fresh parsley
1 medium onion, cut into wedges	1 cup frozen corn
4 cloves of garlic, chopped	3/4 cup corn bread stuffing
1 red bell pepper, thinly sliced	

Cook the pasta using package directions. Sprinkle the chicken with salt and pepper. Heat the olive oil in a deep skillet over medium heat. Add the chicken; sauté until brown, about 3 minutes per side. Remove the chicken; set aside. Reduce the heat to low. Pour off all but 1 tablespoon of the oil; add the onion, garlic, red pepper and green pepper to the skillet. Cook, stirring often, for about 6 minutes. Stir in the pizza sauce and taco sauce. Add the water and parsley. Return the chicken to the skillet. Bring the sauce to a simmer; reduce heat to low. Simmer, covered, for 20 minutes, turning the chicken after 10 minutes. Stir in the corn; simmer for 10 minutes. Turn into a serving dish; sprinkle with the stuffing. Serve over pasta. Yield: 4 servings.

Gloria Scherrer, Preceptor Alpha Xi
Green Valley, Arizona

PEPPERONI CHICKEN PASTA

Serve with any fresh in-season vegetable—especially zucchini.

4 boneless skinless whole chicken breasts	1 (15-ounce) can diced tomatoes, undrained
2 tablespoons olive oil	1 (28-ounce) jar prepared spaghetti sauce
Garlic powder to taste	
Salt to taste	
1 green pepper, chopped	1½ cups shredded mozzarella cheese
8 ounces fresh mushrooms, chopped	½ cup Parmesan cheese
1 small yellow onion, chopped	Pepperoni slices to taste
1 (8-ounce) can large black olives, sliced	16 ounces pasta of choice, cooked

Cut the chicken breasts into large pieces. Sauté the chicken in the olive oil with the garlic powder and salt. Add the green pepper, mushrooms and onion; sauté for 10 minutes. Add the olives, tomatoes and spaghetti sauce. Cover with mozzarella cheese, Parmesan cheese and pepperoni slices. Simmer for 30 minutes. Serve over cooked pasta. Yield: 8 servings.

Marge Wehman, Xi Eta Eta
Harrison City, Pennsylvania

THREE CHEESE CHICKEN LASAGNA

It is not necessary to precook the noodles in this recipe.

½ cup chopped onion	8 ounces lasagna noodles
½ cup chopped green pepper	1½ cups dry cottage cheese
1 (10-ounce) can cream of chicken soup	2 cups chopped cooked chicken
1 (4-ounce) can sliced mushrooms, drained	1½ cups shredded mild Cheddar cheese
½ cup pimientos, drained	½ cup grated Parmesan cheese
⅓ cup milk	
½ teaspoon basil	

Preheat the oven to 350 degrees. Sauté the onion and green pepper in a small amount of water until tender; drain. Add the soup, mushrooms, pimientos, milk and basil. Layer half the noodles, half the soup mixture, half the cottage cheese, half the chicken, half the Cheddar cheese and half the Parmesan cheese in a 9-by-13-inch baking dish. Layer the remaining noodles, soup mixture, cottage cheese and chicken over that. Bake, covered, for 45 minutes. Sprinkle with the remaining Cheddar cheese and Parmesan cheese; bake uncovered for 2 minutes. Yield: 10 servings.

Donna Ramsey, Psi Master
Fort Collins, Colorado

GARLIC CHICKEN LASAGNA

3 (10-ounce) cans cream of mushroom soup	2 tablespoons cornstarch
2 (10-ounce) cans water	4 boneless skinless whole chicken breasts
2 green onions, chopped	
8 ounces mushrooms, chopped	1 clove of garlic, minced
1 tablespoon chopped parsley	8 ounces spinach lasagna noodles
¼ cup cold water	4 cups shredded Monterey Jack cheese

Preheat the oven to 350 degrees. Pour the soup into a large kettle. Add the cans of water, green onions, mushrooms and parsley. Simmer for 10 to 15 minutes or until the mushrooms are soft. Blend cold water and cornstarch; add to the soup. Simmer until thick, stirring constantly. Remove from heat. Cut the chicken into bite-size pieces; sauté with the garlic. Cook the noodles al dente, using package directions. Line a 9-by-13-inch baking pan with 1 ladle of soup mix. Layer half the noodles, half the mushroom sauce, half the chicken and half the cheese in the pan; repeat the layers. Bake until heated through and cheese melts. Cool before serving. Yield: 8 servings.

Robinn Habkirk, Pi
North Vancouver, British Columbia, Canada

Becky Wachs, Theta Sigma, Hays, Kansas, makes Baked Cheese Ravioli with a package of frozen cheese ravioli cooked using package directions and mixed with a large green bell pepper, a small onion chopped and sautéed in a tablespoon of oil, and a 28-ounce can of seasoned tomatoes that have been crushed. Top with a cup of mozzarella cheese and bake in a preheated 350-degree oven for 30 minutes. May add a pound of chopped cooked chicken or browned and drained ground beef.

CHICKEN PRIMAVERA

This is my husband's favorite meal. The vegetables may be chopped ahead of time if you want to prepare a quick meal.

1 boneless skinless whole chicken breast, sliced in strips	1 very small zucchini, finely chopped
5 green onions, finely chopped	1 very small yellow squash, finely chopped
1/2 medium green pepper, finely chopped	1 large carrot, finely chopped
2 celery ribs, finely chopped	2 (15-ounce) cans stewed Italian tomatoes
4 ounces mushrooms, sliced	1 tablespoon oregano
2 teaspoons minced garlic from a jar	Salt and pepper to taste
	Cooked angel hair pasta

Brown the chicken in a large nonstick skillet or wok; remove the chicken and set aside. Place the green onions, green pepper, celery, mushrooms, garlic, zucchini, squash and carrot in the skillet; cook over medium heat, stirring until the vegetables begin to soften. Stir the chicken into the vegetables. Add the tomatoes, oregano, salt and pepper. Simmer for about 15 minutes. Serve over angel hair pasta.
Yield: 4 servings.

Billie Jo Essman
The Plains, Ohio

CHICKEN WITH MUSHROOM PEPPERCORN SAUCE

4 medium boneless skinless chicken breast halves	1/2 cup evaporated skim milk
1 teaspoon olive oil	1 tablespoon all-purpose flour
3 cups sliced fresh mushrooms	2 tablespoons Dijon mustard
1/2 cup chopped onion	2 cups hot cooked fusilli or other pasta
1/2 teaspoon dried peppercorns, crushed	
1 cup reduced-sodium chicken broth	

Rinse the chicken and pat dry. Spray a cold large skillet with nonstick cooking spray. Preheat the skillet over medium heat. Cook the chicken in the hot skillet for about 10 minutes, turning to brown evenly. Remove the chicken from the skillet. Add the oil to the skillet. Add the mushrooms, onion and peppercorns. Cook, stirring, for 4 to 5 minutes or until the vegetables are tender. It may be necessary to add another 1 teaspoon oil while cooking. Stir in the chicken broth. Return the chicken pieces to the skillet. Bring to a boil. Reduce heat, cover and simmer for 20 minutes or until chicken is tender and no longer pink. Remove the chicken from the skillet. Stir the evaporated milk and flour together. Pour into the skillet. Cook, stirring, until thickened and bubbly, then cook and stir for 2 minutes longer. Stir in the mustard. Return the chicken to the skillet and heat through. Serve over hot cooked pasta.
Yield: 4 servings.

Anita M. Wilson, Omega Master
Mansfield, Ohio

CHICKEN FETTUCCINI

This meal can be prepared in 30 minutes

4 boneless chicken breasts	2 cups cream
1 clove of garlic, minced	1 cup sour cream
1 small zucchini, sliced	1 cup grated fresh Parmesan cheese
2 tablespoons melted butter or margarine	1 1/2 (6 ounces) cups shredded mozzarella cheese
1 pound fresh fettuccini noodles	Seasoned salt to taste

Rinse the chicken and pat dry. Dice the chicken. Sauté with the garlic and zucchini in the butter in a skillet over medium heat until chicken is cooked through. Cook the fettuccini noodles using package directions. Heat the cream, sour cream and 1/2 cup of the Parmesan cheese in a saucepan until the mixture is hot but not boiling. Add seasoned salt. Stir together the noodles, chicken mixture, cream sauce, mozzarella cheese and the remaining 1/2 cup Parmesan cheese. Yield: 4 servings.

Lynda Kinberg, Xi Alpha Zeta
Renton, Washington

CHICKEN MOZZARELLA

4 boneless skinless chicken breast halves	1 cup chicken broth
1/4 cup all-purpose flour	1/2 teaspoon oregano leaves
1 1/2 teaspoons salt	10 ounces uncooked spaghetti
1/4 cup vegetable oil	1 cup (4 ounces) shredded mozzarella cheese (regular or fat-free)
1 small onion, diced	
1 clove of garlic, minced	
2 (8-ounce) cans tomato sauce	

Rinse the chicken and pat dry. Coat the chicken with a mixture of flour and salt. Brown the chicken in the oil in a large skillet over medium heat; drain on paper towels. Cook the onion and garlic in the same skillet over low heat for 5 to 10 minutes or until tender. Pour off the oil. Return the chicken to the skillet. Combine the tomato sauce, chicken broth and oregano in a medium bowl; pour into the skillet. Simmer, covered, for 1 hour. Cook the spaghetti until tender using package directions. Turn the hot spaghetti into a serving dish. Cover it with the hot chicken and sauce; top with the mozzarella cheese. The spaghetti and chicken should be hot enough to melt the cheese. Yield: 4 servings.

Sara Ussery, Xi Delta Rho
Brentwood, Tennessee

CHICKEN BREASTS WITH SUN-DRIED TOMATO SAUCE

1/4 cup coarsely chopped sun-dried tomatoes	*2 tablespoons dry red wine*
1/2 cup chicken broth	*1 teaspoon olive oil*
4 boneless skinless chicken breast halves	*1/2 cup skim milk*
1/2 cup sliced fresh mushrooms	*2 teaspoons cornstarch*
2 tablespoons chopped green onions	*2 teaspoons chopped fresh basil or 1/2 teaspoon dried basil*
2 cloves of garlic, minced	*2 cups hot cooked fettuccini*

Combine the sun-dried tomatoes and chicken broth in a bowl; let stand for 30 minutes. Rinse the chicken and pat dry. Trim the fat. Cook the mushrooms, green onions, garlic and wine in a medium skillet over medium heat for 3 minutes; remove the mixture from the skillet. Pour the olive oil into the skillet. Brown the chicken in the olive oil over medium heat. Simmer, covered, for 10 minutes, stirring occasionally. Remove the chicken; keep warm. Mix the milk, cornstarch and basil; stir into the tomato mixture. Bring to a boil, stirring constantly. Boil, stirring, for 1 minute. Stir in the mushroom mixture; heat through. Serve over chicken and fettuccini. Yield: 4 servings.

Christine A. Stevenson, Beta Chi
Independence, Iowa

Ruth Newmann, Preceptor Gamma Epsilon, De Kalb, Illinois, makes Seaside Macaroni by mixing 1 1/2 cups cooked macaroni with a 19-ounce can of chunky clam chowder, an 8-ounce can of drained tomatoes, 1 teaspoon dry mustard, 1/2 cup Cheddar cheese, and 2 tablespoons Parmesan cheese. Bake in a preheated 350-degree oven for 30 minutes. Stir the mixture, top with an additional 1/2 cup Cheddar cheese, and bake until melted.

QUICK CHICKEN PASTA

I have been preparing this dish for our Woman of the Year Dinner for several years, and I am always asked for the recipe. Now it is time to share it with everyone.

2 boneless skinless whole chicken breasts	*1 small onion, chopped*
1/2 cup fat-free Italian salad dressing	*1/4 cup all-purpose flour*
1 red bell pepper, chopped	*1 tablespoon dried parsley*
6 to 8 medium mushrooms, sliced	*2 tablespoons soy sauce*
1 small zucchini, cut in 1-inch sticks	*1/2 teaspoon salt*
	1/2 teaspoon pepper
	4 cups cooked rotini or penne pasta

Rinse the chicken and pat dry. Cut into bite-size pieces. Marinate in the salad dressing while preparing the vegetables. It can be marinated for 8 to 10 hours. Sauté the chicken in a large skillet over medium heat for about 10 minutes. Add the red bell pepper, mushrooms, zucchini and onion; sauté until partially cooked. Sprinkle in the flour; mix into the chicken and vegetables. Add enough water to cover the chicken and vegetables. Increase the heat and cook for 2 minutes, stirring gently. Stir in the parsley, soy sauce, salt and pepper. Add the pasta and simmer for 3 to 4 minutes or until the pasta soaks up the sauce. Yield: 6 servings.

Sharon T. Cole, Laureate Rho
Vancouver, British Columbia, Canada

CRAWFISH FETTUCCINI

1 1/2 cups margarine	*3 pounds crawfish tails*
3 medium onions, chopped	*4 pints half-and-half*
3 ribs celery, chopped	*8 ounces process cheese*
1 green pepper, chopped	*Salt and pepper to taste*
1/4 cup all-purpose flour	*16 ounces fettuccini noodles*
4 tablespoons parsley	

Preheat the oven to 350 degrees. Melt the margarine in a skillet. Add the onions, celery and green pepper; cook for 10 minutes over medium-low heat. Add the flour; blend well. Cook, covered, for 10 minutes stirring often. Add the parsley and crawfish; cook for 15 minutes. Add the half-and-half and cheese; mix well. Add the salt and pepper. Cook the noodles in salted water using package directions. Drain and add to the sauce. Pour into a 12-by-16-inch baking dish. Bake for 30 minutes. Yield: 15 servings.

Miriam Langford, Alpha Zeta Theta
Missouri City, Texas

LINGUINI AND CLAM SAUCE

2 (7-ounce) cans
  chopped clams
1 (7-ounce) can whole
  clams
2 tablespoons extra-
  virgin olive oil
5 to 6 cloves of garlic,
  minced
2 teaspoons anchovy
  paste
4 tablespoons finely
  chopped fresh parsley

1 (16-ounce) can diced
  peeled tomatoes in
  juice
1/8 teaspoon freshly
  ground black pepper
2 teaspoons freshly
  squeezed lemon juice
6 to 8 ounces dry
  linguini, cooked al
  dente
Parsley for garnish
  (optional)

Drain the chopped clams and whole clams, reserving the juice. Cover the drained clams tightly and set aside. Heat the olive oil in a heavy nonaluminum saucepan over medium heat. Add the minced garlic; cook until it starts to sizzle. Stir in the anchovy paste; mix well. Add the parsley, reserved clam juice, tomatoes and pepper; mix well. Bring to a boil. Reduce heat to low and simmer, uncovered, for 25 minutes, stirring occasionally. Add the clams and lemon juice and heat through, about 1 to 2 minutes. Do not boil the sauce or the clams will become tough. Place hot cooked pasta into warm bowls. Top each serving with a cup of the clam sauce, garnishing with parsley; or toss the sauce with the pasta. Yield: 4 servings.

Cyril Hennum, Xi Beta Xi
San Diego, California

VERMICELLI WITH SMOKED SALMON

6 ounces smoked salmon
  (lox)
1 large clove of garlic,
  minced
3 tablespoons olive oil
2 1/4 cups Roma
  tomatoes, seeded,
  chopped
1/4 cup white wine

3 tablespoons capers,
  drained
1 1/2 teaspoons dillweed
1 1/2 teaspoons basil
8 ounces vermicelli or
  spaghettini
1/2 cup grated Parmesan
  cheese
Parsley (optional)

Cut the salmon into 1/2-inch-wide strips. Set aside. Sauté the garlic in the olive oil in a large skillet over medium heat until golden. Add 2 cups of the tomatoes, wine, capers, dillweed and basil; cook until mixture is hot. Cook the pasta using package directions; drain and place in a large serving bowl. Pour the sauce over the pasta. Add the salmon and Parmesan cheese; toss gently. Garnish with the remaining 1/4 cup tomatoes and the parsley. Yield: 4 servings.

Lori Richardson
Penticton, British Columbia, Canada

PASTA AND SHRIMP ALFREDO

3 quarts water
12 ounces spaghetti or
  linguine
2 medium zucchini,
  quartered lengthwise,
  sliced crosswise
1 tablespoon olive oil
1 pound medium shrimp,
  shelled, deveined

1/4 teaspoon salt
1/4 teaspoon pepper
2 medium tomatoes,
  diced
2 cups Alfredo sauce
Chopped parsley
Grated Parmesan cheese

Bring the water to a boil in a large covered kettle. Add the pasta to the water and cook uncovered, stirring often, for 7 minutes. Add the zucchini. Cook for about 3 minutes longer or until the pasta is al dente and the zucchini is tender. Drain. Heat the olive oil in a large deep skillet over medium-high heat. Add the shrimp, salt and pepper. Sauté until the shrimp turns pink. Add the pasta-zucchini mixture, the tomatoes and the Alfredo sauce. Stir gently until blended and heated through. Sprinkle with parsley. Serve immediately with Parmesan cheese. Yield: 4 to 5 servings.

Lorene Brown
Prosser, Washington

❖ SHRIMP IN ANGEL HAIR PASTA

1 tablespoon butter or
  margarine
2 eggs
1 cup plain yogurt
1 cup half-and-half
1/2 cup (4 ounces)
  shredded Swiss
  cheese
1/3 cup crumbled feta
  cheese
1/3 cup chopped parsley
1/4 cup chopped fresh
  basil or 1 teaspoon
  crushed dried basil

1 teaspoon crushed dried
  oregano leaves
1 (9-ounce) package
  uncooked fresh angel
  hair pasta
1 (16-ounce) jar mild
  thick-and-chunky
  salsa
1 pound medium shrimp,
  peeled, deveined
1 cup (4 ounces)
  shredded Monterey
  Jack cheese

Preheat the oven to 350 degrees. Grease an 8-by-12-inch baking dish with the butter. Combine the eggs, yogurt, half-and-half, Swiss cheese, feta cheese, parsley, basil and oregano in a medium bowl; mix well. Cook the pasta using package directions. Spread half the pasta in the baking dish. Cover with salsa. Add half the shrimp. Cover with the remaining pasta. Spread the egg mixture over the pasta and top with the remaining shrimp. Sprinkle with Monterey Jack cheese. Bake for 30 minutes or until bubbly. Let stand for 10 minutes. Yield: 6 servings.

Anita Hanson
Boulder, Colorado

Distinctive Side Dishes

In many a meal, the entrée
is the main attraction—
stealing the show from every day
side dishes that may play minor,
supporting roles. But side dishes
don't have to be ordinary.
In fact, the distinctive dishes we've
assembled here are all star players that can
light up any menu and add spice to every meal!
Peruse this section to put pizzazz in your potatoes—
or add color and flavor to tried-and-true vegetables.
Discover new ways to perk up perennial favorites,
and your side dishes may soon
upstage even the most
show-stopping entrées!

STUFFED ARTICHOKES

4 to 6 medium-to-large artichokes	1/2 cup bread crumbs
1 clove of garlic, crushed	3 tablespoons olive oil
1/2 small onion, chopped	1 egg, beaten
1 tablespoon olive oil	Salt and pepper to taste
1/2 cup grated Parmesan cheese	Dried parsley to taste
	1/2 cup water
	1/4 cup olive oil

Preheat the oven to 325 degrees. Trim the artichokes. Soak them in warm salted water for 20 minutes; rinse, and plunge into cold water. Drain well. Sauté the garlic and onion in the 1 tablespoon olive oil. Mix the sautéed onion and garlic, Parmesan cheese, bread crumbs, the 3 tablespoons olive oil, egg, salt, pepper and parsley in a medium bowl. Stuff the bread crumb mixture into the leaves of the artichokes. Place the stuffed artichokes in a baking dish with a lid. Pour the water and remaining 1/4 cup olive oil over the mixture. Bake, covered, for 1 hour.
Yield: 4 to 6 servings.

Marcy Marino
Ransomville, New York

SICILIAN ARTICHOKES

4 artichokes	Dash of salt
4 cloves of garlic	Dash of pepper
8 ounces Monterey Jack cheese, sliced	4 tablespoons olive oil
	1/2 to 3/4 cup water

Wash the artichokes. Cut off the tops, bottoms and thorny edges. Place a clove of garlic in the center of each artichoke. Stuff each artichoke with 1/4 of the Jack cheese slices. Sprinkle with the salt and pepper and pour 1 tablespoon olive oil over each. Place them in a large, deep skillet; add water and cover. Simmer until the artichokes are done, or until the leaves pull out easily. Yield: 4 servings.

Lucy A. Igna, Preceptor Beta Nu
Hacienda Heights, California

RANCH STYLE BEANS

1 pound lean ground beef	2 teaspoons butter or margarine
1 (16-ounce) can kidney beans, drained	2 tablespoons prepared mustard
2 (16-ounce) cans pork and beans in tomato sauce	1 envelope onion soup mix
1 cup catsup	2 teaspoons cider vinegar
1/2 cup water	

Preheat the oven to 400 degrees. Brown the ground beef; drain. Place the kidney beans, pork and beans and catsup in a bean pot or large covered baking dish; blend well. Add the water, butter, mustard, onion soup mix and vinegar; stir well. Bake for 30 to 40 minutes. Yield: 6 to 8 servings.

Patricia A. Astle, Preceptor Chi
Baraboo, Wisconsin

AUNT MARY'S BEANS

1 small onion, chopped	2 tablespoons chili powder
1 small green pepper, chopped	1/2 teaspoon salt
4 medium tomatoes, peeled, diced	Dash of pepper
2 tablespoons butter or margarine	Dash of hot pepper sauce
4 cups cooked kidney beans, drained	3 cups shredded sharp Cheddar cheese
	6 slices bacon, crisp-fried, crumbled

Sauté the onion, green pepper and tomatoes in the butter until tender-crisp. Stir in the kidney beans, chili powder, salt, pepper and hot pepper sauce. Heat thoroughly. Stir in the Cheddar cheese and bacon. Serve immediately or keep in an oven on low heat until serving time. Yield: 6 servings.

Mary Hays, Xi Alpha Eta
Torrington, Wyoming

BROCCOLI SOUFFLE

Even your children will like this broccoli! Everything can be mixed ahead of time and refrigerated until ready to bake. Once cooked, it can be kept warm in the turned-off oven.

2 (10-ounce) packages frozen chopped broccoli	1 small onion, chopped
2 eggs	1 cup shredded sharp Cheddar cheese
1/2 cup margarine, softened	1 (10-ounce) can cream of mushroom soup
1 scant cup mayonnaise	1/4 cup crumbled cheesy crackers

Preheat the oven to 325 degrees. Cook the broccoli according to package directions; drain well. Mix the eggs, margarine, mayonnaise, onion, Cheddar cheese and cream of mushroom soup in a bowl. Stir the drained broccoli into the mixture; pour into a greased 2-quart baking dish. Sprinkle the crumbled crackers over the mixture. Bake for 45 minutes or until lightly set. Yield: 10 to 12 servings.

Cindy Looper, Xi Mu
Clear Lake, Iowa

JANE'S DELMONICO POTATOES

This is a great dish to take to a potluck because it holds well after baking.

1/4 cup butter or margarine	Dash of pepper
1 cup slightly crushed cornflakes	1 1/2 cups milk
3 tablespoons all-purpose flour	1 (32-ounce) package frozen crinkle-cut French fries
1/2 teaspoon salt	10 ounces shredded Cheddar cheese

Preheat the oven to 375 degrees. Melt the butter in a saucepan. Blend 1 tablespoon of the melted butter with the cornflakes; set aside. Stir the flour, salt and pepper into the remaining butter in the saucepan. Add the milk; cook over medium heat, stirring constantly until it is a smooth, thick white sauce. Spread half the French fries over the bottom of a 9-by-12-inch baking dish; pour half the white sauce over the French fries; sprinkle half the cheese over the sauce. Repeat these layers, then sprinkle the cornflakes over the top. Bake, covered, for 1 hour or until heated throughout. Yield: 12 servings.

Sharon Kern, Laureate Delta Epsilon
Lodi, California

LEMON ROASTED POTATOES

8 to 10 potatoes (about 4 pounds), peeled	3 cloves of garlic, minced
1 cup water	2 teaspoons salt
1/2 cup lemon juice	2 teaspoons oregano
1/3 cup olive oil	1 teaspoon pepper

Preheat the oven to 325 degrees. Cut the potatoes lengthwise into thick wedges. Place them in a 9-by-13-inch baking dish. Whisk together the water, lemon juice, olive oil, garlic, salt, oregano and pepper. Pour the lemon juice mixture over the potatoes, turning them to coat evenly. Bake, occasionally turning gently to keep the potatoes well moistened, for about 2 hours or until potatoes are very tender and most of the liquid has evaporated. Yield: 8 to 12 servings.

Brenda Yuzdepski, Epsilon
Saskatoon, Saskatchewan, Canada

GARLIC MASHED POTATOES

10 medium potatoes, peeled, diced large	1 cup heavy whipping cream
5 cloves of garlic	1/2 pound unsalted butter, softened
2 tablespoons salt	
1 teaspoon black or white pepper	

Place the potatoes, garlic, salt and pepper in a large skillet of boiling water. Boil until potatoes are soft to the touch; drain well. Place the potatoes in a mixer bowl. Add the whipping cream and the butter in 2 stages, using a whipping attachment at medium speed. Whip until smooth. Yield: 10 to 12 servings.

Susan Gagnea, Xi Alpha Xi
Hueytown, Alabama

TWICE-BAKED GARLIC CHEESE POTATOES

Save time by microwaving the potatoes; or prepare ahead of time and pop into the oven when ready to bake.

4 large russet potatoes	1 teaspoon seasoned salt
1/2 cup melted butter or margarine	1/2 teaspoon lemon pepper
2 or 3 cloves of garlic, crushed	1 teaspoon chopped parsley
3/4 cup sliced green onion	1 cup shredded Cheddar cheese
2/3 cup regular or low-fat sour cream	1 cup shredded mozzarella cheese
1 teaspoon dillweed	

Preheat the oven to 350 degrees. Microwave the potatoes on High for about 15 to 20 minutes, depending on the size of the potatoes, or until potatoes are tender. Cut each potato in half. Scoop out the middle of each potato into a bowl, leaving a 1/4-inch layer of potato inside the skin. Place the potato shells in a 9-by-13-inch baking pan that has been sprayed with nonstick cooking spray. Stir the butter, garlic, green onion, sour cream, dillweed, seasoned salt, lemon pepper, parsley, half the Cheddar cheese and half the mozzarella cheese into the scooped-out potato in the bowl; mix well. Fill the potato shells with the mixture. Sprinkle with the remaining Cheddar cheese and remaining mozzarella cheese. Bake for about 30 minutes or until hot and bubbly.
Yield: 6 to 8 servings.

Nancy Boggio, Zeta Iota
Loveland, Colorado

Sandy Larson, Preceptor Zeta, Fayetteville, Arkansas, makes Baked Potato Wedges by cutting 4 medium scrubbed potatoes into wedges and coating with a mixture of 3/4 cup ranch dressing and 1 teaspoon pepper and baking in a preheated 425-degree oven for 30 minutes, turning several times. Serve with a dipping sauce of 1/2 cup ranch dressing, 1/4 cup sour cream, and 1/4 cup salsa.

NORWEGIAN NACHOS

This recipe is best when you use large russet potatoes, uniformly sliced.

8 to 10 potatoes	8 ounces sour cream
Salt and pepper to taste	1/2 cup milk
8 slices smoked bacon	1 envelope ranch
1/2 cup water	dressing mix
1 (16-ounce) box process	
cheese	

Preheat the oven to 350 degrees. Slice the unpeeled potatoes crosswise and stack in a greased 9-by-13-inch pan until the pan is full. Salt and pepper as desired. Lay the smoked bacon slices across the potato slices. Pour in 1/2 cup water. Cover the pan tightly with aluminum foil. Bake for about 45 minutes or until potatoes are done (they should remain a little firm, not extremely soft). While the potatoes are baking, melt together the process cheese, sour cream and milk in the microwave or on the stove; stir in the ranch dressing mix. Remove the potatoes from the oven. Remove the bacon strips from the potatoes and microwave on High until crispy. Pour the sour cream mixture over the potatoes; crumble the bacon strips over the sauced potatoes. Cover the pan with aluminum foil. Return to the oven for 5 minutes. Serve smoking hot. Yield: 10 to 12 servings.

Sheila Syurud
Rock Springs, Wyoming

ONION PIE

Serve this pie with steak and a fresh vegetable salad. Omit the Cheddar cheese if you are using cheese in another part of the meal.

3 large sweet onions,	Salt and pepper to taste
finely chopped	2 eggs, beaten
1/2 cup butter or	1 recipe (2-crust) pie
margarine	pastry
3 to 4 tablespoons	1/2 cup shredded Cheddar
all-purpose flour	cheese (optional)
1/2 pint cream	

Preheat the oven to 350 degrees. Sauté the onions in the butter until golden brown. Sprinkle in the flour and stir in the cream. Add the salt and pepper. Stir until the mixture thickens. Remove from heat and stir in the eggs. Pour into an unbaked pie shell. Sprinkle the shredded cheese over the pie filling before adding the top pastry. Cover with the top pastry, sealing the edges. Bake for 30 minutes.
Yield: 6 to 8 servings.

Marjorie A. Harrity
Missoula, Montana

BLOOMIN' ONION

Bloomin' Onion	1/4 teaspoon dried
Dipping Sauce	oregano
1 egg, beaten	1/8 teaspoon dried thyme
1 cup milk	1/8 teaspoon cumin
1 cup all-purpose flour	1 giant Spanish onion
1 1/2 teaspoons salt	(3/4 pound or more)
1 1/2 teaspoons cayenne	Vegetable oil for deep
pepper	frying
1/2 teaspoon ground	
black pepper	

Prepare the Dipping Sauce; keep it covered in the refrigerator until needed. Combine the egg and milk in a medium bowl. Combine the flour, salt, cayenne pepper, black pepper, oregano, thyme and cumin in a separate bowl. Now it's time to slice the onion—this is the tricky part. Slice 3/4 to 1 inch off the top and bottom of the onion. Remove the papery skin. Use a thin knife to cut a 1-inch-diameter core out of the onion. Use a very sharp, large knife to slice the onion several times down the center to form the "petals": Slice through the center of the onion about 3/4 down. Turn the onion 90 degrees and slice again the same way, forming an "X" across the first slice. Keep slicing the sections in half, very carefully, until you've cut the onion 16 times. Remember not to cut down to the bottom. The last 8 slices are usually difficult—just use a steady hand and don't worry if your onion doesn't look like a perfect flower. It will still taste good. Spread apart the "petals" of the onion. The onion sections tend to stick together; separate them to make coating easier. Dip the onion in the milk mixture. Coat liberally with the flour mixture, separating the "petals" and sprinkling the mixture between them. Once you're sure the onion is well coated, dip it back into the milk mixture, then coat it with the flour mixture again. Double-coating this way ensures a well-coated onion, and less coating will float off when the onion is fried. Let the onion rest, covered, in the refrigerator for at least 15 minutes while you get the oil ready. Heat the oil in a deep fryer or deep pot to 350 degrees. Make sure you use enough oil to completely cover the onion when it fries. If the hot oil does not reach the inside of the onion, the coating will be gooey and will not brown. Fry the onion right side up in the oil for 10 minutes or until brown. Remove it from the oil and let it drain on a rack or paper towels. Open the onion wider from the center to form a place for a small dish of the Bloomin' Onion Dipping Sauce; use plain catsup if you don't like hot sauce. Yield: 4 to 6 servings.

BLOOMIN' ONION DIPPING SAUCE

3/4 cup mayonnaise	*Dash of cayenne pepper*
1/4 teaspoon paprika	*2 tablespoons cream-*
Dash of ground black	*style horseradish*
pepper	*1/8 teaspoon dried*
2 teaspoons catsup	*oregano*
1/4 teaspoon salt	*1 teaspoon sugar*

Combine the mayonnaise, paprika, black pepper, catsup, salt, cayenne pepper, horseradish, oregano and sugar in a bowl.

Sherri Cowan, Xi Epsilon Gamma
Edinburgh, Indiana

HEAVENLY ONIONS

To make this recipe low in salt and fat, use low-sodium soy sauce, skim milk, and low-fat cheese and soup.

3 or 4 large white	*10 slices French bread,*
onions, cut up (not	*buttered on both*
chopped)	*sides*
8 ounces mushrooms,	*1 (10-ounce) can cream*
canned or fresh	*of chicken soup*
1/4 cup margarine	*1/2 cup milk*
8 ounces shredded Swiss	*3 teaspoons soy sauce*
cheese	

Sauté the onions and mushrooms in the margarine just until tender. Arrange the sautéed vegetables in the bottom of a greased 9-by-13-inch pan. Cover with the Swiss cheese. Cover with the French bread slices. Mix the cream of chicken soup, milk and soy sauce; pour the mixture over the top of the bread layer. Chill, covered, in the refrigerator for 8 to 10 hours. Preheat the oven to 350 degrees. Bake, uncovered, for 30 to 40 minutes or until lightly browned. Yield: 12 to 15 servings.

Constance Creary
Knoxville, Iowa

ROASTED ROOTS

This delicious recipe is wonderful with freshly baked bread and other vegetarian delights.

5 fresh beets, quartered	*3/4 (32-ounce) bag baby*
2 sweet potatoes, thinly	*carrots*
sliced	*Other root vegetables if*
6 small red-skinned	*desired*
potatoes, quartered	*5 shallots, peeled, sliced*
5 small turnips,	*3 cloves of garlic,*
quartered	*peeled, sliced*
2 leeks, thinly sliced	*Salt and pepper to taste*
1/2 pound brussels	*3 tablespoons olive oil*
sprouts, halved	*Fresh rosemary to taste*

Preheat the oven to 500 degrees. Scrub and trim the beets, sweet potatoes, red-skinned potatoes, turnips and leeks. Mix in an oiled 11-by-13-inch glass baking dish with the brussels sprouts, carrots, shallots and garlic. Add the salt and pepper. Sprinkle with the olive oil and the rosemary. Bake, uncovered, for 3 minutes; reduce the heat to 350 degrees and bake for 1 hour. Yield: 6 to 8 servings.

Starr Byrne, Theta Upsilon
Peachtree City, Georgia

RATATOUILLE CASSEROLE

This makes a great meal served with warm French bread to dip in the vegetable juices.

4 medium tomatoes	*2 red or green bell*
1 medium onion,	*peppers, cut into*
chopped	*1/2-inch pieces*
1 medium eggplant,	*3 cloves of garlic, minced*
cubed	*2 tablespoons rosemary,*
3 medium zucchini,	*chopped*
cut into 1/2-inch	*1/3 cup fresh basil,*
pieces	*chopped*
3 medium yellow	*Salt and pepper to taste*
bottleneck squash,	*3 tablespoons olive oil*
cut into 1/2-inch	*1/4 cup grated Parmesan*
pieces	*cheese*

Preheat the oven to 350 degrees. Place the tomatoes in a kettle with enough water to cover the tomatoes; bring to a boil. Remove immediately from heat; drain. Peel off the tomato skins. Chop the tomatoes and place in a 3-quart lidded glass baking dish prepared with nonstick cooking spray. Add the onion, eggplant, zucchini, squash, bell pepper, garlic, rosemary, basil, salt and pepper; mix together. Pour the olive oil over the top. Sprinkle the Parmesan over the top. Bake for 40 to 50 minutes. Yield: 6 servings.

Dana Payne, Alpha Gamma
Omaha, Nebraska

Norma Jean Jones, Epsilon Master, Broken Arrow, Oklahoma, says everyone will love Popeye Spinach prepared this way: Use fresh spinach in any amount. Rinse the spinach well and discard stems. Have a large pot of rapidly boiling water ready. Add the spinach and boil for exactly 2 minutes. Pour into a colander and rinse with cold water for 30 seconds to stop cooking and set the color. Drain well or gently squeeze. Melt some butter in a pan. Add the spinach and salt and pepper to taste, and heat just to serving temperature. Serve immediately.

SPINACH SOUFFLE

1 (10-ounce) package frozen chopped spinach	*1 cup grated Parmesan cheese*
1 tablespoon grated onion	*1 tablespoon all-purpose flour*
2 eggs, beaten	*2 tablespoons butter or margarine, softened*
½ cup sour cream	*Salt and pepper to taste*

Preheat the oven to 350 degrees. Warm the spinach and the onion in a small amount of water in a saucepan over medium-low heat until the spinach is thawed. Drain well. Combine the eggs, sour cream, Parmesan cheese, flour, butter, salt and pepper; mix well. Stir in the spinach and onion. Pour into a greased 1½-quart baking dish. Bake for 25 to 30 minutes or until center is set. Do not overcook or the soufflé will separate. Serve warm. Yield: 4 servings.

Lois M. Broyles
Bedford, Texas

GOLDEN ACORN SQUASH WITH BLUEBERRIES

2 golden acorn squash	*4 tablespoons light brown sugar*
3 tablespoons water	
4 tablespoons margarine	*1 cup fresh or frozen blueberries*

Pierce each squash 4 or 5 times with a sharp knife. Microwave each squash on High on a paper towel for 6 to 8 minutes. Carefully cut the squash in half and scoop out the seeds. Place the squash halves, cut side down, in a shallow baking dish. Add 3 tablespoons of water. Cover the dish with plastic wrap. Microwave on High for 6 to 8 minutes or until squash tests done. Cut a slice off the curved side of each squash half so it will stand securely. Arrange the squash halves in a baking dish and fill each half with 1 tablespoon of the margarine, 1 tablespoon of the brown sugar and ¼ cup of the blueberries. Microwave on High, for 4 minutes if using frozen berries, 3 minutes if using fresh. Yield: 4 servings.

Carlie Schmidt, Xi Tau Tau
Santa Clarita, California

SPANISH SQUASH

2 pounds yellow squash, sliced	*½ cup mayonnaise-type salad dressing*
1 medium onion, chopped	*¼ cup cracker crumbs*
2 eggs, beaten	*1 (4-ounce) can chopped green chiles*
12 ounces shredded sharp Cheddar cheese	*Salt and pepper to taste*

Preheat the oven to 350 degrees. Cook the squash and onion in as little water as possible in a saucepan over medium-low heat just until the squash is tender, about 10 minutes. Drain well. Combine the squash mixture, eggs, cheese, salad dressing, cracker crumbs, green chiles, salt and pepper in a bowl. Pour into a greased 9-by-12-inch baking dish. Bake for 20 to 25 minutes or until set. Yield: 6 to 8 servings.

Marge Moon, Laureate Zeta Sigma
Lubbock, Texas

HARVEST SQUASH

2 medium acorn squash, halved, seeds removed	*1 tablespoon lemon juice*
	¼ cup margarine
2 medium tart apples, pared, thinly sliced	*¼ cup cornstarch*
	1 teaspoon cinnamon
½ cup slivered almonds	*½ teaspoon nutmeg*
½ cup raisins	*¼ teaspoon salt*
1 cup maple syrup	

Preheat the oven to 350 degrees. Place the squash halves cut side down in a 9-by-12-inch baking pan. Bake for 30 minutes. Remove from oven and turn right side up. Combine the apples, almonds and raisins; fill the squash with this mixture. Combine the maple syrup, lemon juice, margarine, cornstarch, cinnamon, nutmeg and salt in a small saucepan. Cook, stirring, over low heat until thickened. Pour the syrup mixture over the filled squash. Bake for 25 minutes or until squash is tender. Yield: 4 servings.

Nina Rohlfs, Preceptor Tau
Unadilla, Nebraska

SQUASH TEASE

This is a great dish for kids who think they don't like squash.

1 (1½-pound) yellow squash, cooked	*1½ cups shredded Cheddar cheese*
1 tablespoon margarine	*1½ cups cheese puffs, slightly crushed*
2 eggs, slightly beaten	*1 (3-ounce) can French-fried onion rings*
1 teaspoon salt	

Preheat the oven to 350 degrees. Mash the cooked squash in a bowl. Add the margarine, eggs, salt, cheese and cheese puffs; mix well. Pour into a greased 8-by-8-inch baking dish. Bake for 30 minutes or until firm. Sprinkle the onion rings over the top. Bake for 5 minutes longer. Yield: 6 servings.

Kris Jandora, Zeta Lambda
Martinsburg, West Virginia

AMARETTO SWEET POTATOES

3 (17-ounce) cans sweet potatoes, undrained	1/2 cup amaretto
1/2 cup packed light brown sugar	1/2 cup sugar
2 tablespoons orange juice	1/2 cup melted butter or margarine
	1 cup miniature marshmallows

Preheat the oven to 350 degrees. Heat the sweet potatoes in their juice in a saucepan until very hot; drain well and whip with an electric mixer. Beat in the brown sugar, orange juice, amaretto, sugar and butter. Pour into a well-greased 2½- to 3-quart baking dish. Top with the marshmallows. Cover and bake for 30 minutes. Yield: 6 to 9 servings.

Carole Y. Parrott, Zeta Eta
Salisbury, North Carolina

❖ SWEET POTATOES IN APRICOT SAUCE

6 medium sweet potatoes, cooked, peeled, halved lengthwise	1 teaspoon grated orange peel
	1/2 teaspoon cinnamon
	1 cup apricot nectar
1¼ cups firmly packed light brown sugar	1 cup canned apricot halves
1½ tablespoons cornstarch	1/2 cup chopped pecans
	2 tablespoons margarine

Preheat the oven to 375 degrees. Arrange the sweet potatoes in a single layer in a greased 9-by-13-inch baking dish. Combine the brown sugar, cornstarch, orange peel and cinnamon in a saucepan. Stir in the apricot nectar. Cook over medium heat, stirring constantly, until thick and clear. Stir in the apricots, pecans and margarine. Pour the mixture over the sweet potatoes. Bake for 25 minutes or until hot and bubbly. Yield: 6 to 8 servings.

Pauline Dennis
Dallas, Texas

SWEET POTATOES IN ORANGE SHELLS

3 medium oranges, halved	3 tablespoons packed light brown sugar
1 (16-ounce) can sweet potatoes, undrained	1/2 teaspoon salt
	1/4 cup flaked coconut
2 tablespoons melted butter or margarine	6 miniature marshmallows

Preheat the oven to 350 degrees. Squeeze the oranges, saving the juice. Remove the membranes from the orange shells with a sharp knife. Mash the sweet potatoes. Blend 3 tablespoons reserved orange juice, butter, brown sugar and salt; combine with the sweet potatoes. Stir in the coconut. Spoon the mixture into the orange shells. Arrange the stuffed shells in a shallow baking pan. Bake for 20 to 30 minutes or until lightly browned. Top each stuffed shell with a marshmallow. Return to the oven and bake for 5 minutes longer to brown the marshmallows. Yield: 6 servings.

Betty Prusaczyk, Lambda Master
Harrisburg, Illinois

CORNY TOMATO DELIGHT

4 medium tomatoes, sliced	2½ cups milk
1 (16-ounce) can corn, drained	1½ cups all-purpose flour
1/4 cup melted unsalted butter	1/4 teaspoon chili powder
3 eggs	1/4 teaspoon salt
	1/2 cup Parmesan cheese

Preheat the oven to 400 degrees. Drain the sliced tomatoes on paper towels for 10 minutes. Spray a 9-by-13-inch baking pan with nonstick cooking spray. Spread the corn in the prepared pan. Top with the tomatoes. Pour the butter over the vegetables. Combine the eggs, milk, flour, chili powder, salt and Parmesan cheese in a blender container; process until smooth. Pour over the buttered vegetables. Sprinkle extra Parmesan over the top if desired. Bake for 45 minutes. Yield: 8 servings.

Anita J. Mawer
Simi Valley, California

❖ ZUCCHINI STUFFING CASSEROLE

4 medium zucchini, sliced 1/2 inch thick	1 (10-ounce) can cream of chicken soup
3/4 cup shredded carrot	1/2 cup sour cream
1/2 cup chopped onion	3/4 cup herbed stuffing cubes
4 tablespoons butter or margarine	2 tablespoons melted butter or margarine
1½ cups herbed stuffing cubes	

Preheat the oven to 350 degrees. Cook the zucchini in boiling salted water for 5 to 10 minutes or until tender. Drain. Sauté the carrot and onion in the 4 tablespoons butter until tender. Remove from heat and stir in the 1½ cups stuffing cubes, cream of chicken soup and sour cream. Gently stir in the zucchini; turn into a 1½-quart baking dish. Toss the 3/4 cup stuffing cubes with the 2 tablespoons melted butter; spread over the top of the casserole. Bake for 30 to 40 minutes. Yield: 5 to 6 servings.

Carol J. Means, Preceptor Xi Beta
Fresno, California

DONNA'S FAMOUS BARBECUE SAUCE

This won a blue ribbon at the Lincoln County Fair.

1/2 cup minced onion	2 tablespoons light
1/2 cup minced green	brown sugar
pepper	1 tablespoon
2 tablespoons margarine	Worcestershire sauce
3/4 cup catsup	1 teaspoon salt
2 tablespoons vinegar	1 teaspoon chili powder
2 tablespoons prepared	1/2 teaspoon pepper
mustard	1/4 teaspoon paprika

Sauté the onion and green pepper in the margarine in a skillet over low heat until the vegetables are tender. Add the catsup, vinegar, mustard, brown sugar, Worcestershire sauce, salt, chili powder, pepper and paprika; simmer, uncovered, for at least 20 minutes. Yield: 1 1/2 cups.

Donna Oden, Xi Alpha
Kemmerer, Wyoming

HOT APPLE SALAD

1 (20-ounce) can	2/3 cup shredded Cheddar
pineapple tidbits	cheese
5 large apples, peeled,	1/2 cup melted margarine
sliced	1/2 cup sliced almonds
3/4 cup sugar	1/2 cup pineapple juice
1/3 cup all-purpose flour	

Preheat the oven to 350 degrees. Combine the pineapple, apples, sugar, flour and cheese. Spread the mixture in a 9-by-13-inch baking dish. Combine the margarine, almonds and pineapple juice in a small bowl. Pour over the apple-pineapple mixture. Bake for 45 to 50 minutes or until steaming hot and just beginning to brown. Yield: 12 servings.

Cindy Kruckenberg, Xi Theta Zeta
Gilbert, Iowa

"MODERN" CRANBERRY CHUTNEY

Give this to special friends as a holiday gift—they'll love it!

1 (20-ounce) can	1 cup golden raisins
pineapple chunks in	1/2 teaspoon cinnamon
own juice, drained,	1/4 teaspoon ginger
juice reserved	1/4 teaspoon allspice
1 1/2 cups sugar	3/4 cup walnuts, coarsely
1 (12-ounce) bag fresh	chopped, toasted
cranberries	

Combine the reserved pineapple juice with the sugar, cranberries, raisins, cinnamon, ginger and allspice in a medium saucepan. Bring to a boil. Reduce heat to medium low and simmer, covered, for 25 to 30 min-

utes or until the cranberries are tender. Stir in the pineapple chunks and walnuts; mix well. Refrigerate, covered, for at least 4 hours or until completely chilled. Yield: 8 servings.

Helen N. Woods, Alpha Master
Riverside, California

❖ CRANBERRY PEAR SALSA

Bosc pears are a good choice for this salsa. Serve alongside any meat.

1 (12-ounce) bag fresh	1 teaspoon minced
cranberries	orange zest
2 cups chopped pears	2 tablespoons fresh
1 cup chopped red, green	orange juice
and yellow bell	1 tablespoon vegetable
peppers	oil
1/4 cup honey	Pinch of salt
1/2 cup sugar	
1 jalapeño chile, seeded,	
minced	

Chop the cranberries or pulse them in a food processor until coarse. Combine the cranberries with the remaining ingredients in a large bowl; toss gently. Yield: 5 cups.

Betty Erickson, Preceptor Psi
Walnut, California

HOT FRUIT CASSEROLE

1/2 (22-ounce) box dried	1 (15-ounce) can pitted
apricots	black cherries,
1/4 cup Grand Marnier	drained
1/2 cup sugar	2 or 3 large bananas, cut
2 teaspoons cinnamon	in large chunks
3 pounds apples, peeled,	1 cup frozen orange juice
sliced	concentrate, thawed
1 (20-ounce) can	2 tablespoons
pineapple chunks,	cornstarch
drained	

Soak the apricots in the Grand Marnier for 8 to 10 hours. Drain the apricots, reserving the soaking liquid. Preheat the oven to 350 degrees. Combine the sugar and cinnamon. Layer the apples, pineapple chunks, cherries, bananas and apricots in an 11-by-13-inch baking dish, sprinkling each layer with some of the sugar-cinnamon mixture. Combine the orange juice concentrate and cornstarch; pour the mixture over the fruit. Pour the reserved Grand Marnier soaking liquid over the fruit. Bake, tightly covered with foil, for 1 hour. Yield: 8 to 10 servings.

Janet Wheeler
Londonderry, New Hampshire

Bountiful Breads

Bread is standard fare at
almost every meal—
whether it's a nutrient-filled
slice of toast in the morning,
a muffin at brunch, hearty sandwiches
at lunchtime, or buttery yeast rolls
served with dinner. But nothing beats
the flavor and the taste-tempting aroma
of homemade bread taken hot from the oven!
If you've been intimidated by the complexities of bread
baking, try these easy-to-make breads that can
be prepared in thirty minutes or less.
Dust a little flour on your hands,
face, and countertop, and
they'll think you fussed
and slaved for hours!

BACON BREAD RING

This recipe is quick, easy, and yummy. It does require a little time and a few tears to chop an onion—but you can use dry minced onion instead!

8 to 12 slices bacon, crisp-fried, crumbled	2 (5-count) packages refrigerated
1/2 cup Parmesan cheese	buttermilk biscuits
1/4 cup diced onion	1/2 cup melted butter or margarine

Preheat the oven to 350 degrees. Mix bacon, cheese and onion in a shallow bowl. Roll the biscuits in the bacon mixture and stand them on end in a greased bundt pan until the pan is full. Pour the melted butter over the biscuits. Bake for 20 to 30 minutes or until puffed and crusty. Yield: 10 servings.

Kass Witt, Alpha Chi
Glendive, Montana

MONKEY BREAD

1/2 cup melted butter or margarine	1 tablespoon cinnamon
1/2 teaspoon vanilla extract	2 (6-count) cans extra-large refrigerated biscuits
1/3 cup sugar	1/3 cup chopped pecans
1/3 cup packed light brown sugar	

Preheat the oven to 350 degrees. Spray a bundt pan with nonstick cooking spray. Add the vanilla to the melted butter. Combine the sugars and cinnamon in a reclosable plastic bag. Cut the biscuits into quarters and place in the plastic bag with the sugar mix. Shake the closed bag until all the biscuits are coated. Place half the coated biscuits in the bundt pan, sprinkle half the pecans on top and drizzle half the butter over the pecans. Place the remaining coated biscuits in the pan, sprinkle with remaining pecans and drizzle remaining butter on top. Bake for 30 minutes. Remove from the oven and cool. Invert the bread on a plate. Yield: 12 servings.

Jean McClammy
Nederland, Texas

Nancy Tosetti, Omicron Delta, Witt, Illinois, makes Cheddar Biscuits by mixing 2 cups baking mix, 2/3 cup milk, and 1/2 cup shredded Cheddar cheese, dropping by tablespoonfuls onto an ungreased baking sheet, baking in a preheated 450-degree oven for 8 to 10 minutes, and brushing with a mixture of 1/4 cup melted butter and 1/2 teaspoon garlic powder.

ICE CREAM BISCUITS

These biscuits are quick, inexpensive, and easy to make.

1 cup chopped pecans	1 cup packed light brown sugar
3 (10-count) cans refrigerator biscuits	1/4 cup margarine
1 cup vanilla ice cream	

Preheat the oven to 400 degrees. Spray a 9-by-13-inch baking pan with nonstick cooking spray and scatter the pecans in the bottom of the pan. Place the biscuits in 3 rows, slightly overlapping, in the pan. Bring the ice cream, brown sugar and margarine to a boil; pour over the biscuits and bake for 15 minutes. Let the biscuits cool slightly in the pan. Invert them on a platter. Yield: 20 to 30 servings.

Jeanne Birkenholz, Mu Chi
Newton, Iowa

JIFFY CHERRY COFFEE CAKE

Never get caught short—keep this coffee cake in the freezer for emergencies. This recipe offers quick preparation for a busy parent and refreshments for a meeting in minutes. The cake is best served warm. You can heat a frozen cake in a foil wrap in a 350-degree oven until warmed through, about 30 to 35 minutes. Open the foil wrap during the last 10 minutes of heating.

1 1/4 cups sifted all-purpose flour	3 tablespoons milk
1/2 cup sugar	1 teaspoon vanilla extract
1 1/2 teaspoons baking powder	1 (21-ounce) can cherry pie filling
1/4 teaspoon salt	Brown Sugar Topping
1/4 cup butter or margarine	Whipped cream (optional)
1 egg, beaten	Orange peel (optional)

Preheat the oven to 350 degrees. Sift the flour, sugar, baking powder and salt together into a large bowl. Cut in the butter until the mixture resembles coarse crumbs. Combine the egg, milk and vanilla; add to the ingredients in the bowl and mix well. Spread the mixture into a greased 7-by-11-inch baking pan. Spoon the cherry pie filling over the mixture. Sprinkle Brown Sugar Topping over the cherry pie filling. Bake for 45 to 50 minutes or until a tester inserted in the center comes out dry and clean. Top with whipped cream and orange peel if desired. Yield: 8 servings.

BROWN SUGAR TOPPING

½ cup sifted all-purpose
  flour
¼ cup packed light
  brown sugar

½ teaspoon cinnamon
¼ cup butter or
  margarine

Mix the first 3 ingredients in a bowl; cut in the butter until mixture resembles coarse crumbs.

Elaine Sills, Beta Gamma Master
El Paso, Texas

CREAM CHEESE BISCUITS

2 cups sifted all-purpose
  flour
2½ teaspoons baking
  powder
¼ teaspoon baking soda
¼ teaspoon salt

3 tablespoons whipped
  cream cheese
2 tablespoons unsalted
  margarine
⅔ cup skim milk

Preheat the oven to 425 degrees. Combine the flour, baking powder, baking soda and salt in a large bowl. Work in the cream cheese and margarine with a pastry blender until the mixture resembles coarse meal. Stir in all but 1 tablespoon of the milk; the dough should be firm but not dry. Turn the dough onto a lightly floured surface. Knead 2 or 3 times until smooth. Roll the dough ½ inch thick. Cut out rounds of dough, using a 2-inch floured biscuit cutter. Spray a baking sheet with nonstick cooking spray. Place biscuits on sheet and brush the remaining tablespoon of milk over the top of the biscuits. Bake for 12 minutes or until golden brown. Yield: 12 biscuits.

Shaunna Machtolff, Nu Kappa
Guthrie, Oklahoma

APPLE DOUGHNUTS

1½ cups all-purpose
  flour
1¾ teaspoons baking
  powder
½ teaspoon salt
½ teaspoon nutmeg
½ cup sugar

⅓ cup vegetable oil
1 egg, beaten
¼ to ½ cup milk
½ cup chopped apples
½ cup melted butter
1 teaspoon cinnamon
½ cup sugar

Preheat the oven to 350 degrees. Mix the first 5 ingredients in a bowl. Add the oil and stir until the mixture resembles coarse meal. Stir in the egg and milk. Mix in the apple. Bake in greased muffin tins for 18 to 25 minutes or until golden brown. Remove doughnuts from the muffin tins and roll in the melted butter. Roll in a mixture of cinnamon and ½ cup sugar. Yield: 12 servings.

Elaine McCulloch
Lamar, Missouri

BLUEBERRY CREAM MUFFINS

I got this recipe from a good friend in Wyoming. I like to use big Texas-style muffin tins and serve the muffins for summer breakfasts.

2 cups sugar
4 eggs, beaten
1 cup vegetable oil
1 teaspoon vanilla
  extract
4 cups flour

1 teaspoon salt
2 teaspoons baking
  powder
2 cups (16 ounces) sour
  cream
2 cups blueberries

Preheat the oven to 400 degrees. Add the sugar to the eggs and mix well. Slowly add the oil and the vanilla. Stir together the flour, salt and baking powder. Add the dry mixture to the egg mixture alternately with the sour cream in thirds, stirring after each addition. Fold in the blueberries. Spoon into a muffin tin and bake for 20 minutes or until light brown.
Yield: 12 to 24 servings.

Deb Hawkinson, Xi Xi
Tioga, North Dakota

BRAN NUT MUFFINS

This batter can be made and refrigerated for up to 5 days.

18 ounces bran
5 cups skim milk
¼ cup lemon juice
1⅓ cups canola oil
2⅞ cups packed light
  brown sugar
2½ teaspoons vanilla
  extract
2¾ cups plus
  2 tablespoons
  all-purpose flour

2½ teaspoons baking
  soda
2 tablespoons baking
  powder
5 ounces sliced almonds
5 ounces chopped
  walnuts
5 ounces raisins

Preheat the oven to 350 degrees. Mix the bran, milk and lemon juice in a large bowl and let soak for 10 minutes. Add the oil, brown sugar and vanilla; mix well. Combine the flour, baking soda and baking powder and add to the bran mixture. Fold in the almonds, walnuts and raisins. Spray large muffin tins with nonstick cooking spray. Fill the muffin cups ¾ full. Bake for 10 minutes and rotate the pan; then bake for 15 minutes longer or until lightly browned. Let the muffins stand for 5 minutes, then remove from the muffin tins. Yield: 20 servings.

Ramona Zeigler, Oregon Pi Master
Eugene, Oregon

CRANBERRY MUFFINS

My son Dwayne loves these muffins.

1 cup chopped raw cranberries	1/4 teaspoon salt
1/2 cup sugar	1/4 cup sugar
2 cups all-purpose flour	1 egg
3/4 teaspoon baking soda	1/4 to 1/2 cup buttermilk
	1/4 cup melted shortening

Preheat the oven to 350 degrees. Combine the cranberries with 1/2 cup sugar and set aside. Combine the flour, soda, salt and 1/4 cup sugar in a large bowl. Combine the egg, buttermilk and shortening in a smaller bowl; pour into the center of the dry ingredients. Stir just until mixed. Add more buttermilk if the batter seems too dry. Gently fold in the cranberry mixture. Spoon the batter into a greased muffin tin, filling each cup 2/3 full. Bake for 20 minutes or until a toothpick inserted in the center comes out clean. Yield: 12 servings.

Judith A. Courtney, Preceptor Nu
Salina, Kansas

HEARTHSIDE INN MUFFINS

These muffins were warmly received by faculty and staff at a preschool meeting. They may be served with whipped topping if desired. They can be frozen successfully.

2 1/2 cups sugar	2 apples, shredded
4 cups all-purpose flour	1 cup pecans, chopped
4 teaspoons cinnamon	1 (8-ounce) can crushed pineapple
4 teaspoons baking soda	
1 teaspoon salt	6 eggs, lightly beaten
1 cup shredded coconut	2 cups vegetable oil
1 cup raisins	1 teaspoon vanilla extract
4 cups shredded carrots	

Preheat the oven to 375 degrees. Mix the sugar, flour, cinnamon, baking soda and salt in a large bowl. Add the coconut, raisins, carrots, apples, pecans and pineapple; stir well. Add the eggs, oil and vanilla, stirring only until blended (not beaten). Spoon into greased muffin tins. Bake for 20 minutes or until browned. Yield: 20 to 24 muffins.

Jane Hajdukiewicz, Eta Master
Tallahassee, Florida

Julie Conway, Xi Epsilon Mu, Lee's Summit, Missouri, makes Strawberry Butter by beating 1 1/2 cups softened butter with a 10-ounce package of thawed frozen strawberries and 1 1/2 cups sifted confectioners' sugar. Store, covered, in the refrigerator.

NEW MEXICAN BREAKFAST MUFFINS

These muffins are always a favorite at my church hospitality table.

1 3/4 cups sifted all-purpose flour	1/3 cup bacon drippings
	3/4 cup bacon, crisp-fried, crumbled
2 1/2 teaspoons baking powder	
1/2 teaspoon salt	1/4 cup fresh chopped green chiles
1 egg, well beaten	
1 cup milk	1 cup shredded Cheddar cheese

Preheat the oven to 400 degrees. Sift the flour, baking powder and salt into a large mixing bowl; make a well in the center of the ingredients. Combine the egg, milk and bacon drippings and add all at once to the dry ingredients. Stir quickly only until the dry ingredients are moistened. Quickly fold in the bacon, green chile and cheese. Fill muffin cups 2/3 full. Bake for 18 to 20 minutes. Yield: 12 muffins.

Alana M. Jantzen, Xi Nu
Los Alamos, New Mexico

SOUR CREAM PEACH MUFFINS

After canning peaches all day, these muffins are a real treat with a cup of peach tea.

1 cup chopped peaches	1/2 teaspoon salt
1 teaspoon lemon juice	1/4 teaspoon cinnamon
1 cup milk	3 teaspoons baking powder
1 egg	
1/4 cup melted shortening	2 cups unsifted all-purpose flour
2/3 cup sugar	

Preheat the oven to 450 degrees. Sprinkle the peaches with the lemon juice; stir and set aside. Mix the milk, egg, shortening, sugar, salt, cinnamon, baking powder and flour in a large bowl. Fold in the peaches just before baking. Fill greased muffin tins 2/3 full. Bake for 20 minutes or until lightly browned.
Yield: 12 to 15 muffins.

Candy Falk
La Center, Washington

FLOUR TORTILLAS

5 cups all-purpose flour	1/3 cup vegetable oil or melted lard
2 teaspoons salt	
5 teaspoons baking powder	2 1/2 cups hot tap water

Mix the flour, salt, baking powder and oil together with your hand. Add the hot water until a soft ball is formed. Knead the flour ball about 25 strokes. Form into 12 balls, then roll each ball into a flat circle with a rolling pin. Bake on a hot griddle, turning to cook both sides. Yield: 12 tortillas.

Joan Perez, Zeta Iota
Bayard, New Mexico

GREEN CHILE CHEDDAR CORN BREAD IN A FLOWERPOT

You may make more loaves with smaller flowerpots. If you use flowerpots that are 4½ inches in diameter and 4 inches tall, place ⅔ cup of the batter in each pot and bake for 30 minutes. You may bake the bread in greased wide-mouth 1-pint jars, using 1 cup of batter for each jar and baking at 425 degrees for 30 minutes. If used as gifts, wrap each flowerpot or jar in colored cellophane. Gather the cellophane into a bunch and tie with a ribbon.

2½ cups buttermilk	1 (8-ounce) can cream-
1 teaspoon baking soda	style corn
3 eggs, beaten	1 cup shredded Cheddar
1 cup vegetable oil	cheese
2 cups cornmeal	1 small raw potato,
1 cup all-purpose flour	peeled, grated
1 tablespoon baking	1 (4-ounce) can chopped
powder	green chiles
¼ cup sugar	1 small onion, chopped
1 teaspoon salt	

Preheat the oven to 450 degrees. Combine buttermilk and baking soda in a small bowl; mix well. Mix eggs and oil together in a separate bowl. Blend the cornmeal, flour, baking powder, sugar and salt in a large bowl with a wire whisk. Add egg mixture to cornmeal mixture; mix slightly. Add the buttermilk mixture, corn, cheese, potato, chiles and onion; stir gently until moistened. Line 4 new clay flowerpots (6 inches in diameter, 5½ inches tall) with heavy foil, letting the foil extend over the sides. Spray the foil with nonstick cooking spray. Place 1¾ cups batter in each flowerpot. Bake for 45 minutes. Let cool. Cover the top of the corn bread with the extending foil. Yield: 4 loaves.

Gladys Kelly, Xi Omicron Nu
Friendswood, Texas

Tomilie Sullivan, Alpha Zeta Master, Denton, Texas, makes Hearty Broccoli Corn Bread with two 7-ounce packages of corn bread mix, 1 cup melted butter, 4 eggs, 16 ounces cottage cheese, a chopped onion, and 10-ounce package chopped broccoli that has been thawed and drained. Bake in a greased 9-by-13-inch baking pan in a preheated 350-degree oven for 30 minutes.

SANTA FE CORN AND CHEESE SQUARES

2 (8-ounce) packages	1 cup sour cream
corn bread mix	¾ cup melted margarine
1 teaspoon salt	4 eggs, beaten
1 cup chopped green	1 (16-ounce) package
onions	frozen corn with red
½ cup chopped fresh	and green peppers,
cilantro	thawed, drained
3 tablespoons chopped	1 cup shredded Cheddar
jalapeños	cheese

Preheat the oven to 400 degrees. Combine the corn bread mix, salt, green onions, cilantro and jalapeños in a bowl. Add the sour cream, margarine and eggs; mix well. Add the corn and cheese; mix well. Spread in a greased 9-by-13-inch baking pan. Bake for 34 to 42 minutes or until golden brown. Let stand for 10 minutes. Cut into squares. Yield: 12 servings.

Sherilyn Brooks, Xi Theta Sigma
Bay City, Texas

SPOON BREAD

1¼ cups cornmeal	3 eggs, beaten
3 cups milk	1¾ teaspoons baking
1 teaspoon salt	powder
2 tablespoons butter	

Preheat the oven to 350 degrees. Gradually stir the cornmeal into the milk in a saucepan over medium-high heat. Bring to a boil. Add the salt and butter, remove from heat; let cool. Add the eggs and baking powder; beat well. Pour into a glass 8-by-8-inch baking pan. Bake for 30 minutes. Yield: 6 to 8 servings.

Ruth Baker
Hazard, Kentucky

Jeannette Brown, Laureate Beta Phi, Council Bluffs, Iowa, makes Spumoni Coffee Cake. Cream ¾ cup butter with 1½ cups sugar. Add 3 eggs, 1½ cups sour cream, and 3 cups flour mixed with 1½ teaspoons baking powder. Beat 2 cups batter with ¼ cup milk and 1 small package chocolate instant pudding mix. Beat 2 cups batter with 1 small package pistachio instant pudding mix. Mix remaining batter with ½ cup chopped maraschino cherries and 2 tablespoons cherry juice. Drop by spoonfuls into a greased and floured bundt pan. Bake in a preheated 325-degree oven for 1¼ hours. Cool for 10 minutes. Invert onto a plate. Drizzle with a mixture of 1 cup confectioners' sugar and 2 tablespoons milk.

SPINACH BREAD

I never tell that this bread has spinach in it until everyone has tasted it. Once it has been tasted, it becomes everyone's favorite.

½ cup margarine, softened	1 (9-ounce) package quick corn muffin mix, dry
1 egg	
1 (8-ounce) container sour cream	1½ cups shredded Cheddar cheese
1 (10-ounce) can cream of onion soup	
1 (10-ounce) box frozen chopped spinach, thawed and drained	

Preheat the oven to 375 degrees. Mix the margarine, egg, sour cream and soup in a medium bowl with a wooden spoon. Squeeze the excess liquid from the spinach and add to the soup mixture. Stir in the corn muffin mix. Pour into a greased 9-by-9-inch baking pan. Bake for 30 to 40 minutes or until lightly browned. Sprinkle the cheese on top and bake until the cheese melts. Yield: 12 to 16 servings.

Debbie Durnil
Washington, Indiana

CORN FRITTERS

Don't mix the batter ahead of time.

1 cup all-purpose flour	2 eggs, well beaten
¼ cup sugar	1 (8¾-ounce) can cream-style corn
1 teaspoon baking powder	Shortening for frying
Pinch of salt	

Sift the flour, sugar, baking powder and salt together in a large bowl. Blend the eggs and corn together. Gradually stir the corn mixture into the flour mixture. Lower spoonfuls of the batter into hot shortening a few at a time, frying until golden brown and turning once. Yield: 4 servings.

Kay Sidwell, Preceptor Beta Omicron
Rella, Missouri

Hazel I. Ivey, Brackettville, Texas, makes Texas-Style Beer Bread by mixing 3 cups self-rising flour with 1 cup sugar, adding a 12-ounce can of beer, letting it foam, and stirring until mixed. Pour into a greased loaf pan, brush with an egg beaten with 1 tablespoon water, bake in a preheated 350-degree oven for 40 to 45 minutes, and brush with 1 tablespoon butter.

APPLE BREAD

3 cups all-purpose flour	½ cup orange juice
1½ teaspoons salt	4 unpeeled apples, finely chopped
1 teaspoon baking soda	
2 cups sugar	1 teaspoon vanilla extract
1 teaspoon cinnamon	
4 eggs, well beaten	1 cup chopped pecans
1 cup vegetable oil	

Preheat the oven to 350 degrees. Combine the first 8 ingredients in a large bowl; mix well. Stir in the apples, vanilla and pecans. Pour into 2 greased and floured 5-by-9-inch loaf pans. Bake for 50 to 60 minutes. Cool for 15 minutes. Invert onto a wire rack to cool completely. Yield: 20 to 24 servings.

Lise Pinkerton
Mercedes, Texas

❖ PRALINE APPLE BREAD

1 cup sugar	½ teaspoon salt
1 (8-ounce) container sour cream	1½ cups chopped tart apples
2 eggs	1 cup pecans, chopped
2 teaspoons vanilla extract	¼ cup butter or margarine
2 cups all-purpose flour	¼ cup packed light brown sugar
2 teaspoons baking soda	

Preheat the oven to 350 degrees. Combine the first 7 ingredients in a large bowl; mix well. Stir in the apples and half the pecans. Turn into a greased 5-by-9-inch loaf pan. Sprinkle with the remaining pecans; press into the batter. Bake for 50 to 60 minutes. Boil the butter and brown sugar in a small saucepan for 1 minute. Drizzle over the bread. Remove the bread from the pan after it has cooled. Yield: 12 servings.

Patricia Nicely, Laureate Zeta
Roanoke, Virginia

Carol Sassin, Xi Psi Beta, Beeville, Texas, makes Filled Garlic Loaf. Cut a loaf of French bread in half lengthwise; scoop out the centers, forming shells. Sauté 2 to 8 cloves of garlic, 7 teaspoons sesame seeds, and bread centers in 6 tablespoons butter. Mix 1½ cups sour cream, 2 cups Monterey Jack cheese, ¼ cup Parmesan cheese, 2 tablespoons parsley, and 2 teaspoons lemon pepper together. Stir in the garlic and bread mixture and a 14-ounce can of drained and chopped artichoke hearts. Spoon into the shells, sprinkle with 1 cup shredded Cheddar cheese, and bake in a preheated 350-degree oven for 30 minutes.

❖ SARAH'S SURPRISE BANANA BREAD

This bread started out as a plain banana bread which seemed to get more boring every time I served it. So I added dried cranberries and walnuts and served it to my sorority sisters. Many asked for the recipe. I mash the bananas right into the creamed sugar and butter and eggs.

1¼ cups sugar	2½ cups all-purpose
½ cup butter, softened	flour
2 large eggs	1 teaspoon baking soda
1½ cups mashed	½ teaspoon salt
bananas	1 cup dried cranberries
1 (8-ounce) carton sour	1 cup chopped walnuts
cream	
1 teaspoon vanilla	
extract	

Preheat the oven to 350 degrees. Cream the sugar and butter in a large bowl until light and fluffy. Stir in the eggs and beat until blended. Add the bananas; beat a little more. Add the sour cream and vanilla; beat until smooth. Stir in the flour, baking soda and salt. Add the cranberries and nuts; mix well. Pour into a greased 5-by-9-inch loaf pan. Bake for up to 1 hour and 25 minutes or until loaf tests done. *1 hr + 25 min* Yield: 12 to 14 servings.

makes a very full loaf pan

Sarah B. Hunsucker
Wichita Falls, Texas

CHOCOLATE CHIP BANANA NUT BREAD

My daughters and I enjoy baking this bread together. If you sift together all the dry ingredients before mixing, the batter will be easier to prepare.

½ teaspoon baking soda	½ cup vegetable oil
½ teaspoon salt	2 eggs
2 teaspoons baking	1 cup mashed bananas
powder	1 cup semisweet
1¾ cups sifted all-	chocolate chips
purpose flour	1 cup chopped walnuts
¾ cup sugar	or pecans

Preheat the oven to 325 degrees. Mix the first 4 ingredients in a small bowl. Combine the sugar, oil and eggs in a large bowl; beat until frothy. Add the bananas to the sugar mixture and blend well. Fold in the flour mixture. Stir in the chocolate chips and nuts. Pour the batter into a greased loaf pan. Bake for 1 hour until the crust is golden brown and a toothpick comes out clean. Yield: 1 loaf.

Kelly Evanoff, Epsilon Theta
Salem, Oregon

BLUEBERRY LEMON BREAD

⅓ cup margarine,	1 teaspoon salt
softened	½ cup milk
1 cup sugar	1 cup blueberries
3 tablespoons fresh	2 tablespoons grated
lemon juice	lemon rind
2 eggs	½ cup chopped pecans
1½ cup sifted all-	¼ cup lemon juice
purpose flour	½ cup sugar
1 teaspoon baking	
powder	

Preheat the oven to 350 degrees. Cream the margarine, 1 cup sugar and 3 tablespoons lemon juice in a large bowl until light and fluffy. Beat in the eggs. Mix the flour, baking powder and salt in a medium bowl. Add the flour mixture to the margarine mixture in thirds alternately with the milk. Stir just enough to blend. Toss the blueberries in a small amount of flour to coat; stir into the batter with the lemon rind and nuts. Pour the batter into a greased and floured 5-by-9-inch loaf pan. Bake for about 70 minutes. Blend ¼ cup lemon juice and ½ cup sugar to make a glaze; drizzle it over the top of the bread while it is still warm. Yield: 10 to 12 servings.

Katie Disney, Preceptor Alpha Gamma
Ridgway, Illinois

EGGNOG BREAD

3 cups all-purpose	1¾ cups canned or dairy
flour	eggnog
½ cup sugar	½ cup vegetable oil
4 teaspoons baking	½ cup chopped pecans
powder	½ cup golden raisins
½ teaspoon salt	½ cup sifted
½ teaspoon nutmeg	confectioners' sugar
1 egg, beaten	2 to 3 teaspoons eggnog

Preheat the oven to 350 degrees. Combine the flour, sugar, baking powder, salt and nutmeg in a large bowl. Combine the egg, 1¾ cups eggnog and oil and add to the dry ingredients, stirring just until combined. Stir in the nuts and raisins. Turn into a greased 5-by-9-inch loaf pan. Bake for 60 to 70 minutes; if the bread browns quickly, cover with aluminum foil after 50 minutes. Cool in the pan for 10 minutes. Remove from the pan and cool completely on a wire rack. Wrap and store overnight. Before serving, mix the powdered sugar and 2 to 3 teaspoons eggnog and drizzle over the bread. Yield: 9 (1-inch-thick) slices.

Tonia Fraze, Alpha Sigma
New Salisbury, Indiana

HAWAIIAN COCONUT BREAD

½ cup butter or margarine, softened	¼ teaspoon salt
	2 eggs
1 cup sugar	½ cup mashed bananas
2 cups flour	½ cup crushed pineapple
1 teaspoon baking powder	¼ cup shredded coconut
½ teaspoon baking soda	

Preheat the oven to 350 degrees. Cream the butter and sugar in a large bowl until light and fluffy. Add the flour, baking powder, baking soda, salt, eggs, bananas, pineapple and coconut; beat until well blended. Pour the batter into a greased 5-by-9-inch loaf pan. Bake for 60 to 70 minutes. Cool completely before slicing. Yield: 12 slices.

Jennifer Jacobs
Baytown, Texas

LEMON LOAF

I bake several times a year for seniors and this is a favorite. It tastes great, and baking it makes me happy because I am helping others. If you want to use miniature loaf pans, bake for only 30 to 35 minutes.

⅓ cup vegetable oil	1½ teaspoons baking powder
1 cup sugar	
Grated rind of 1 lemon	1 teaspoon salt
2 eggs, beaten	½ cup milk
1½ cups sifted all-purpose flour	Juice of 1 lemon
	¼ cup sugar

Preheat the oven to 350 degrees. Cream the oil and 1 cup sugar in a large bowl; beat in the lemon rind and eggs. Combine the flour, baking powder and salt in a small bowl. Add the dry ingredients in thirds to the egg mixture, alternating with thirds of the milk. Spoon into a well-greased 5-by-9-inch loaf pan. Let the batter stand for 20 minutes. Bake for 1 hour. Remove from the oven and drizzle with a mixture of the lemon juice and ¼ cup sugar. Cool for 10 minutes. Remove the loaf from the pan and put it bottom down on a wire rack. Yield: 12 slices.

Alyce E. Huff, Xi Tau Tau
Saugus, California

Barbara Bowden, Tampa, Florida, makes a delicious Pecan Date Spread for crackers, tea bread, or muffins by creaming ⅓ cup margarine and 3 ounces cream cheese and adding ¼ cup chopped dates, ¼ cup chopped pecans, and a tablespoon of apple juice. Store in the refrigerator.

ORANGE BREAD

My mother and I used to make this bread for special occasions. My mother loved to bake, and she made sure that my sister and I knew how to make her special recipes. Sometimes I use soup cans or vegetable cans for baking. I fill them half full with the batter and bake at 350 degrees for 30 to 40 minutes or until an inserted toothpick comes out clean.

1½ cups all-purpose flour	2 eggs, beaten
	¼ cup melted butter or margarine
½ cup sugar	
2 teaspoons baking powder	½ cup orange juice
	2 tablespoons grated orange peel
½ teaspoon baking soda	
½ teaspoon salt (optional)	2 tablespoons water
	1 cup chopped walnuts

Preheat the oven to 350 degrees. Combine the flour, sugar, baking powder, baking soda and salt in a large bowl. Combine the eggs, butter, orange juice, orange peel and water in a small bowl. Add the egg mixture to the flour mixture, stirring just until blended. Stir in the walnuts. Spoon into a greased 4½-by-8½-inch loaf pan. Bake for 50 minutes or until a toothpick inserted in the loaf comes out clean. Cool in the pan for 10 minutes. Remove from the pan and cool completely on a wire rack. Yield: 10 to 12 servings.

Beverly Raze
Ontario, Oregon

PISTACHIO BREAD

1 (2-layer) package yellow cake mix	1 cup sour cream
	¾ cup chopped maraschino cherries
1 (3-ounce) package pistachio instant pudding mix	½ cup chopped walnuts
	¼ cup sugar
4 eggs	Cinnamon to taste
2 tablespoons cold water	

Preheat the oven to 350 degrees. Combine the cake mix, pudding mix, eggs, water, sour cream, cherries and walnuts in a large bowl; mix well with a spoon. Stir together the sugar and cinnamon to make a sugar topping. Grease two 5-by-9-inch loaf pans and sprinkle ¼ of the sugar topping in the bottom of each pan. Place dough in the pans and sprinkle the rest of the sugar topping over each loaf. Bake for 45 minutes. Let cool after removing from the oven. Remove the loaves from the pans and wrap in foil. Place them in the refrigerator. Yield: 24 slices.

Dayle Nelson, Beta Master
Cheyenne, Wyoming

LEMON POPPY SEED BREAD

Every time I use this recipe I think of Mamie, a good friend of mine who used to serve it with hot tea. It keeps well for a week when refrigerated, or it can be kept frozen for a month.

2²/₃ cups all-purpose flour	4 teaspoons grated lemon peel
1¹/₂ teaspoons baking powder	1¹/₂ teaspoons vanilla extract
1 teaspoon salt	3 large eggs
¹/₄ cup poppy seeds	¹/₃ cup milk
1 cup butter or margarine	¹/₂ cup fresh lemon juice
1¹/₄ cups sugar	¹/₂ cup sugar

Preheat the oven to 350 degrees. Sift the flour, baking powder and salt into a medium bowl; stir in the poppy seeds. Cream butter and 1¹/₄ cups sugar in a large bowl until light and fluffy; beat in the lemon peel and the vanilla. Beat in the eggs 1 at a time. Add the milk and beat until combined. Add the flour mixture and beat just until combined. Divide the batter among 4 greased and floured 3¹/₄-by-5¹/₄-inch loaf pans. Bake for 40 to 45 minutes or until a tester comes out clean. To make a syrup, combine the lemon juice and ¹/₂ cup sugar in a small saucepan. Bring to a boil, stirring until the sugar is dissolved. Keep the syrup warm. After removing the loaves from the oven, poke them immediately with a skewer in several places and brush with some of the syrup. Let cool for 5 minutes. Invert on a wire rack, poke all sides with the skewer and brush with syrup. Brush the tops with the remaining syrup. Let cool.
Yield: 24 servings.

Drusilla Emery
Colenburn, Maine

POPPY SEED BREAD

This bread is a hit when I make it for family and friends at Christmastime. To make a variety of shapes and sizes, I bake it in soup or coffee cans. This bread freezes well.

3 eggs, beaten	3 cups all-purpose flour
2¹/₂ cups sugar	1¹/₂ teaspoons salt
1¹/₂ cups milk	1¹/₂ teaspoons baking powder
1 cup vegetable oil	2 tablespoons poppy seeds
1¹/₂ teaspoons vanilla extract	Almond Glaze
1¹/₂ teaspoons almond extract	
1¹/₂ teaspoons butter extract	

Preheat the oven to 350 degrees. Combine the first 8 ingredients in a large bowl; beat well. Mix in the flour, salt, baking powder and poppy seeds. Pour into 3 greased 3-by-7-inch loaf pans. Bake for 50 to 55 minutes. Brush Almond Glaze over the hot loaves. Let cool. Remove from the pans; wrap in plastic wrap. Yield: 24 slices.

ALMOND GLAZE

¹/₂ teaspoon vanilla extract	¹/₂ teaspoon butter extract
¹/₂ teaspoon almond extract	³/₄ cup sugar
	¹/₄ cup orange juice

Combine the vanilla, almond extract, butter extract, sugar and orange juice.

Laurie Siddall, Mu Chi
Newton, Iowa

RHUBARB BREAD

1¹/₂ cups packed light brown sugar	1 teaspoon salt
²/₃ cup vegetable oil	1¹/₂ to 2 cups finely chopped rhubarb
1 cup buttermilk	¹/₂ cup walnuts or pecans
1 egg	¹/₂ cup sugar
1 teaspoon vanilla extract	1 tablespoon butter or margarine, melted
2¹/₂ cups all-purpose flour	1 teaspoon cinnamon
1 teaspoon baking soda	

Combine the first 10 ingredients in order listed, mixing well after each addition. Pour the batter into 2 greased and floured 5-by-9-inch loaf pans. Combine the sugar, butter and cinnamon; sprinkle over batter. Bake for 45 minutes or until a wooden pick inserted in the centers comes out clean. Yield: 24 slices.

Annette Byman, Xi Nu
Mason City, Iowa

Joycee Davis, Preceptor Zeta, Lowell, Arkansas, submits a recipe from her husband, George, that he serves for poker parties. His Spicy Cheese Bread is made by pressing a 10-ounce package of refrigerated pizza dough into a 5-by-14-inch rectangle, sprinkling a 4-ounce can of drained chopped green chiles, 1 cup each sharp Cheddar cheese and pepper Jack cheese down the center, folding the ends and the sides over to seal, sprinkling with ¹/₂ teaspoon garlic powder, and baking in a preheated 375-degree oven for 15 to 20 minutes. Easy to double or triple.

SESAME CHEESE CASSEROLE BREAD

3 tablespoons sesame
  seeds
1 egg
1½ cups milk
1 cup shredded Cheddar
  cheese

3¾ cups baking mix
1 tablespoon snipped
  parsley
¼ teaspoon pepper
  (optional)

Preheat the oven to 350 degrees. Grease a 2-quart baking pan; sprinkle the sesame seeds evenly on the bottom and sides. Beat the egg in a large mixer bowl on low speed. Add the milk, cheese, baking mix, parsley and pepper, beating on medium speed for 30 seconds. Pour into the baking dish. Bake for 40 to 45 minutes or until a wooden pick inserted in the center comes out clean. Immediately invert and remove from the pan. Yield: 12 to 15 servings.

June Hamann
Pasco, Washington

CARAWAY SPINACH BREAD

My mom always served this with her fried chicken on Sundays.

3 cups baking mix
1 (10-ounce) can
  Cheddar cheese soup
3 large eggs
1 tablespoon caraway
  seeds

¼ cup vegetable oil
1 (10-ounce) box frozen
  chopped spinach,
  thawed and squeezed
  dry

Preheat the oven to 350 degrees. Grease a 5-by-9-inch loaf pan. Mix the baking mix, soup, eggs, caraway seeds and oil in a large bowl until well blended, about 1 minute. Stir in the spinach until well blended. Pour the batter into the pan. Bake for 1 hour or until a toothpick or knife inserted in the center comes out clean. Let cool and remove from the pan. Yield: 12 to 15 servings.

Judy M. Diltz, Xi Sigma Omicron
Marysville, California

STRAWBERRY BREAD

2 cups sugar
1 teaspoon baking soda
½ teaspoon salt
1 teaspoon cinnamon
4 eggs
1 cup vegetable oil
2 (10-ounce) packages
  frozen strawberries,
  drained, juice
  reserved

3 cups all-purpose flour
1 (8-ounce) package
  cream cheese,
  softened
½ cup confectioners'
  sugar
⅓ cup butter or
  margarine
⅓ cup juice from frozen
  strawberries

Preheat the oven to 325 degrees. Mix the sugar, baking soda, salt and cinnamon in a large bowl. Add the eggs, oil and strawberries; mix well. Add the flour and mix well. Spoon the batter into 2 greased 5-by-9-inch loaf pans. Bake for 30 to 40 minutes or until a wooden pick inserted in the center of the loaves comes out clean. Remove from pans and cool. Blend the cream cheese, confectioners' sugar, butter and strawberry juice until smooth. Serve with the bread. Yield: 12 servings.

Della Jo Pickett, Preceptor Lambda Delta
Kilgore, Texas

ZUCCHINI BREAD

This recipe was given to me by a friend from Sweden many years ago. My son has requested it for his birthday for over 10 years. Buy large zucchini for easier grating. Instead of 1 large loaf, you can bake 3 small loaves, testing after 40 minutes to see if they are done. You can also double the recipe, using large bowls or Dutch ovens for mixing.

1½ cups grated unpeeled
  zucchini
1 cup sugar
1 egg
½ cup vegetable oil
1½ cups all-purpose
  flour
¼ teaspoon grated
  lemon peel

1 teaspoon ground
  cinnamon
½ teaspoon salt
½ teaspoon baking soda
½ teaspoon nutmeg
¼ teaspoon baking
  powder
½ cup chopped walnuts

Preheat the oven to 325 degrees. Mix the zucchini, sugar, egg and oil in a large bowl. Set aside. Mix the flour, lemon peel, cinnamon, salt, baking soda, nutmeg and baking powder in a medium bowl. Slowly blend the flour mixture into the zucchini mixture. Fold in the walnuts. Pour the batter into a greased and floured 5-by-9-inch loaf pan. Bake for 60 to 65 minutes or until a toothpick inserted into the center of the bread comes out clean. Yield: 12 slices.

Jeanette Christy, Preceptor Mu Omicron
Rancho Santa Margarita, California

❖ STUFFED FRENCH TOAST

1 (8-ounce) package
  cream cheese,
  softened
¼ cup crushed pineapple
½ cup chopped pecans
1 (16-ounce) loaf French
  bread
4 large eggs

1 cup whipping cream
½ teaspoon vanilla
  extract
1 teaspoon ground
  ginger
1 (12-ounce) jar apricot
  preserves
½ cup orange juice

Beat the cream cheese and pineapple at medium speed with an electric mixer until light and fluffy. Stir in the pecans. Cut the bread into 12 (1½-inch-thick) slices; cut into the top crust of each slice, forming a pocket. Stuff each slice evenly with the cream cheese mixture. Combine the eggs, whipping cream, vanilla and ginger, stirring well with a wire whisk. Dip the bread slices in the egg mixture, coating on all sides. Bake on a lightly greased griddle over medium-high heat for 3 minutes on each side or until golden brown. Combine the preserves and orange juice in a saucepan; cook over low heat, stirring constantly. Serve over the hot French toast. The toast may also be served with maple syrup. Yield: 6 servings.

Beverly J. Neff, Laureate Tau
South Charleston, West Virginia

JALAPENO BREAD

This bread is great for potluck gatherings. It has an unusual texture that makes it a conversation piece, so almost everyone tries it. For a milder bread, remove the seeds from the jalapeños before chopping.

2 (1-pound) loaves frozen bread dough, thawed	2 tablespoons taco seasoning mix
1 (9-ounce) can whole kernel corn, drained	1 (2-ounce) jar sliced pimientos, drained
1 egg, beaten	1½ teaspoons vinegar
1 (3½-ounce) can whole jalapeños, chopped	

Preheat the oven to 350 degrees. Cut the bread dough into 1-inch pieces. Place the dough pieces, corn, egg, jalapeños, seasoning mix, pimientos and vinegar in a large bowl; toss to coat the dough. Spoon the mixture into 2 greased 4-by-8-inch loaf pans. Cover and let stand for 15 minutes. Bake for 35 to 40 minutes until golden brown. Cool in pans for 10 minutes before removing to a wire rack. Serve warm if desired. Yield: 24 servings.

Ann M. Lobenstein
Tomah, Wisconsin

PEPPERONI BREAD

1 (1-pound) loaf frozen bread dough	1 teaspoon salt
1 egg	8 ounces sliced pepperoni
1 teaspoon oregano	1 cup shredded mozzarella cheese
¼ teaspoon black pepper	Sesame seeds
1 teaspoon parsley	

Preheat the oven to 375 degrees. Follow the package directions to prepare the dough to the final rising stage. Spread the dough into a rectangle on a greased baking sheet. Make an egg wash by mixing the egg, oregano, pepper, parsley and salt. Spread half the egg mixture on the dough almost to the edges. Layer the pepperoni and cheese down the center of the dough. Fold the sides of the dough over the filling and press to seal. Place seam side down on a baking sheet. Spread with the remaining egg wash. Sprinkle with sesame seeds. Bake for 25 minutes. Yield: 12 servings.

Dianna Hawkins, Nu Sigma
Tarkio, Missouri

BIG JOHN'S ROLLS

These rolls are great when served with chili or vegetable soup. You may use another type of cheese instead of the Cheddar if you desire. You may use frozen crescent rolls instead of the frozen bread (crescent rolls do not require rising time). When John needs a dish to take to his office, this is what everyone requests. In fact, someone writes "Big John's Rolls" next to his name on the list.

1 (16-ounce) loaf frozen bread	1 (4-ounce) can chopped mushrooms
8 ounces sliced pepperoni	1 (4-ounce) can chopped black olives
1 cup shredded Cheddar cheese	1 (4-ounce) can chopped green olives

Preheat the oven to 350 degrees. Set out the frozen bread dough to thaw and rise. Pull off 3 dozen chunks of dough the size of golf balls. Flatten each piece of dough to ¼ inch thick on a floured board. Place several pepperoni slices in one corner of a piece of flattened dough and spread the dough with 1 teaspoon each of cheese, mushrooms, black olives and green olives. Roll up like a jelly roll and press the ends together. Place the rolls on 2 or 3 baking sheets. Bake 15 minutes or until the tops are light brown. Yield: 3 dozen rolls.

Jane Walsh
Alachua, Florida

Carol Winiger, Xi Iota, Butler, Wisconsin, makes Casserole Pizza Bread by dissolving 2 envelopes yeast in 2 cups warm water. Mix 2 tablespoons each sugar and butter, ½ cup Parmesan cheese, 1½ tablespoons oregano, and 4½ cups flour. Mix in dissolved yeast, pour into a greased 8-inch casserole, and bake in a preheated 375-degree oven for 55 minutes.

SAUSAGE BREAD

This recipe was given to me by a coworker in 1981, and it has been requested by all family members at Christmastime ever since. You can use boxed baking mix instead of the frozen bread; the bread will turn out drier.

1 (16-ounce) loaf frozen bread dough, thawed	2 eggs
1 pound sausage, fried, crumbled, drained	½ cup Parmesan cheese
1 cup shredded sharp Cheddar cheese	Pinch of oregano
	Pinch of parsley flakes
	Melted margarine

Let the bread dough rise. Preheat the oven to 350 degrees. Brown the sausage; remove as much fat as you can with paper towels. Let cool. Add the Cheddar cheese, eggs, Parmesan cheese, oregano and parsley to the sausage; mix well. Roll the bread dough ¾ inch thick on a floured board. Spread the sausage mixture on the dough, and roll up like a jelly roll, pinching the ends together. Bake for 45 minutes. Brush the loaf with melted margarine after removing from the oven. Do not slice until ready to serve; do not cover with foil while hot. Yield: 12 to 15 servings.

*Connie Daggett
Topeka, Kansas*

CRUNCHY GARLIC BREAD

This bread tastes great with vegetable lasagna and a tossed green salad.

2 teaspoons olive oil	2 teaspoons chopped fresh marjoram or ¾ teaspoon dried marjoram
2 cloves of garlic, minced	
2 tablespoons chopped fresh parsley	½ teaspoon paprika
2 tablespoons chopped fresh thyme or 2 teaspoons dried thyme	2 tablespoons grated Parmesan cheese
	2 small loaves French or Italian bread

Preheat the oven to 350 degrees. Combine the oil and garlic in a small bowl. Combine the parsley, thyme, marjoram and paprika in a separate bowl; add the Parmesan and mix well. Cut each loaf crosswise into diagonal slices without cutting all the way through. Brush cut sides with the garlic oil. Sprinkle the herb mixture between the slices. Wrap each loaf in foil and place them on a baking sheet. Bake for 10 to 15 minutes or until heated through. Unwrap the loaves and place them in a basket. Serve immediately.
Yield: 24 servings.

*Jackie Gitthens, Laureate Psi
Havelock, North Carolina*

HERB BREAD

I served this bread at a chapter party with great success. I get requests for the recipe every time there is a get-together. I usually use 2 packages of buns so there will be more bread. You may use garlic purée instead of fresh garlic, but I think the fresh has much better flavor.

1 (8-count) package hot dog buns	¼ teaspoon thyme
1 or more large cloves of garlic	½ cup melted butter or margarine
¼ teaspoon basil	
½ teaspoon crushed rosemary	

Preheat the oven to 200 degrees. Cut each bun into 6 sticks. Crush the garlic in a garlic press. Add the garlic, basil, rosemary and thyme to the melted butter; mix well. Brush the seasoned butter on all sides of the sticks and bake for 1½ to 2 hours or until light brown and crisp. Yield: 6 to 12 servings.

*Emilie M. Reynolds, Xi Epsilon
Gulfport, Mississippi*

ZESTY SWISS MUSHROOM BREAD

We first had this delicious bread at my husband's class reunion golf tournament. We've been enjoying it ever since! You may substitute two small cans of mushrooms for the fresh mushrooms if you like.

1 cup butter or margarine, softened	2 (16-ounce) loaves French bread
2 tablespoons minced onion	4 ounces fresh mushrooms, sliced
1 teaspoon seasoned salt	2 cups shredded Swiss cheese
½ teaspoon lemon juice	
1 tablespoon dry mustard	

Preheat the oven to 350 degrees. Mix the butter, onion, seasoned salt, lemon juice and mustard in a bowl and set aside. Slice a long V-shaped piece out of the top of each loaf of bread. Spread the butter mixture on the cut sides of the V-shaped piece and the loaf. Replace the V-shaped piece and cut the loaf crosswise into diagonal slices without cutting all the way through the bottom. Stuff the sliced crevices with the sliced mushrooms and Swiss cheese. Double-wrap the bread with aluminum foil. Bake for 20 minutes. Yield: 12 to 15 servings.

*Cindee Wachter, Xi Beta Omicron
Columbus, Nebraska*

SPINACH BREAD

This bread that resembles a spinach pizza can be served with a meal or as a hearty appetizer. An electric knife does a speedy job of slicing; use a serrated knife if you do not have an electric one. If there happen to be any leftovers, wrap them in foil and refrigerate or freeze for reheating at a later time.

1 loaf French bread	1½ tablespoons
1 cup margarine,	Worcestershire sauce
softened	1¼ teaspoons Creole
1½ cups chopped onion	seasoning
1 (10-ounce) package	1¼ cups shredded
frozen chopped	mozzarella cheese
spinach, thawed,	⅓ cup grated Parmesan
squeezed to drain	cheese
1 (8-ounce) roll garlic	
cheese	

Preheat the oven to 400 degrees. Cut the bread in half lengthwise. Spread the cut surfaces with ½ cup of the margarine. Place the remaining ½ cup margarine in a skillet and heat until bubbling. Add the chopped onions and sauté until tender. Stir in the spinach, garlic cheese, Worcestershire sauce and Creole seasoning. Continue to cook and stir until the cheese is melted. Spread the spinach mixture evenly on the buttered bread. Sprinkle with the mozzarella and Parmesan cheeses. Place the bread on a large baking sheet and heat in the oven for 10 minutes or until the cheese is melted. Cut into pieces before serving. Yield: 32 slices.

Sondra Wineinger, Xi Nu Phi
Cuero, Texas

CINNAMON RING ROLL

This recipe was given to me by my mother, Mildred Hunt. It is a favorite breakfast bread for my entire family.

1 envelope active dry	2 eggs, beaten
yeast	½ teaspoon salt
¼ cup warm water	3¼ cups all-purpose
¾ cup milk, scalded and	flour
cooled	1 cup sugar
4 tablespoons	4 teaspoons cinnamon
shortening	Melted butter
2 tablespoons sugar	

Dissolve the yeast in the warm water and add to the milk. Cream the shortening and 2 tablespoons sugar in a large bowl. Add the eggs. Add the milk mixture, salt and flour; blend well. Let rise until doubled in bulk. Preheat the oven to 350 degrees. Mix 1 cup sugar and cinnamon in a bowl. Punch down the dough. Pinch off pieces of the dough, forming 1-inch balls. Dip the balls into the melted butter; roll in the cinnamon mixture. Layer the balls in a greased tube pan. Let rise for 1 hour. Bake for 30 minutes. Yield: 8 to 12 servings.

Mary Lou Hunt, Beta Master
Wilmington, Ohio

HAWAIIAN SWEET BREAD

1 cup pineapple juice	2 teaspoons vanilla
3 eggs	extract
6½ to 7 cups all-purpose	2 envelopes active dry
flour	yeast
¼ cup potato flakes	1 cup milk
⅔ cup sugar	½ cup water
1 teaspoon salt	½ cup butter or
½ teaspoon ginger	margarine

Allow the pineapple juice and eggs to come to room temperature. Combine 3 cups of the flour, potato flakes, sugar, salt, ginger, vanilla and yeast in a large bowl. Heat the milk, water and butter until very warm. Add the milk mixture, pineapple juice and eggs to the flour mixture. Blend with an electric mixer at low speed until moist, then beat at medium speed for 4 minutes. Stir in 3 cups of flour by hand; knead for 5 to 8 minutes, adding ½ to 1 cup of flour to prevent sticking. Place the dough in a greased bowl. Let rise, loosely covered, for 1½ hours or until doubled in bulk. Punch dough down and divide into 3 portions. Form each portion into a ball and place in a 9-inch round pie plate. Preheat the oven to 375 degrees. Allow the dough to rise until doubled. Bake for 25 to 35 minutes. Yield: 36 servings.

Lynette Stenzel, Mu Phi
Ness City, Kansas

HONEY APPLESAUCE GRAIN BREAD

If you have one of the smaller bread machines, you may have to cut this recipe in half.

1 envelope active dry	½ cup rolled oats
yeast	2 tablespoons nonfat
3 cups bread flour	dry milk
½ cup whole wheat	1 teaspoon salt
flour	⅓ cup applesauce
½ cup cornmeal	¼ cup honey
½ cup raw wheat bran	1⅓ cups warm water

Put the ingredients into a bread-making machine, in the order listed. Select the Whole Wheat setting on the machine and press Start. Yield: 15 servings.

Marge Hefty
Tucson, Arizona

MUENSTER BREAD

2 envelopes active dry
  yeast
1 cup warm milk (110 to
  115 degrees)
½ cup butter or
  margarine, softened
2 tablespoons sugar
1 teaspoon salt

3¼ to 3¾ cups all-
  purpose flour
1 egg plus 1 egg yolk
4 cups (16 ounces)
  shredded Muenster
  cheese
1 egg white, beaten

Dissolve the yeast in the milk in a large bowl. Add the butter, sugar, salt and 2 cups of the flour; beat until smooth. Stir in enough of the remaining flour to form a soft dough. Turn onto a floured board; knead until smooth and elastic, about 6 to 8 minutes. Place in a greased bowl, turning over once to grease the top. Cover and let rise in a warm place until doubled, about 1 hour. Preheat the oven to 375 degrees. Beat the egg and yolk in a large bowl; stir in the cheese. Punch down the dough and roll it into a 16-inch circle. Place in a greased 9-inch round cake pan, letting the dough drape over the edges. Spoon the cheese mixture into the center of the dough. Gather the dough up over the filling in 1½-inch pleats. Gently squeeze the pleats together at the top and twist to form a topknot. Let rise for 10 to 15 minutes. Brush the loaf with the egg white. Bake for 45 to 50 minutes. Cool on a wire rack for 20 minutes. Serve warm. Yield: 24 servings.

Carey Stubblefield, Alpha
Springfield, Missouri

OATMEAL BREAD

1½ cups milk
1½ cups water
4 teaspoons salt
2 tablespoons
  shortening
2 cups quick-cooking
  oats
2 envelopes active dry
  yeast

1½ cups warm water
½ cup molasses
1 cup packed light
  brown sugar
2 to 7 cups all-purpose
  flour
Butter

Mix the milk, water, salt, shortening and oats in a saucepan; bring to a boil over medium heat. Let cool. Dissolve the yeast in the warm water and add to the pan along with the molasses, brown sugar and 2 cups of the flour; stir well. Add enough of the remaining flour to form a dough and turn out on a floured counter. Knead until firm (not sticky). Put the dough in a greased bowl and rub a little melted shortening on top. Let rise until doubled in size, 1 hour or more. Preheat the oven to 350 degrees. Punch down the dough and shape into 2 loaves in place in greased 5-by-9-inch loaf pans. Rub a little shortening on top of the loaves. Let rise for 30 minutes. Bake for 45 to 60 minutes or until tapping on the side of bread removed from pan makes a hollow sound. Rub butter on top of the baked bread. Yield: 2 loaves.

Joan Lee McAdam
Clewiston, Florida

OLD-FASHIONED OATMEAL BREAD

I have been baking this bread for 20 years and have never had a failure. It makes wonderful toast!

2 cups water
1 cup rolled oats
4 tablespoons
  shortening
2 envelopes fast-rising
  yeast
½ cup warm water

⅔ cup packed light
  brown sugar
1 tablespoon sugar
1 egg
1 teaspoon salt
5½ to 6 cups all-purpose
  flour

Mix the water, oats and shortening in a saucepan; bring to a boil, remove from heat and let cool. Dissolve the yeast in the ½ cup water. Add the brown sugar, sugar, egg, salt and dissolved yeast to the oats mixture. Add flour to make a soft dough. Knead the dough on a floured board for 5 to 10 minutes, adding flour as necessary to keep the dough from sticking. Place in a well-greased bowl, turning once to grease the top of the dough. Cover with a cloth and let rise until doubled in bulk, 1 to 2 hours. Turn onto the floured board and knead for 5 minutes. Shape into 2 loaves and place in 5-by-9-inch loaf pans. Preheat the oven to 375 degrees. Let the dough rise for 1 hour. Bake for 40 to 45 minutes. Slice with an electric knife. Yield: 2 loaves.

Irene Linvill, Kappa Sigma Phi Master
Neodesha, Kansas

ONION BATTER BREAD

My mom used to bake this bread. My family would eat the entire loaf before it even cooled off!

2 cakes yeast
2 cups lukewarm water
2 teaspoons sugar
1 teaspoon salt
3 tablespoons butter or
  margarine, softened

4½ cups all-purpose
  flour
1 package onion soup
  mix
Butter, melted

Dissolve the yeast in the water with the sugar in a large bowl. Add the salt, butter, 3 cups of the flour and the onion soup mix; beat for 2 minutes. Add the remaining flour and beat until well blended. Cover and let rise until doubled, about 30 minutes.

Stir down the dough and pour into a well-buttered 1½-quart baking dish. Let rise, covered, until doubled or until the batter reaches the top of the dish. Preheat the oven to 375 degrees. Bake for 50 to 55 minutes or until browned. Turn onto a wire rack and brush with melted butter. Yield: 24 servings.

Robin W. Morley, Delta Omega
Danville, Kentucky

RYE BREAD

2 cups boiling water	½ cup warm water
2 teaspoons salt	2 cups sifted rye flour
⅓ cup shortening	6 to 7 cups all-purpose
¾ cup molasses	flour
1 envelope active dry	1 egg, beaten
yeast	1 tablespoon water

Stir together the boiling water, salt, shortening and molasses in a large bowl. Dissolve the yeast in ½ cup warm water. Add the rye flour to the molasses mixture and beat well. Add 2 cups of the all-purpose flour; beat well and let cool. Add the dissolved yeast to the mixture, then add the remaining 4 to 5 cups of flour to make a thick, heavy dough. Turn out on a floured board and let rest for 10 minutes. Knead until the dough is smooth and satiny, about 10 minutes. Place in a greased bowl, cover and allow to rise until double in size. Preheat the oven to 350 degrees. Punch down the dough and let it rise again. Turn out onto a floured board. Divide into 3 equal parts. Knead each part and place it in a greased 8-inch round cake pan. Allow the 3 loaves to rise until the pans are full and the dough is rounded nicely. Before baking, brush the dough lightly with the egg beaten with 1 tablespoon water. Bake for 30 minutes or until the bread tests done. Yield: 36 servings.

Louise Long, Laureate Beta Lambda
Bethany, Missouri

BEST EVER YEAST ROLLS

Best Ever Yeast Rolls are served at Spencer Heights Resort, Poudre Canyon, Colorado, where we always stop after skiing. People come from all over for these rolls! This recipe can be doubled, and it makes excellent cinnamon rolls.

1 envelope active dry	⅓ cup vegetable oil
yeast	1 cup milk, scalded,
½ teaspoon salt	cooled
1 tablespoon sugar	1 egg, beaten
½ cup warm water	4 to 5 cups all-purpose
⅓ cup sugar	flour

Dissolve the yeast, salt and 1 tablespoon sugar in the warm water in a small bowl. Add the ⅓ cup sugar and the oil to the cooled milk in the large bowl. Add the egg to the yeast mixture and combine with the milk mixture. Add 3 cups of the flour; beat well and add enough remaining 1 to 2 cups flour to make soft dough. Knead on lightly floured surface until smooth and elastic. Place in a greased bowl, turning to coat surface. Let rise, covered, until doubled in bulk. Preheat the oven to 375 degrees. Punch dough down. Let rise until doubled. Shape rolls and place in a greased 9-by-13-inch pan. Bake for 12 minutes or until lightly browned. Yield: 16 rolls.

Tenny Collins, Laureate Beta
Cheyenne, Wyoming

BURGER BUNS

4 cups all-purpose flour	1 teaspoon salt
2 cups warm water	¾ cup oil
2 envelopes active dry	3 eggs, beaten
yeast	2 cups whole wheat
½ cup sugar	flour

Place the flour in a large bowl. Mix the warm water, yeast, sugar and salt in a small bowl and let stand for 5 minutes. Beat the oil and eggs together. Make a well in the flour and add the yeast mixture; mix well. Add the egg mixture. Start working in the whole wheat flour by hand, kneading well. If the dough is sticky, add more all-purpose flour until you have a soft, easily handled dough. Cover and let rise until doubled in bulk. Preheat the oven to 350 degrees. Punch dough down, place on a floured surface and knead for 5 minutes. Divide into 12 equal portions. Shape into balls. Place on a greased baking sheet, pressing down with a can or glass. Cover and let rise until doubled. Bake for 30 minutes or until golden brown. Yield: 12 servings.

Ava Swan, Rho Master
Odessa, Texas

Gayna M. Dunsmore, Alpha Theta, Oak Hill, Virginia, makes Buttermilk Syrup by combining 1½ cups sugar, ¾ cup buttermilk, ½ cup butter, 2 tablespoons corn syrup, and 1 teaspoon baking soda and boiling for 7 minutes. Remove from heat. Stir in 2 teaspoons vanilla extract. Serve it on a German Pancake made by processing 6 eggs, 1 cup milk, 1 cup flour, ½ teaspoon salt, and 2 tablespoons butter in a blender and baking in a greased 9-by-13-inch pan in a preheated 400-degree oven for 20 minutes.

BUTTER CRESCENTS

1/2 cup milk, scalded	1/2 cup warm water
1/2 cup butter or	(105 to 115 degrees)
margarine, softened	1 large egg, beaten
1/3 cup sugar	3 1/2 to 4 cups all-purpose
1/2 teaspoon salt	flour
1 envelope active dry	1 large egg, lightly
yeast	beaten

Combine the milk, butter, sugar and salt in a large bowl; stir well. Cool until it is warm. Dissolve the yeast in the warm water in a small bowl; let stand until foamy, about 5 minutes. Beat the yeast mixture and the egg into the milk mixture. Beat in 2 cups of the flour at low speed until smooth. Mix in more flour until the dough pulls away from the sides of the bowl. Knead the dough for 2 to 3 minutes until elastic. Place it in a greased bowl, turning to coat. Cover loosely with a damp cloth and let rise for 1 hour. Preheat the oven to 400 degrees. Punch down the dough and divide into halves on a floured surface. Let rest for 10 minutes. Grease 2 baking sheets. Roll each dough half into a 12-inch circle, using a floured rolling pin. Cut each circle into 12 wedges. Beginning at the side opposite the point, roll up each wedge. Place the rolls point-side down on greased baking sheets. Curve the ends of each roll to form a crescent. Cover with a damp cloth. Let rise until doubled. Brush the crescents with 1 large egg, lightly beaten. Bake for 15 minutes or until golden. Place on a wire rack to cool. Yield: 24 crescents.

Diana Boman
Thornton, Colorado

BUTTERHORNS

4 cups all-purpose flour	1 teaspoon cinnamon
1 teaspoon salt	1 tablespoon sugar
2 tablespoons sugar	1/2 cup chopped pecans
1 cup shortening	or walnuts
1 1/4 cups milk, scalded	1/4 cup melted butter or
1-ounce yeast cake	margarine
3 egg yolks (or 2 whole	Powdered Sugar
eggs), beaten	Frosting
1 teaspoon sugar	

Combine the flour, salt and the 2 tablespoons sugar in a large bowl. Cut the shortening into the dry ingredients until the mixture resembles coarse meal. Cool the scalded milk to lukewarm and add the yeast, beaten eggs and the 1 teaspoon sugar. Combine the milk mixture with the flour mixture; knead for a few minutes. Let rise until double. Divide the dough into 4 parts. Roll each part into a circle about 1/4 inch thick. Combine the cinnamon, 1 tablespoon sugar, nuts and 1/4 cup melted butter; spread the mixture over the dough circles. Cut each circle into 6 pie-shaped wedges. Roll the wedges into crescent shapes. Preheat the oven to 400 degrees. Place the crescents on a baking sheet; let rise until doubled. Bake for 15 minutes or until light brown. Glaze with Powdered Sugar Frosting while still hot. Yield: 24 crescents.

POWDERED SUGAR FROSTING

3 tablespoons butter or	Hot water
margarine, melted	1/2 teaspoon vanilla
3/4 cups confectioners'	extract
sugar	

Blend the confectioners' sugar into the melted butter. Add hot water, a tablespoon at a time, until of spreading consistency. Stir in the vanilla.

Lois Burant
Milwaukee, Wisconsin

MAMA'S DINNER ROLLS

These rolls are always served at our family gatherings. They melt in your mouth, and there are never enough to go around! The dough will keep for several days in the refrigerator. You can melt the shortening in 1 cup water in the microwave to save time. This dough also makes delicious cinnamon buns.

1 envelope active dry	1 tablespoon salt
yeast	1/4 cup sugar
1 cup lukewarm water	5 to 6 cups all-purpose
1 cup boiling water	flour
1 cup shortening	Butter or margarine
2 eggs, well beaten	

Dissolve the yeast in the cup of lukewarm water. Pour the boiling water over the shortening in a large bowl, melting the shortening. Stir until cool. Add the yeast mixture, eggs, salt and sugar. Add 3 to 4 cups of the flour to the liquid mixture, using an electric mixer to beat until smooth and creamy. Stir in the remaining flour (up to 6 cups total), then cover tightly and refrigerate for at least 4 hours. Spoon desired amount of the dough onto a floured surface and pat to a 1/2-inch thickness. Cut circles with a 2 1/2-inch glass. Fold each circle in half with a small pat of butter inside and pinch ends together. Place the rolls in a large greased 2-inch-deep baking pan. Preheat the oven to 400 degrees. Let rise, covered with plastic wrap, for 1 1/2 to 2 hours or until doubled in bulk. Bake for 10 minutes or until golden. Yield: 5 to 6 dozen rolls.

Marianne Pruitt
Suches, Georgia

Divine Desserts

Delight your sweet tooth
with this scrumptious array
of desserts—from the extravagant,
to-die-for variety to the
no-frills, down-home favorites
Grandma use to make.
Are you looking for something dramatic
to serve at a party? Tasty cookies for your
family to nibble? Perhaps you're pining for a luscious,
low-calorie treat that won't expand your waistline.
Here's a spectacular selection of desserts
that are as fun to make as they are to eat—
simply wonderful for snacking and
the fitting finale for any meal!

APRICOT COGNAC TEA CAKE

I have served this delectable cake at many parties. It is always a big hit—and each serving has only 159 calories!

½ cup cognac or water
1 cup dried apricots, chopped
1 cup apricot jam
1 (2-layer) package lowfat yellow cake mix
1⅓ cups plus 2 tablespoons apricot soaking liquid

3 egg whites or 3/4 cup frozen egg substitute
1 small package sugar-free vanilla instant pudding
½ cup skim milk
1 (8-ounce) container light whipped topping

Preheat the oven to 350 degrees. Heat the cognac in a saucepan until hot. Remove from heat and stir in the dried apricots; soak for 15 minutes. Strain the apricots, reserving the apricot soaking liquid. Combine the soaked apricots and apricot jam to make the filling. Lightly grease and flour two 9-inch round cake pans. Place the cake mix, 1⅓ cups apricot soaking liquid and egg whites in a mixer bowl. Mix at low speed with an electric mixer; then beat at high speed for 2 minutes. Pour the batter into the pans and bake for 20 to 30 minutes or until a toothpick inserted in the center of the cake comes out clean and dry. Let the cake cool for 15 minutes in the pans; remove from the pans and cool completely. Slice each cake layer in half horizontally. Place one cake layer, cut side up, on a serving plate; spread with ⅓ of the filling. Repeat with the second and third cake layers and the remaining filling. Top with the fourth cake layer, cut side down. To make the frosting, combine the pudding mix, milk, and 2 tablespoons apricot soaking liquid; blend well. Add the whipped topping and beat on low speed for 2 minutes. Frost the top and sides of the cake. Chill, covered, for at least 2 hours before serving. Yield: 16 servings.

Cynthia Brunkhorst, Xi Gamma Chi
Palisade, Nebraska

CARAMEL BUNDT CAKE

1 (2-layer) package caramel cake mix
1 (4-ounce) package vanilla instant pudding mix

4 eggs
1 cup water
⅓ cup vegetable oil
1 (16-ounce) can caramel icing

Preheat the oven to 350 degrees. Combine the caramel cake mix, pudding mix, eggs, water and oil in a mixer bowl. Beat for 2 minutes at medium speed. Pour the batter into a greased and floured bundt pan.

Bake for 50 to 60 minutes or until cake tests done. Melt the caramel icing in ½ cup portions for 10 to 15 seconds in the microwave; drizzle over the cooled cake. Yield: 16 servings.

Jeannie Pitluck, Xi Zeta Epsilon
St. Joseph, Missouri

CAPTIVATING CARROT CAKE

My sisters command me to make this cake for sorority functions. I have never served it to anyone who didn't ask for the recipe.

2 cups all-purpose flour
2 teaspoons baking soda
½ teaspoon salt
2 teaspoons ground cinnamon
3 eggs, well beaten
¾ cup vegetable oil
¾ cup buttermilk
2 cups sugar
2 teaspoons vanilla extract

1 (8-ounce) can crushed pineapple, drained
2 cups shredded carrots
1 (3½-ounce) can flaked coconut
1 cup chopped walnuts or pecans
Buttermilk Glaze
Orange Cream Cheese Frosting

Preheat the oven to 350 degrees. Combine the flour, baking soda, salt and cinnamon in a small bowl and set aside. Combine the eggs, oil, buttermilk, sugar and vanilla in a large bowl and beat until smooth. Stir the flour mixture and the crushed pineapple, carrots, coconut and nuts into the egg mixture. Pour the batter into 2 greased and floured 9-inch round cake pans. Bake for 35 to 40 minutes or until a toothpick inserted in the center comes out clean. While the cake is baking, make the Buttermilk Glaze and the Orange Cream Cheese Frosting. When the cake is done, remove from the oven and immediately spread the Buttermilk Glaze evenly over the layers. Cool in the pans 15 minutes; remove from pans and cool completely. Spread the Orange Cream Cheese Frosting over the top and sides of each layer. Yield: 16 servings.

BUTTERMILK GLAZE

1 cup sugar
½ teaspoon baking soda
1 tablespoon light corn syrup

½ cup buttermilk
1 teaspoon vanilla extract

Combine the sugar, baking soda, light corn syrup and buttermilk in a Dutch oven. Bring to a boil; cook 4 minutes, stirring often. Remove from heat. Stir in the vanilla.

ORANGE CREAM CHEESE FROSTING

1/2 cup butter or
  margarine, softened
1 (8-ounce) package
  cream cheese,
  softened
1 teaspoon vanilla
  extract
2 cups sifted
  confectioners' sugar
1 teaspoon grated
  orange rind
1 teaspoon orange juice

Combine the butter and cream cheese, beating until light and fluffy. Add the vanilla, confectioners' sugar, orange rind and orange juice; beat until smooth.

Sharon Chalmers, Xi Delta Tau
Lynchburg, Virginia

❖ AMAZING CORN CAKE

Sweet corn tastes sweeter than ever in this Amazing Corn Cake. The cake always gets rave reviews at potluck dinners and sorority meetings. It can be frosted in the pan so it is easy to carry.

1 (17-ounce) can cream-
  style corn
1/2 cup packed light
  brown sugar
3/4 cup sugar
3 eggs
1 cup vegetable oil
1 tablespoon baking
  powder
2 1/4 cups all-purpose
  flour
1 teaspoon baking soda
1 teaspoon salt
1 teaspoon cinnamon
1/2 cup golden raisins
1/2 cup chopped nuts
Caramel Frosting

Preheat the oven to 350 degrees. Combine the corn and sugars in a large bowl; add the eggs and oil and beat until well blended. Combine the baking powder, flour, baking soda, salt and cinnamon; add to the batter and mix well. Stir in the raisins and nuts. Pour into a greased 9-by-13-inch baking pan. Bake for 30 to 35 minutes or until cake tests done. Cool thoroughly. Frost the cake with Caramel Frosting.
Yield: 12 to 15 servings.

CARAMEL FROSTING

4 tablespoons butter or
  margarine
1/2 cup packed dark
  brown sugar
1/4 cup cream
2 to 3 cups sifted
  confectioners' sugar

Bring the butter and brown sugar to a boil in a saucepan over medium heat. Stir in the cream. Stir in confectioners' sugar until the frosting is desired consistency.

R. Gene Farley, Laureate Gamma Iota
Tallahassee, Florida

CHOCOLATE ALMOND ZUCCHINI CAKE

3 eggs
1 cup sugar
1 cup packed light
  brown sugar
1 cup vegetable oil
1 teaspoon vanilla
  extract
2 cups shredded zucchini
1 teaspoon almond
  extract
2 cups all-purpose flour
2 (1-ounce) squares
  unsweetened
  chocolate, melted
1 teaspoon salt
1 teaspoon cinnamon
1/4 teaspoon baking
  powder
1 teaspoon baking soda
Cocoa Frosting

Preheat the oven to 375 degrees. Cream eggs, sugars, oil and vanilla in a large bowl until light and fluffy. Mix in the zucchini and almond extract. Add the flour, chocolate, salt, cinnamon, baking powder and baking soda; mix well. Pour into a well greased and floured bundt pan. Bake for 40 to 50 minutes or until cake tests done. Frost with Cocoa Frosting while cake is still hot. Yield: 12 servings.

COCOA FROSTING

3 tablespoons milk
1/4 cup margarine
2 tablespoons
  cocoa
1 (16-ounce) box
  confectioners' sugar
1 teaspoon vanilla
  extract

Heat the milk, margarine and cocoa over low heat until melted. Blend the confectioners' sugar and vanilla into the cocoa mixture.

Aliene Gribas, Laureate Iota
Havre, Montana

KAHLUA CAKE

This cake tastes even better the day after baking, and it is well worth the wait! My best friend, Beth, made it for my birthday once. It was by far the best chocolate cake I have ever had.

1 (2-layer) package
  devil's food cake mix
4 eggs
3/4 cup vegetable oil
1 cup sour cream
1 cup kahlúa liqueur
1 (6-ounce) package
  semisweet chocolate
  chips

Preheat the oven to 350 degrees. Place cake mix, eggs, oil, sour cream and kahlúa in a mixing bowl and beat thoroughly with an electric mixer. Stir in the chocolate chips. Pour the batter into a greased and floured bundt cake pan. Bake for 50 to 60 minutes until the cake tests done; do the toothpick test first at 50 minutes. Yield: 16 servings.

Stacy A. Smith, Xi Iota Delta
Denver City, Texas

QUILT CAKE

1 (2-layer) package
   German chocolate
   cake mix
1 (5-ounce) can
   evaporated milk
1 (12-ounce) jar caramel
   topping for ice cream
1 (8-ounce) package
   whipped topping
Heath candy bars,
   crushed, or Heath
   chips

Bake the cake mix in a sheet cake pan using package directions. Let cool completely. Poke holes in the top of the cake with a fork or skewer. Mix the evaporated milk and caramel topping together and spread over the cake. Spread the whipped topping over the caramel mixture. Sprinkle the Heath candy over the whipped topping. Refrigerate, covered, until ready to serve. Yield: 12 to 16 servings.

Tara Wall, Beta Eta Upsilon
Sherman, Texas

CHOCOLATE CHIP CAKE

My sister, who recently died of cancer, passed this recipe on to me. I cannot bake this cake without calling it "Kay's cake." It is good for taking to potlucks or to serve when you have weekend guests. The icing is baked into the cake. You may serve it with whipped topping if you like.

1 cup dates
1½ cups boiling water
1½ teaspoons baking
   soda
¾ cup shortening
1 cup sugar
2 eggs, beaten
1½ cups all-purpose
   flour
¾ teaspoon baking soda
½ teaspoon salt
1 (12-ounce) package
   semisweet chocolate
   chips
¼ cup sugar
1 cup chopped walnuts
   or pecans

Preheat the oven to 325 degrees. Combine the dates, boiling water and baking soda; let stand until cool. Cream the shortening and 1 cup sugar in a large mixer bowl until light and fluffy. Stir in the eggs, then the date mixture. Add the flour, baking soda and salt; mix on low speed for 2 minutes. Pour into a greased 9-by-13-inch glass baking dish. Sprinkle the chocolate chips, ¼ cup sugar and nuts over the batter. Bake for 40 to 45 minutes. Yield: 12 to 15 servings.

Trudy Grandt, Beta Omega
Kankakee, Illinois

OATMEAL CHOCOLATE CHIP CAKE

I always make this popular cake to take to Boy Scout and football dinners. The shortening and flour used to prepare a pan sometimes lingers on baked goods— I prefer to use a nonstick baker's spray. All the ingredients should be mixed in by hand.

1¾ cups boiling water
1 cup uncooked quick
   oats
½ cup margarine,
   softened
1 cup lightly packed
   light brown sugar
1 cup sugar
2 eggs
1 teaspoon baking soda
1¾ cups all-purpose
   flour
1 tablespoon cocoa
½ teaspoon salt
1 (12-ounce) package
   semisweet chocolate
   chips
1½ cups chopped pecans
   or walnuts

Preheat the oven to 375 degrees. Pour the boiling water over the oats in a large bowl. Let stand for 10 minutes. Add the margarine and allow to melt. Add the sugars and the eggs. Sift together the baking soda, flour, cocoa and salt in a separate bowl; add these ingredients to the oat mixture. Stir in half the chocolate chips and half the nuts. Pour into a greased and floured 9-by-13-inch baking pan or a jelly roll pan. Bake for 35 to 40 minutes. Remove from the oven and sprinkle with the remaining chocolate chips and nuts. Yield: 15 servings.

Peggy Wallis, Laureate Delta
Pueblo, Colorado

LIGHT FRUITCAKE

I have made this cake every year for 45 years. I make it in early November and freeze it until it is needed. Even people who usually do not like fruitcake love this one. The recipe was given to me 45 years ago by a lovely lady who made me promise not to give it to anyone until she died.

1 pound butter or
   margarine, softened
1 pound sugar (2 cups)
9 eggs, separated
2 teaspoons vanilla
   extract
3 cups all-purpose flour
3 teaspoons baking
   powder
1 teaspoon salt
1 pound light golden
   raisins
1 pound currants
2 ounces orange peel
2 ounces lemon peel
2 ounces candied
   pineapple
2 ounces citron
2 ounces chopped
   candied cherries
1 pound chopped
   walnuts

Preheat the oven to 250 degrees. Cream the butter and sugar in a large bowl until light and fluffy. Add the egg yolks and vanilla to the mixture; blend well. Sift the flour with the baking powder and salt. Toss the raisins, currants, orange peel, lemon peel, pineapple and citron with enough of the flour mixture to coat. Mix into the batter. Stir in the remainder of the flour mixture. Beat the egg whites until stiff and fold into the batter. Pour the batter into 5 lightly greased loaf pans. Press the cherries and walnuts into the batter. Bake for 1½ hours or until a tester inserted in the cake comes out clean. Yield: 5 fruitcakes.

Antoinette Olff, Laureate Beta Sigma
Marietta, Ohio

MOONSHINER'S DELIGHT CAKE

1 pound candied cherries	*6 eggs, separated*
½ pound white raisins	*5 cups all-purpose flour*
1 pint whiskey	*2 teaspoons nutmeg*
1½ cups margarine	*1 teaspoon baking*
2 cups sugar	*powder*
1 cup packed light	*1 pound chopped pecans*
brown sugar	

Soak the candied cherries and raisins in the whiskey for at least several hours. Preheat the oven to 275 degrees. Cream the margarine and both sugars in a large bowl until light and fluffy. Beat in the egg yolks. Beat in the flour, nutmeg and baking powder. Beat the egg whites until stiff; blend into the cake mixture. Stir in the soaked fruit and pecans. Pour into a well-greased and floured 7½-inch bundt pan. Bake for 3½ hours. Yield: 16 servings.

Jessie R. Neighbors
Montgomery, Alabama

FRUIT COCKTAIL CAKE

¼ cup packed light	*Pinch of salt*
brown sugar	*1 (16-ounce) can fruit*
1 cup chopped walnuts	*cocktail*
or pecans	*¾ cup sugar*
1½ cups sugar	*½ cup margarine*
2 cups all-purpose flour	*½ cup evaporated milk*
2 teaspoons baking soda	

Preheat the oven to 350 degrees. Mix the brown sugar and nuts in a small bowl. Mix 1½ cups sugar, flour, baking soda, salt and fruit cocktail in a large mixer bowl. Beat for 2 minutes at medium speed. Pour into a greased 9-by-13-inch baking dish. Sprinkle the batter with the nut mixture. Bake for 45 minutes. To make the icing, put ¾ cup sugar, margarine and evaporated milk in a saucepan and bring to a boil; boil for 2 minutes. Pour the icing over the cake as soon as it is removed from the oven. Yield: 15 servings.

Joyce H. Joslin, Xi Kappa Pi
O'Fallon, Illinois

ITALIAN CREAM CAKE

I found this recipe 20 years ago in a cookbook that was dedicated to all the men and women who served our country in the military services. It is a very, very special cake.

½ cup butter or	*1 cup buttermilk*
margarine, softened	*1 teaspoon vanilla*
½ cup shortening	*extract*
2 cups sugar	*1 (3½-ounce) can flaked*
5 eggs, separated	*coconut*
2 cups flour	*1 cup chopped pecans*
1 teaspoon baking soda	*Cream Cheese Frosting*

Preheat the oven to 350 degrees. Cream the butter and shortening in a large bowl until light and fluffy. Add the sugar gradually, beating well. Add the egg yolks 1 at time, beating well after each addition. Stir together the flour and baking soda. Add the flour mixture alternately with the buttermilk, a third at a time, beating well after each addition. Stir in the vanilla. Add the coconut and pecans, reserving some of the coconut and pecans to sprinkle over finished cake if desired; blend well. Beat the egg whites until stiff. Fold into the batter. Pour the batter into 3 greased and floured 9-inch cake pans. Bake for 20 to 25 minutes. Cool in the pans for 10 minutes; remove from pans and cool completely. Frost with Cream Cheese Frosting. You may decorate the top with desired amounts of pecans and coconut.
Yield: 12 servings.

CREAM CHEESE FROSTING

½ cup butter or	*1 teaspoon vanilla*
margarine, softened	*extract*
1 (8-ounce) package	*1 (16-ounce) box*
cream cheese,	*confectioners' sugar*
softened	

Cream the butter and cream cheese in a bowl. Mix in the vanilla and confectioners' sugar, beating until smooth.

Glo Snyder, Alpha Delta Phi
Lowry City, Missouri

LEMON CAKE

This delectable cake is from an old Swedish recipe. It is even better when baked the day before serving—the flavor deepens overnight.

5 tablespoons melted butter or margarine	2 teaspoons grated lemon zest (only the yellow)
1 cup sugar	
2 eggs	1/2 cup chopped walnuts or almonds (optional)
1 1/2 cups all-purpose flour	
1 teaspoon baking powder	3 tablespoons freshly squeezed lemon juice
1 teaspoon salt	1/3 cup sugar
1/2 cup milk	

Preheat the oven to 350 degrees. Butter and flour a 5-by-9-inch loaf pan and set aside. Combine the butter, 1 cup sugar and eggs in a large bowl. Sift together the flour, baking powder and salt. Add to the butter-sugar mixture alternately with the milk. Stir in the lemon zest and nuts. Pour the batter into the prepared pan and bake for 40 to 45 minutes. Prepare a lemon glaze while the cake is baking. Combine the lemon juice and 1/3 cup sugar in a nonmetallic saucepan; heat gently to dissolve the sugar. Remove from heat and let stand at room temperature. As soon as the cake is taken from the oven, spoon the glaze over the top. Cool in the pan for 20 minutes. Remove from the pan and cool completely. Yield: 10 servings.

Barbara Stalfort, Laureate Phi
Sun City West, Arizona

MARDI GRAS KING CAKE

The King Cake is made to honor the Three Wise Men who brought gifts to the baby Jesus. The sugar colors represent the gold, frankincense, and myrrh that were given to Jesus. I was raised in the tradition that Mardi Gras parties begin on January 6 (Epiphany or the Feast of the Three Kings). Whoever finds the piece of cake with the baby in it at the first party will have the next party and serve the next cake. The parties continue until Mardi Gras.

1 envelope active dry yeast	1 cup butter or margarine, softened
1/4 cup warm water (105 to 115 degrees)	3/4 cup sugar
	1/4 teaspoon salt
6 tablespoons milk, scalded and cooled	4 eggs
	Plastic toy baby or small red bean
4 to 5 cups all-purpose flour	Mardi Gras Frosting

Dissolve the yeast in the warm water in a small bowl. Stir in the milk and enough of the flour to form a soft dough. Combine the butter, sugar, salt and eggs in a mixer bowl, using an electric mixer to blend thoroughly. Add the soft ball of yeast dough to the butter mixture; mix thoroughly. Add about 3 1/2 cups of the flour gradually to the mixture, stirring by hand to make a medium dough that is neither too soft nor too stiff. Don't be afraid to add more flour if necessary. Place the dough in a greased bowl and brush with butter. Cover with a damp cloth and set aside to rise until double in bulk, about 3 hours. If the room temperature is low, you can put the bowl of dough in an unheated oven with a pan of hot water under the bowl to help the rising. Knead the dough and form it into a rope. (You may want to divide the dough and make 2 cakes from this recipe.) Place on a greased 14-by-17-inch baking sheet, connecting the ends of the rope to form an oval. Preheat the oven to 325 degrees. Hide a plastic toy baby or a small red bean in the dough. Cover with a damp cloth; let rise until doubled. Bake for 30 to 40 minutes. When cooled, decorate with Mardi Gras Frosting.
Yield: 48 servings.

MARDI GRAS FROSTING

1 1/2 cups sugar	3 tablespoons water
Purple, green and yellow food coloring	3 tablespoons confectioners' sugar

To make the frosting, place 1/2 cup of the sugar into a small jar. Add a few drops of the yellow food coloring, cap the jar tightly and shake well. The sugar should turn a deep gold color; add more coloring if necessary. Repeat the process for the other 2 colors. Combine the 3 tablespoons water and 3 tablespoons confectioners' sugar to create a slightly runny paste that is not too thick. Brush the mixture onto the top of the cake. While the mixture is still wet, sprinkle on the colored sugar in alternating bands of purple, green and gold.

Michelle Vyles, Beta Epsilon Theta
The Colony, Texas

ORANGE CAKE

My aunt always made this cake for our family reunions.

1 cup butter or margarine, softened	3 cups all-purpose flour
2 cups sugar	2 tablespoons grated orange rind
4 eggs	Pinch of salt
1 teaspoon baking soda	1 cup orange juice
1 1/4 cups buttermilk	2 cups sugar

Preheat the oven to 350 degrees. Cream the butter and 2 cups sugar in a medium bowl until light and fluffy. Add the eggs 1 at a time, beating well after each addition. Stir the baking soda into the buttermilk. Add the flour and buttermilk to the creamed mixture. Add the orange rind and salt; stir well. Put the batter into a greased angel food cake pan. Bake for 45 to 50 minutes or until the cake tests done. Make a glaze by mixing the orange juice with 2 cups sugar; let stand. After removing the cake from the oven, slowly pour the glaze over the hot cake. Keep stirring the glaze as you pour. Let the cake cool before removing from the pan. Yield: 12 servings.

Betty J. Buckles, Laureate Phi
Phoenix, Arizona

ORANGE VODKA CAKE

1 (2-layer) package
  orange cake mix
1 (4-ounce) package
  vanilla instant
  pudding mix
1/2 cup vegetable oil

3/4 cup orange juice
4 eggs
1/4 cup vodka
1/4 cup galliano
Vodka Glaze

Preheat the oven to 350 degrees. Combine the cake mix, pudding mix, oil, orange juice, eggs, vodka and Galliano in a large mixer bowl. Beat for 4 minutes on medium speed. Pour the batter into a greased, lightly floured bundt pan. Bake for 40 to 50 minutes or until cake tests done. Cool in the pan for 10 minutes before turning onto a cooling rack. Pour the Vodka Glaze over the warm cake. Yield: 12 to 16 servings.

VODKA GLAZE

1 cup confectioners'
  sugar
1 tablespoon orange
  juice

1 tablespoon vodka
1 tablespoon light corn
  syrup

Combine the confectioners' sugar, orange juice, vodka and corn syrup in a bowl; blend well.

Joyce Johnson, Laureate Mu
Tombstone, Arizona

MANDARIN ORANGE CAKE

1 (2-layer) package
  butter-recipe
  cake mix
4 eggs
1/2 cup vegetable
  oil

1 (8-ounce) can
  mandarin oranges,
  undrained
Pineapple Frosting
Slivered almonds
  (optional)

Preheat the oven to 350 degrees. Combine the cake mix, eggs, oil and mandarin oranges in a large mixer bowl. Mix on low speed for 3 minutes or until the oranges are broken up and mixed in well. Pour the batter into 3 greased 8-inch round cake pans or a greased 9-by-13-inch baking pan. Bake according to package directions. While the cake is baking, prepare the Pineapple Frosting and place, covered, in the refrigerator. Frost the cooled cake and sprinkle with almonds. Yield: 15 servings.

PINEAPPLE FROSTING

1 (16-ounce) carton
  whipped topping
1 (10-ounce) can crushed
  pineapple, drained

1 (4-ounce) package
  vanilla instant
  pudding mix

Combine whipped topping, pineapple and pudding mix in a bowl; blend well.

Sara S. Cornette
Chesapeake, Virginia

PEACH UPSIDE-DOWN CAKE

The half of the cake batter that is not used for this recipe can be used to make a single cake layer in an 8-inch round pan—or double the peach mixture and use all the cake batter in a 9-by-13-inch pan.

1/4 cup melted butter or
  margarine
1/2 cup packed light
  brown sugar
1 (16-ounce) can sliced
  peaches in heavy
  syrup, drained
2 1/4 cups sifted all-
  purpose flour
3 1/2 teaspoons baking
  powder

1 teaspoon salt
1 1/2 cups sugar
1/2 cup butter or
  margarine, softened
1 cup milk
1 teaspoon vanilla
  extract
2 eggs, beaten

Preheat the oven to 350 degrees. Stir together the melted butter and brown sugar; pour in the bottom of a 6-by-10-inch glass pan. Arrange the sliced peaches over the butter mixture. Set aside. Sift the flour, baking powder, salt and sugar into a large mixer bowl. Add the butter, milk and vanilla. Beat on medium speed for 2 minutes. Add the eggs; beat for 1 minute longer. Pour half the cake batter over the peaches in the pan. Bake for 35 to 40 minutes or until cake tests done. Yield: 6 servings.

Phyllis Kraich
Akron, Colorado

PEANUT CRUNCH CAKE

I serve this cake warm with hot chocolate after sledding. Delicious!

1 (2-layer) package
   yellow cake mix
1 cup peanut butter
1/2 cup packed light
   brown sugar
1 cup water
3 eggs

1/4 cup vegetable oil
1/2 to 3/4 cup semisweet
   chocolate chips
1/2 to 3/4 cup peanut
   butter chips
1/2 cup chopped peanuts

Preheat the oven to 350 degrees. Place the cake mix, peanut butter and brown sugar in a mixer bowl and beat on low speed until crumbly. Set aside 1/2 cup of the mixture. Add the water, eggs and oil to the remaining crumb mixture; blend on low speed until moistened. Beat on high speed for 2 minutes. Stir in 1/4 cup each of chocolate and peanut butter chips. Pour into a greased 9-by-13-inch baking pan. Combine the peanuts, reserved crumb mixture and the remaining chips; sprinkle over the batter. Bake for 40 to 45 minutes or until a toothpick inserted near the center comes out clean. Let cool completely. Yield: 12 to 16 servings.

Teresa Boudreau
Manhattan, Kansas

ROASTED PECAN CAKE

4 extra-large eggs
1/2 cup sugar
3/4 cup extra-virgin olive
   oil

1 cup sour cream
1 (2-layer) package
   butter cake mix
2 cups roasted pecans

Preheat the oven to 350 degrees. Beat the eggs until light and fluffy. Stir in the sugar, oil and sour cream. Add the cake mix, stirring to blend. Fold in the pecans. Spray a bundt pan with nonstick cooking spray. Pour the batter into the pan. Bake for 45 to 60 minutes or until a toothpick inserted near the center comes out clean. Don't overbake! Yield: 16 servings.

Jean Pauline Nowak
Pompano Beach, Florida

PECAN CAKE

This cake is perfect for the holidays or those sorority meetings when a pie just isn't enough.

2 cups sugar
2 cups packed light
   brown sugar
1 1/2 cups butter or
   margarine, softened
6 eggs, lightly beaten

1 teaspoon salt
2 teaspoons vanilla
   extract
2 cups all-purpose flour
2 to 3 cups coarsely
   chopped pecans

Preheat the oven to 300 degrees. Cream the sugar, brown sugar and butter in a large bowl until light and fluffy. Stir in the eggs, salt, vanilla, flour and pecans. Spray a 9-by-13-inch pan with nonstick baking spray. Pour the batter into the pan; batter will be thick. Bake for 2 to 2 1/2 hours or until a toothpick inserted near the center comes out clean. (Start checking for doneness after 1 1/2 hours of baking, but do not underbake.) Yield: 15 servings.

Cricket Allison Hough
Holden, Missouri

HAWAIIAN TREASURE CAKE

You may decorate this cake with banana slices, kiwifruit, strawberries, or mandarin oranges.

1 (2-layer) white or
   yellow cake mix
1 (4-ounce) package
   vanilla instant
   pudding mix
1 (20-ounce) can crushed
   pineapple, undrained

1 (8-ounce) package
   cream cheese,
   softened
1 (16-ounce) package
   whipped topping,
   thawed
Coconut

Bake a white or yellow cake mix in a 9-by-13-inch baking pan using package directions. Let cool. Mix the pudding mix, pineapple and cream cheese; spread over top of cake. Spread the whipped topping over the pudding mixture. Sprinkle the coconut on the whipped topping. Yield: 15 servings.

Beverly Attebery
Weiser, Idaho

PINEAPPLE CAKE

This cake is delicious served warm or cold. It can be served plain or with whipped cream or ice cream.

1 1/2 cups sugar
2 cups flour
1 teaspoon baking soda
1 (15-ounce) can crushed
   pineapple, undrained
2 eggs

1/2 cup packed light
   brown sugar
1/4 cup chopped walnuts
   or pecans
Vanilla Icing

Preheat the oven to 350 degrees. Mix the sugar, flour and baking soda in a bowl. Add the pineapple and eggs. Mix well and pour into a greased and floured 9-by-13-inch baking pan. Combine the brown sugar and nuts and sprinkle over the batter. Bake for 30 minutes or until the cake tests done. While the cake is baking, prepare the Vanilla Icing. Remove the cake from the oven, and pour the hot icing over the hot cake. Yield: 12 to 18 servings.

VANILLA ICING

½ cup margarine
½ cup sugar
1 cup cream

1 teaspoon vanilla
extract

Bring margarine, sugar, cream and vanilla to a rolling boil in a saucepan. Boil for 2 to 3 minutes.

Nina Walker, Iota Eta
Ennis, Texas

SWEDISH PINEAPPLE PAN CAKE

1 (20-ounce) can crushed
unsweetened
pineapple, undrained
2 cups sugar
2 cups flour
2 teaspoons baking soda

1 teaspoon vanilla
extract
2 eggs, beaten
Vanilla Cream Cheese
Icing

Preheat the oven to 350 degrees. Blend the pineapple in a blender for 1 minute or until it is finely crushed. Mix the blended pineapple, sugar, flour, baking soda, vanilla and eggs in a large bowl. Pour into a greased 9-by-13-inch baking pan. Bake for 30 to 40 minutes or until cake tests done. Spread the Vanilla Cream Cheese Icing on the warm cake. Yield: 15 servings.

VANILLA CREAM CHEESE ICING

1 (8-ounce) package
cream cheese,
softened
½ cup margarine,
softened

1 teaspoon vanilla
extract
2 cups confectioners'
sugar

Blend the cream cheese, margarine, vanilla and confectioners' sugar; beat until smooth.

Marianne Hays, Xi Alpha Mu
Terre Haute, Indiana

PURPLE PLUM CAKE

This cake won a second-place ribbon in the County Fair in San Bernardino County, California. I use nonstick cooking spray to grease the pan. This cake freezes well. If you do freeze it, glaze the cake after thawing.

1 (20-ounce) can purple
plums, or 2 (15-ounce)
cans whole plums
1½ cups sugar
3 eggs
¾ cup vegetable oil
½ cup whole milk
2½ cups sifted
all-purpose flour

1 teaspoon baking soda
1 teaspoon salt
½ teaspoon each ground
cinnamon, nutmeg
and ginger
½ cup chopped pecans
(optional)
Purple Plum Glaze

Preheat the oven to 350 degrees. Drain the plums, reserving the plum syrup for the glaze. If the plums are whole, cut each into 4 pieces and pit. Combine the sugar and eggs, beating until foamy and light. Add the oil and milk. Beat for 1 minute longer. Sift together the flour, baking soda, salt, cinnamon, nutmeg and ginger. Gradually add to the egg mixture, beating until smooth. Gently fold in the nuts and plums. Pour the batter into a greased bundt pan or angel food cake pan. Bake for 50 to 60 minutes. Turn onto a wire rack. When cool, spoon warm Purple Plum Glaze over the top. Yield: 12 servings.

PURPLE PLUM GLAZE

½ cup sugar
1 tablespoon cornstarch

1 cup purple plum syrup

Combine the sugar, cornstarch and the purple plum syrup from the canned plums. Bring to a boil in a saucepan and cook until thickened and clear.

Janet R. Medlock
Apple Valley, California

ALMOND POPPY SEED POUND CAKE

I'm known as the "Poppy Seed Cake Lady." I bake as many as 13 of these cakes for my son's teachers at Christmastime and for other holidays as well. I bake 3 at a time. They freeze well. Ovens bake differently, so start checking the cake for doneness after 30 minutes.

1 (2-layer) yellow cake
mix
1 (4-ounce) vanilla
instant pudding mix
1 cup hot water
½ cup vegetable oil

4 eggs
1 teaspoon almond
extract
4 tablespoons poppy
seeds

Preheat the oven to 350 degrees. Combine yellow cake mix, pudding mix, water and vegetable oil in a mixer bowl; mix on low speed. Add the eggs and almond extract to the mixture; mix on low speed. Add the poppy seeds to the mixture; mix on low speed until smooth. Pour batter into a greased bundt pan. Bake for 40 minutes or until the cake springs back after you touch it. Turn the cake out of the pan, turning it right side up on the serving plate. The pudding in the cake is moist on top and it will stick to the plate if the cake is turned upside down. Yield: 12 servings.

Charlene Torrence
Hallsville, Texas

POPPY SEED CAKE

1 (2-layer) package
  yellow cake mix
1/2 cup sugar
3/4 cup vegetable oil

1 cup buttermilk
4 eggs
1/4 cup poppy seeds

Preheat the oven to 350 degrees. Spray the inside of a bundt pan with nonstick cooking spray and dust the sprayed area with sugar. Combine the cake mix, sugar, oil and buttermilk in a large bowl. Add the eggs 1 at a time, beating after each addition. Stir in the poppy seeds. Pour the batter into the prepared bundt pan. Bake for 45 minutes to 1 hour or until the cake tests done. Yield: 16 servings.

Amy Terry
Lake Jackson, Texas

COCONUT POUND CAKE

3 cups sugar
1 1/2 cups butter or
  margarine, softened
6 eggs, separated
1 1/2 teaspoons almond
  extract
1 1/2 teaspoons coconut
  flavoring

3 cups cake flour or
  2 5/8 cups all-purpose
  flour
1/2 teaspoon baking
  powder
1 cup milk
2 cups flaked coconut

Preheat the oven to 300 degrees. Reserve 3 tablespoons of the sugar and set aside. Cream the rest of the sugar and the butter in a bowl until light and fluffy. Stir the egg yolks into the sugar mixture. Beat the egg whites until stiff, adding the reserved 3 tablespoons of sugar. Add the almond extract and coconut flavoring to the sugar mixture. Stir together the flour and baking powder. Add the flour mixture to the sugar mixture alternately with the milk 1/3 at a time. Fold in the egg whites and coconut. Bake for 2 hours in a greased and floured tube or bundt pan. Test for doneness after 1 1/2 hours. Yield: 16 servings.

Camille Burt, Alpha Rho Nu
Huffman, Texas

LEMON POUND CAKE

1 cup butter or
  margarine, softened
1/4 cup shortening or
  margarine
3 cups sugar
1 cup milk
1/4 teaspoon baking
  powder

3 cups all-purpose flour
5 eggs
1 teaspoon vanilla
  extract
2 teaspoons lemon
  flavoring

Preheat the oven to 325 degrees. Cream the butter, shortening and sugar in a bowl until light and fluffy.

Add the milk. Sift together the baking powder and flour and stir into the butter mixture. Add the eggs 1 at a time, beating after each addition. Stir in the vanilla and lemon flavoring. Pour into a greased and floured bundt pan. Bake for 1 hour 20 minutes or until the cake tests done. Yield: 16 servings.

Billie Fitts, Xi Alpha Gamma Lambda
Palestine, Texas

POUND CAKE PERFECTION

1 cup butter or
  margarine, softened
1 cup shortening
3 cups sugar
3 cups cake flour
1/2 teaspoon baking
  powder

1/2 teaspoon salt
1 cup milk
5 eggs
1 teaspoon vanilla
  extract

Preheat the oven to 350 degrees. Cream the butter, shortening and sugar in a bowl until light and fluffy. Sift together the flour, baking powder and salt 3 times. Add the flour mixture alternately with the milk to the sugar mixture. Add the eggs and vanilla; beat well. Bake in a large greased tube pan for 1 hour 20 minutes or in 2 loaf pans 35 to 40 minutes. Yield: 18 to 24 servings.

Linda Bond, Xi Beta Lambda
Dover, New Jersey

PRALINE POUND CAKE

This pound cake can be made in mini-loaves for Christmas gifts. Everyone will want the recipe! This is a great recipe, well worth the effort . . . but to make it seem like less work, make the pralines ahead of time. There are a couple of ways to determine when a mixture reaches the soft-ball stage. If you spoon a drop of the boiling syrup into a cup of ice water, it will form a soft ball that flattens easily between your fingers. Another method is to use a candy thermometer; when the mixture reaches 234 to 240 degrees Fahrenheit on the candy thermometer, it is at the soft-ball stage.

2 sticks butter or
  margarine, cubed,
  softened
1 1/4 cups sugar
5 eggs, separated
1 teaspoon vanilla
  extract
2 cups all-purpose flour
1/2 teaspoon baking
  powder

Pinch of salt
1 cup crumbled pralines
2 tablespoons dark rum
2 pints praline ice cream
1 cup store-bought
  caramel sauce,
  warmed
Confectioners' sugar for
  sprinkling
Sprigs of fresh mint

Preheat the oven to 350 degrees. Butter a 5-by-9-inch loaf pan. Cream the butter and sugar with an electric mixer until light and fluffy, occasionally scraping down the sides of the bowl. Beat the egg yolks with the vanilla in a small bowl until light and frothy. Add the egg yolk mixture gradually to the butter mixture and mix on medium-low speed for about 4 minutes. Combine the flour, baking powder and salt in another bowl. With the mixer running, add the flour alternately with the egg whites to the butter mixture, a third at a time. Scrape down the sides of the bowl as you mix. Fold in the pralines and rum. Pour the batter into the prepared pan. Bake for 1 hour and 10 minutes or until golden and firm to the touch. Remove the pan from the oven and cool on a wire rack for 10 minutes. Remove the cake from the pan and cool on the wire rack. The cake can be served warm or cooled completely—for this recipe, the cake should be slightly warm. Line a 5-by-9-inch loaf pan with plastic wrap. Spread the ice cream evenly in the pan and cover the ice cream with the ends of the plastic wrap. Place in the freezer and freeze until firm. Cut the cake into 12 slices. Place 1 slice of the pound cake in the center of each plate. Place a slice of the ice cream on top of the cake. Top the ice cream with another piece of pound cake, forming a sandwich. Drizzle the entire sandwich with warm caramel sauce. Garnish each sandwich with confectioners' sugar and mint. Yield: 6 servings.

PRALINES

1 cup plus 2 tablespoons packed light brown sugar	Pinch of salt
1/4 cup plus 2 tablespoons evaporated milk	1 1/2 teaspoons butter or margarine
	1 cup chopped pecans

Mix the brown sugar, evaporated milk, salt and butter in a heavy-bottomed saucepan. Cook over low heat until the sugar dissolves, stirring constantly with a wooden spoon. Stir in the pecans and cook over medium heat until the mixture reaches the soft-ball stage. Remove the pan from the heat and stir rapidly until the mixture thickens. Drop by teaspoons 1 inch apart on baking sheets lined with parchment paper. Let cool completely until firm. Store in an airtight container. Yield: 1 dozen.

Pam Stewart, Alpha Alpha Eta
West Columbia, Texas

PUMPKIN ROLL

3 eggs	1 tablespoon ground cinnamon
3/4 cup sugar	1/2 teaspoon ground nutmeg
1/4 cup packed light brown sugar	1 cup finely chopped pecans
1 cup mashed pumpkin	2 to 3 tablespoons confectioners' sugar
1 cup all-purpose flour	Cream Cheese Filling
1 teaspoon baking powder	
1/2 teaspoon salt	

Preheat the oven to 375 degrees. Beat the eggs, sugar and brown sugar in a mixer bowl at high speed until smooth. Blend in the pumpkin. Mix the flour, baking powder, salt, cinnamon and nutmeg. Add to the pumpkin mixture and mix until smooth. Spread evenly in a shallow 10-by-15-inch jelly roll pan. Sprinkle with the pecans. Bake for 12 to 15 minutes or until the top springs back when lightly touched. Sprinkle the confectioners' sugar evenly on a tea towel. Loosen the edges of the cake with a knife. Invert the cake carefully onto the towel. Roll as for jelly roll in the towel. Cool completely. Unroll and spread with Cream Cheese Filling to within 1/2 inch of the edges. Reroll carefully without the towel. Chill before serving. Yield: 8 to 12 servings.

CREAM CHEESE FILLING

1 1/4 cups confectioners' sugar	1/4 cup lightly salted butter, softened
1 (8-ounce) package cream cheese, softened	1 teaspoon vanilla extract

Combine the confectioners' sugar, cream cheese, butter and vanilla in a mixer bowl. Beat at medium speed until smooth.

Becky Castellari, Preceptor Delta
Centralia, Illinois

Elaine Sills, Beta Gamma Master, El Paso, Texas, makes Chocolate Cherry Bundt Cake by beating a devil's food cake mix with 1/2 can cherry pie filling, 1 cup water, 3 eggs, 1/3 cup vegetable oil, and 2 teaspoons almond extract for 2 minutes. Pour half the batter into a greased and floured bundt pan. Spoon remaining pie filling on batter—don't touch the pan. Pour remaining batter on top. Bake in a preheated 375-degree oven for 35 to 40 minutes. Cool for 10 minutes, invert onto plate, and sprinkle with confectioners' sugar.

RED VELVET CAKE

When I was growing up in the South, this was always a special Christmas cake—delicious and colorful.

1½ cups sugar
1½ cups vegetable oil
1 teaspoon vinegar
2 eggs, beaten
2½ cups self-rising flour
1 teaspoon baking soda

1 cup buttermilk
1 teaspoon vanilla
   extract
2 ounces red food
   coloring
Red Velvet Filling

Preheat the oven to 350 degrees. Combine the sugar, oil, vinegar and eggs in a bowl; mix well. Sift the flour and baking soda together; add to the egg mixture. Stir in the buttermilk slowly. Stir in the vanilla and red cake coloring. Bake in 3 greased 8- or 9-inch round cake pans for 25 minutes or until cake tests done. Let cool. Spread the Red Velvet Filling between the cake layers; use it to frost the sides and the top. Yield: 16 servings.

RED VELVET FILLING

3/4 cup butter or
   margarine
1½ (8-ounce) packages
   cream cheese

1½ (16-ounce) boxes
   confectioners' sugar
2 cups finely chopped
   pecans

Melt the butter and the cream cheese in a saucepan over low heat. Add the confectioners' sugar; mix well. Add the pecans; mix well. Use while still warm.

Ellen Lakin, Xi Gamma Upsilon
Alma, Nebraska

RICOTTA CAKE

1 (2-layer) package
   butter-recipe yellow
   cake mix
1 (15-ounce) container
   ricotta cheese
3 eggs
2 teaspoons vanilla
   extract

3/4 cup sugar
Cream Cheese Topping
1 (15-ounce) can crushed
   pineapple, drained
Coconut (optional)
Chopped walnuts or
   pecans (optional)

Preheat the oven to 350 degrees. Grease and flour a 9-by-13-inch pan. Prepare the cake mix according to package directions. Pour into the prepared pan. Beat the ricotta, eggs, vanilla and sugar together; pour over the cake batter. Bake for 55 minutes or until the cake tests done. Cool thoroughly. Spread the top with the Cream Cheese Topping. Top with the pineapple. Sprinkle with coconut and nuts. Yield: 8 to 10 servings.

CREAM CHEESE TOPPING

1 (4-ounce) package
   vanilla pudding mix
1 cup 2% milk
1 (8-ounce) package
   cream cheese,
   softened

1 (8-ounce) container
   whipped topping

Prepare the pudding with the milk using package directions. Beat the cream cheese in a bowl until light and fluffy. Fold in whipped topping and pudding.

Katrine Krempecke, Iota Iota
Blairsville, Georgia

RUM CAKE

4 eggs, beaten
½ cup vegetable oil
½ cup water
½ cup rum or sherry
1 (2-layer) package
   butter-recipe
   cake mix

1 (4-ounce) package
   vanilla instant
   pudding mix
½ cup chopped pecans
Rum Glaze

Preheat the oven to 325 degrees. Mix the eggs, oil, water and rum in a large bowl. Add the cake mix and pudding mix; beat well. Pour into a greased bundt pan. Bake for 50 to 60 minutes or until cake tests done. Pour Rum Glaze over the hot cake and let stand for 30 minutes. Invert the cake onto a plate. Yield: 8 to 10 servings.

RUM GLAZE

¼ cup sugar
¼ cup rum
¼ cup water

2 tablespoons butter or
   margarine

Combine sugar, rum, water and butter in a saucepan. Heat and stir until all ingredients are dissolved.

Loucille J. Swaim, Laureate Sigma
Asheboro, North Carolina

Nita Chambers, Claremore, Oklahoma, makes Flourless Pecan Torte by beating 6 egg whites with ¼ cup sugar until stiff peaks form and setting aside. Beat 6 egg yolks with 3/4 cup sugar until doubled in bulk and beat in 1 teaspoon vanilla. Fold in beaten egg whites and 2 cups very finely ground pecans. Pour into an oiled 8-inch springform pan. Bake in a preheated 325-degree oven for 65 minutes. Cool, chill overnight, and remove side of pan. Serve with ice cream or sweetened whipped cream and fresh fruit.

SPICE CAKE IN A JAR

If you use canning jars and lids, this cake will have a shelf life of 6 months. Decorate the lid to make a nice gift.

2/3 cup shortening	2 teaspoons baking soda
2 2/3 cups sugar	1/2 teaspoon baking
4 eggs	powder
2 cups unsweetened	1 1/2 teaspoons salt
applesauce	1 teaspoon cinnamon
2/3 cup water	1 teaspoon ground
2 cups whole wheat	cloves
flour	2/3 cup chopped walnuts
1 1/3 cups all-purpose	or pecans (optional)
flour	

Preheat the oven to 325 degrees. Cream the shortening, sugar and eggs in a large bowl until light and fluffy. Add the applesauce and water; mix well. Mix the whole wheat flour, all-purpose flour, baking soda, baking powder, salt, cinnamon and cloves in another bowl. Add to the first mixture and blend. Stir in nuts if desired. Spray wide-mouth pint jars with nonstick cooking spray and fill half-full with batter. Bake for 45 minutes. Remove the jars from the oven 1 at a time and quickly screw a lid on each one. They will keep, refrigerated, for 6 months.
Yield: 7 to 8 jars of cake.

Nancy Strickland
Brunswick, Georgia

PINTO SPICE CAKE

2 cups warm cooked	1/2 teaspoon ground
pinto beans	cloves
1/4 cup bean liquid	1/2 teaspoon allspice
1/2 cup butter or	1/2 teaspoon mace
margarine, softened	1 teaspoon baking soda
1 cup sugar	1 teaspoon cinnamon
1 egg	2 cups chopped peeled
2 teaspoons vanilla	apples
extract	1/2 cup seedless raisins
1 cup sifted flour	1/2 cup chopped walnuts
1/2 teaspoon salt	Cream Cheese Icing

Preheat the oven to 350 degrees. Beat the undrained pinto beans in a bowl until smooth. Cream butter and sugar in large bowl until light and fluffy. Beat the egg and vanilla into the butter mixture; stir in the mashed beans. Combine the flour, salt, cloves, allspice, mace, baking soda and cinnamon in a bowl; mix well. Add half the flour mixture to the creamed mixture; beat well. Stir in the apples, raisins, nuts and remaining flour mixture; beat just until mixed. Pour into a buttered 9-inch tube pan. Bake for 1 hour. Cool. Frost with Cream Cheese Icing. Yield: 12 servings.

CREAM CHEESE ICING

1/2 cup butter or	1 teaspoon vanilla
margarine, softened	extract
1 (8-ounce) package	4 cups confectioners'
cream cheese,	sugar
softened	

Cream butter, cream cheese and vanilla in a bowl until light and fluffy. Add the confectioners' sugar 1 cup at a time, beating well after each addition.

Hazel R. French, Preceptor Alpha Upsilon
Maybeury, West Virginia

STRAWBERRY ALMOND SHORTCAKE

2 cups all-purpose flour	1 egg, beaten
3 teaspoons baking	1/2 cup water
powder	2 teaspoons almond
2 tablespoons sugar	extract
1/2 teaspoon salt	1 quart strawberries
4 tablespoons	Sugar to taste
shortening	Whipped cream

Preheat the oven to 475 degrees. Sift together the flour, baking powder, sugar and salt in a bowl. Add the shortening and mix it in with a fork. Combine the egg, water and almond extract. Add slowly to the flour mixture, stirring to make a soft dough. Roll and pat the dough by hand on a floured board until 1/2 inch thick. Cut with a large biscuit cutter dipped in flour. Place the shortcakes in a greased baking pan. Bake for 10 to 12 minutes or until lightly browned. Chop the strawberries in a bowl and add sugar to taste. Split the shortcakes while hot. Spoon strawberries onto the bottom layer and add the top layer. Spoon on more strawberries and top with whipped cream. Yield: 8 servings.

Julie Schultz, Pi Psi
Bryan, Texas

Hope Marlene Dukeshire, Xi Theta Psi, Santa Ana, California, shares her Mother-in-Law's Secret Fruitcake. Cook a 9-ounce package of compressed mincemeat with 1/2 cup water in a large saucepan, breaking up clumps. Boil for 1 minute and cool. Add 1 cup chopped nuts, 1 cup mixed candied fruit, 1 egg, 1 can sweetened condensed milk, 3/4 cup flour, and 1/2 teaspoon baking soda. Pour into a greased and waxed-paper-lined loaf pan. Bake in a preheated 350-degree oven for 1 1/2 hours, or use several small pans and bake for 30 minutes.

LOW-FAT STRAWBERRY YOGURT CAKE

Try this cake topped with fruit, fruit-flavored apple-sauce or with different flavors of yogurt. Nobody will ever guess it is low in fat!

1 (2-layer) white low-fat supermoist cake mix	2 (8-ounce) containers low-fat or fat-free strawberry yogurt
3/4 cup water	1 (8-ounce) container
1/3 cup applesauce	low-fat whipped
2 egg whites	topping, thawed

Preheat the oven to 350 degrees. Combine cake mix, water, applesauce and egg whites in a bowl, mixing until smooth and blended. Stir in 1 of the containers of yogurt. Spray a 9-by-13-inch baking pan with non-stick cooking spray. Pour the batter into the pan. Bake for 30 minutes or until cake tests done. Let cool. Mix the second container of yogurt with the whipped topping. Spread over the cake. Refrigerate until serving time. Top with fruit if desired. Yield: 12 to 15 servings.

Suzanne Seger
Columbus, Indiana

WINE CAKE

1 (2-layer) package yellow cake mix	3/4 cup sherry
	4 eggs
1 (4-ounce) package vanilla instant pudding mix	1 teaspoon nutmeg
	Confectioners' sugar and sherry for glaze
3/4 cup vegetable oil	

Preheat the oven to 350 degrees. Combine the cake mix, pudding mix, oil, sherry, eggs and nutmeg in a mixer bowl. Beat for 5 minutes. Pour the batter into a greased tube or bundt pan. Bake for 40 to 50 minutes. Stir a few tablespoons confectioners' sugar together with enough sherry to make a glaze. Glaze the cake while still hot. Yield: 12 servings.

Fran Maulding
Helena, Montana

BUTTER BRICKLE

1 cup sugar	2 tablespoons water
1 cup butter (not margarine)	1 cup chopped pecans
	4 or 5 (7-ounce)
1 teaspoon vanilla extract	Hershey's candy bars

Combine the sugar, butter, vanilla and water in a heavy saucepan. Bring to a boil, stirring constantly. Cook to the hard-crack stage on a candy thermometer. Spread the pecans on a baking sheet; cover with hot mixture. Lay the candy bars on top; spread across

the brickle when melted. Cool completely. Break into bite-size pieces. Yield: 15 to 20 servings.

Patricia M. Janulewicz, Laureate Psi
Grand Island, Nebraska

YUMMY CARAMELS

2 cups sugar	1 cup butter (not margarine)
1 cup packed light brown sugar	1 teaspoon vanilla extract
1 cup light corn syrup	1/2 cup chopped pecans
1 cup cream	
1 cup milk	

Cook the sugar, brown sugar, corn syrup, cream, milk and butter in a heavy saucepan over low heat to 248 degrees on a candy thermometer, stirring frequently. Remove from the heat. Stir in the vanilla and pecans. Pour into a buttered 9-by-13-inch pan. Cool. Cut into squares; wrap in waxed paper. Yield: 48 servings.

Elaine Long, Preceptor Tau
Weiser, Idaho

CANTONESE FUDGE

If you like the taste of candied or crystallized ginger, you will love this fudge.

2 1/4 cups packed light brown sugar	3/4 cup evaporated milk
1 tablespoon light corn syrup	1 teaspoon vanilla extract
1 tablespoon butter or margarine	1/4 cup finely chopped candied ginger

Mix the sugar, corn syrup, butter and milk in a heavy saucepan. Cook over medium heat to the soft-ball stage or to 237 degrees on a candy thermometer, stirring constantly. Cool. Stir in the vanilla and ginger. Beat until crystalline. Turn onto a greased baking sheet and mark into squares. Store in airtight bags. Yield: 20 servings.

Shasta L. Anker, Omicron Master
Los Angeles, California

Sue Altimore, Preceptor, Anderson, Texas, makes Candy Jewels by mixing a can of sweetened condensed milk, 8 ounces coconut, and 8 ounces gumdrops and boiling until the gumdrops look transparent. Remove from heat. Stir in 1 teaspoon vanilla, a pound of confectioners' sugar, and 1 cup pecans until thickened. Drop by teaspoonfuls onto waxed paper.

FANNY FARMER FUDGE

I gave this recipe to a sorority sister at Christmastime. Twenty of her friends and relatives made it, and all said it was the best fudge they ever had.

4½ cups sugar	3 teaspoons vanilla
1 (12-ounce) can	extract
evaporated milk	½ to 1 cup chopped
1 cup butter or	pecans or walnuts
margarine	
3 (6-ounce) bags	
semisweet chocolate	
chips	

Bring the flour, evaporated milk and butter to a boil in a large saucepan. Cook for 6 minutes. Remove from heat. Add the chocolate chips, stirring until dissolved and creamy smooth. Add the vanilla and nuts, stirring regularly until the consistency of frosting. Spread in a greased 9-by-13-inch pan or place in fancy foil mini-muffin cups. Refrigerate, covered, until set. Yield: 80 servings.

Pam Niederhauser, Preceptor Pi
Columbia, Missouri

PATIENCE CANDY

You will know why this is called Patience Candy after stirring until it reaches the soft ball stage.

1 cup milk	1 cup pecans
3 cups sugar	
3 tablespoons butter or	
margarine	

Heat the milk and 2 cups of the sugar in a saucepan, stirring constantly until a soft ball forms when a spoonful is dropped in cool water. Brown the remaining sugar and stir into the milk mixture. Remove from heat. Add the butter. Beat until creamy. Stir in the pecans. Pour onto buttered platters. Break into pieces. Yield: 50 servings.

Pamela Smith, Xi Alpha
Albuquerque, New Mexico

EASY PRALINES

1 cup sugar	1 (4-ounce) package
½ cup packed light	butterscotch pudding
brown sugar	mix (not instant)
½ cup evaporated milk	1 cup pecans
1 tablespoon margarine	

Combine the sugar, brown sugar, milk, margarine and pudding mix in a 6- to 8-quart saucepan. Heat over medium heat, stirring constantly, until all ingredients are dissolved. Bring to a boil; boil for 5 minutes or until the mixture forms a soft ball. Remove from heat; continue to beat the mixture until it thickens slightly. Stir in the pecans. Drop the mixture quickly by teaspoons to form pralines on waxed paper. Yield: 15 to 18 servings.

Jolene Broussard
Sulphur, Louisiana

MICROWAVE PECAN PRALINES

If the pecan pieces are larger than I want them to be, I put them in a storage bag and crush them with a rolling pin.

1 cup packed light	2 tablespoons butter or
brown sugar	margarine
1 cup sugar	2 cups pecan pieces or
¾ cup evaporated milk	halves

Mix the brown sugar, sugar, evaporated milk, butter and pecans in a glass dish. Microwave on High for 3 minutes; remove from the microwave and stir. Continue to microwave the mixture (remove and stir after 3-minute intervals) until total cooking time is 12 minutes. At the end of the 12 minutes, stir until the gloss on the mixture begins to dull. Pour quickly over a baking sheet lined with waxed paper. Cool completely. Break into pieces. Yield: 12 servings.

Jean S. Kyle, Preceptor Delta
Montgomery, Alabama

SUGARPLUMS

Sugarplums are an ancient treat that originated in the Middle East. Crystallized ginger can be found in the bottled spice section of the grocery store.

3 pounds dried mixed	½ pound crystallized
figs, dates, raisins	ginger
and currants	Grated rinds of 2 oranges
1½ pounds blanched	2 to 3 tablespoons
almonds or walnuts	brandy
½ pound pistachio nuts	Sugar

Finely chop the dried fruit, almonds, pistachio nuts, ginger and orange rind, using a food grinder (preferred) or food processor. Add the brandy to make the mixture stick together. Form the mixture into small balls and roll in sugar. Store the sugarplums in a lightly covered container in the refrigerator for a few days while the flavors meld. They will keep in the refrigerator for a month or more. Yield: 4 dozen.

Janice J. Sartore, Laureate Beta Phi
Findlay, Ohio

SNICKER BARS

1 cup milk chocolate
 chips
1/4 cup butterscotch
 chips
1/4 cup creamy peanut
 butter

Marshmallow Filling
Caramel
Butterscotch Icing

Combine the chocolate chips, butterscotch chips and peanut butter in a small saucepan. Stir over low heat until melted and smooth. Spread over the bottom of a lightly greased 9-by-13-inch baking pan. Refrigerate, covered, until set. Spread the Marshmallow Filling over the chilled first layer. Refrigerate, covered, until set. Spread the Caramel over the chilled peanut butter filling. Refrigerate, covered, until set. Pour the Butterscotch Icing over the chilled caramel layer. Refrigerate, covered, for at least 1 hour. Cut into bars. Yield: 8 dozen.

MARSHMALLOW FILLING

1/4 cup butter or
 margarine
1 cup sugar
1/4 cup evaporated milk
1 1/2 cups marshmallow
 creme

1/4 cup creamy peanut
 butter
1 teaspoon vanilla
 extract
1 1/2 cups chopped salted
 peanuts

To make the filling, melt the butter in a heavy saucepan over medium heat. Add the sugar and milk. Bring to a boil and boil for 5 minutes. Remove from heat. Stir in the marshmallow creme, peanut butter and vanilla. Add the peanuts.

CARAMEL

14 ounces caramels

1/4 cup whipping cream

Combine the caramels and whipping cream in a saucepan. Stir over low heat until melted and smooth.

BUTTERSCOTCH ICING

1 cup milk chocolate
 chips
1/4 cup butterscotch
 chips

1/4 cup creamy peanut
 butter

Combine the chocolate chips, butterscotch chips and peanut butter in a saucepan. Stir over low heat until melted and smooth.

Shirley Fitch, Preceptor Rho
Flagstaff, Arizona

FRESH APPLE BARS

3 eggs
1 3/4 cups sugar
1 cup vegetable oil
2 cups all-purpose flour
1 teaspoon salt
1 teaspoon baking soda

1/2 teaspoon cinnamon
2 cups packed diced
 peeled apples
1 cup chopped pecans
1 cup raisins
Thin Vanilla Icing

Preheat the oven to 350 degrees. Combine the eggs, sugar and oil in a large bowl; beat thoroughly. Sift together the flour, salt, baking soda and cinnamon. Add to the egg mixture; beat well. Fold in the apples, pecans and raisins. Pour into a greased and floured 9-by-13-inch baking pan. Bake for 40 to 50 minutes. Remove from oven. Frost with Thin Vanilla Icing. Cut into bars when cool. Yield: 1 to 2 dozen.

THIN VANILLA ICING

1 1/2 cups confectioners'
 sugar
1 1/4 teaspoons vanilla
 extract

Milk

Combine the confectioners' sugar and vanilla. Beat in enough milk to make a thin icing.

Estelle Hite, Mu Epsilon
Royalton, Illinois

APPLE BROWNIES

3 eggs
1 3/4 cups sugar
1 cup vegetable oil
2 cups sifted all-purpose
 flour
1 teaspoon salt
1 teaspoon cinnamon

1 teaspoon baking soda
1 cup chopped peeled
 apples
1 cup walnuts or pecans
 (optional)
Cream Cheese Icing

Preheat the oven to 350 degrees. Mix the eggs, sugar, oil, flour, salt, cinnamon, baking soda, apples and nuts in a large bowl. Bake in a greased 9-by-13-inch baking pan for 35 to 40 minutes. When cool, frost with Cream Cheese Icing. Cut into squares. Yield: 16 servings.

CREAM CHEESE ICING

1/4 cup margarine,
 softened
1 (3-ounce) package
 cream cheese,
 softened
1 3/4 cups confectioners'
 sugar

1 teaspoon vanilla
 extract
1 cup walnuts or pecans
 (optional)

Cream margarine and cream cheese in a bowl until light and fluffy. Add confectioners' sugar, vanilla and nuts, beating in gradually. Use to ice a cooled cake.

Mary E. Blanchard, Alpha Gamma Master
Gambier, Ohio

BLACK-BOTTOM BANANA BARS

1/2 cup margarine, softened
1 cup sugar
1 egg
1 teaspoon vanilla extract
1 1/2 cups mashed bananas
1 1/2 cups all-purpose flour
1 teaspoon baking powder
1 teaspoon baking soda
1/2 teaspoon salt
1/4 cup cocoa

Preheat the oven to 350 degrees. Cream the margarine and sugar in a large bowl until light and fluffy. Add the egg and vanilla; beat until combined. Blend in the bananas. Combine the flour, baking powder, baking soda and salt in a medium bowl. Add to the creamed mixture; mix well. Divide the batter in half. Stir the cocoa into 1 of the halves. Spread the cocoa batter into a greased 9-by-13-inch baking pan. Spoon the remaining batter on top. Swirl with a knife. Bake for 25 minutes. Cut into bars. Yield: 3 dozen.

Sherri Smith, Delta Chi
Blue Springs, Missouri

HEAVENLY BANANA BARS

3 eggs
1/2 cup butter or margarine, softened
2 cups sugar
1 teaspoon vanilla extract
3 medium ripe bananas
2 cups all-purpose flour
1 teaspoon baking soda
Cream Cheese Frosting

Preheat the oven to 350 degrees. Cream the eggs, butter and sugar in a large bowl until light and fluffy. Add the vanilla, bananas, flour and baking soda; beat well. Pour into a greased 11-by-16-inch baking pan. Bake for 25 minutes. Let cool. Frost with Cream Cheese Frosting. Cut into bars. Yield: 6 dozen.

CREAM CHEESE FROSTING

1/2 cup butter or margarine, softened
1 (8-ounce) package cream cheese, softened
4 cups confectioners' sugar
2 teaspoons vanilla extract

Beat butter, cream cheese, confectioners' sugar and vanilla together in a bowl.

Lisa Deimel, Pi Lambda
Olney, Illinois

LOW-CHOLESTEROL BUTTERSCOTCH BROWNIES

1/4 cup olive oil
1 cup packed light brown sugar
1 egg or 2 egg whites
1 teaspoon vanilla extract
2/3 cup flour
1/4 teaspoon salt
1 teaspoon baking powder
1/2 cup nuts (any kind)

Preheat the oven to 350 degrees. Blend the oil, brown sugar, egg and vanilla in a large bowl. Mix in the flour, salt and baking powder. Add the nuts. Spread in a greased 9-inch square baking pan. Bake for 25 minutes. Cool. Frost if desired. Cut into squares. Yield: 9 servings.

Virginia Fast, Kappa Master
Knoxville, Iowa

CARAMEL TOFFEE SQUARES

1/2 cup plus 2 teaspoons butter or margarine, softened
1/4 cup sugar
1 1/4 cups all-purpose flour
1/2 cup packed light brown sugar
1/2 cup butter or margarine
2 tablespoons light corn syrup
1/2 cup sweetened condensed milk
1 cup semisweet chocolate chips
2 teaspoons butter or margarine

Preheat the oven to 350 degrees. Mix 1/2 cup plus 2 teaspoons butter, sugar and flour in a bowl. Press into a greased 9-by-9-inch baking pan. Bake for 20 minutes. Cool. Combine the brown sugar, 1/2 cup butter, corn syrup and condensed milk in a heavy saucepan. Bring to a boil. Boil for 5 minutes. Remove from heat. Beat well and pour over the cooled base. Chill, covered, until set. Melt 2 teaspoons butter and chocolate chips over low heat. Pour over the filling. Refrigerate or freeze. Cut into squares.
Yield: 16 servings.

Laverne Rose Teasdale, Omega
East Selkirk, Manitoba, Canada

Pat McCourry, Preceptor Gamma Theta, Canton, Ohio, makes Superfast Triple Fudge Brownies by preparing a small package of chocolate instant pudding mix with 2 cups milk, whisking in a chocolate cake mix and 2 cups semisweet chocolate chips and baking in a greased 10-by-15-inch pan in a preheated 350-degree oven for 30 to 35 minutes.

CONFETTI BARS

1 (12-ounce) package
  butterscotch chips
1 cup peanut butter
1/4 cup margarine
1 1/2 cups colored
  miniature
  marshmallows

1/2 cup chopped walnuts
  (optional)
1/2 cup shredded coconut
  (optional)
2 1/2 to 3 cups crispy rice
  cereal
Brown Sugar Icing

Grease a 9-by-13-inch baking pan. Melt the butterscotch chips, peanut butter and margarine in a double boiler over hot water. Remove from heat; add the marshmallows. Stir in the nuts and coconut. Add the cereal to butterscotch mixture; mix well. Pour into prepared pan. Spread Brown Sugar Icing quickly over the baked layer. Cut into bars. Yield: 3 dozen.

BROWN SUGAR ICING

2 tablespoons butter or
  margarine
4 tablespoons cream or
  evaporated milk

1/4 cup packed light
  brown sugar
1 to 1 1/2 cups
  confectioners' sugar

Melt the butter in a small saucepan. Add the cream and brown sugar; bring to a boil. Remove from heat and add the confectioners' sugar. Beat well by hand to a spreading consistency.

Elinor Sanderson, Preceptor Beta Iota
Colorado Springs, Colorado

HOOSIER BARS

2 cups all-purpose flour
2 teaspoons baking
  powder
1 teaspoon baking soda
1/2 teaspoon salt
1/2 cup shortening
1/2 cup sugar
1/2 cup packed light
  brown sugar
1 teaspoon vanilla
  extract

2 eggs, separated
3 to 5 tablespoons cold
  water
1 (6-ounce) package
  semisweet chocolate
  chips
1 cup packed light
  brown sugar
3/4 cup chopped walnuts

Preheat the oven to 325 degrees. Sift the flour, baking powder, baking soda and salt together. Cream the shortening, sugar and 1/2 cup brown sugar in a large bowl. Blend the vanilla and egg yolks together; add to the sugar mixture. Add the cold water alternately with the sifted dry ingredients to the sugar mixture. Press the dough into a greased and floured 9-by-13-inch baking pan. Sprinkle the chocolate chips over the dough; press gently. Beat the egg whites until foamy; gradually add 1 cup brown sugar. Beat until stiff. Spread the egg white mixture over the chocolate

chips. Top with the walnuts. Bake for 30 to 35 minutes. Cut into bars while warm. Yield: 3 dozen.

Mary H. Kennedy, Preceptor Upsilon
South Windsor, Connecticut

PUMPKIN BLACK-BOTTOM BROWNIE SQUARES

1/2 cup butter or
  margarine, softened
2/3 cup sugar
2 eggs
1 1/2 cups all-purpose
  flour
1 teaspoon baking
  powder
1/2 teaspoon baking soda
1/4 teaspoon salt

1/4 cup cocoa
1/2 cup sugar
1 teaspoon vanilla
  extract
3/4 cup canned pumpkin
  pie filling
1 teaspoon pumpkin pie
  spice
1 cup chopped nuts
  (optional)

Preheat the oven to 350 degrees. Cream the butter, 2/3 cup sugar and eggs in a large mixer bowl until light and fluffy. Mix the next 4 ingredients; gradually add to the creamed mixture. Pour half the batter into a separate bowl. Combine the cocoa and 1/2 cup sugar. Stir the cocoa mixture into 1 of the bowls of batter; blend in the vanilla. Spread the cocoa batter evenly in a greased 8-by-8-inch baking pan. Add the pumpkin pie filling and pumpkin pie spice to the other half of the batter. Spoon the pumpkin batter over the cocoa batter. Sprinkle with the nuts. Bake for 40 minutes. Cut into squares. Yield: 16 squares.

Denise Ackerman, Zeta Chi
Portland, Oregon

RASPBERRY CHOCOLATE BARS

2 1/2 cups all-purpose
  flour
1 cup sugar
3/4 cup finely chopped
  pecans
1 cup butter or
  margarine, softened

1 egg
1 (2-ounce) jar seedless
  raspberry jam
1 2/3 cups semisweet
  chocolate chips

Preheat the oven to 350 degrees. Combine the flour, sugar, pecans, butter and egg in a large bowl; stir until crumbly. Reserved 1 1/2 cups of the mixture. Press the remaining mixture into the bottom of a greased 9-by-13-inch pan. Spread with the raspberry jam. Sprinkle with the chocolate chips; top with the reserved crumb mixture. Bake for 40 to 45 minutes or until lightly browned. Cool completely in the pan on a wire rack. Cut into bars. Yield: 3 dozen.

Bonnie Carroll, Xi Nu
Evansville, Indiana

PEANUT BUTTER BARS

If you like the "peanut butter cups" candy, you will like this recipe. It is much cheaper than the candy and every bit as good. It keeps well, refrigerated, for an indefinite period of time.

1 cup margarine
1 cup peanut butter
1 cellophane package (1/3 regular box) graham crackers, crushed

1 (16-ounce) package confectioners' sugar
1 1/4 cups semisweet chocolate chips, melted

Melt the margarine in a 9-by-13-inch baking pan. Stir in the peanut butter. Add the graham cracker crumbs and the powdered sugar to the margarine and peanut butter, stirring until the mixture has a uniform texture. Press firmly to make an even layer on the bottom of the pan. Chill, covered, in the refrigerator just until cool. Melt the chocolate chips in a saucepan over very low heat; spread them evenly and quickly over the chilled layer. Return briefly to the refrigerator to cool. Cut before the chocolate hardens, running a knife around the outside of the bars and cutting into the desired number of servings. Refrigerate until serving time. Yield: 3 to 4 dozen.

Rose Mary Coakes, Laureate Alpha Rho
Marshall, Michigan

TANTALIZING TOFFEE BARS

Saltine crackers
1 cup butter (not margarine)
1 cup packed light brown sugar

1 (6-ounce) package semisweet chocolate chips

Preheat the oven to 350 degrees. Grease a cookie sheet. Arrange one layer of the saltine crackers, salt side up, on the cookie sheet, completely covering the sheet. Heat the butter in a saucepan over medium heat. Add the brown sugar; mix well. Bring the mixture to a boil, stirring constantly. Remove from heat; continue stirring for 1 minute. Pour the hot mixture over the saltines, spreading evenly. Sprinkle with the chocolate chips. Bake for 5 minutes. Remove from the oven and spread the chocolate evenly. Let cool, covered in the refrigerator for 1 hour or until the chocolate is firm. Cut into bars. Yield: 3 to 4 dozen.

Rebecca Hahn
Pembroke Pines, Florida

APRICOT BISCOTTI

3 cups sifted all-purpose flour
1 1/2 cups sugar
1/2 stick chilled butter or margarine, diced
2 1/2 teaspoons baking powder
1 teaspoon salt
1 teaspoon ground ginger
4 ounces white chocolate

1 1/2 cups whole almonds, toasted
6 ounces dried apricots, diced
2 eggs
1/3 cup apricot-flavored brandy
1 teaspoon almond extract

Cover a baking sheet with buttered and floured foil or parchment paper. Combine the flour, sugar, butter, baking powder, salt and ginger in a food processor or mixer; process until a fine meal forms. Pour into a bowl. Process the white chocolate until finely chopped; add to the flour mixture. Chop the almonds coarsely; add with the diced apricots to the flour mixture. Beat the eggs, brandy and almond extract together; add to the flour mixture. Process until a moist dough forms. Shape into three 12-inch logs on the prepared baking sheet. Moisten the fingertips and shape each log into a 2-inch-wide strip. Refrigerate for 1 1/2 hours or until firm. Preheat the oven to 350 degrees. Bake on center rack for 25 to 30 minutes or until golden. Remove the baking sheet to a wire rack to cool completely. Reduce oven temperature to 300 degrees. Use a sharp knife to cut each log crosswise into 3/4- to 1-inch-wide slices. Arrange cut side down on a greased cookie sheet. Bake for 10 minutes; turn the cookies over and bake for 10 minutes longer. Cool on a wire rack. Yield: 3 to 4 dozen.

Rosalie R. King, Preceptor Eta Eta
Lompoc, California

Nancy Cummings, Xi Kappa Pi, Belleville, Illinois, makes Caramel Banana Pizza by slicing an 18-ounce package of refrigerated sugar cookie dough and pressing over a 12-inch pizza pan, shaping a rim. Bake in a preheated 375-degree oven for 10 to 12 minutes. Cool. Blend 3/4 cup caramel topping with 2 cups whipped cream. Slice 3 to 4 bananas, arrange over cookie crust, and spread caramel mixture over bananas, covering completely. Drizzle with additional caramel topping and sprinkle with 1/2 cup toasted sliced almonds.

BON BON COOKIES

Mom and Dad made these cookies together at Christmastime. Dad always made sure the color of the gumdrop inside the cookie matched the color of the outside gumdrop.

1/2 cup butter or margarine, softened	1 1/2 cups all-purpose flour
3/4 cup confectioners' sugar	1/8 teaspoon salt
1 tablespoon vanilla extract	Gumdrops, halved, and/or nuts
	Tinted Icing

Preheat the oven to 350 degrees. Combine the butter, sugar and vanilla in a large bowl. Blend in the flour and salt with your hands. Make sure the ingredients are thoroughly blended. Wrap a tablespoon of the dough around a piece of nut or the bottom half of a small gumdrop. Bake 1 inch apart on an ungreased cookie sheet for 12 to 15 minutes or until set. Dip the tops of the warm cookies in the Tinted Icing. Press a piece of nut or the top half of the gumdrop into the icing. Yield: 2 dozen.

TINTED ICING

1 cup confectioners' sugar	1 teaspoon vanilla extract
2 tablespoons milk	Food coloring

Mix the confectioners' sugar, milk and vanilla in a bowl. Stir in food coloring as desired.

Carol Ann Ferguson
Marion, Ohio

VIENNESE BON BON RIBBONS

I won first prize with these cookies at our town's Cookie Bakeoff: the Wilson Borough Jubilee.

1 cup butter or margarine	6 tablespoons red currant jelly
1 cup sugar	4 tablespoons apricot jam
4 eggs, separated	
2 cups sifted flour	Vanilla Cream Frosting
1 cup sour cream	Tinted sugars
1/2 cup finely chopped walnuts	

Preheat the oven to 350 degrees. Cream the butter in a large bowl until light; gradually add the sugar in thirds, creaming well after each addition. Add the egg yolks all at once; beat well. Sir in the flour until it completely disappears. Beat the egg whites in a medium bowl until stiff enough to form soft peaks; fold into the batter. Invert a shallow 10-by-15-inch jelly roll pan; lightly butter and flour the underside. Measure 1/3 of the batter into the center of the pan; spread thinly, almost to the pan's edges. Bake for 10 minutes or until golden brown around the edges. Carefully cut in half crosswise. Remove to a wire rack to cool. Repeat the spreading and baking procedure twice to make 6 very thin layers. Combine the sour cream and walnuts. Place a cake layer, top side up, on a cutting board. Spread thinly with 2 tablespoons of the red currant jelly, then with a generous 2 tablespoons of the sour cream mixture. Top with a second layer, spreading with 2 tablespoons of the apricot jam and 2 tablespoons of the sour cream mixture. Continue to add layers and filling, alternating currant jelly and apricot jam until you have stacked 6 layers. Do not spread jelly or sour cream mixture on the top layer. Top with a second board to weigh down the layers. Chill for 8 to 10 hours. Prepare the tinted sugars by stirring food coloring into sugar as desired. Remove the cookie layers from the refrigerator and trim off the crust edges. Spread the Vanilla Cream Frosting thinly on the top layer. Sprinkle lightly with tinted sugar. Cut crosswise into 12 strips, each about 3/4 inch wide. Cut each strip into 4 lengths to make 48 ribbons. Yield: 48 servings.

VANILLA CREAM FROSTING

3 tablespoons butter or margarine, softened	1 tablespoon cream
	Dash of salt
1 1/2 cups confectioners' sugar	1 teaspoon vanilla extract

Cream the butter in a bowl until soft. Stir in 3/4 cup of the confectioners' sugar, cream, salt and vanilla. Gradually add the remaining 3/4 cup confectioners' sugar until the mixture spreads easily.

Kathe Ingham, Laureate Epsilon Kappa
Easton, Pennsylvania

BUTTER COOKIES

1 cup butter, softened	1/2 cup confectioners' sugar
3/4 cup cornstarch	
1 cup all-purpose flour	

Preheat the oven to 320 degrees. Cream the butter in a bowl. Add the cornstarch, flour and confectioners' sugar a little at a time as you continue to cream the mixture. Roll into small balls and flatten. Bake on an ungreased cookie sheet for 12 minutes. When the cookies are cool, frost them with cream cheese frosting or any favorite frosting. Yield: 3 dozen.

Theresa Viola, Pi Iota
Prairie Village, Kansas

GRANDMA'S HONEY COOKIES

1 cup sugar	1 teaspoon salt
1 cup shortening	1 teaspoon cinnamon
1 cup honey	2 teaspoons baking soda
1 egg	½ cup water
5 cups all-purpose flour	Milk

Preheat the oven to 375 degrees. Cream the sugar and shortening in a bowl until light and fluffy. Stir in the honey. Stir in the egg. Combine the flour, salt and cinnamon in a separate bowl. Dissolve the baking soda in the water. Add the flour mixture to the sugar mixture alternately with the baking soda mixture, beating well after each addition. The dough will be stiff. Drop by teaspoonfuls onto a greased cookie sheet. Use fork tines to flatten each cookie; brush with milk. Bake for 15 minutes or until light brown. Yield: 5 dozen.

Nancy Ray
Richmond, Indiana

HIGH TEA LEMON COOKIES

The frosting recipe makes almost enough for 2 batches of cookies. The cookies freeze well and so does the frosting.

2 cups butter or margarine, softened	½ teaspoon vanilla extract
⅔ cup confectioners' sugar	2 cups all-purpose flour
1 teaspoon grated lemon zest	1½ cups cornstarch
	Lemon Frosting

Preheat the oven to 350 degrees. Beat the butter until creamy. Add the confectioners' sugar; beat until light and fluffy. Add the lemon zest and vanilla; beat well. Stir the flour and cornstarch into the butter mixture; beat well. Roll the dough into 1-inch balls and place on an ungreased cookie sheet. Bake for 15 minutes or until the bottoms of the cookies are light brown. Remove carefully from the oven and cool. Spread Lemon Frosting over the cooled cookies. Yield: 6 dozen.

LEMON FROSTING

⅓ cup butter or margarine, softened	⅓ cup fresh lemon juice
1 teaspoon grated lemon zest	4 cups confectioners' sugar

Combine the ingredients; mix well. May substitute orange zest and juice for the lemon zest and juice.

Kreta Saathoff, Xi Sigma
Ridgefield, Washington

MILKY WAY SURPRISE

2 cups all-purpose flour	¼ teaspoon salt
½ cup sugar	½ cup shortening
½ cup packed light brown sugar	2 eggs
1 teaspoon baking powder	2 tablespoons milk
	7 (2-ounce) Milky Way candy bars

Preheat the oven to 350 degrees. Combine flour, sugar, brown sugar, baking powder, salt, shortening, eggs and milk in a mixer bowl. Beat on medium speed for 2 minutes. Place the candy bars in a food processor container; process to a very fine crumble. Stir the candy bar crumbs into the batter. Line muffin tins with paper liners or spray with nonstick cooking spray. Fill the muffin cups half full. Bake for 15 to 20 minutes or until light golden. Let cool for 10 minutes before serving. Yield: 18 to 24 servings.

Daphne McClure, Preceptor Nu
Trenton, Missouri

MUD COOKIES

My daughter used to love to eat Mud Cookies when she was small. She delighted in telling her friends, "Mom lets me eat mud." For a creamy mixture and a smoother taste, mix the peanut butter and vanilla before stirring into the batter.

½ cup butter or margarine	½ cup peanut butter
2 cups sugar	3 cups quick-cooking oats
3 tablespoons cocoa	1 teaspoon vanilla extract
½ cup milk	

Heat butter, sugar, cocoa and milk in a saucepan. Bring to a boil and boil hard for 1 minute. Remove from the heat. Stir in the peanut butter, oats and vanilla. Drop by spoonfuls onto waxed paper or a cookie sheet. Let cool. Yield: 4 dozen.

Linda Ridgley-Getz
Belleville, Illinois

Lisa Carter, Gamma Gamma, Pensacola, Florida, makes Easy Oatmeal Brownies by pressing a mixture of a 12-ounce package of oatmeal cookie mix, 1 teaspoon butter, and 1 egg into a 9-by-9-inch baking pan. Bake in a preheated 350-degree oven for 10 minutes. Pour a mixture of an 8-ounce package of brownie mix, 1 egg, and 1 tablespoon water over the oatmeal crust and bake for 25 to 30 minutes. Cool and frost with canned chocolate frosting. Top with pecans or miniature peanut butter cups.

BISCOCHOS (Mexican Wedding Cookies)

Serve these cookies at a wedding reception for good luck.

6 cups all-purpose flour	1/2 teaspoon salt
2 teaspoons ground anise	2 3/4 cups sugar
2 teaspoons cinnamon	1/2 (3-pound) can shortening
1/4 teaspoon ground cloves	1 egg
1/4 teaspoon baking powder	2 tablespoons vanilla extract
	Cinnamon and sugar

Preheat the oven to 350 degrees. Combine the flour, anise, cinnamon, cloves, baking powder and salt in a bowl. Combine the sugar, shortening, egg and vanilla in a large bowl; beat with an electric mixer until creamy. Add the flour mixture gradually to the sugar mixture. Knead the dough until smooth. Let rest for 5 to 10 minutes. Roll out dough 1/4 inch thick. Cut the cookies into shapes. Bake on greased cookie sheets for 10 to 15 minutes or until lightly browned. Cool on a wire rack. Dip the cooled cookies in a mixture of 1 part cinnamon and 1 part sugar. Yield: 6 dozen.

Martha Muñoz, Zeta Iota
Santa Clara, New Mexico

LACY OATIES

These delicious cookies spread a great deal while baking, so be sure to allow plenty of room on the cookie sheets.

2 tablespoons all-purpose flour	1 egg, lightly beaten
1/4 teaspoon baking powder	1/2 cup melted margarine
1/4 teaspoon salt	1 teaspoon vanilla extract
1/2 cup sugar	1/2 cup honey-roasted nuts, chopped
1 cup rolled oats	

Preheat the oven to 325 degrees. Combine the flour, baking powder, salt, sugar and rolled oats in a large bowl. Beat together the egg, margarine and vanilla in a small bowl. Add the egg mixture to the flower mixture and stir until blended. Stir in the chopped nuts. Drop by spoonfuls onto a greased cookie sheet. Bake for 12 minutes or until the edges begin to brown. Yield: 30 servings.

Betty Kotlar, Gamma Master
Pueblo, Colorado

CHOCOLATE CHIP OATMEAL PEANUT BUTTER COOKIES

1 cup butter-flavor shortening	2 cups all-purpose flour
1 cup packed light brown sugar	1 teaspoon baking soda
1 cup sugar	1 teaspoon baking powder
2 eggs	1 teaspoon salt
1 teaspoon vanilla extract	1 cup rolled oats
1 cup crunchy peanut butter	1 (12-ounce) package semisweet chocolate chips

Preheat the oven to 350 degrees. Cream the shortening, brown sugar and sugar in a large bowl until light and fluffy. Add the eggs and vanilla; mix well. Fold in the peanut butter. Combine the flour, baking soda, baking powder, salt and oats in a separate bowl. Add the flour mixture to the sugar mixture; stir until blended. Fold in the chocolate chips. Drop by teaspoonfuls onto a cookie sheet. Bake for exactly 10 minutes. Cool completely before removing from the cookie sheet. Yield: 5 to 6 dozen.

Kelley Allison
Pinckney, Michigan

CRISP OATMEAL COOKIES

This family recipe was given to me by a college roommate about 60 years ago. For immediate baking, skip the chilling step and drop the dough by spoonfuls on the cookie sheet.

1 cup shortening	1 1/2 cups all-purpose flour
1 cup packed light brown sugar	1 teaspoon salt
1 cup sugar	1 teaspoon baking soda
2 eggs, beaten	3 cups quick-cooking oats
1 teaspoon vanilla extract	1/2 cup chopped walnuts

Cream the shortening, brown sugar, sugar, eggs and vanilla in a large bowl until light and fluffy. Sift the flour with the salt and baking soda. Add the flour mixture to the sugar mixture. Blend in oats 1 cup at a time. Fold in the walnuts. Form into long rolls and chill, covered, in the refrigerator for at least 2 hours. Preheat the oven to 350 degrees. Slice the chilled dough into 1/4-inch-thick rounds. Bake on an ungreased cookie sheet for 10 minutes. Yield: 5 to 6 dozen.

Thelma Cofer Stranahan
Missoula, Montana

OATMEAL CHOCOLATE CHIP COOKIES

2 cups butter or
margarine, softened
2 cups sugar
2 cups packed light
brown sugar
4 eggs
2 teaspoons vanilla
extract
4 cups all-purpose flour
5 cups rolled oats

1 teaspoon salt
2 teaspoons baking
powder
2 teaspoons baking soda
2 (12-ounce) packages
semisweet chocolate
chips
Nuts (optional)
Grated chocolate
(optional)

Preheat the oven to 375 degrees. Cream the butter, sugar and brown sugar in a large bowl until light and fluffy. Beat in the eggs and vanilla. Combine the flour, oats, salt, baking powder and baking soda in a separate bowl. Add the flour mixture to the butter mixture and blend thoroughly. Fold in the chocolate chips. Add nuts and grated chocolate if desired. Arrange small golf ball-size balls of dough on ungreased cookie sheets. Bake for 5 minutes. Yield: 100 cookies.

Marilynn Thivierge
Gananoque, Ontario, Canada

SALTED PEANUT COOKIES

1 cup butter or
margarine, softened
2 cups packed light
brown sugar
2 eggs
1 teaspoon vanilla
extract

2 cups all-purpose flour
1 teaspoon baking
powder
1 teaspoon baking soda
1½ cups rolled oats
1½ cups salted peanuts
1 cup flaked-corn cereal

Preheat the oven to 375 degrees. Cream the butter and brown sugar in a large bowl until light and fluffy. Blend in the eggs and vanilla. Add the flour, baking powder and baking soda; mix well. Add the oats, peanuts and cereal; mix well. Drop by teaspoons onto greased cookie sheets. Bake for 9 to 12 minutes or until the cookies begin to brown. Yield: 4 to 5 dozen.

Clara Jo Bolin, Laureate Alpha Kappa
Oregon City, Oregon

AUNT SHARON'S PECAN DROPS

½ cup butter or
margarine, softened
⅔ cup sugar
1 egg yolk
½ teaspoon vanilla
extract

⅛ teaspoon cream of
tartar
1 cup all-purpose flour
⅓ cup finely chopped
pecans
Pecan halves

Preheat the oven to 300 degrees. Cream the butter and sugar in a mixer bowl. Add the egg yolk and vanilla; beat until light and fluffy. Beat in the cream of tartar. Stir in the flour and chopped pecans. Drop by teaspoonfuls 1 inch apart onto a cookie sheet sprayed with nonstick cooking spray. Press a pecan half into the center of each. Bake for 23 to 25 minutes or until the cookies are a rich golden color. Remove to a wire rack to cool. Yield: 3 dozen.

Sharon L. Hartford, Omega
Las Cruces, New Mexico

PUMPKIN WHOOPIE PIES

2½ cups packed light
brown sugar
1 cup vegetable oil
2 eggs
1 (15-ounce) can
pumpkin
1 teaspoon vanilla
extract
3 cups all-purpose flour

1 teaspoon each
cinnamon, ginger and
cloves
1 teaspoon nutmeg
1 teaspoon salt
1 teaspoon baking
powder
1 teaspoon baking soda
Whoopie Filling

Preheat the oven to 350 degrees. Cream the brown sugar, oil and eggs in a large bowl. Add the pumpkin and vanilla; mix well. Mix dry ingredients together. Add to the sugar mixture; stir until blended. Drop by rounded teaspoonfuls 2 inches apart onto a nonstick cookie sheet. Bake for 10 minutes or just until cookies begin to brown. Remove to a wire rack to cool. Make cookie sandwiches by spreading Whoopie Filling between two cookies. Yield: 2 dozen.

WHOOPIE FILLING

2 egg whites
2 teaspoons vanilla
extract
1 (16-ounce) box
confectioners' sugar

4 tablespoons milk
4 tablespoons all-
purpose flour
1 cup shortening

Combine the egg whites, vanilla, 2 tablespoons of the confectioners' sugar, milk, flour and shortening. Add the rest of the confectioners' sugar; mix until smooth.

Waneta L. Merry, Xi Gamma Kappa
Slidell, Louisiana

Vickie J. Bender, Alpha Lambda, Carroll, Iowa, says Last Minute Cookies are incredibly easy. Mix a cake mix of any flavor with 1 egg and 8 ounces whipped topping, shape into balls, roll in confectioners' sugar, and place 2 inches apart on a greased cookie sheet. Bake in a preheated 325-degree oven for 8 minutes.

JO'S BOURBON PIE

I always grind up a large box of graham crackers and put the crumbs in a freezer bag. When I'm ready to make a crust, the crumbs are all ready too.

5 egg yolks	2 cups whipping cream,
3/4 cup sugar	whipped
1 envelope unflavored	1 baked (9-inch) graham
gelatin	cracker crust, cooled
1/4 cup cool water	1/2 ounce unsweetened
1/3 cup bourbon	chocolate

Beat the egg yolks until thickened. Add the sugar gradually to the yolks. Beat constantly until the mixture turns a very pale yellow color. Soften the gelatin in the water, then heat until the gelatin is dissolved. Cool slightly. Add the gelatin mixture to the egg yolk mixture; blend by hand, mixing well. Fold in the bourbon; fold in the whipped cream. Pour the filling into the pie shell. Shave the chocolate over the top. Refrigerate at least 12 hours. Yield: 8 servings.

Jo Ann Hansler, Laureate Beta Omega
Port Orchard, Washington

COFFEE PIE

My mother-in-law gave me this wonderful recipe. She got it from a four-star restaurant in Chicago.

2 egg, separated	1/2 (16-ounce) package
1/2 cup sugar	large marshmallows
1/4 teaspoon salt	1/2 cup water
1/2 cup finely chopped	1 pint whipping cream
nuts	1/2 teaspoon almond
2 tablespoons instant	extract
coffee granules	

Preheat the oven to 400 degrees. Beat the egg whites until very stiff, adding the sugar and salt while beating. Fold in the chopped nuts. Use a fork to press the egg white mixture against the bottom and sides of a 9-inch pie pan, forming a shell. Bake for 12 minutes. Let cool. To make the filling, combine the coffee, marshmallows and water in a saucepan. Cook over medium heat, stirring constantly for 3 to 4 minutes. Remove from heat. Beat the egg yolks slightly and stir into the coffee mixture. Return to the heat and cook for 1 to 2 minutes longer or until the mixture begins to thicken. Fold in the whipped cream and almond extract. Beat at medium speed until smooth. Pour into the pie shell. Chill, covered, in the refrigerator for at least 2 hours. Serve. Yield: 6 to 8 servings.

Robbie Murta, Laureate Kappa
Great Bend, Kansas

GERMAN CHOCOLATE PIE

This dessert tastes even better when it has been prepared a day before you serve it. Serve it with a scoop of vanilla ice cream.

4 ounces sweet baking	1 teaspoon vanilla
chocolate	extract
2 ounces butter or	1/8 teaspoon salt
margarine	2 baked (9-inch) pastry
1 1/3 cups sweetened	shells, cooled
condensed milk	1/2 cup pecans
2 eggs	1/2 cup shredded coconut
1/2 cup hot water	

Preheat the oven to 350 degrees. Melt the chocolate and butter in a heavy saucepan over low heat. Combine the condensed milk and the warm chocolate mixture in a large bowl. Add the eggs, hot water, vanilla and salt; mix well. Pour half the mixture into each pie shell. Sprinkle pecans and coconut over top of pies. Bake 35 to 40 minutes. Let cool. Chill 3 to 4 hours before serving. Refrigerate unused servings. Yield: 12 to 16 servings.

Melissa Sportsman, Gamma Phi
Brookfield, Missouri

FRUIT PIE

1 (15-ounce) can tart	1 (3-ounce) package
red cherries,	cherry gelatin mix
undrained	3 bananas, mashed
1 (8-ounce) can crushed	1 cup chopped pecans
pineapple, undrained	2 baked (9-inch) graham
1/4 cup all-purpose flour	cracker crusts
2/3 cup sugar	Whipped topping

Combine cherries, pineapple, flour and sugar in a saucepan. Cook over medium heat until thick. Add the gelatin mix; blend well. Stir in the bananas and nuts. Pour into the graham cracker crusts. Refrigerate until serving time. Top with whipped topping before serving. Yield: 12 to 16 servings.

Patricia G. Kelley, Preceptor Iota
Greenville, South Carolina

GREEN TOMATO PIE

4 cups diced peeled green	4 tablespoons
tomatoes	all-purpose flour
1 cup sugar	2 unbaked (9-inch) pie
1 teaspoon cinnamon	shells
1 teaspoon nutmeg	2 tablespoons melted
1 teaspoon vanilla	butter or margarine
extract	Melted butter for
1/4 teaspoon salt	brushing crust

Preheat the oven to 350 degrees. Combine the tomatoes, sugar, cinnamon, nutmeg, vanilla and salt in a large bowl. Stir in the flour. Pour the mixture into 1 of the pie shells. Sprinkle with the 2 tablespoons melted butter. Use the other pie shell as a top crust. Add the top crust to the pie, sealing the edges, and brush with melted butter. Slit the top crust. Bake for 1 hour or until crust turns golden. Yield: 6 servings.

Doris J. Bain, Xi Epsilon
Chattanooga, Tennessee

LEMON PIE

I have two lemon trees, and I am always on the lookout for delicious ways to use the lemons.

1 large lemon	1 tablespoon butter or
3 eggs, separated	margarine
1 cup sugar	1 (8-inch) pie shell

Preheat the oven to 325 degrees. Grate the lemon to get 1 to 1½ teaspoons lemon peel, yellow part only. Juice the lemon. Set the lemon peel and juice aside. Beat the egg whites in a small bowl until foamy. Add 1 teaspoon of the sugar and beat until stiff and glossy. Combine the egg yolks, butter, lemon juice, lemon peel and the rest of the sugar in a large bowl. Gently fold in the egg whites. Pour into an unbaked pie shell. Bake for 45 minutes. Yield: 6 to 8 servings.

Caroline Driessen, Preceptor Omicron Alpha
Dana Point, California

SOUR CREAM LEMON PIE

1 cup sugar	3 egg yolks, slightly
3 tablespoons	beaten
cornstarch	1 cup cultured sour
¼ cup butter or	cream
margarine	1 baked (8- or 9-inch)
1 tablespoon grated	graham cracker crust
lemon rind	1 cup heavy cream,
¼ cup fresh lemon juice	whipped, or whipped
1 cup milk	topping

Combine the sugar and cornstarch in a 1½-quart saucepan. Add the butter, lemon rind, lemon juice, milk and egg yolks; stir over medium heat until the mixture boils. Boil, stirring, until very thick. Remove from the heat and fold in the sour cream. Pour into the graham cracker crust. Refrigerate at least several hours until thoroughly chilled. Top with whipped cream or whipped topping. Yield: 8 servings.

Susan K. Green
Derby, Kansas

LEMON SPONGE PIE

This pie with its sweet-tart taste is especially good after a meal such as lasagna or spaghetti.

1 cup sugar	Juice of 1 lemon
Dash of salt	1 tablespoon melted
1 tablespoon plus	butter or margarine
1 teaspoon	1 cup hot milk
all-purpose flour	1 unbaked (9-inch) pie
3 eggs, separated	shell
Grated peel of 1 lemon	

Preheat the oven to 325 degrees. Combine the sugar, salt and flour in a large bowl. Add 2 of the egg yolks; beat until light. Add the lemon peel and lemon juice. Stir in the melted butter. Stir in the hot milk. Beat the 3 egg whites until soft peaks form; fold into the lemon mixture. The whites will float to the top, and the mixture will look curdled—that's OK. Pour the mixture into the pie shell. Bake for 1 hour until top is brown. Yield: 6 to 8 servings.

Joan M. Pompei, Laureate Beta
East Petersburg, Pennsylvania

PINEAPPLE CHESS PIE

An excellent and unusual pie . . .

4 tablespoons all-	1 (20-ounce) can crushed
purpose flour	pineapple, drained
3 cups sugar	1 (7-ounce) bag shredded
3 eggs, beaten	coconut
½ cup margarine,	2 unbaked (9-inch) pie
softened	shells

Preheat the oven to 300 degrees. Combine the flour and sugar in a large bowl. Beat in the eggs and margarine. Stir in the pineapple and coconut. Pour the mixture into the pie shells. Bake for 1¼ hours. Pies can be frozen. Yield: 12 to 16 servings.

Terry Bohn, Gamma Omicron
Liberal, Kansas

Lillie Dittfurth, Athens, Texas, makes Apple Blossom Pie by partially baking a pie shell in a preheated 375-degree oven for 5 minutes, then spreading a can of apple pie filling in the pie shell and sprinkling with a small package of mixed fruit-flavored gelatin. The topping is made of ⅓ cup flour, ¼ cup sugar, and ¼ teaspoon salt mixed with ¼ cup margarine until crumbly and sprinkled over the top. Bake for 25 to 30 minutes or until filling is bubbly and topping is brown. Serve warm or chilled.

SNICKERS PIE

1 unbaked (9-inch) pie shell	2 eggs
5 (2-ounce) Snickers candy bars	1/3 cup sour cream
1/2 cup sugar	1/3 cup creamy peanut butter
4 (3-ounce) packages cream cheese, softened	3 tablespoons heavy cream
	2/3 cup chocolate chips

Preheat the oven to 450 degrees. Bake the pie shell for 5 to 7 minutes or until it is a very light golden brown. Let cool. Reduce the oven temperature to 325 degrees. Cut the candy bars in half lengthwise; cut the halves into 1/4-inch pieces. Place the candy bar pieces over the bottom of the partially baked shell. Combine the sugar and cream cheese in a small bowl; beat until smooth. Beat in the eggs 1 at a time. Add the sour cream and peanut butter, beating until the mixture is smooth. Pour the mixture over the candy bar pieces. Bake for 30 to 40 minutes or until the center is set. Cool completely. Heat the heavy cream in a saucepan until very warm. Remove from heat and add the chocolate chips, stirring until the chips melt and the mixture is smooth. Spread over the top of the cooled pie. Chill, covered, in the refrigerator for 2 to 3 hours before serving. Yield: 7 servings.

Jessica Christensen
Eagle Grove, Iowa

DIET DOUBLE LAYER PUMPKIN PIE

This low-fat, low-sugar pie is very good—you will not think it is a diet pie! It is great for summer. For diabetics, a serving is equal to 2 starch exchanges.

4 ounces low-fat cream cheese	1 (16-ounce) can pumpkin
1 cup plus 1 tablespoon 2% milk	1 small package sugar-free instant vanilla pudding and pie filling mix, dry
1 tablespoon sugar substitute	1 teaspoon cinnamon
8 ounces whipped topping	1/2 teaspoon ground ginger
1 baked (9-inch) graham cracker crust	1/4 teaspoon ground cloves
1 cup cold 2% milk	

Combine the cream cheese, 1 tablespoon of the milk and the sugar substitute in a large bowl, beating with a wire whisk until smooth. Gently stir in 1 1/2 cups of the whipped topping. Spread the mixture over the bottom of the crust. Pour 1 cup milk into a large bowl. Add the pumpkin, pudding and pie mix, cinnamon, ginger and cloves; beat with a wire whisk until well mixed (the mixture will be thick). Spread

over the cream cheese layer. Chill, covered, in the refrigerator for 4 hours. Top with the remaining whipped topping before serving. Yield: 8 servings.

Wanda Kirk, Xi Delta Kappa
Scott City, Kansas

ORANGE CREAM PIE

1 cup sugar	1 tablespoon butter or margarine
1/2 cup all-purpose flour	3 eggs, separated
1/4 teaspoon salt	3 tablespoons sugar
Grated rind of 1 orange	1 baked (9-inch) pie shell
1 1/2 cups orange juice	
1 tablespoon lemon juice	

Preheat the oven to 350 degrees. Combine the sugar, flour, salt, orange rind, orange juice and lemon juice in a double boiler over boiling water. Cook for 10 minutes or until thickened, stirring constantly. Beat the egg yolks slightly and add with the butter to the juice mixture. Cook for 2 minutes. Let cool. Pour into the pie shell. Beat the egg whites with the 3 tablespoons sugar until stiff peaks form. Spread over the pie. Bake for 12 to 15 minutes or until lightly browned. Yield: 6 to 8 servings.

Sonya Leavitt, Mu Omega
Mercedes, Texas

SWEET POTATO PIE

I refused to eat sweet potatoes as a child, yet I loved pumpkin pie. When Mom baked this pie, I believed it was pumpkin, and I loved it! You can use canned sweet potatoes and a prepackaged pie shell if you like.

1 cup sugar	1 cup mashed sweet potatoes
2 teaspoons cornstarch	1/2 cup chopped pecans
1/2 teaspoon salt	3 eggs, slightly beaten
1/4 teaspoon nutmeg	1 unbaked (9-inch) pie shell
1/8 teaspoon cloves	
3/4 cup dark corn syrup	
3 tablespoons margarine	

Preheat the oven to 400 degrees. Combine the sugar, cornstarch, salt, nutmeg, cloves, corn syrup, margarine, sweet potatoes and pecans in a medium saucepan. Cook over low heat for 3 to 5 minutes or until thickened, stirring constantly. Remove from heat. Add the eggs; mix well. Spoon the mixture into the pie shell. Bake for 15 minutes. Reduce the oven heat to 350 degrees and bake for 1 hour. Yield: 6 to 8 servings.

Ginny M. Tawzer, Laureate Mu
Lexington, South Carolina

PECAN CHESS PIE

1/2 cup melted margarine	1 tablespoon vinegar
1 1/4 cups sugar	3 eggs
1 tablespoon cornmeal	1 unbaked (9-inch) pie
1 teaspoon vanilla	shell
extract	Pecan halves

Preheat the oven to 350 degrees. Combine the margarine, sugar and cornmeal in a large bowl, stirring well. Stir in the vanilla and vinegar. Add the eggs; mix well. Pour the filling into the pie shell. Add pecan halves to cover the pie top. Bake for 45 to 50 minutes. Yield: 6 to 8 servings.

Wendy Bahr, Iota Eta
Columbia, Missouri

OATMEAL MOCK PECAN PIE

This economical pie tastes like pecan pie!

1 cup milk	1 1/2 cups rolled oats
1 1/2 cups dark corn syrup	1 tablespoon vanilla
1/2 teaspoon salt	extract
4 eggs	1/2 cup butter or
1 (7-ounce) package	margarine, softened
shredded coconut	2 unbaked (9-inch) pie
2 cups sugar	shells

Preheat the oven to 350 degrees. Combine the milk, corn syrup, salt, eggs, coconut, sugar, oats, vanilla and margarine in a large bowl; mix well. Pour the mixture into the pie shells. Bake for 1 hour. Yield: 12 to 16 servings.

Wanda J. Wright, Pi Xi
Overland Park, Kansas

MOCK PECAN PIE

My son-in-law requested this pie for his birthday cake! It calls for 14 crackers, no more, no less. To crush the crackers, place them between 2 pieces of waxed paper and roll with a rolling pin.

14 butter crackers,	1/2 teaspoon baking
crushed fine	powder
1 cup sugar	3/4 cup chopped walnuts
3 egg whites, beaten stiff	1 cup whipped topping

Preheat the oven to 350 degrees. Combine the crackers, sugar, egg whites, baking powder and walnuts in a medium bowl; mix well. Pour into a greased 8- or 9-inch pie plate. Bake for 35 minutes. Let cool. Spread the whipped topping over the cooled pie. Yield: 6 to 8 servings.

Doris M. Pelrine, Laureate Delta
Andover, Massachusetts

PINEAPPLE COCONUT PIES

4 eggs, separated	1 (16-ounce) can crushed
3/4 cup evaporated milk	pineapple, drained
1/2 cup melted margarine	2 unbaked (9-inch) pie
2 1/2 cups sugar	shells
1/3 cup all-purpose flour	Shredded coconut

Preheat the oven to 325 degrees. Beat the egg whites until stiff and set aside. Combine the egg yolks, evaporated milk, margarine, sugar, flour and pineapple in a large bowl; mix well. Fold in the beaten egg whites. Pour into pie shells. Sprinkle with coconut. Bake for 35 to 45 minutes or until set. Yield: 12 to 16 servings.

Marla Weber, Preceptor Nu
Hobbs, New Mexico

TAFFY APPLE PIZZA

1 (18-ounce) package	1/2 cup water
refrigerated sugar	2 to 3 teaspoons lemon
cookie dough	juice
2 tablespoons creamy	3 medium Granny
peanut butter	Smith apples
1 (8-ounce) package	Ground cinnamon
cream cheese, softened	(optional)
1/2 cup packed light	2 tablespoons caramel
brown sugar	ice cream topping
1 teaspoon vanilla	
extract	

Preheat the oven to 350 degrees. Reserve 4 ounces of the cookie dough for another use. Roll remaining dough 1/4 inch thick on waxed paper; place in a 9-by-13-inch cake pan. Bake for 11 to 14 minutes or until lightly browned. Cool completely. Mix the peanut butter, cream cheese, brown sugar and vanilla until smooth. Spread on the cooled cookie. Peel, core and slice the apples; dip into a mixture of water and lemon juice to prevent browning. Arrange the apple slices on the cream cheese mixture. Sprinkle with cinnamon; drizzle with caramel topping. Yield: 16 servings.

Renee Rupp, Omicron Sigma
Rolfe, Iowa

Judy Hanners, Delta Alpha Omicron, Bonne Terre, Missouri, makes Frozen Lemonade Pie by beating a 6-ounce can of partially thawed frozen lemonade concentrate with 2 cups softened vanilla ice cream and folding in 8 ounces whipped topping. Spread in a graham cracker pie shell and freeze for several hours. Top with favorite fruit or fruit sauce.

SWEET APPLE CRISP

6 large Granny Smith
  apples, peeled, sliced
1/2 cup orange juice
1/2 teaspoon ground
  cinnamon

1 cup sugar
3/4 cup all-purpose flour
6 tablespoons butter or
  margarine

Preheat the oven to 350 degrees. Arrange apple slices in a greased 8-by-8-inch baking dish. Pour the orange juice over apple slices. Combine the cinnamon with 1/2 cup of the sugar; sprinkle over the apple slices. Combine the flour and the remaining sugar in a medium bowl. Cut the butter into flour mixture until crumbly. Spoon the mixture over apple slices. Bake for 1 hour or until golden brown. Yield: 6 servings.

Sandra Gellner
Lubbock, Texas

SUGARLESS APPLE CRUNCH

3 tablespoons
  cornstarch
Artificial sweetener
  equal to 1 cup sugar
3/4 teaspoon cinnamon

1/2 teaspoon nutmeg
1/4 teaspoon salt
8 cups sliced apples
Sugarless Topping for
  Apple Crunch

Mix the cornstarch, artificial sweetener, cinnamon, nutmeg, salt and sliced apples in a bowl. Pour the mixture into a greased 8-by-8-inch baking pan. Sprinkle Sugarless Topping over the apples. Bake for 1 hour or until lightly browned. Yield: 8 servings.

SUGARLESS TOPPING FOR APPLE CRUNCH

1/2 cup all-purpose flour
1/2 cup rolled oats
1/2 cup butter or
  margarine

Artificial sweetener
  equal to 1/2 cup sugar

Mix the flour, oats, butter and artificial sweetener in a bowl until crumbly.

Sabina Beckett, Laureate Alpha Kappa
Milwaukie, Oregon

Neva Sheeley, Epsilon Master, Vancouver, Washington, makes Cranberry Cream Cheese Pie. Mix 1 1/2 cups vanilla wafer crumbs with 6 tablespoons melted butter and press into a pie plate. Process a can of sweetened condensed milk, 8 ounces cream cheese, a 16-ounce can of whole cranberry sauce, 1/3 cup lemon juice, and 1/2 teaspoon vanilla in a blender. Pour into the crumb pie shell and freeze, covered with plastic wrap and foil, overnight.

APPLE DUMPLINGS

I sometimes bake these in individual foil tart pans to share with neighbors.

2 cups sugar
2 cups water
1/4 teaspoon cinnamon
1/4 teaspoon nutmeg
1/4 cup margarine
8 Granny Smith apples
2 cups all-purpose flour
1/2 teaspoon salt

1 teaspoon baking
  powder
3/4 cup shortening
1/2 cup milk
8 teaspoons sugar
Cinnamon
8 pats of margarine

Preheat the oven to 350 degrees. Combine the sugar, water, cinnamon and nutmeg. Cook over medium heat for 5 minutes. Stir in the margarine; set aside. Peel and core the apples, leaving the apples whole. Sift the flour, salt and baking powder together; cut in the shortening until the texture of coarse meal. Add the milk all at once; stir just until the flour is moistened. Divide the dough into 8 balls. Roll each ball flat, large enough to encase an apple. Before wrapping the dough around an apple, put 1 teaspoon sugar, a sprinkle of cinnamon and a pat of margarine in the center of the apple. Place the apple in the center of the rolled piece of dough and bring the dough to the top of the apple, pinching edges together. Arrange the wrapped apples in a 9-by-13-inch baking dish. Pour the sugar sauce over the apples. Bake for 1 hour or until golden brown. Yield: 8 servings.

Frances S. Wright, Laureate Tau
Tarboro, North Carolina

APPLE DUMPLING DESSERT

4 cups all-purpose
  flour
2 teaspoons salt
1 1/3 cups shortening
8 to 9 tablespoons cold
  water
8 cups chopped peeled
  tart apples
3/4 teaspoon ground
  cinnamon

1/4 cup sugar
2 cups water
1 cup packed light
  brown sugar
Whipped topping or
  vanilla ice cream
  (optional)
Mint leaves (optional)

Preheat the oven to 400 degrees. Combine the flour and salt in a large bowl; cut in the shortening until the mixture resembles coarse crumbs. Sprinkle with water, 1 tablespoon at a time, and toss with a fork until the dough can be formed into a ball. Divide the dough into 4 parts. Roll one part on a lightly floured surface to fit the bottom of an ungreased 9-by-13-inch baking dish. Place the dough in the dish; top with a third of the apples. Combine the cinnamon and sugar. Sprinkle a third of the cinnamon sugar over the apples. Repeat the layers of pastry, apples, and cinnamon sugar twice. Roll out the remaining dough to fit the dish; place on top. Cut 2-inch slits through the top 3 layers using a sharp knife. Bring the 2 cups water and brown sugar to a boil. Cook and stir until the sugar is dissolved. Pour the syrup over the top crust. Bake for 35 to 40 minutes or until browned and bubbly. Serve warm with whipped topping or ice cream. Garnish with mint leaves if desired. Yield: 12 servings.

Sandi Keim, Alpha Mu Master
Wooster, Ohio

MEXICAN APPLE PIES

1½ cups sugar	2 teaspoons ground
2 cups water	cinnamon
½ cup butter or	10 (6-inch) flour
margarine, melted	tortillas
4 cups diced peeled	Whipped cream
Delicious apples	Cinnamon to sprinkle
½ teaspoon allspice	

Preheat the oven to 350 degrees. Combine the sugar and water in a small saucepan. Cook over medium heat until the sugar melts. Pour the melted butter into a 9-by-13-inch baking pan. Combine the apples, allspice and cinnamon; stir until the apples are coated. Spread ½ cup of the apple mixture down the center of each tortilla. Roll up each tortilla and place seam side down in the baking pan. Pour the sugar mixture over the top of the tortillas. Cover with foil. Bake for 30 minutes. Uncover and bake for 25 to 30 minutes longer. Serve warm with whipped cream sprinkled lightly with cinnamon. Yield: 10 servings.

Debbie Guynn, Xi Delta Rho
Miami, Florida

NORWEGIAN APPLE PIE

1½ cups sugar	½ teaspoon salt
2 eggs	1 cup chopped walnuts
2 teaspoons vanilla	3 cups diced peeled
extract	apples
1 cup all-purpose flour	Vanilla ice cream
2 teaspoons baking	Hot Cinnamon Sauce
powder	

Preheat the oven to 350 degrees. Beat the sugar and eggs in a large bowl until light and fluffy. Stir in the vanilla. Stir in the flour, baking powder and salt. Fold in the walnuts and apples. Pour into a greased and floured 9-by-13-inch baking dish. Bake for 35 minutes. Cut into squares. Top with vanilla ice cream. and Hot Cinnamon Sauce. Yield: 12 servings.

HOT CINNAMON SAUCE

2 tablespoons	2 cups boiling water
cornstarch	4 tablespoons butter or
1 cup sugar	margarine
2 teaspoons cinnamon	Dash of nutmeg

Combine the cornstarch, sugar, cinnamon, boiling water, butter and nutmeg in a saucepan over medium heat; stir until thickened.

Trudy Smith, Laureate Pi
Tacoma, Washington

APPLE SOUFFLE

2 cups chopped peeled	Pinch of salt
cored apples	2 tablespoons
1 teaspoon lemon juice	cornstarch
¼ cup plus 3	2 teaspoons brandy
tablespoons sugar	extract (optional)
6 egg whites	¼ teaspoon nutmeg or
¼ teaspoon cream of	cardamom
tartar	½ teaspoon cinnamon

Preheat the oven to 425 degrees. Toss the apples with the lemon juice and ¼ cup sugar in a saucepan. Simmer for 15 minutes or until tender. Pour the warm apples into a blender and purée. Cool completely. Beat the egg whites with the cream of tartar and salt until stiff, but not dry peaks form; blend in the cornstarch. Add the brandy extract, nutmeg and cinnamon to the apple purée; gently fold in the egg whites. Pour the apple mixture into a 2-quart soufflé dish sprayed with nonstick cooking spray. Place the dish in a pan of hot water in the oven. Bake for 10 minutes. Reduce the oven temperature to 375 degrees. Bake for 20 minutes longer. Sprinkle 3 tablespoons sugar over the top. Serve immediately. Yield: 8 servings.

Helen Robbins, Xi Phi Sigma
Coleville, California

Debbie Talkington, Delta Pi, Scipio, Indiana, makes Brownie Chocolate Cheesecake by preparing a 20-ounce package of brownie mix by package directions for chewy brownies, spreading in a greased 9- or 10-inch springform pan and baking in a preheated 350-degree oven for 30 minutes. Beat 24 ounces cream cheese while adding a can of sweetened condensed milk, 3 eggs, and 2 teaspoons vanilla and stir in ½ cup miniature semisweet chocolate chips. Pour over brownie layer and bake at 300 degrees for 50 to 60 minutes. Cool, then chill, remove side of pan, and garnish as desired.

❖ CHOCOLATE-GLAZED TRIPLE LAYER CHEESECAKE

This is my family's "special" cheesecake that I shared with my sisters at our annual Christmas cookie and secret sister ornament exchange a couple of years ago. Following this recipe's baking instructions exactly will eliminate the crack that usually occurs in cheesecake tops.

1 (8½-ounce) package chocolate wafer cookies, crushed	2 ounces semisweet chocolate, melted
¼ cup plus 1 tablespoon melted butter or margarine	1⅓ cups sour cream
	⅓ cup packed dark brown sugar
¾ cup sugar	1 tablespoon all-purpose flour
2 (8-ounce) packages cream cheese, softened	¼ cup chopped pecans
	5 ounces cream cheese, softened
3 eggs	¼ teaspoon almond extract
1 teaspoon vanilla extract	Chocolate Glaze

Preheat the oven to 325 degrees. Mix the cookie crumbs, butter and ¼ cup of the sugar. Press into the bottom and 2 inches up the side of a 9-inch springform pan. Combine half the cream cheese with ¼ cup of the sugar; beat until light and fluffy. Add 1 of the eggs and ¼ teaspoon of the vanilla; blend well. Stir in the chocolate and ⅓ cup of the sour cream. Spoon the mixture into the crust. Combine the brown sugar, flour and the remaining 8 ounces cream cheese; beat until fluffy. Add another egg and ½ teaspoon of the vanilla; blend well. Stir in the pecans. Spoon into the prepared springform pan. Combine the 5 ounces cream cheese and the remaining ¼ cup sugar; beat until fluffy. Add the remaining egg and blend well. Stir in the remaining sour cream, almond extract and remaining vanilla. Spoon the mixture gently over the pecan layer. Bake for 1 hour. Turn off the oven and leave the cheesecake in the oven for 30 minutes. Partially open the oven door, leaving the cheesecake in the oven for 30 minutes. Remove to a wire rack to cool. Chill, covered, in the refrigerator for 8 hours. Remove from the pan. Spread warm Chocolate Glaze over the top, allowing the glaze to spill slightly over the edges. Yield: 12 servings.

CHOCOLATE GLAZE

6 ounces semisweet chocolate	¾ cup confectioners' sugar
¼ cup butter or margarine	1 teaspoon vanilla extract
2 tablespoons water	

Combine the chocolate and butter in a small saucepan over low heat. Heat until melted. Remove from heat. Stir in the water, confectioners' sugar and vanilla; stir until smooth.

Laura Amundson, Xi Alpha Delta
Verona, Wisconsin

SENSUAL WHITE CHOCOLATE CHEESECAKE

2 (8-ounce) packages cream cheese, room temperature	1 ready-to-use (9-inch) chocolate cookie crumb pie crust
1 cup sugar	½ cup miniature semisweet chocolate chips
2 eggs	
2 tablespoons milk	
1 (12-ounce) package white chocolate squares, melted	1 pint red raspberries or blueberries
	1 cup cherry juice

Preheat the oven to 350 degrees. Mix the cream cheese, ½ cup of the sugar, eggs, milk and white chocolate in a large bowl; beat until fluffy and light. Spread the miniature chocolate chips over the crumb crust. Pour the creamed mixture over the chocolate chips. Bake for 10 minutes. Turn the oven temperature down to 250 degrees and bake for 50 minutes longer. Allow to cool slowly. Arrange the raspberries around the perimeter and in the center of the pie to make an artful design. To make a shiny glaze, boil the cherry juice and the remaining ½ cup sugar for 1 minute. Let cool. Brush the berries lightly with the glaze. Yield: 8 servings.

Laura J. Hannan
Hays, Kansas

COCONUT MACAROON CHEESECAKE

1 cup flaked coconut, toasted	¼ teaspoon almond extract
½ cup ground pecans	3 eggs
2 tablespoons butter or margarine, melted	1 egg white
	½ teaspoon vanilla extract
3 (8-ounce) packages cream cheese, softened	⅓ cup sugar
	⅔ cup flaked coconut, toasted
½ cup sugar	Strawberries
½ teaspoon vanilla extract	

Preheat the oven to 350 degrees. Combine 1 cup of the toasted coconut, pecans and melted butter in a small bowl. Press the mixture into the bottom of a 9-inch springform pan. Set aside. Beat the cream cheese on low speed in a mixer bowl. Continue to beat while gradually adding ½ cup sugar, ½ teaspoon vanilla and the almond extract; beat until light and fluffy. Add the 3 whole eggs; beat on low speed until combined. Pour the mixture into the pan. Bake for 35 minutes. Beat the egg white and 1/2 teaspoon vanilla in a small bowl until soft peaks form. Gradually beat in 1/3 cup sugar until stiff. Fold in 2/3 cup toasted coconut. Carefully spread the topping over the cheesecake. Bake for 20 minutes. Cool on a wire rack for 15 minutes. Loosen the sides. Cool completely. Chill, covered, in the refrigerator for 4 hours. Garnish with strawberries and more coconut just before serving. Yield: 12 to 16 servings.

Ella Leinwebber, Alpha Delta Master
Spokane, Washington

LEMON CHEESECAKE

The first time my grandmother made this cheesecake, my grandfather liked it so much after tasting it that he insisted they eat it before the meal. To this day our family eats this dessert before the meal!

1 1/2 cups graham cracker crumbs	2 cups milk
3 tablespoons sugar	1 (4-ounce) package lemon instant pudding mix
1/3 cup melted butter or margarine	
1 (8-ounce) package cream cheese, softened	

Preheat the oven to 350 degrees. Combine the graham cracker crumbs and sugar in a bowl. Add the melted butter; mix thoroughly. Reserve 1/4 cup of the graham cracker mixture. Press the rest of the mixture firmly and evenly against the bottom and sides of a 9-inch pie pan. Bake for 10 minutes. Cool before filling. Beat the cream cheese until soft. Blend in 1/2 cup of the milk. Add the remaining 1 1/2 cups milk and the lemon pudding mix. Beat for 1 minute or until blended. Pour the filling into the crumb crust. Chill for 2 hours. Sprinkle reserved graham cracker crumbs over the cheesecake. Yield: 6 servings.

Mary Bushnell
Russell, Kansas

Peggy Patterson, Nu Eta, Owasso, Oklahoma, makes Cranberry Cheesecake Shakes by processing 1 egg or the equivalent egg substitute for 15 to 30 seconds in a blender, adding 3 ounces cream cheese, 1/2 cup milk, 2 cups vanilla ice cream, an 8-ounce can jellied cranberry sauce, and 1 cup cranberries and processing until smooth. Pour into frosty glasses and serve immediately.

MEXICAN CHEESECAKE

2 (8-ounce) packages cream cheese, softened	1 egg
1 (20-ounce) can crushed pineapple, drained well	1 tablespoon water
1/4 cup sugar	12 to 15 (10- or 12-inch) flour tortillas
	Oil for deep frying
	Cinnamon sugar (optional)

Beat the cream cheese, pineapple and sugar in a mixer bowl until light and fluffy. Whip the egg and water together to make an egg wash. Place a tablespoon or more of the pineapple mixture down the center of each tortilla. Brush the egg wash around the edges of the tortilla. Fold each tortilla and secure with a toothpick. Deep fry until golden brown. Roll in cinnamon sugar while still hot if desired. Remove the toothpicks and serve. Yield: 12 to 15 servings.

Irene Hitzeman, Laureate Beta Epsilon
Lisle, Illinois

PEACHES AND CREAM CHEESECAKE

3/4 cup all-purpose flour	1 (15- to 20-ounce) can sliced peaches
1 teaspoon baking powder	1 (8-ounce) package low-fat cream cheese, softened
1/2 teaspoon salt	1/2 cup sugar
1 (3-ounce) package vanilla pudding mix (not instant)	3 tablespoons peach syrup
3 tablespoons butter, softened	1 tablespoon sugar
1/2 cup milk	1/2 teaspoon cinnamon
1 egg	

Preheat the oven to 350 degrees. Combine the flour, baking powder, salt, pudding mix, butter, milk and egg in a large bowl. Blend at low speed until moist. Beat for 2 minutes at medium speed. Pour the mixture into a greased 9-inch deep-dish pie pan. Drain the peaches, reserving 3 tablespoons of the syrup. Arrange the peach slices over the batter. Combine the cream cheese, sugar and reserved peach syrup in a small bowl; beat for 2 minutes at medium speed. Spoon the mixture over the peaches, spreading to 1 inch from outer edge of crust. Combine the sugar and cinnamon; sprinkle over the filling. Bake for 30 to 35 minutes or until the top is golden brown. Store, covered, in the refrigerator. Yield: 6 servings.

Linda C. Johnson
Ames, Iowa

❖ WHITE CHOCOLATE MOUSSE WITH RED RASPBERRY COULIS

4 (10-ounce) packages
    frozen raspberries,
    thawed, undrained
Juice of 1 lemon
1/2 cup sugar
4 tablespoons
    cornstarch
1 1/2 cups cold water
2 tablespoons Grand
    Marnier or other
    liqueur (optional)

2 teaspoons unflavored
    gelatin
1/2 cup milk
10 ounces white
    chocolate, broken
3 cups heavy whipping
    cream
Berries for garnish,
    partially frozen or
    fresh

Combine the raspberries and lemon juice in a food processor container; process until smooth. Press the mixture with the back of a spoon through a strainer into a medium bowl. Add the sugar, cornstarch, 1 cup of the cold water and liqueur; blend well. Pour into a saucepan over medium heat; bring to a boil, stirring often. Boil for 1 minute, continuing to stir. Remove from heat and let cool until ready to use. Sprinkle the gelatin over the remaining 1/2 cup cold water in a glass measuring cup; the mixture will soften in a minute or so. Microwave on High for 20 to 40 seconds; let stand for 2 minutes or until the gelatin granules are dissolved. Pour the milk into a small saucepan over medium heat and bring to the simmering point. Remove from heat; add the white chocolate, stirring until smooth. Stir the gelatin into the white chocolate mixture. Chill, covered, in the refrigerator about 10 minutes or until slightly thickened. Whip the cream until stiff peaks form. Fold the white chocolate mixture into the whipped cream. Alternate layers of raspberry sauce and mousse in tall parfait glasses. Chill, covered, in the refrigerator for 2 hours. Garnish with berries. Yield: 8 servings.

Polly A. Patton, Xi Epsilon Beta
Woodstock, Virginia

CHERRY THING

You may substitute any other type of fruit pie filling for the cherry filling if you like.

1 1/2 cups all-purpose
    flour
2 tablespoons sugar
1 cup margarine, melted
3/4 cup chopped pecans
1/2 cup milk
2 cups confectioners'
    sugar

1 (8-ounce) container
    whipped topping
1 (8-ounce) package
    cream cheese,
    softened
1 (21-ounce) can cherry
    pie filling

Preheat the oven to 375 degrees. Stir together the flour, sugar, melted margarine and pecans. Press the mixture over the bottom of a 9-by-13-inch baking pan. Bake for 20 minutes or until slightly brown. Cool completely. Combine the milk, confectioners' sugar, whipped topping and cream cheese; pour over the baked crust. Spread cherry pie filling over the cream cheese layer. Chill, covered, in the refrigerator until ready to serve. Yield: 15 servings.

Marlene Willis
Rusk, Texas

FABULOUS CREAM PUFFS

1 cup water
1/2 cup butter (not
    margarine)
1 cup all-purpose flour
1/4 teaspoon salt
4 eggs
1/2 cup sugar
1/3 cup flour

1/4 teaspoon salt
3 egg yolks, beaten
3 cups 2% milk
3/4 teaspoon vanilla
    extract
3/4 teaspoon almond
    extract
Chocolate Topping

Preheat the oven to 400 degrees. Bring the water and 1/2 cup butter to a rolling boil. Remove from heat; add 1 cup flour and 1/4 teaspoon salt. Stir vigorously to form a ball. Add the eggs 1 at a time, beating well after each addition. Form the dough into round puffs the size of golf balls. Bake for 35 to 40 minutes or until the puffs are firm to the touch. To make the filling, combine the sugar, 1/3 cup flour and 1/4 teaspoon salt in a medium saucepan. Combine the beaten egg yolks and the 3 cups milk in a bowl; stir well. Stir a small amount of the milk mixture into the flour mixture to make a paste. Place the saucepan over medium heat. Add the remaining milk, stirring constantly, being careful not to scorch the mixture. Bring to a boil; boil for 1 minute. Stir in the vanilla and almond extract. Remove from heat. Cover with plastic wrap and let cool. When ready to serve, slice off the top 1/3 of each puff. Remove the inside dough from each puff, leaving the shell intact. Fill the puff with a large spoonful of the filling, then replace the top of the puff. Spoon Chocolate Topping over the cream puffs. Serve immediately. Yield: 12 servings.

CHOCOLATE TOPPING

2 tablespoons melted
    butter or margarine
1/4 cup cocoa
1/8 teaspoon salt
1/4 cup milk

1/2 teaspoon vanilla
    extract
1 1/2 cups confectioners'
    sugar

Combine the melted butter, cocoa and salt in a medium bowl. Add the milk and vanilla. Stir in the confectioners' sugar ½ cup at a time. Mix until smooth and creamy.

Laura Wallace, Nu Alpha
Rock Valley, Iowa

JUMBO CREAM PUFF

1 cup water
½ cup margarine
1 cup all-purpose flour
4 eggs
1 (8-ounce) package
   cream cheese, softened
2½ cups milk
2 (4-ounce) packages
   vanilla instant
   pudding and pie
   filling

1 (8-ounce) container
   whipped topping
Chocolate ice cream
   topping that hardens
   to a shell

Preheat the oven to 400 degrees. Bring the water and margarine to a boil in a medium saucepan. Lower the heat. Stir in the flour. Add the eggs 1 at a time, beating thoroughly after each addition and allowing the mixture to heat through. Spread the dough in a 9-by-13-inch baking pan. Bake for 25 minutes. Let cool. Do not be concerned about the "hills and valleys" in the baked dough. Beat together the cream cheese and ½ cup of the milk. Stir in the remaining milk and the dry pudding mix, beating until thickened. Spread over the dough. Spread whipped topping over the cream cheese layer and drizzle with ice cream topping. Yield: 8 to 12 servings.

Carol Dathe, Chi Kappa
Cape Canaveral, Florida

DUTCH FRITTERS (Ollie Bollen)

1 cup currants
7 cups all-purpose flour
2 cups sugar
1 tablespoon salt
9 teaspoons baking
   powder
3 eggs, beaten

3 cups milk
¼ cup vegetable oil
1½ cups chopped peeled
   apples
Vegetable oil for frying
Sugar for rolling fritters

Place the currants with enough water to cover in a saucepan. Bring to a simmer over medium heat; simmer for 10 minutes or until currants are plump. Drain and set aside. Combine the flour, sugar, salt and baking powder in a large bowl. Stir in the eggs, milk and ¼ cup oil. Stir in the apples and currants. Drop by spoonfuls into the oil in a deep fryer; fry until golden brown. They will turn themselves when done on 1 side. Place on paper towels to drain. Roll in sugar. Yield: 30 servings.

Delinda Tjoelker, Epsilon Rho
La Crescenta, California

ALMOST SUGARLESS BANANA ICE CREAM

7 eggs
52 packets artificial
   sweetener
2 pints whipping cream
6 bananas, mashed

1 teaspoon vanilla
   extract
About ½ gallon lowfat
   milk

Break the eggs into a large bowl and beat well with an electric mixer. Add the artificial sweetener, whipping cream, bananas and vanilla, in that order, stirring after each addition. Pour the mixture into an electric ice cream freezer. Add the milk to the fill line. Add ice and salt to the freezer tub and allow the freezer to run until it turns itself off.
Yield: 1 gallon ice cream.

Cheryl A. Baxley, Zeta Theta
Hobbs, New Mexico

HEAVENLY CHOCOLATE ICE CREAM

Betty Wish, our Beta sister who passed away in 1995, used to bring a freezer of this delicious chocolate ice cream to our ice cream parties.

10 (2-ounce) Milky Way
   bars or 2 (10-ounce)
   bars
1 (14-ounce) can
   sweetened condensed
   milk

About 3 quarts whole
   milk
1 (5-ounce) can
   chocolate syrup

Combine the candy and condensed milk in a large microwave-safe bowl. Microwave on Medium, stirring occasionally, until the candy is melted. Let cool. Stir in about 1 quart of the whole milk; mix well with an electric mixer. Pour the mixture into an ice cream freezer. Stir in the chocolate syrup. Fill the freezer with milk to within 4 inches of the top. Freeze according to the freezer manufacturer's directions.
Yield: 1 gallon ice cream.

Carlene Miller
Clarksville, Arizona

Linda Todd, Coldwate, Michigan, makes Ice Cream Sandwich Delight by lining a 9-by-13-inch pan with 12 ice cream sandwiches, cutting as necessary to cover the bottom completely. Add layers of whipped topping, chopped pecans, caramel topping, and chocolate syrup. Repeat the layers, cover tightly, and freeze until firm. Linda also suggests an easy way to melt chocolate chips—just place in a plastic zip-top bag, place in boiling water for 20 to 30 seconds, and cut a tiny corner off the bag to drizzle the chocolate.

OLD-FASHIONED CRANK ICE CREAM

This is the best ice cream recipe I've ever used. It takes a while, but the end result is worth all the effort. It can be made just as well in an electric ice cream maker.

1½ cups milk	2 eggs or 3 egg yolks
¾ cup sugar	½ teaspoon vanilla
2 tablespoons all-	extract
purpose flour	½ cup heavy cream
A few grains of salt	

Scald the milk in the top of a double boiler. Mix the sugar, flour and salt in a bowl; stir in enough of the scalded milk to make a smooth paste. Stir this mixture into the rest of the milk in the double boiler. Cook, stirring constantly, until thickened. Cook, covered, 10 minutes longer. Beat the eggs slightly; stir into the milk mixture in the double boiler. Cook for 1 minute, stirring. Let cool. Stir in the vanilla and cream. Freeze in an ice cream freezer that is 2 quarts or larger until the handle is difficult to turn. Allow to stand, or "ripen," until firm. Drain off the water when firm. Pack with ice for 2 hours. Yield: ½ gallon.

You can make a number of varieties by making the following substitutions.

- *French Vanilla:* Substitute 6 egg yolks for the eggs.
- *Peach:* Before freezing, add 1½ cups mashed peaches combined with ¼ cup additional sugar (or enough to sweeten). Add a few drops of almond extract.
- *Strawberry:* Reduce the amount of milk to 1 cup. When the milk and egg mixture has cooled, add 1 quart washed, hulled and mashed strawberries. Sweeten with ¼ cup additional sugar; blend well. Add the cream after that.
- *Pistachio:* Add ¾ teaspoon almond extract and ½ cup chopped, blanched pistachio nuts. Tint a delicate green with food coloring.
- *Pineapple:* Substitute 1 tablespoon lemon juice for the vanilla. Just before freezing, add 2 cups well-drained crushed pineapple.
- *Peppermint:* Omit the vanilla. Add 1 drop peppermint extract, or 1½ cups finely crushed peppermint stick candy. If you use the candy, omit the sugar and add the candy to the milk before scalding. Tint the ice cream a delicate pink or green.
- *Raspberry:* Before freezing, add 1½ cups crushed raspberries mixed with ¼ cup additional sugar and a few drops almond extract.
- *Bisque:* Substitute 3 tablespoons sherry for the vanilla. When ready to freeze, add 1 cup fine macaroon crumbs.
- *Coffee:* Substitute ¾ cup cold strong coffee for ¾ cup of the milk.
- *Chocolate:* Add 2 squares unsweetened chocolate to the milk before scalding. When the chocolate is melted, beat by hand until smooth.

Janet Walker, Preceptor Alpha Alpha
Tempe, Arizona

BRICKLE BRACKLE ICE CREAM CRUMBLE

This is a great dessert to keep on hand in the freezer for unexpected company.

2 cups all-purpose flour	½ cup melted margarine
½ cup rolled oats	1 (12-ounce) jar caramel
½ cup packed light	or chocolate topping
brown sugar	1 gallon ice cream
1 cup chopped pecans	

Preheat the oven to 400 degrees. Mix the flour, oats, brown sugar, pecans and melted margarine in a large bowl. Pat the mixture onto a greased baking sheet. Bake for 10 minutes. Crumble while still hot. Pat half the mixture on the bottom of a 9-by-13-inch baking pan. Drizzle half the caramel topping over the mixture. Slice the ice cream in 1-inch slices and layer over the caramel topping. Pat the remaining crumbs over the ice cream. Drizzle the remaining caramel topping over the crumbs. Store in a freezer. Remove from the freezer and let rest a few minutes before serving. Yield: 12 to 14 servings.

Betty Byatt, Tau Master
Stratford, Ontario, Canada

DECADENT CHOCOLATE PEANUT BUTTER SWIRL

1½ cups chocolate	½ cup sugar
cookie crumbs	4 eggs
2 tablespoons peanut	2 teaspoons vanilla
butter	extract
½ cup chopped walnuts	½ cup crunchy peanut
or pecans	butter
¼ cup melted margarine	1 (16-ounce) container
2 (8-ounce) packages	whipped topping
cream cheese,	Small jar chocolate
softened	fudge ice cream sauce

Combine the chocolate crumbs, 2 tablespoons peanut butter, nuts and melted margarine. Press into an 8-inch springform pan, reserving 3 tablespoons for topping. Beat together the cream cheese and sugar. Beat in the eggs 1 at a time. Beat in the vanilla and ½ cup peanut butter. Fold in the whipped topping. Pour over the crumb crust. Top with 4 dollops of ice cream sauce. Swirl to marbleize. Sprinkle with the reserved crumb mixture. Freeze until ready to serve. Yield: 12 servings.

Marge Smalyga, Xi Theta
Fonthill, Ontario, Canada

ICE CREAM DESSERT

Use any ice cream or pie filling.

6 cups rice Chex cereal
1 cup chopped nuts
1 cup coconut
3/4 cup butter or
margarine

1 cup packed light
brown sugar
Hot Topping
1/2 gallon vanilla ice
cream, softened

Crush the rice cereal. Mix the crushed cereal, nuts and coconut in a medium bowl. Bring the butter and brown sugar to a boil in a medium saucepan; boil until caramelized. Pour over the cereal mixture; mix well. Pat 3/4 of the mixture in the bottom of a 9-by-13-inch pan and spread with the softened ice cream. Sprinkle with the remaining cereal mixture. Freeze until serving time. Cut into squares and cover with Hot Topping. Yield: 12 to 16 servings.

HOT TOPPING

1 cup hot water
1/2 tablespoon
cornstarch
1 tablespoon almond
extract

1 (21-ounce) can cherry
pie filling

Mix the water and cornstarch in a saucepan. Bring to a boil. Boil, stirring constantly. Add the almond extract and cherry pie filling.

Judy Leshovsky, Alpha Epsilon
Minneapolis, Minnesota

Jean Pessano, Ocean City, New Jersey, makes Miniature Ice Cream Bombes by arranging chocolate-covered cherry candies 2 inches apart on a waxed paper-lined tray. Scoop ice cream with a medium ice cream scoop, level off, and press slowly over each candy until scoop rim touches paper. Remove scoop carefully. Freeze for 3 hours. Peel off paper and place on wire rack. Pour hard shell chocolate over scoops. Place in waxed paper-lined airtight container to store in the freezer for up to 2 weeks. For a beautiful presentation, cut each bombe into halves and place on dessert plates in a pool of raspberry sauce.

DIVINE LEMON DESSERT

1 1/2 cups all-purpose
flour
3/4 cup margarine
2/3 cup finely chopped
pecans
1 cup confectioners'
sugar
1 (8-ounce) package
cream cheese, softened

1 (16-ounce) container
whipped topping
2 (4-ounce) packages
lemon instant
pudding mix, dry
2 cups milk

Preheat the oven to 350 degrees. Combine the flour, margarine and pecans using a pastry cutter. Press the mixture into a 9-by-13-inch baking pan. Bake for 30 minutes. Let cool. Beat the confectioners' sugar, cream cheese and half the whipped topping at medium speed for 2 minutes. Spread the mixture over the cooled crust. Stir together the pudding mix and milk; spread the mixture over the cream cheese layer. Spread the remaining whipped topping over the top. Refrigerate until serving time. Yield: 15 servings.

Helen A. Robinson, Laureate Psi
Royal Center, Indiana

PINK LEMONADE DESSERT

About 60 butter
crackers, crushed
1/2 cup melted butter or
margarine
1/2 cup confectioners'
sugar
1 (6-ounce) can frozen
pink lemonade
concentrate

14 ounces heavy cream,
whipped, or
1 (16-ounce)
container whipped
topping
1 (14-ounce) can
sweetened condensed
milk

Combine the crushed crackers, melted butter and confectioners' sugar in a medium bowl; mix well. Press the cracker mixture over the bottom of a 9-by-13-inch baking pan, reserving some to sprinkle over the top. Combine the lemonade concentrate, whipped cream and condensed milk in a bowl; mix well. Pour over the cracker crust. Sprinkle with the reserved cracker mixture. Chill, covered, in the refrigerator until set. Yield: 12 to 20 servings.

Christy Hutchinson, Tau Delta
Corona, California

Elizabeth Kauffmann, Xi Theta, Pocatello, Idaho, suggests serving cream puffs with a filling of your favorite ice cream, hot fudge sauce, whipped cream, and nuts for Surprise Cream Puffs.

KAREN'S FORGOTTEN CAKE

6 egg whites, at room
  temperature
½ teaspoon cream of
  tartar
¼ teaspoon salt
1½ cups sugar
1 teaspoon vanilla
  extract
1½ cups whipping
  cream, whipped
1 (10- to 16-ounce)
  carton frozen
  sweetened
  strawberries, thawed

Preheat the oven to 425 degrees. Beat the egg whites until foamy. Add the cream of tartar and salt, continuing to beat until the egg whites are stiff. Add the sugar gradually, beating well. The more you beat the egg whites, the higher they will rise during baking. Fold in the vanilla. Spoon the mixture into a greased 9-by-13-inch baking pan. Place in the preheated oven, close the oven door, and immediately turn off the oven. Keep the oven door closed overnight and don't open it until the next morning or afternoon. Spread the whipped cream over the cake. Chill, covered, in the refrigerator until time to serve. Top with the strawberries. Yield: 8 to 10 servings.

Carolyn Schott
Scottsdale, Arizona

HOWDY PEAR PANDOWDY

I tasted this dessert for the first time in a Mennonite restaurant in Sarasota, Florida. It is simply delicious, easy to make, and great for using up overripe pears.

6½ cups sliced peeled
  pears
½ cup sugar
½ teaspoon allspice
½ teaspoon ground
  ginger
½ cup light molasses
3 tablespoons water
2 teaspoons melted
  butter or margarine
1 recipe (1-crust) pie
  pastry
1 tablespoon milk
Sugar for topping

Preheat the oven to 350 degrees. Combine the pears, sugar, allspice and ginger in a medium bowl. Pour the pear mixture into a buttered 9-by-13-inch baking dish. Combine the molasses, water and melted butter; pour over the pear mixture. Cover with the pastry dough. Brush the top of the pastry with milk and sprinkle with sugar. Bake for 30 minutes. Remove from the oven. Use a knife or spoon to break the crust into pieces and to press the pieces gently into the filling. Bake for 25 to 30 minutes longer until the pears are tender and the crust is a golden brown. Yield: 12 to 15 servings.

Myrtle Pion
Lakeland, Florida

CHEESE AND PEAR PIZZA

This experiment in using fresh pears was a great success. To toast the pecans, spread whole pecans on a baking sheet and bake for 3 to 5 minutes at 350 degrees, stirring once. Slice after toasting.

2 d'Anjou pears, peeled
Fruit-Fresh
1 sheet puff pastry,
  thawed
1 (15-ounce) carton
  ricotta cheese
1 (3-ounce) package
  cream cheese,
  softened
½ cup confectioners'
  sugar
1 teaspoon grated lemon
  peel
¼ cup toasted sliced
  pecans

Preheat the oven to 450 degrees. Slice the pears into ¹⁄₁₆-inch slices; toss with Fruit-Fresh to keep them from turning brown. Set aside. Bake the puff pastry on an ungreased baking sheet for 10 minutes. Allow to cool. Combine the ricotta cheese, cream cheese, ¼ cup of the confectioners' sugar and the lemon peel; beat well. Spread the cheese mixture on the cooled puff pastry. Arrange the pear slices over the cheese. Sprinkle the pecans over the pears. Yield: 10 servings.

Cari Harper, Xi Omega
Bend, Oregon

BREADED APPLE PUDDING

You may substitute peaches or pears for the apples, but if you do, towel-dry the fruit or cut back on the milk. Peaches and pears are juicy!

1 egg or egg substitute
1 quart evaporated skim
  milk
1 teaspoon vanilla
  extract
1 cup white grape juice
2 teaspoons cinnamon
½ teaspoon nutmeg
8 cups bread crumbs
3 Fuji apples, cored and
  sliced
1 cup raisins
Peanuts, walnuts, or
  sliced almonds
  (optional)

Mix the first 7 ingredients in a large bowl. Let the mixture soak, covered, for about 4 hours in the refrigerator. Preheat the oven to 350 degrees. Spray a 9-by-13-inch baking pan with nonstick cooking spray. Line the pan with half the apple slices and half the raisins. Layer the bread crumb mixture over the apples and raisins. Arrange the remaining apples and raisins over the bread crumb mixture. Sprinkle with nuts if desired. Bake for 30 to 35 minutes or until a knife inserted near the center comes out clean. Yield: 12 servings.

Dorothy H. Ebert, Laureate Zeta
Hope, Idaho

CREAMY BANANA PUDDING

This pudding can be layered in individual serving dishes.

1 (14-ounce) can
   sweetened condensed
   milk
1½ cups cold water
1 (4-ounce) package
   instant vanilla
   pudding mix, dry

2 cups whipping cream,
   whipped
36 vanilla wafers
3 medium bananas,
   sliced, dipped in
   lemon juice and
   drained

Combine the condensed milk and water in a large bowl. Add the pudding mix; beat well. Chill for 5 minutes. Fold in the whipped cream. Spoon 1 cup of the pudding mixture into a 2½-quart glass serving bowl. Layer ⅓ of the wafers, ⅓ of the bananas and ⅓ of the pudding mixture over the first layer of pudding mixture. Repeat the layers twice. Chill, covered, in the refrigerator until set. Refrigerate any leftovers. Yield: 8 to 12 servings.

Amy Nachtolff, Nu Kappa
Guthrie, Oklahoma

BODACIOUS BREAD PUDDING

This is best when you use day-old bread. My mother used to throw in leftover biscuits as well. Serve hot or cold, plain or with a lemon or vanilla sauce. I turn off the oven and let the pudding cool in the oven.

1 cup margarine
10 slices white bread,
   lightly toasted
4 eggs
1¾ cups sugar
2 teaspoons vanilla
   extract

4 cups milk
1 teaspoon nutmeg
1 teaspoon cinnamon
½ cup raisins

Preheat the oven to 400 degrees. Melt the margarine in an 11-by-13-inch baking pan. Break the toasted bread into bite-size pieces and place in the pan of melted margarine. Mash down the bread pieces until they have soaked up all the margarine. Beat the eggs and sugar in a 2-quart bowl. Stir in the vanilla and milk; mix well. Pour over the bread; mash down the bread to soak up the egg mixture. Sprinkle the nutmeg, cinnamon and raisins over the top and push them down into the soaked bread. Bake for 30 to 40 minutes or until firm. Yield: 14 to 16 servings.

Doris J. Bain, Xi Epsilon
Chattanooga, Tennessee

LEMON PUDDING CUSTARD WITH FRUIT TOPPING

¼ cup plus
   2 tablespoons sugar
2 tablespoons all-
   purpose flour
¼ teaspoon salt
3 eggs
2 tablespoons lemon
   juice

1 cup skim milk
2 teaspoons grated
   lemon zest
1 teaspoon vanilla
   extract
Fresh strawberries or
   strawberry pie filling
Fresh mint sprigs

Preheat the oven to 350 degrees. Spray four 6-ounce ovenproof custard cups with nonstick baking spray. Combine the sugar, flour and salt in a medium bowl. Beat the eggs at high speed in a mixer bowl for 1 to 2 minutes. Add lemon juice, milk, lemon zest and vanilla, beating at medium speed until blended. Gradually add the flour mixture; beat thoroughly. Pour the batter into the custard cups. Place the cups in a shallow baking dish; fill the dish with 1 inch of hot water. Bake for 40 minutes or until set. Remove from the oven and allow to set for 3 to 5 minutes before unmolding. Garnish with strawberries. Yield: 4 servings.

Gina Flynn, Alpha Epsilon
Washington, Indiana

RICOTTA PUDDING

If you don't have a food processor, you can beat the ingredients in a mixing bowl with an electric mixer.

2 cups ricotta cheese
⅓ cup heavy cream
½ cup confectioners'
   sugar
1 teaspoon grated
   orange or lemon zest

¼ teaspoon vanilla
   extract
Cinnamon for garnish

Combine the ricotta cheese, cream, confectioners' sugar, orange zest and vanilla in a food processor container; process until smooth. Pour into serving cups. Chill, covered, in the refrigerator for 30 minutes or longer. Sprinkle a pinch of cinnamon over the top at serving time. Yield: 4 to 6 servings.

Betty L. Levin
Buffalo, New York

Patty Enos, Xi Eta Phi, Pittsburgh, Pennsylvania, makes an Easy Lincoln Log by blending whipped topping with apple butter and stacking vanilla wafers 5 or more high with filling between, turning the stack on its side, and spreading with filling on all sides.

RHUBARB PUDDING

It is a good idea to put a cookie sheet or foil under the pan while baking this juicy, delicious dessert.

1 egg	2¹/₂ cups sugar
1 tablespoon butter or margarine, softened	Dash of salt
	¹/₂ cup milk
1 cup all-purpose flour	4 cups raw rhubarb
1 teaspoon baking powder	1¹/₂ cups boiling water

Preheat the oven to 375 degrees. Mix the egg, butter, flour, baking powder, ¹/₂ cup of the sugar, salt and milk in a bowl. Pour into a greased 9-by-13-inch baking pan. Mix the rhubarb, boiling water and the remaining 2 cups sugar in a bowl. Pour over the batter in the pan. Bake for 40 minutes or until bubbly. Yield: 12 to 16 servings.

Mary Ann Williams
Summerfield, Illinois

SWEET POTATO EGGNOG PUDDING

2 (1-pound) cans sweet potato or 2¹/₂ pounds fresh sweet potato, cooked	¹/₂ teaspoon salt
	¹/₂ teaspoon cinnamon
	¹/₂ teaspoon ground ginger
2 tablespoons melted butter or margarine	2 tablespoons grated orange rind
1 cup eggnog	¹/₂ cup finely chopped walnuts
³/₄ cup sugar	

Preheat the oven to 375 degrees. Beat the sweet potatoes with a rotary beater until thoroughly mashed. Add the melted butter, eggnog, sugar, salt, cinnamon and ginger. Beat until well blended and fluffy. Fold in the orange rind and walnuts. Pour into a greased 1¹/₂-quart baking dish. Bake for 40 minutes. Yield: 10 to 12 servings.

Rosemarie Dann, Preceptor Beta Sigma
Fountain Hills, Arizona

RASPBERRY DELIGHT

2¹/₄ cups all-purpose flour	¹/₄ teaspoon salt
2 tablespoons sugar	16 ounces whipped topping
³/₄ cup butter or margarine, softened	1 (6-ounce) package raspberry gelatin mix
1 (8-ounce) package cream cheese, softened	2 cups boiling water
	2 (15-ounce) packages frozen raspberries
1 cup confectioners' sugar	Whipped topping for garnish (optional)
1 teaspoon vanilla extract	Fresh mint leaves (optional)

Preheat the oven to 300 degrees. Combine the flour and sugar in a bowl. Blend in the butter until smooth. Press into an ungreased 9-by-13-inch baking pan. Bake for 20 to 25 minutes; the crust will not brown. Let cool. Combine the cream cheese, confectioners' sugar, vanilla and salt in a mixer bowl; beat at medium speed until smooth. Fold in the whipped topping. Spread over the crust in the baking pan. Dissolve the gelatin in the boiling water; stir in the raspberries. Chill, covered, in the refrigerator for 20 minutes or until the mixture begins to thicken. Spoon the topping over the cream cheese filling; refrigerate until set. Cut in bars. Garnish with whipped topping and mint. Yield: 16 servings.

Evelyn Ickes
Alliance, Ohio

STRAWBERRY TORTE

3 egg whites	1 teaspoon vanilla extract
1 cup sugar	
20 butter crackers, crushed	8 ounces whipping cream
¹/₂ cup chopped pecans	1 cup sweetened strawberries, well drained
¹/₂ teaspoon baking powder	

Preheat the oven to 325 degrees. Beat the egg whites until stiff and dry, adding the sugar 1 tablespoon at a time. Fold in the crushed crackers, pecans, baking powder and vanilla. Spread the mixture in a well-greased 8-by-8-inch baking pan. Be sure the bottom and sides are covered with the mixture to form a shell. Bake for 30 to 35 minutes. Cool for 4 hours. Whip the whipping cream until very stiff. Fold in the strawberries. Spread over the cooled torte. Yield: 9 servings.

Phyllis Craig
Trenton, Missouri

TORTILLA SURPRISE

1¹/₂ tablespoons cinnamon	1 cup milk
1 cup sugar	1 (8-ounce) package cream cheese, softened
1 (10-count) package large soft flour tortillas	1 (16-ounce) container whipped topping
Melted butter for brushing tortillas	Chocolate syrup
	Maraschino cherries
1 (6-ounce) package vanilla pudding mix	

Preheat the oven to 350 degrees. Spray muffin tins with nonstick cooking spray. Mix the cinnamon and sugar. Brush 1 side of each tortilla shell with melted butter and sprinkle with the cinnamon mixture. Flip over and repeat on the other side. Cut each shell into 4 quarters. Position each quarter gently in muffin cup. Bake for 8 to 10 minutes or until golden. Blend the pudding mix, milk and cream cheese in a bowl. Fold in the whipped topping. Fill each shell with 1 tablespoon of the cream cheese filling. Drizzle with chocolate syrup and top with a maraschino cherry just before serving. Yield: 40 servings.

Sandra McCalmon
Port Colborne, Ontario, Canada

DREAM DESSERT FOR A CROWD

1 (2-layer) package
yellow cake mix
3 (4-ounce) packages
vanilla instant
pudding mix
4 cups cold milk
1½ teaspoons coconut
extract

1 (8-ounce) package
cream cheese,
softened
1 (10-ounce) can crushed
pineapple, drained
1 (16-ounce) container
whipped topping
2 cups flaked coconut

Preheat the oven to 350 degrees. Prepare the cake batter as directed on the package. Pour into two 9-by-13-inch sprayed and floured baking dishes. Bake until done. Cool completely. Combine the pudding mix, milk and coconut extract in a large mixer bowl; beat for 2 minutes on medium speed. Add the cream cheese; beat well. Fold in the pineapple. Spread the mixture over the cooled cakes. Top with the whipped topping and sprinkle with coconut. Chill, covered, in the refrigerator for 2 hours. Yield: 24 servings.

Floy M. Grabner, Preceptor Iota Alpha
Citrus Heights, California

JUMBLE COOKIE SALAD DESSERT

1 cup buttermilk
1 (4-ounce) package
vanilla instant
pudding mix
8 ounces whipped
topping

1 (16-ounce) can crushed
pineapple, drained
1 (16-ounce) can fruit
cocktail, drained
1 package fudge-stripe
cookies, crushed

Mix the buttermilk and pudding mix in a medium bowl. Blend in the whipped topping. Add the pineapple and fruit cocktail; mix well. Stir half the crushed cookies into the fruit mixture. Sprinkle the remaining crushed cookies over the top. Chill for several hours. Yield: 8 servings.

Sara Risseeuw, Mu Chi
Newton, Iowa

TROPICAL FRUIT SURPRISE

1 (8-ounce) package
cream cheese,
softened
¼ cup sugar
1 (8-ounce) container
lowfat whipped
topping
1 (4-ounce) jar brandied
or regular maraschino
cherries, drained,
chopped

1 (8-ounce) can crushed
pineapple, drained
1 (8-ounce) can
mandarin oranges,
drained, chopped
1 small jar macadamia
nuts, chopped
Sliced mango

Cream the cream cheese and sugar in a medium bowl until light and fluffy. Fold in the whipped topping. Stir in the maraschino cherries, pineapple, mandarin oranges and macadamia nuts. Refrigerate for a few hours before serving. Serve on a bed of sliced mango. Yield: 8 servings.

Marie Purdy, Preceptor Eta Phi
West Melbourne, Florida

TWINKIES DESSERT

1 (6-ounce) package
lowfat vanilla
instant pudding mix
1 package reduced-fat
Twinkies

1 (8-ounce) can crushed
pineapple, drained
6 or 7 bananas, sliced
1 (12-ounce) container
whipped topping

Prepare the pudding according to package directions. Cut the Twinkies in half lengthwise; use them to line a 9-by-13-inch baking pan. Layer half the pineapple, half the sliced bananas and half the pudding over the Twinkies; repeat the layers. Top with the whipped topping. Chill, covered, in the refrigerator for several hours. Yield: 12 or more servings.

Rebecca Isbel, Xi Alpha Beta Zeta
Waco, Texas

Lucylee Lively, Preceptor Iota Sigma, Dallas, Texas, makes Frosty Pumpkin Gingerbread by preparing and baking a 14-ounce package of gingerbread mix in a 9-by-13-inch pan. Prepare a small package of butterscotch instant pudding mix with ¾ cup milk, adding a 15-ounce can of pumpkin and 3 cups whipped topping to spread over the cooled gingerbread. Top with additional whipped topping, ½ cup chopped pecans, and a sprinkle of nutmeg and cinnamon.

TROPICAL TRIFLE

This recipe is perfect for a summer potluck or barbe-cue, and is virtually fat (guilt)-free!

1 frozen fat-free pound cake, thawed	**1 small package fat-free white chocolate pudding mix**
1 (15-ounce) can crushed pineapple, drained	**1 (12-ounce) container fat-free whipped topping**
1 (8-ounce) can mandarin oranges, drained	**Shredded coconut**
1 cup milk	

Cut the pound cake into 1-inch pieces. Place half the cake pieces in the bottom of a trifle bowl or other large serving bowl. Sprinkle half the pineapple and half the mandarin oranges over the pound cake pieces. Mix the milk and pudding mix until smooth. Stir the whipped topping into the pudding mixture; pour half the resulting mixture over the cake and fruit. Repeat the layer of pound cake, pineapple, oranges and pudding mix in that order. Top with shredded coconut. Refrigerate for 1 to 2 hours before serving to firm the trifle and allow the flavors to blend. Yield: 10 to 12 servings.

Jessica Cece
Albuquerque, New Mexico

CHOCOLATE RASPBERRY TRUFFLE TORTE

1/2 cup sifted cake flour	**Raspberry Sauce**
1/4 cup Dutch process cocoa	**Chocolate Truffle Filling**
4 eggs, at room temperature	**Chocolate Glaze**
1/2 cup sugar	**Fresh raspberries**
2 tablespoons butter or margarine	**Hazelnuts, whole**

Place a baking rack in the center of the oven and preheat the oven to 350 degrees. Line a 9-inch spring-form pan with parchment paper. Grease and flour the parchment lightly. Sift the cake flour and cocoa together. Beat the eggs and sugar in a large mixer bowl until triple in volume and the texture of soft whipped cream. Sift the cocoa mixture 1/3 at a time over the egg mixture and fold in gently. Reserve 1/2 cup of the batter. Soften the butter in a small bowl. Fold the reserved batter into the butter; fold the butter mixture into the remaining batter. Pour into prepared springform pan. Bake for 25 to 28 minutes or until the cake pulls from the side of the pan. Cool on a wire rack for 10 minutes. Remove the outer ring. Let stand until cooled, then remove the pan bottom. Cut the cake horizontally into 2 thin layers. Spread 1/3 cup of the Raspberry Sauce over the cut surface of the top layer to within 1/2 inch of the edge. Spread the Chocolate Truffle Filling over the other cut surface. Place the 2 layers together with the Raspberry Sauce and Chocolate Truffle Filling touching. Frost the top and side with a thin base coat of the Chocolate Glaze. Refrigerate the torte until firm. Soften the remaining Chocolate Glaze over hot water until of pouring consistency. Pour into the center of the torte and tilt the cake to allow the glaze to run down the side; spread with a knife only if necessary. Let stand until firm. Cut the torte into wedges and serve on dessert plates in a pool of Raspberry Sauce. Garnish with fresh raspberries and whole hazelnuts. Yield: 12 servings.

RASPBERRY SAUCE

16 ounces fresh or frozen raspberries	**1/3 to 1/2 cup sugar**
	1 tablespoon cornstarch

Heat the raspberries in a small saucepan just until the berries release 1 cup of their juice. Press the berries through a sieve and return the juice to the saucepan. Reserve 2 tablespoons of the juice. Blend the desired amount of sugar with the juice in the saucepan. Dissolve the cornstarch in the reserved juice. Cook the sweetened berry juice over medium-high heat until reduced by a third, stirring frequently. Whisk the cornstarch mixture into the hot syrup and cook until thickened, whisking constantly.

CHOCOLATE TRUFFLE FILLING

1/3 cup shelled hazelnuts	**6 ounces semisweet chocolate**
1 egg yolk	
1/3 cup whipping cream	

Spread the hazelnuts in a shallow pan. Roast at 375 degrees for 20 to 30 minutes or until the skins crack. Rub the warm nuts with a rough cloth to remove the skins; cool and chop. Whisk egg yolk with whipping cream in a small saucepan. Cook over medium heat to 160 degrees on a candy thermometer, whisking constantly; remove from the heat. Add the chocolate and stir until chocolate melts and blends well. Fold in hazelnuts. Cool to spreading consistency.

CHOCOLATE GLAZE

6 ounces semisweet chocolate	**1/4 cup unsalted butter or margarine**
1/4 cup whipping cream	

Combine the chocolate, whipping cream and butter in a small saucepan. Heat over low heat until smooth and well blended. Let stand until slightly thickened but pourable.

Photograph for this recipe is on the Cover.

Gentlemen's Choice

What comes out of a kitchen
when the man of the house
puts on the apron?
Intriguing ethnic dishes!
Adventuresome entrées.
Robust flavors and extra-hearty portions!
Manly munchies for armchair quarterbacks
and their Game Day guests!
Whether he's a guru at the grill or a maverick
who dabbles in spicy flavors and exotic combinations,
he'll love our Gentlemen's Choice recipes—
all submitted by men who love to cook—
and eat, of course!

DAVE'S BIG KICK BEEF DIP

We tried this recipe at a Super Bowl party a few years ago, and it's been a hit ever since. Dave likes it the most, so we let him have the kitchen and prepare it. It is easily doubled for a larger crowd. Serve it with regular or nacho-flavored taco chips.

¼ cup finely chopped green onions	1 (16-ounce) package process cheese, cubed
1 pound ground beef	Dash of garlic powder
1 (8-ounce) can tomato sauce	1 (4-ounce) can chopped chile peppers or dash of cayenne pepper
1 teaspoon Worcestershire sauce	

Preheat the oven to 350 degrees. Panfry the green onions and ground beef until beef is browned and crumbly; drain. Place in a reheatable 2-quart casserole; stir in the tomato sauce, Worcestershire sauce, process cheese, garlic powder and chile peppers. Heat in the oven until the cheese melts. Keep hot on a warming tray. Yield: 4 servings.

Dave (Debra) Hall, Eta Phi
Burns Lake, British Columbia, Canada

RICKY'S SALSA

I love to see my husband in the kitchen making this salsa! Serve it with tortilla chips.

2 ripe medium Roma tomatoes, chopped	2 cloves of garlic
½ medium onion, chopped	Juice of ½ lime
Pinch of fresh cilantro	½ tomatillo, chopped
½ fresh basil sprig	1 jalapeño pepper, seeded
	Salt and pepper to taste

Combine the Roma tomatoes, onion, cilantro, basil, garlic, lime juice, tomatillo, jalapeño pepper, salt and pepper in a food processor fitted with a metal blade. Process until finely chopped. Yield: 1 cup.

Ricky (Deborah) Smith
Olton, Texas

TOM'S SALSA

To make a milder salsa, remove the seeds from the hot peppers or reduce the number of peppers.

25 medium tomatoes	2 teaspoons cumin
18 jalapeño peppers	¼ cup sugar
5 green peppers	1 cup vinegar
2 habenero peppers	6 tablespoons salt
3 medium white onions	6 cloves of garlic
1 bunch cilantro	

Wash all ingredients. Combine the tomatoes, jalapeño peppers, green peppers, habenero peppers, onions and cilantro in the container of a food processor fitted with a metal blade; process until chopped. Pour the contents of the food processor container into a large kettle. Stir in the cumin, sugar, vinegar, salt and garlic. Cook over medium heat for 30 to 45 minutes or until mixture is desired consistency. Ladle into hot sterilized jars, leaving ½ inch headspace; seal with 2-piece lids. Process in a boiling water bath for 10 minutes. Yield: 10 pints.

Tom (Kay) Harmon
Holyoke, Colorado

❖ ART'S TOXIC WASTE

This recipe can be made even hotter by using the hot forms of the sauces.

1 cup (4 ounces) shredded Cheddar cheese	1 (24-ounce) jar picante sauce
1 cup (4 ounces) mozzarella cheese	1 (24-ounce) jar salsa
1 (16-ounce) can pork and beans, pork removed	Jalapeño peppers (optional)
	1 (20-ounce) bag tortilla chips

Combine the Cheddar cheese, mozzarella cheese, pork-and-beans, picante sauce, salsa and jalapeño peppers in a large bowl; mix well. Serve with tortilla chips. Yield: 10 cups.

Art (Stacey) Vonderschmidt
Hiawatha, Kansas

DAN'S NORTH OF BUFFALO WINGS

4 pounds jumbo chicken wings	1 tablespoon ground cumin
Oil for deep frying	1 teaspoon cayenne pepper
1 (16-ounce) bottle Russian salad dressing	10 to 15 drops Louisiana hot sauce, or to taste
2 tablespoons chili powder	4 ounces apricot jam

Deep-fry the chicken wings for 6 to 8 minutes. While they are frying, combine the salad dressing, chili powder, cumin, cayenne pepper and hot sauce in a medium saucepan. Bring to a boil over medium-high heat. Add the jam; stir until dissolved. Remove from heat. Preheat the broiler. Dip the cooked wings in the sauce; arrange on a baking sheet. Broil a few minutes on each side. Yield: 2 to 4 servings.

Dan (Lynda) Coulton, Alpha
Saint John, New Brunswick, Canada

JOHN'S PUNCH

This punch tastes the same whether you use the liquor or not!

1 (10-ounce) can frozen orange juice, thawed
1 (8-ounce) can frozen lemonade, thawed
1 quart pineapple juice
1 (1-liter) bottle ginger ale
2 (6-ounce) bottles sweet and sour mix
Small bottle grenadine
1.75 liters rum or vodka (optional)

Combine the orange juice, lemonade, pineapple juice, ginger ale, sweet and sour mix, grenadine and rum in a 5-gallon container. Serve in a punch bowl with an ice ring. Yield: 5 gallons.

John (Diana) Embrey
Falmouth, Virginia

BEN'S HAMBURGER SOUP

My grandmother made this soup when I was a little boy (says Ben). Except she threw everything into the pot and boiled it together—even the raw hamburger!

1 pound lean ground beef
1 medium onion, chopped
4 large potatoes, cubed
1 bay leaf
1 teaspoon parsley
1/2 teaspoon rosemary
1 teaspoon red pepper, crushed
1 teaspoon black pepper

Brown the ground beef in a skillet, stirring until crumbly; drain. Combine the ground beef, onion, potatoes, bay leaf, parsley, rosemary, red pepper and black pepper in a 4- to 6-quart kettle. Add enough water to barely cover ingredients. Bring to a boil; simmer for 20 to 30 minutes. Yield: 4 to 6 servings.

Ben (Sharon) Goodman, Preceptor Alpha Kappa
Glendale, Arizona

THE WORLD'S BEST CAESAR FOR TWO

Freshly ground pepper
1 clove of garlic
2 fillets of anchovy
1 teaspoon Dijon mustard
2 egg yolks
1/4 to 1/2 cup olive oil
Dash of hot pepper sauce
Juice of 1/2 lemon
1 teaspoon Worcestershire sauce
1 teaspoon red wine vinegar
1/2 head of romaine lettuce, cleaned, torn
1/2 cup grated Parmesan cheese
1/2 cup croutons

Crush the ground pepper in a salad bowl. Add the garlic and anchovy fillets; crush well. Add the Dijon mustard; mix to form a paste. Add the egg yolks; mix well. Pour the oil into the bowl in a slow, steady stream, beating vigorously with two forks; dressing will thicken slightly. Add the hot pepper sauce, lemon juice, Worcestershire sauce and red wine vinegar; mix well. Add the lettuce; toss to coat. Add the Parmesan cheese and croutons; toss again. Rub 2 serving plates with the squeezed lemon half. Serve salad on plates; sprinkle with freshly ground pepper. Yield: 2 servings.

Gordon (Bonnie) Wilson
Whitby, Ontario, Canada

STEVE'S CONFETTI PASTA SALAD

2 cups cooked linguini, rinsed in hot water
1/2 cup mayonnaise
2 tablespoons Dijon mustard
1/4 cup chopped green onions
1/4 cup sliced radishes
1/4 cup diced lean precooked ham
1/2 cup diced Swiss cheese
1 hard-cooked egg, chopped

Place the linguini in a 4-quart bowl. Fold in the mayonnaise, Dijon mustard, green onions, radishes, ham, cheese and egg. Chill, covered, until ready to serve. Yield: 4 to 6 servings.

Steve (Barb) Roberts
Astoria, Oregon

ED'S BEEF BURGUNDY

1 medium onion, chopped
2 tablespoons vegetable oil
2 pounds sirloin tip or top round steak
2 tablespoons all-purpose flour
2 envelopes brown gravy mix
1/2 cup burgundy wine
Salt and pepper to taste
2 (4-ounce) cans mushrooms, drained
Dash of oregano
Dash of rosemary
Dash of garlic salt
Cooked noodles or rice

Sauté the onion in the oil in a large skillet or Dutch oven over medium-low heat for 5 to 10 minutes. Cut the beef into 1-inch cubes; toss with the flour. Add the beef to the onion in the skillet and brown. Prepare the gravy using package directions, substituting the wine for 1/2 cup of the water. Stir the gravy mixture into the meat mixture in the skillet. Add salt, pepper, mushrooms, oregano, rosemary and garlic salt, stirring well. Simmer for 45 minutes, stirring occasionally. Serve over noodles or rice. Yield: 4 servings.

Ed (Mary Joyce) Fahey, Laureate Gamma Rho
Winter Haven, Florida

❖ KEVIN'S TOURNEDOS WITH ARTICHOKES AND MUSHROOM SAUCE

1 (8-ounce) can tomatoes, drained, liquid reserved
2 (9-ounce) packages frozen artichoke hearts
2 large onions, cut into ½-inch slices
6 tablespoons butter or margarine
16 ounces large mushrooms, thickly sliced
½ cup water
3 tablespoons brandy or dry sherry
1 tablespoon minced fresh basil
2 beef-flavored bouillon cubes
8 (1-inch-thick) beef tenderloins

Dice the tomatoes. Cook the artichoke hearts using package directions; set aside. Cook the onions in 3 tablespoons of the butter in a 12-inch skillet over medium heat for 5 to 10 minutes or until onions are tender. Remove the onions. Cook the mushrooms in the remaining butter in the skillet over high heat for 5 to 10 minutes or until tender. Preheat the broiler. Return onions to the skillet with the mushroom. Stir in the tomatoes, tomato liquid, water, brandy, basil and bouillon cubes. Cook over medium heat, stirring constantly, until mixture thickens. Stir in the artichokes; heat through. Broil the tenderloins for 10 to 15 minutes or until desired doneness. Serve with the artichoke sauce. Yield: 8 servings.

Kevin (Elizabeth) Bailey
Belle Fourche, South Dakota

ED'S ITALIAN BEEF AND SPINACH PIE

1 unbaked (9-inch) pie shell
½ pound lean ground beef
¼ pound ground Italian turkey sausage
¾ cup chopped bell peppers, red, yellow or green
½ cup sliced fresh mushrooms
1 clove of garlic, minced
½ cup chopped green onions
1 cup water
½ cup tomato paste
1½ teaspoons dried Italian seasoning
½ teaspoon salt
1 (10-ounce) package frozen chopped spinach, thawed, drained
⅔ cup light ricotta cheese
¾ cup shredded mozzarella or Colby cheese
1 cup chopped tomatoes

Preheat the oven to 450 degrees. Line the pie shell with a double thickness of aluminum foil. Bake for 8 minutes. Remove the foil. Bake for 4 minutes longer or until shell is set and dry; set aside. Reduce oven temperature to 350 degrees. Combine the ground beef, sausage, bell peppers, mushrooms, garlic and green onions in a medium skillet over medium heat; cook until beef is brown and vegetables are tender. Drain well. Stir in the water, tomato paste, Italian seasoning and salt; bring to a boil. Simmer, covered, for 10 minutes. Combine the spinach, ricotta cheese and ¼ cup of the mozzarella cheese in a medium bowl. Spoon the spinach mixture into the baked crust. Spread the meat mixture over the spinach layer. Cover the edges of the pie shell with aluminum foil to prevent overbrowning. Bake for 30 minutes. Remove from oven. Cover with the chopped tomatoes and the remaining ½ cup mozzarella cheese. Return to oven to bake 2 minutes longer. Remove from oven. Allow to stand for 10 minutes before serving. Yield: 8 servings.

Ed (Rose Marie) Netzer, Zeta Beta
Timberon, New Mexico

RICHARD'S CHICKEN-FRIED STEAK

2 cloves of garlic, minced
1 tablespoon red pepper
1½ tablespoons black pepper
2 teaspoons salt
2 cups milk
1½ to 2 pounds steak, cut in 6 to 8 pieces
1 egg
1 cup all-purpose flour
Vegetable oil for panfrying

Combine the garlic, half the red pepper, half the black pepper and the salt with the milk. Marinate the steak, covered, in the refrigerator for at least 8 hours. When ready to cook, stir the egg into the steak mixture. Place the flour in a shallow bowl. Heat ¼ to ½ inch of oil in a cast iron skillet until oil is almost smoking. Shake the milk mixture off the steak pieces. Dredge the steak 1 piece at a time in the flour. Drop 1 or 2 steak pieces at a time in the hot oil. Cook quickly over medium heat, 2 to 3 minutes per side, until steak is golden brown. Yield: 4 servings.

Richard (Helen) Beach, Laureate Lambda
Augusta, Maine

LORAN'S POOR MAN'S STEW

You may prepare this stew ahead of time and freeze portions to save for a cold winter's day. Serve with corn bread.

1½ pounds ground beef
2 (16-ounce) cans Veg-All
1 (15-ounce) can tomatoes with green chiles
1 (4-ounce) can chopped green chiles
1 (8-ounce) can tomato sauce
Salt to taste
Garlic salt to taste

Brown the ground beef in a Dutch oven over medium heat until crumbly; drain. Add the Veg-All, tomatoes with green chiles, green chiles, tomato sauce, salt and garlic salt to the beef. Bring to a boil. Simmer, partially covered, for 30 minutes. Yield: 8 servings.

Loran McMahon (Melba Gonzales), Alpha Phi
Roswell, New Mexico

BERNIE'S DREAMY STYLE SPAGHETTI

7 ounces spaghetti	2 cups small curd
1½ pounds ground	cottage cheese
beef	1 (8-ounce) package
2 tablespoons butter or	cream cheese,
margarine	softened
2 (8-ounce) cans tomato	¼ cup sour cream
sauce	2 tablespoons chopped
1 (4-ounce) can	green pepper
mushrooms	¼ cup chopped onion

Cook the spaghetti using package directions; set aside. Brown the ground beef in a skillet until crumbly; drain. Stir the butter, tomato sauce and mushrooms into the beef; heat through and set aside. Combine the cottage cheese, cream cheese, sour cream, green pepper and onions in a bowl. Place half the cooked spaghetti in the bottom of a 2- to 3-quart casserole dish. Layer the cheese mixture over the spaghetti. Cover cheese mixture with remaining spaghetti. Cover with the meat mixture. Refrigerate, covered, for at least 1 hour, 8 to 10 hours if possible. Preheat the oven to 350 degrees. Bake, uncovered, for 45 minutes. Yield: 10 servings.

Bernie (Monica) Bystrzycki, Xi Alpha Theta
Milwaukee, Wisconsin

ZACK'S CORNED BEEF DINNER

Serve with corn bread.

3 pounds corned beef	8 small whole onions
1 bay leaf	8 small carrots
6 whole cloves	½ head cabbage,
¼ teaspoon pepper	quartered
8 small new potatoes	

Rinse the beef. Place in a 6-quart Dutch oven. Add the bay leaf, cloves and pepper. Cover with hot water. Bring to a boil, covered, over high heat. Reduce heat to low when steam begins to escape from the cover. Simmer, covered, for about 3 hours or until beef is almost tender. Skim if necessary. Forty minutes before the beef is done, arrange the potatoes, onions and carrots around the beef in the Dutch oven; place the cabbage on top. Increase the heat to high. Heat until steam escapes from the cover.

Reduce heat to low. Cook until vegetables are tender, about 45 minutes. Place the meat on a serving platter; arrange the vegetables around it.
Yield: 6 to 8 servings.

Zack (Sue) Byrns, Preceptor Tau
Merritt Island, Florida

KENNY'S PEKING PORK ROAST

1 (3- to 5-pound) pork	1 cup vinegar
roast	2 cups strong coffee
Green onions to taste	2 cups water
Chopped garlic to taste	Salt and pepper to taste

Stuff the roast with the green onions and garlic. Place the roast in a bowl; pour the vinegar over the roast. Chill, covered, in the refrigerator for 24 hours, basting occasionally. Remove from the refrigerator; drain off the vinegar. Brown the roast in a skillet. Place the roast in a Dutch oven; add the coffee, water, salt and pepper. Cook, covered, over low heat for 6 hours on the stovetop. Yield: 4 to 6 servings.

Kenny (Rene) Folmar, Delta Omega
Albuquerque, New Mexico

EDWIN'S HAM LOAF

3 pounds ground smoked	1 cup milk
ham	Salt and pepper to taste
½ pound fresh ground	1½ cups packed light
pork	brown sugar
2 eggs	1 tablespoon dry
1 cup ground graham	mustard
crackers	½ cup vinegar

Preheat the oven to 350 degrees. Mix the smoked ham, ground pork, eggs, graham cracker crumbs, milk, salt and pepper in a bowl. Shape into 2 large or 8 small loaves and place in 2 large or 8 small loaf pans. Bake for 45 minutes. Combine the brown sugar, mustard and vinegar to make a sauce. Pour the sauce over the loaves. Bake for 45 minutes longer.
Yield: 8 to 12 servings.

Edwin (Frances) Ayers, Alpha Gamma
Mt. Vernon, Ohio

Bob (Joanne) Mohr, Preceptor Alpha Rho, Brunswick, Georgia, makes Anytime Tortilla Rollups for breakfast, snacks, or dessert by placing raisins or dates, a little pancake syrup, a sprinkle of cinnamon-sugar, and a bit of butter on flour tortillas, rolling them up tightly to enclose the filling, and baking at 350 degrees for 10 to 15 minutes.

BEST BARBECUE RIBS IN WYOMING

This whole meal can be baked in a portable electric oven and served right from the pan (says Kent). My wife used to prepare it every Wednesday evening for a local chuck wagon. Cowboys came from miles around to eat this dish.

15 to 20 pounds short ribs, trimmed	**4 tablespoons dry mustard**
1 (20-ounce) can catsup	**2 tablespoons liquid smoke**
1/2 (20-ounce) can water	
1 pound light brown sugar	**2 cups finely chopped onions**
3/4 cup lemon juice	**Seasoned salt or onion salt to taste**
1/2 (10-ounce) bottle Worcestershire sauce	**(up to 4 tablespoons)**

Preheat the oven to 400 degrees. Bake the ribs in a large roasting pan for 2 hours; drain well. Reduce oven heat to 350 degrees. Combine the catsup, water, brown sugar, lemon juice, Worcestershire sauce, mustard, liquid smoke, onions and seasoned salt in a large bowl; mix well. Cover the ribs generously with the sauce. Return to oven to bake, covered with foil, for 2 hours or until meat is tender. Yield: 30 servings.

Kent (Virginia) Reindahl, Laureate Sigma Story, Wyoming

HENRY'S JAZZ RIBS

These ribs have been eaten and endorsed by renowned jazz musicians all over the world. The Secret Jazz Sauce should be prepared while listening to music. The ribs must be completely sealed during baking so that no juices will escape (no peeking!). Should you and your friends have the urge to listen to jazz music after eating these ribs, do not panic—this is normal.

4 pounds (1 slab) beef or pork ribs	**2 ounces white vinegar**
2 tablespoons salt	**Secret Jazz Sauce**

Cut the slab of ribs in half. Add the salt to a large kettle of boiling water. Add the vinegar. Boil the ribs in the water for about 5 minutes. Drain. Rinse ribs with cold water; drain and pat dry. Cover the ribs liberally with Secret Jazz sauce. Marinate, covered, in the refrigerator for about 2 hours, turning ribs frequently. Preheat the oven to 250 degrees. Place the ribs and sauce in a large baking pan. Cover and seal the pan completely with aluminum foil. Bake for 2 1/2 to 3 hours. Begin to check the meat after 2 1/2 hours. The meat should be tender and almost falling off the bone. Yield: 8 to 12 servings.

SECRET JAZZ SAUCE

1 (6-ounce) can tomato paste	**1 medium yellow onion, finely chopped**
2 to 3 tablespoons Worcestershire sauce	**3 tablespoons light brown sugar**
1 (10-ounce) can frozen orange juice concentrate, thawed	**1 tablespoon dry mustard powder**
1 to 2 teaspoons cayenne pepper	**6 to 8 cloves of garlic, minced**
1 to 2 ounces dry wine (red or white)	**1 to 2 tablespoons red wine vinegar**
1 to 2 teaspoons freshly ground black pepper	**1 tablespoon hickory smoke (optional)**
3 tablespoons prepared mustard	

Combine the tomato paste, Worcestershire sauce, orange juice concentrate, cayenne pepper, wine, black pepper, prepared mustard, onion, brown sugar, mustard powder, garlic, vinegar and hickory smoke.

Henry (Yvonne) Young, Preceptor Alpha Kappa North Vancouver, British Columbia, Canada

TINY'S BURGOO

1 pound ground beef	**2 (16-ounce) cans red kidney beans**
1 pound ground pork	
1 pound ground chicken	**2 (16-ounce) cans spaghetti and meatballs in sauce**
2 (8-ounce) cans mushrooms, drained	
1/2 pound onions, chopped	**2 (14-ounce) bottles hot catsup**
Salt and pepper to taste	**1 (16-ounce) can Parmesan cheese**
1 tablespoon vegetable shortening	**Red pepper to taste**
1 (28-ounce) can tomatoes	**Sugar to taste**
2 (15-ounce) cans chili with beans	**Paprika to taste**

Cook the ground beef, ground pork, ground chicken, mushrooms, onions, salt and pepper in vegetable shortening in a large skillet until meat is browned and well done. Turn into a large stainless steel cooker. Stir in the tomatoes, chili, kidney beans, spaghetti, catsup, Parmesan cheese, red pepper, sugar, paprika and more salt if necessary. Heat until thickened, stirring constantly to prevent scorching. Yield: 6 quarts.

Ralph "Tiny" Preston, father of Pat Preston, Xi Alpha Psi Paintsville, Kentucky

SHISH KABOB

Leg of lamb, skinned,
  boned, cut into
  medium chunks
Salt and pepper to taste
1 medium onion, sliced
2 tablespoons vinegar
3 tablespoons vegetable
  oil

1 to 2 tablespoons
  chopped parsley
Soy sauce to taste
Mushrooms, cherry
  tomatoes and small
  onions

Sprinkle the lamb with salt and pepper. Combine the sliced onion, vinegar, oil, parsley and soy sauce; pour over the lamb. Chill, covered, in the refrigerator for 8 to 10 hours, stirring once or twice. Preheat the grill. Skewer the marinated meat, mushrooms, tomatoes and small onions. Grill over hot coals for 30 minutes, turning the skewers every 5 minutes.
Yield: 8 to 12 servings.

Father of Ercell Gray, Preceptor Lambda Pi
Visalia, California

ANTHONY'S CHICKEN BREASTS WITH PARMESAN CRUST

I prepare this dish for my wife when she needs some TLC (says Anthony).

1/3 cup fine bread crumbs
1/4 cup grated Parmesan
  cheese
1 teaspoon dried basil
  leaves
1 egg white

2 teaspoons Dijon
  mustard
6 boneless skinless
  chicken breast halves
1 tablespoon vegetable
  oil

Mix bread crumbs, Parmesan cheese and basil in a medium bowl. Beat the egg white in a separate bowl; stir in the Dijon mustard. Dip the chicken in the egg white mixture; coat with the bread crumb mixture. Cook the chicken in the oil in a large skillet over medium heat for 10 minutes on each side or until fork-tender. Yield: 6 servings.

Anthony (Debbie) Bastiaanssen, Eta Mu
Westbank, British Columbia, Canada

Don (Linda) Jobin, Xi Eta Omicron, Windsor, Ontario, Canada, makes Turkey Pizza for poker nights by pressing refrigerated crescent roll dough into a 9-by-12-inch baking pan, adding cooked and well-drained ground turkey and a cup of salsa, sprinkling with 1/4 cup shredded Cheddar cheese, and baking at 450 degrees for 18 to 20 minutes.

LEO'S CHICKEN CHALUPA CASSEROLE

2 (10-ounce) cans cream
  of chicken soup
2 (4-ounce) cans
  chopped green chiles
1 medium onion, grated
  or chopped
1 pint sour cream
4 whole chicken breasts,
  cooked, cubed

3 cups (12 ounces)
  shredded Monterey
  Jack cheese
8 small flour tortillas,
  cut in strips
3 cups (12 ounces)
  shredded Cheddar
  cheese
Paprika

Combine the cream of chicken soup, chiles, onion, sour cream, chicken and Monterey Jack cheese. Layer the tortilla strips, Cheddar cheese and soup mixture 1/2 at a time in a greased 9-by-13-inch baking dish. Finish with layers of the remaining tortilla strips, soup mixture and Cheddar cheese, in that order. Sprinkle with paprika. Chill, covered, in the refrigerator for 8 to 10 hours. Preheat the oven to 350 degrees. Bake for 45 minutes. Allow to stand for at least 15 minutes before serving. Yield: 10 servings.

Leo (Joyce) Boor, Theta Master
Great Bend, Kansas

GARY'S DRUNKEN CHICKEN

2 pounds boneless
  skinless chicken
  breasts or tenders
2 cups water
1 cup dry sherry
1 1/2 teaspoons salt
1 1/2 teaspoon curry
  powder
1 medium onion,
  chopped

1/2 cup chopped celery
2 (6-ounce) boxes long
  grain wild rice
1 (10-ounce) can cream
  of mushroom soup
1 (4-ounce) can chopped
  mushrooms, drained
1 cup sour cream
1/4 cup slivered almonds
Paprika

Combine the chicken with the water, sherry, salt, curry powder, onion and celery. Boil for 1 hour. Remove the chicken and chop into bite-size pieces. Cook the rice using package directions, substituting the chicken broth for the water. Preheat the oven to 350 degrees. Combine the chicken, cream of mushroom soup, mushrooms, rice and sour cream in a large bowl. Spread in a 9-by-13-inch baking pan coated with nonstick cooking spray. Sprinkle with the almonds and paprika. Bake, covered, for 1 hour. Yield: 6 servings.

Gary (Frances) Inman, Xi Mu
Knoxville, Tennessee

JOHN'S SAUSAGE AND CHICKEN JAMBALAYA

10 chicken thighs
3 medium onions, chopped
4 ribs celery
5 cloves of garlic
2 green peppers
1 to 2 tablespoons olive oil
1 pound smoked sausage, sliced
1 (6-ounce) can tomato paste
1 (28-ounce) can tomatoes
Cayenne pepper to taste
Chili powder to taste
Parsley flakes to taste
Worcestershire sauce to taste
Hot pepper sauce to taste
Salt and pepper to taste
1 cup white long grain rice, uncooked
3 bay leaves

Rinse chicken and pat dry. Simmer in water to cover until tender. Drain, reserving broth. Sauté the onions, celery, garlic and green peppers in the olive oil. Remove chicken from bone and add to the sautéed vegetables with the sausage. Stir in the tomato paste and tomatoes. Add the next 7 ingredients. Simmer, uncovered, for 30 to 45 minutes over low heat, stirring occasionally. Stir in the rice and 2 to 2½ cups of the reserved broth. Add the bay leaves. Simmer, covered, for 15 to 20 minutes or until the rice is tender. Remove bay leaves. Yield: 10 to 12 servings.

John (Page) Meyer, Jr.
Greer, South Carolina

❖ FRANK'S PASTA JAMBALAYA

½ cup chopped onion
½ cup chopped red bell pepper
1 clove of garlic, minced
1 teaspoon Cajun seasoning
1 (15-ounce) can black beans, rinsed, drained
1 (10-ounce) can diced tomatoes with green chiles, undrained
3 ounces turkey kielbasa, halved lengthwise, thinly sliced
7 cups hot cooked penne pasta
½ cup (2 ounces) shredded Mexican-recipe 4-cheese blend (Sargento brand)

Sauté the onion, red bell pepper and garlic in a large nonstick skillet coated with nonstick cooking spray over medium-high heat for 5 minutes. Add Cajun seasoning; sauté for 1 minute. Add black beans, tomatoes and kielbasa; bring to a boil. Simmer for 10 minutes or until thick. Combine the bean mixture and pasta in a large bowl. Sprinkle with the cheese. Yield: 8 servings.

Frank (Terrie) Stamey
Social Circle, Georgia

DUANE'S OYAKUDOMBURI

1 cup sake
3 medium yellow onions, sliced
½ pound mushrooms, sliced
¼ cup water
2 pounds boned chicken, cut in bite-size pieces
3 teaspoons light brown sugar
Soy sauce to taste
3 or 4 eggs, beaten
Cooked rice (optional)

Pour sake in skillet. Add the onions, mushrooms and water. Cook for 5 minutes over medium-low heat. Add chicken and brown sugar; mix well and cook for 5 minutes longer. Add the soy sauce (should make mixture a brownish color). Continue to cook, stirring, over medium-low heat until chicken is cooked completely. Add the eggs. Serve alone or over rice. Yield: 6 to 8 servings.

Duane (Shayne) Yocum, Preceptor Beta Lambda
Lowell, Michigan

JAMES' GRILLED DUCK WITH RED CURRANT SAUCE

½ cup olive oil
4 dashes teriyaki sauce
4 dashes soy sauce
Garlic powder to taste
2 dashes Italian seasoning
2 dashes hot pepper sauce
12 duck breasts
Red Currant Jelly Sauce

Combine the olive oil, teriyaki sauce, soy sauce, garlic powder, Italian seasoning and hot pepper sauce to make the marinade. Place marinade and duck breasts in a sealable plastic bag. Marinate the breasts in the refrigerator for at least 4 hours. Grill the duck breasts on a charcoal grill. Serve with hot Red Currant Jelly Sauce. Yield: 12 servings.

RED CURRANT JELLY SAUCE

1 cup red currant jelly
2 tablespoons Dijon mustard
1½ teaspoons red wine vinegar
¾ teaspoon Worcestershire sauce
¼ teaspoon ground cumin
Ground pepper to taste

Combine the red currant jelly, Dijon mustard, red wine vinegar, Worcestershire sauce, ground cumin and ground pepper in a saucepan. Heat slowly until jelly melts, stirring occasionally.

James (Peg) McVitty, Laureate Beta Mu
Forest, Ohio

KAVIN'S BBQ SHRIMP

*1 cup melted butter or
   margarine*
*3 pounds large shrimp,
   unpeeled*
1/4 cup olive oil
Garlic salt to taste

Lemon to taste
1/2 cup barbecue sauce
Black pepper to taste
1/2 cup rum
French bread

Preheat the broiler. Cover the bottom of a large shallow pan with half the melted butter. Add the unpeeled shrimp. Pour the remaining melted butter over the shrimp. Sprinkle the shrimp with the olive oil, garlic salt, lemon and barbecue sauce. Sprinkle heavily with the black pepper. Broil shrimp in the pan on a center or lower oven rack for about 5 minutes. Turn shrimp over and broil for 5 minutes longer. Remove pan from oven. Sprinkle shrimp with the rum. Broil for 1 minute. Serve with French bread. Yield: 8 servings.

*Kavin (Ronett) Jones, Alpha Beta Chi
Clinton, Missouri*

BURKE'S SHRIMP PASTA

*1 teaspoon vegetable or
   olive oil*
1/2 cup chopped onion
2 cloves garlic, crushed
*1/2 pound raw shrimp,
   shelled, deveined*
*1 (16-ounce) can whole
   peeled tomatoes,
   undrained*
1 teaspoon pepper

*1 teaspoon dried basil
   leaves*
1/2 teaspoon salt
1/4 cup chopped parsley
*1 (8-ounce) package
   spaghetti, cooked*
*1/2 cup pitted black ripe
   olives*
Grated Parmesan cheese

Heat the oil in a medium-sized skillet over moderately high heat. Add the onion and garlic; sauté, stirring constantly, until the vegetables are tender. Add the shrimp and cook for 4 minutes or until shrimp turn pink. Remove the shrimp and set aside. Add the tomatoes, pepper, basil and salt. Bring the mixture to a boil over moderately high heat; reduce heat and simmer, uncovered, for 5 minutes. Add the shrimp and parsley; continue heating until warm. Pour the shrimp and sauce over the cooked spaghetti; toss until spaghetti is well coated. Arrange on a serving platter and garnish with black olives. Serve with Parmesan cheese. Yield: 4 servings.

*Burke (Eleanor Jane) Deiter, Xi Alpha Pi
Gambrills, Maryland*

REGGIE'S FIESTA MORNING

4 tablespoons olive oil
1/2 cup chopped onions
*1 1/2 to 2 cups sliced
   mushrooms*
Salt to taste
Pepper to taste
8 eggs (or egg substitute)

4 tablespoons milk
*2 tablespoons
   Worcestershire sauce*
2/3 cup salsa
*2/3 cup shredded Cheddar
   cheese*

Coat the bottom of a 12-inch skillet with the olive oil. Sauté the onions and mushrooms in the skillet over medium heat until the onions are translucent. Sprinkle with the salt and pepper. Meanwhile, slightly beat the eggs, milk and Worcestershire sauce in a medium bowl. Stir the salsa into the egg mixture. Add the egg-salsa mixture to the sautéed onions and mushrooms. Heat the mixture, stirring, until the eggs are set. Drain excess liquid. Stir in the cheese until it melts. Yield: 4 servings.

*Reggie (Carolyn) Clauze, Xi Gamma Rho
Petersburg, West Virginia*

RICHARD'S BAKED BEAN CASSEROLE

*1 (15-ounce) can baked
   beans*
*1 (15-ounce) can pinto
   beans*
*1 (15-ounce) can black
   beans*
1/2 cup catsup
*1/2 cup packed light
   brown sugar*

*1 teaspoon dried
   mustard*
1 teaspoon vinegar
*1/2 pound bacon, cooked,
   chopped*
*1 pound ground beef or
   ground turkey*
Chopped onion to taste

Preheat the oven to 350 degrees. Combine the ingredients in a 2-quart casserole dish or a slow cooker. Bake, uncovered, for 30 minutes; or cook in the slow cooker for 5 to 7 hours. Yield: 8 to 10 servings.

*Richard (Susan) Hutchison, Xi Chi Kappa
Eureka, California*

DAD'S HOT MUSTARD

*1 box Coleman's dry
   mustard*
1/4 cup malt vinegar

3 eggs
1 cup sugar

Mix the mustard and malt vinegar until of the consistency of cake batter, adding more vinegar if necessary. Refrigerate mixture for 8 to 10 hours. Beat the eggs with the sugar. Stir in the mustard mixture. Cook in a double boiler over boiling water until clear, stirring constantly. Pour into glass jars and refrigerate. Yield: variable.

*Ralph (Barbara) Burley
South Daytona, Florida*

TERRY TATERS

8 medium potatoes, cubed
1 onion, chopped
1/2 medium green pepper, chopped

1/2 pound bacon, 1 pound smoked sausage or 1 pound raw shrimp
1 stick margarine, sliced
4 slices American cheese

Preheat the oven to 375 degrees. Layer the first 4 ingredients in a 1-quart casserole dish. Place the margarine slices on top and cook, covered, for 1 hour. Remove casserole from oven and add the cheese. Bake, covered, until cheese melts. Yield: 6 servings.

Terry (Betty) Frederick, Xi Delta Pi
Breaux Bridge, Louisiana

MIKE'S MICROWAVE CROUTONS

3 tablespoons butter or margarine
2 tablespoons grated Parmesan cheese
1/2 teaspoon garlic salt
1/2 teaspoon celery seed

1/2 teaspoon dried oregano
1/2 teaspoon dried basil leaves
3 slices white bread, cut in 1/2-inch cubes

Melt butter in a medium-size microwave-safe bowl. Stir in the next 5 ingredients until blended. Add the bread; toss to coat. Microwave, uncovered, on High for 3 to 5 minutes or until lightly browned and sizzling; stir twice. Spread croutons on paper towels to cool. Store in an airtight container. Yield: 1 to 2 cups.

Mike (Jenny) Poole, Preceptor Mu
Lexington, Kentucky

CHRIS' BUTTERMILK PANCAKES

1 quart buttermilk
3 eggs
3 1/2 cups all-purpose flour
3 1/2 teaspoons baking powder

1/2 teaspoon vanilla extract
3/4 cup sugar
1 1/2 teaspoons baking soda

Mix the ingredients in a bowl. Cook over a hot griddle or skillet. The batter can be kept in the refrigerator for up to a week. Yield: 12 large pancakes.

Chris Stecker, son of Dorrene King, Rho Epsilon Zeta
Atwater, California

BILL'S FRENCH TOAST

1/2 cup fresh or frozen blueberries
1 tablespoon water
1 teaspoon lemon juice
2 packages artificial sweetener

Egg substitute to equal 2 eggs
1 tablespoon water or skim milk
2 slices 40-calorie bread
Cinnamon to taste

Coat a nonstick griddle with nonstick cooking spray. Preheat griddle. Mix the blueberries, 1 tablespoon water, lemon juice and one package artificial sweetener in a saucepan. Cook over medium-low heat until the sauce thickens, stirring constantly. Remove from heat. Combine the egg substitute and 1 tablespoon water in a bowl. Stir. Dip the bread slices in the egg mixture, coating evenly. Place the bread on the hot griddle. Brown on both sides. Place the toast on a plate. Sprinkle with 1 package artificial sweetener. Pour the fruit sauce over the top and sprinkle with cinnamon. Yield: 1 serving.

Bill (Marilyn) Ross, Preceptor Delta Delta
Leawood, Kansas

BILL'S BLUEBERRY BLINTZ

1/2 cup low-fat or 1-percent cottage cheese
1 package artificial sweetener
Few drops of skim milk

Egg substitute to equal 2 eggs
1/4 cup blueberries
Cinnamon to taste (optional)

Coat a nonstick griddle with nonstick cooking spray; heat the griddle. Process the cottage cheese, artificial sweetener and milk in a blender until creamy and set aside. Pour the egg substitute onto the griddle to make a large round pancake. Cook for 1 minute. Pour the blueberries on the pancake in a line down the center of the circle. Cover and cook for 2 minutes or until egg mixture is set to your liking. Sprinkle with cinnamon. Slide the pancake onto a plate. Fill with the sweetened cottage cheese, reserving about a tablespoon. Fold over both edges of the pancake and top with the remaining cheese mixture and a few berries. Yield: 2 servings.

Bill (Marilyn) Ross, Preceptor Delta Delta
Leawood, Kansas

WES AND DYLAN'S ZUCCHINI BROWNIES

1/2 cup melted butter or margarine
1/3 cup vegetable oil
1 3/4 cups sugar
2 eggs
2 1/2 cups all-purpose flour
1/2 teaspoon salt
1 teaspoon baking soda

4 tablespoons cocoa
1/2 cup sour milk
1 teaspoon vanilla extract
2 cups grated raw zucchini
1 cup chopped walnuts
6 ounces semisweet chocolate chips

Preheat the oven to 350 degrees. Combine the butter, oil, sugar and eggs; mix well. Sift the flour, salt, baking soda and cocoa together. Add the flour mixture and sour milk 1/3 at a time to the butter mixture. Add the vanilla and zucchini; mix well. Stir in the walnuts. Pour into a greased 9-by-13-inch baking pan. Sprinkle with the chocolate chips. Bake for 35 minutes or until brownies test done. Let cool. Store covered in the refrigerator. Yield: 30 to 40 brownies.

Wes and Dylan Lancaster, husband and son of Ann Lancaster
Lexington, Kentucky

TRAVIS' CHOCOLATE CHIP COOKIES

2 cups vegetable shortening	5¹/2 cups all-purpose flour
2 cups packed light brown sugar	2 teaspoons baking soda
1 cup sugar	2 teaspoons salt
6 eggs	4 cups semisweet chocolate chips
2 teaspoons vanilla extract	

Preheat the oven to 375 degrees. Combine the shortening, brown sugar and sugar in a large mixer bowl. Add the eggs 1 at a time while mixer is running. Add the vanilla. Combine the flour, baking soda and salt in a separate bowl; add to the creamed mixture. Mix well. Stir in the chocolate chips. Drop by teaspoons on an ungreased cookie sheet. Bake for 9 to 10 minutes or until lightly browned. Remove from the cookie sheet and cool on a wire rack. Yield: 12 dozen.

Travis D. Book, son of Sally M.Book
Council, Idaho

CHRISTOPHER'S CHOCOLATE CHIPPERS

1 cup vegetable shortening	2 cups all-purpose flour
1 cup sugar	1 (12-ounce) package semisweet chocolate chips or 1 (10-ounce) package white chocolate chips
1/2 cup packed light brown sugar	
2 eggs	
2 teaspoons vanilla extract	1 cup chopped walnuts or chopped macadamia nuts
1 teaspoon baking soda	
3/4 teaspoon salt	

Preheat the oven to 375 degrees. Cream the shortening, sugar and brown sugar. Beat in eggs 1 at a time. Add the vanilla, baking soda and salt, beating until well blended. Beat in the flour. Fold in the chocolate chips and nuts. Drop by teaspoons on an ungreased cookie sheet. Bake for 10 to 12 minutes or until lightly browned. Cool on a brown paper bag. Store in an airtight container. Yield: 6 dozen.

Christopher Rossini, son of Mary Jo Rossini, Xi Rho Chi
Orangevale, California

JOHN'S ITALIAN CHOCOLATE CHIP COOKIES

1 cup butter or margarine, softened	3 tablespoons baking powder
1¹/2 cups sugar	2 (12-ounce) bags miniature chocolate chips
6 eggs	
1 (16-ounce) can chocolate syrup	3 (16-ounce) boxes confectioners' sugar
8 cups (2 pounds) all-purpose flour	1 cup hot milk or chocolate milk

Preheat the oven to 350 degrees. Cream the butter and sugar until light and fluffy. Add eggs 1 at a time, beating well after each addition. Stir in the chocolate syrup. Sift the flour and baking powder together. Add the flour mixture gradually to the creamed mixture. Stir in the chocolate chips. Scoop out bite-size cookie dough pieces with a teaspoon or mini-melon baller; arrange on greased cookie sheets. Bake for 6 to 8 minutes, watching carefully so cookies do not dry out. Cool on a wire rack or paper bag. Combine the confectioners' sugar and milk until runny. Drizzle over the cooled cookies. Store in an airtight container. Yield: 8 dozen.

John (Elisabeth Lucas) Rickards, Jr., Zeta
Virginia Beach, Virginia

LYNN'S BROKEN CAKE DESSERT

2 (2-layer) boxes white cake mix	1/2 cup cold water
1 (6-ounce) box strawberry gelatin mix	1 (6-ounce) box instant vanilla pudding
	3 cups 2-percent milk
2 cups boiling water	2 (8-ounce) cartons whipped topping
1 (10-ounce) package frozen strawberries	1/2 cup chopped pecans or walnuts
6 ice cubes	

Bake the cake using package directions. Let cool. Break into pieces. Dissolve the gelatin in the boiling water. Add the strawberries, stirring until thawed. Put the ice cubes in a cup; add cold water to 1/2-cup line. Stir into the gelatin mixture. Add the milk to the instant pudding mix, stirring until thickened. Beat 1 of the containers of whipped topping into the pudding. Layer torn cake pieces, gelatin mixture, more torn cake pieces and pudding in a large glass dish or punch bowl. Repeat the layers. Spread the remaining container of whipped topping over the top. Sprinkle with the nuts. Chill, covered with plastic wrap, in the refrigerator until serving time. Yield: 24 servings.

Lynn (Jane) Neale, Laureate Rho
Powell, Wyoming

Metric Equivalents

A lthough the United States has opted to postpone converting to metric measurements, most other countries, including England and Canada, use the metric system. The following chart provides convenient approximate equivalents for allowing use of regular kitchen measures when cooking from foreign recipes.

Volume

These metric measures are approximate benchmarks for purposes of home food preparation.
1 milliliter = 1 cubic centimeter = 1 gram

Liquid	Dry
1 teaspoon = 5 milliliters	1 quart = 1 liter
1 tablespoon = 15 milliliters	1 ounce = 30 grams
1 fluid ounce = 30 milliliters	1 pound = 450 grams
1 cup = 250 milliliters	2.2 pounds = 1 kilogram
1 pint = 500 milliliters	

Weight	Length
1 ounce = 28 grams	1 inch = $2\frac{1}{2}$ centimeters
1 pound = 450 grams	$\frac{1}{16}$ inch = 1 millimeter

Formulas Using Conversion Factors

When approximate conversions are not accurate enough, use these formulas to convert measures from one system to another.

Measurements	Formulas
ounces to grams:	# ounces x 28.3 = # grams
grams to ounces:	# grams x 0.035 = # ounces
pounds to grams:	# pounds x 453.6 = # grams
pounds to kilograms	# pounds x 0.45 = # kilograms
ounces to milliliters:	# ounces x 30 = # milliliters
cups to liters:	# cups x 0.24 = # liters
inches to centimeters	# inches x 2.54 = # centimeters
centimeters to inches:	# centimeters x 0.39 = # inches

Approximate Weight to Volume

Some ingredients which we commonly measure by volume are measured by weight in foreign recipes. Here are a few examples for easy reference.

flour, all-purpose, unsifted	1 pound = 450 grams = $3^1/_2$ cups
flour, all-purpose, sifted	1 pound = 450 grams = 4 cups
sugar, granulated	1 pound = 450 grams = 2 cups
sugar, brown, packed	1 pound = 450 grams = $2^1/_4$ cups
sugar, confectioners'	1 pound = 450 grams = 4 cups
sugar, confectioners', sifted	1 pound = 450 grams = $4^1/_2$ cups
butter	1 pound = 450 grams = 2 cups

Temperature

Remember that foreign recipes frequently express temperatures in Centigrade rather than Fahrenheit.

Temperatures	Fahrenheit	Centigrade
room temperature	68°	20°
water boils	212°	100°
baking temperature	350°	177°
baking temperature	375°	190.5°
baking temperature	400°	204.4°
baking temperature	425°	218.3°
baking temperature	450°	232°

Use the following formulas when temperature conversions are necessary.

Centigrade degrees x $9/_5$ + 32 = Fahrenheit degrees
Fahrenheit degrees - 32 x $5/_9$ = Centigrade degrees

American Measurement Equivalents

1 tablespoon = 3 teaspoons	12 tablespoons = $3/_4$ cup
2 tablespoons = 1 ounce	16 tablespoons = 1 cup
4 tablespoons = $1/_4$ cup	1 cup = 8 ounces
5 tablespoons + 1 teaspoon = $1/_3$ cup	2 cups = 1 pint
	4 cups = 1 quart
8 tablespoons = $1/_2$ cup	4 quarts = 1 gallon

Merit Winners

Index

Beta Sigma Phi Cookbooks

available from *Favorite Recipes® Press* are chock-full of
home-tested recipes from Beta Sigma Phi members that earn you
the best compliment of all… "More Please!"

Every cookbook includes:

☆ color photos

☆ delicious, family-
pleasing recipes

☆ lay-flat binding

☆ wipe-clean color covers

☆ easy-to-read format

☆ comprehensive index

To place your order,
call our toll-free number
1-800-251-1520
or clip and mail the
convenient form below.

BETA SIGMA PHI COOKBOOKS	Item #	Qty.	U.S. Retail Price	Canadian Retail Price	Total
Fast Feasts	52523		$9.95	$12.95	

Home Sweet Home Cooking:
     Company's Coming
     Family Favorites
	01260
	 01252
			$9.95
			 $9.95
				$12.95
				 $12.95	

Pure & Simple	48798		$9.95	$12.95	
Hearth to Heart	60356		$9.95	$12.95	
Just Desserts	75904		$9.95	$12.95	
Shipping and Handling		1	$1.95	$ 2.95	
TOTAL AMOUNT					

☐ Payment Enclosed
☐ Please Charge My   ☐ MasterCard   ☐ Visa
                       ☐ Discover

Canadian orders: checks or money orders only

Signature _____

Account Number _____

Name _____

Address _____

City _____ State ____ Zip _____

No COD orders please.
Call our toll-free number for
    faster ordering.
Please allow 30 days for delivery.

Mail completed order form to:

Favorite Recipes® Press
P.O. Box 305147
Nashville, TN 37230